THE NEW
GOOD VIBRATIONS
GUIDE TO SEX

Second Edition

THE NEW GOOD VIBRATIONS GUIDE TO SEX

Second Edition

Cathy Winks and Anne Semans

Illustrated by MB Condon

CLEIS PRESS

Published in the United States by Cleis Press Inc.,
P.O. Box 14684, San Francisco, California 94114.

Printed in the United States.
Illustrations: MB Condon
Cover and text design: Karen Huff
Cleis Logo: Juana Alicia
Good Vibrations Logo: MB Condon

Second Edition.
10 9 8 7 6 5

Library of Congress Cataloging-in-Publication Data

Winks, Cathy.
    The new good vibrations guide to sex / Cathy Winks
and Anne Semans. — 2nd ed.
          p. cm.
    Rev. Ed. of: The good vibrations guide to sex, 1st ed.
c1994.
    Includes bibliographical references and index.
    ISBN 1-57344-069-8 (pbk.)
    1. Sex. 2. Sex Instruction. I. Semans, Anne. II. Winks,
Cathy. Good Vibrations Guide to Sex. III. Title.
HQ31.W77346 1997
306.7 – dc21   97-2426
                                                  CIP

Contents

Acknowledgements

We'd like to thank Joani Blank for creating Good Vibrations, Susie Bright for encouraging our writing, and our coworkers at Good Vibrations for sharing tips, techniques and anecdotes. Special thanks go to our longtime friend MB Condon, who spent two action-packed months alone with a box of sex toys producing the beautiful illustrations we're honored to have in our book, and to our beloved mentor Ray Potter, for his infectious enthusiasm, excellent edits, indispensable advice and cheerleading abilities. Lots of love and thanks to Becky, Jeff and Trish for their support and patience.

This book is dedicated to our customers and to anyone who's ever asked or answered a question about sex.

Illustrations

Foreword

As a medical educator, I have been entrusted with the responsibility of educating tomorrow's physicians. It is a challenging task that requires perseverance, imagination and, not infrequently, a thick skin. It also requires patience, for although medicine is advancing rapidly everyday, medical-school curriculums are not. Nutrition, women's health and, of course, human sexuality are subjects that encounter the most noticeable resistance because they lie outside of the traditional structure and organization of modern medicine.

Why should a layperson care how medical students and doctors are trained in human sexuality? Because doctors are the people most likely to be turned to when someone, particularly an adult, has a question. What if a medical professional does not have an answer? What if a person wants to go beyond safer sex (the content most likely to be taught in a medical-school or other health-professions curriculum) to better sex (the content least likely to be taught)?

Fortunately a resource does exist. With the publication of *The New Good Vibrations Guide to Sex,* Cathy Winks and Anne Semans have given the public *and* the professional world what has long been missing: a complete guide to a healthy sex life. By discussing desires and practices that are frequently absent in other books, Winks and Semans provide guidance in an important area of human sexuality: learning to differentiate sexual activities that are "different" from those that are dangerous.

Much of the richness and value of this book is a consequence of the unique backgrounds of the authors. Their accumulated knowledge, garnered from many years of practical experience answering questions and giving advice, is evident in all aspects of their writing. I doubt anyone could read this book and not learn something.

The New Good Vibrations Guide to Sex can and should be read by everyone—men and women, adolescents and elders, laypeople and professionals. One of the highest compliments a book can receive is that it significantly contributes to a person's health and education. *The Good Vibrations Guide to Sex* did that for me, and I am confident that this new edition will do so for many others.

Marc S. Nelson, M.D., Ph.D.
Stanford, California
January 1997

Introduction

Welcome to the expanded, completely updated *Good Vibrations Guide to Sex*, filled with new anecdotes, new ways to enhance your sex life and candid reviews of the latest sex toys and technology.

The first edition of this book has made its way onto the bedside tables of tens of thousands of men and women in the United States, Canada, Britain and Germany. *The Good Vibrations Guide to Sex* is being used in health clinics and in college courses on human sexuality, and it's recommended by sex therapists and medical professionals.

Why This Book?

Ten years of selling sex toys in a women-owned vibrator store, Good Vibrations, have given us a unique perspective. Our experiences talking to strangers and friends about sex have taught us a lot about what real people enjoy doing in bed, and have given us the information that can change your sex life.

People need good sex books. Access to accurate sex information helps all of us to understand ourselves better, to build more intimate relationships and to conquer fear, bias and shame. Not to mention that sex is just good, clean fun, and the more you learn about it, the more pleasurable it becomes.

But getting your hands on the information you need isn't always easy. At Good Vibrations, we've spent years fielding customers' questions about everything from sexual response to enhancing partner sex to selecting vibrators and lubricants. Countless times we wished for a book that offered more detailed answers to the hundreds of questions we were asked. After all, it's not easy to discuss the fine points of sexual techniques and technology during a busy day in a crowded store. For every customer who gathers up the courage to ask a question, we know there are dozens who would rather get their answers from a book—which is still the most accessible way for people to learn about sex.

If you've picked up this book, you're probably curious about expanding your sexual horizons, interested in specific tips and techniques, or searching for reliable advice and answers to general questions about sex. At Good Vibrations, we carry several hundred books about sex, and one of the questions we're asked most frequently by women and men of all ages and orientations is "Can you recommend a good sex manual?" After too many years of explaining that there wasn't a single modern manual that addressed a variety of sexual activities and spoke to a diverse audience, we decided to write one ourselves.

At Good Vibrations, we have the unique privilege of working in an environment where all kinds of people approach us with sexual questions, confessions, concerns, experiences they want to share and tips for us to pass along to other customers. Their healthy, candid curiosity dictates what you'll find here—advice, instruction, definitions, illustrations, anecdotes, encouragement and validation for a variety of sexual interests and activities, courtesy of two women who have been asked a lot of questions about sex.

We're pleased, but not surprised, that folks from a variety of backgrounds enjoy this book and embrace our philosophy. By putting our customers' experiences and interests into writing, we simply acted as messengers attempting to spread the word to a wider community. As letters from our readers confirm, access to good sex information leads to greater health and happiness:

> *After just a quick scan over the oral sex chapter, I had my boyfriend ready to faint. We're looking forward to experiencing many more of the tricks your book has taught us.*

> *I purchased your book three weeks ago and my sex life is headed for an upswing. The warmth and openness of your book (and especially its good humor) helped me to really think about my sexuality. I also found your tips helpful and titillating.*

> *Your advice on communication really hit home. I am in my first relationship after my seven-year marriage ended. My partner is younger and also more experienced than me, but through an honest, spontaneous exchange of what we are feeling and thinking, our time together (both in bed and out) has become richer and much more fulfilling.*

With in-depth answers to the most common questions asked at Good Vibrations, you can expect to learn just about everything there is to know about sex toys in these pages. No other sex book in or out of print has given sex toys their due. Thanks to millions of women and men around the country, sex toys are a billion-dollar business, yet the topic rarely merits more than a dismissive paragraph in sex manuals. Whether you've always been curious about vibrators, but haven't been sure where to begin, or whether you're an old hand who simply wants updates on the latest technology, you'll find sound advice here on how to select the toy that's right for you, where to buy it and tips for safe, creative play.

If you've never considered playing with sex toys, the enthusiastic anecdotes and quotes from our customers may provide all the inspiration you need to try something new. After all, we expand the conventional definition of sex toys to include a variety of erotic accessories. Your idea of sex toys may already include massage oils, vibrators and dildos, but once you read about the fun to be had with food, books, VCRs and telephones, you'll start looking at everyday objects in a whole new way. The bottom line is if it turns you on, it's a sex toy, and we'll happily provide you with all the information and encouragement you need to explore a whole new world of pleasure.

What's New in This Edition

Our experience of human sexuality expands with each new toy, each new scientific discovery and each new sex law, so we've revised, rewritten, rethought and made additions to *The Good Vibrations Guide to Sex* to keep you as up-to-date as possible.

You'll find the lowdown on a cornucopia of new sex toys—including ingenious inventions like a remote-controlled vibrator and a vibrator that plugs into your car lighter—and you'll learn about exciting new trends in the adult industry. We've added an assortment of "GV Tales"—anecdotes that only a sex-toy salesperson could tell. Our updates on safer sex activities and accessories include the latest alternatives to latex. Look for advice on discussing sexual issues with your doctor, enjoying sex during pregnancy, and keeping the flame alive in long-term relationships.

Explore the link between sex and technology—we'll help you navigate the world of on-line sex, steer you toward our favorite websites, and offer advice on selecting adult CD-ROMs. We've added an entirely new chapter on censorship to keep you apprised of the government's ongoing efforts to curb your access to and enjoyment of sexual materials. Finally, we've updated and expanded our resource listings, as well as the bibliography and videography.

Enjoy!

Anne Semans and Cathy Winks
San Francisco
January 1997

CHAPTER 1

About Good Vibrations

The Good Vibrations Philosophy

We are two very lucky women. For over a decade, we've been working at Good Vibrations, the women-run, San Francisco-based sex business. Over the years, we've discussed sex toys, books and videos with hundreds of customers in our retail stores, and we've sent our mail-order catalogs to thousands of people. We're understandably the envy of our friends, as playing with vibrators, reading erotica and reviewing X-rated videos are all in a day's work for us. While our parents or former college professors may sometimes wonder what two nice girls like us are doing peddling porn, we feel fortunate to have jobs that inspire us with missionary zeal, are consistent with our feminist politics and are fun to boot.

What's the mission that fills us with such zeal? Our business was founded on the premise that there's more sexual pleasure available than most people experience, and that achieving this pleasure should not be difficult, dangerous or expensive. Our goal is to provide access to sexual materials and accurate sex information in order to combat the fear, ignorance, bias and insecurity that prevent too many of us from enjoying the sexual pleasure that is our birthright.

Not everyone would agree that selling vibrators and X-rated videos is consistent with a feminist agenda, but we believe that honest communication about sex is a prerequisite to equal rights both in and out of the bedroom. The adult-entertainment industry has traditionally been grounded in male experience and geared toward male consumers. Women who enter adult bookstores often feel like unwelcome intruders, while men shopping with their wives or girlfriends may find that products packaged with photos of porn starlets' genitals are more alienating than inspiring.

Our customers frequently tell us how refreshing it is to shop at a women-owned business, as they feel that our "clean, well-lighted" environment is equally appealing to men and women. Good Vibrations, founded in 1977, is part of the grassroots movement that has been picking up steam since the mid-eighties—more and more women have stepped forward to name their own sexual desires and to produce their own sexual writings, images and products, and in the process they've changed the face of the adult industry for men and women alike.

We take a lot of pride in the revolutionary nature of our work. For one thing, we feel that sex toys are inherently revolutionary. Not only are they self-assertion tools—no dildo is ever going to pressure you into an encounter against your will—but when you plug in a vibrator or cue up an X-rated video, you're affirming that you deserve to experience pleasure for pleasure's sake. This affirmation is a great leap of faith for many of us. There are countless ways to experience sexual pleasure, yet we tend to rate sexual activities in a hierarchy of best, second best or better-than-nothing. Whether consciously or not, many of us are still operating from the belief that sex is okay only if we're motivated by the desire to a) make babies; b) express intimacy; or c) please a partner. The idea that pleasure for pleasure's sake is sufficient motivation for sexual activity, and that no means of experiencing sexual pleasure is morally, aesthetically or romantically superior to another, is the subversive philosophy behind the enjoyment of sex toys.

At Good Vibrations, we also take a revolutionary approach to how we market our products. The vast majority of manufacturers and retailers in the adult industry deal in overpriced, shoddy merchandise. They can count on the fact that their customers are simply too ignorant or embarrassed about sexuality to demand the same quality control from sex toys that they would from household appliances or other products. Good Vibrations was one of the first retailers of sexual products to take a consumer-friendly approach to marketing sex toys. We want our customers to make informed choices, so we acknowledge the drawbacks as well as the advantages of everything we carry.

By holding sex toys to the same standards as any other consumer goods, we've been blessed with an enthusiastic, trusting and loyal customer base. Good Vibrations' success has had a ripple effect—other retailers and catalogers have adopted our straightforward approach to selling sexually explicit materials, and manufacturers and distributors have begun making improvements in their product lines.

We call the products we sell and love "sex toys," rather than "sexual aids" or "marital aids." A lot of the stigma attached to sexual merchandise seems to result from the misconception that vibrators, dildos, lubricants and erotica are "aids" for those troubled by sexual "problems." Certainly sex toys are useful tools for individuals and couples who wish to explore and enhance their sexual imaginations and responses, and they can be immensely helpful to preorgasmic women, men with erectile dysfunctions and couples with desire discrepancies. But identifying sex toys as relevant only to those with special needs, let alone relevant only to married couples, is inaccurate at best.

Our products were created first and foremost for fun, and that's why we call them "toys." You don't need to be experiencing a sexual dysfunction to justify purchasing a sex toy, and you shouldn't feel that purchasing a sex toy exposes you as someone with a "problem." No one would describe a bakery as an establishment that sells "dietary aids"—to us it seems equally illogical to describe Good Vibrations as an establishment that sells "sexual aids." Whether or not you yourself enjoy playing with sex toys, we hope you'll agree that they are among the many "normal" options available in erotic accessories, no more and no less.

Yet the Good Vibrations mission to normalize the purchase of sex toys is just the thin end of the wedge—our ultimate goal is to normalize sex as a vital, life-affirming, primal force in human experience. All of us suffer when the Powers That Be—whether religious, political or social—ignore, repress or distort the free expression of sexual energy. This suffering is most disturbingly evident in sexual abuse and most commonly evident in the shame, discomfort and insecurity many of us feel around sex. Sexual shame is completely unnecessary, and both in our work and in this book, we strive to bring the subject of sex into the light and to encourage a spirit of fun and adventure.

Sex Book Hall of Fame

This book would certainly not be possible without the work of some pioneers in the field of popular sex writing. (By "popular" writing, we mean self-help and sex-education books written for the layperson, not scholarly or scientific publications.) We refer customers to these books regularly—and without hesitation—because these titles meet our criteria for accuracy and sex positivity.

Many were written in the seventies and early eighties, inspired by the sexual revolution and the sex research of Masters and Johnson and Kinsey. Books like Lonnie Barbach's *For Yourself* and Bernie Zilbergeld's *Male Sexuality* gave women and men the permission and the tools to explore their sexuality. These books dispensed basic information on sexual physiology, body image, technique, attitudes, gender stereotypes and common problems in a positive, reassuring and realistic manner.

Independently-published books that focus on singular topics have become the cornerstones of our library at Good Vibrations. Betty Dodson's *Sex for One* (published previously as *Liberating Masturbation* and *SelfLove and Orgasm*) does for masturbation what Betty Crocker did for cooking. We've long felt that all massagers and vibrators should be packaged with the definitive owner's manual, *Good Vibrations: The Complete Guide to Vibrators* by Joani Blank. Jack Morin's one-of-a-kind *Anal Pleasure and Health* earns a place as the anal eroticist's Bible.

Early women's health manuals like *Our Bodies, Ourselves* and *A New View of a Woman's Body,* as well as lesbian primers like *Sapphistry* and the S/M compilation *Coming to Power,* contributed greatly to a growing body of writing on women's sexuality and were among the few volumes to reflect, through their illustrations and language, a diversity in age, size and ethnicity. This representation continues to appear in modern manuals geared toward gay and lesbian audiences.

Skip over the dark ages of the late eighties to the nineties—these days a handful of prolific authors pen a variety of unique sex books. Susie Bright offers witty insights into sex and pop culture *(Susie Bright's Sexual State of the Union),* Margo Anand teaches techniques for sexual enlightenment *(Art of Sexual Magic),* Pat Califia doles out thought-provoking essays *(Public Sex)* and S/M how-to books *(Sensuous Magic),* and Good Vibrations founder Joani Blank promotes sexual self-awareness *(Femalia* and *First Person Sexual).*

Today, there are dozens of excellent books on specific sexual themes. Encyclopedias of sexual terminology, practices and history improve your sexual literacy and offer unique cultural perspectives, while modern guidebooks coach you on subjects as specific as oral technique and craft-it-yourself S/M toys. So whether you're looking for information about your neighbors' sex lives *(Sex: Real People Talk about What They Really Do),* the truth about the condom's origins *(History Laid Bare),* musings on pornography *(Talk Dirty to Me* or *Defending Pornography)* or ejaculatory control techniques *(How to Make Love All Night),* there's a good chance you'll find a book in print on that particular subject.

While each of the books in our Hall of Fame makes a unique contribution to our understanding and experience of sex, they tend to address one specific issue or to speak to a specific population, be it trivia buffs, practitioners of S/M, gays, lesbians or married heterosexuals. For many years, we sought in vain for a comprehensive, general-interest sex manual of Hall of Fame caliber.

The Contemporary Sex Manual

The search for the perfect sex manual is particularly frustrating since dozens of new books appear annually, but many are as alienating as they are educational. Why is this?

Sex manuals proliferated during the seventies and early eighties at the same time Barbach and Zilbergeld were penning their self-help books. The social changes inspired by the women's-, gay- and civil-rights movements were reflected in manuals like *Making Love Better, Joys of Fantasy* and *The Complete Guide to Sexual Fulfillment.* Assumptions of heterosexuality were less prevalent; photographs and illustrations depicted various ethnicities; women's sexual gratification became a right not an inconvenience; and sexual activity, experimentation and tolerance were at an all-time high. Lo and behold, all kinds of different people were shown having sex; they looked natural and seemed to be having fun!

Lest you think this good trend continued, we're sorry to disillusion you, but the eighties saw an end to the heyday of sex manuals with integrity. Perhaps it was the emergence of AIDS combined with a conservative administration and the rise of the so-called Religious Right, but a moral smugness soon infused every issue related to sex. AIDS was proclaimed God's punishment for the sin of nonprocreative sexuality, and the threat of AIDS became the deadly deterrent used to scare the raging hormones out of children. (With limited success, as ever-rising statistics on teen sex and pregnancy would indicate. Yet the debate over providing condoms in public schools rages on.)

How is this reflected in modern sex manuals? For one thing, you rarely see the sexual interests of any population other than monogamous heterosexual adults represented. Popular sex manuals, ostensibly geared toward everyone, barely acknowledge homosexuality. Actual photographs or illustrations representing diversity in age, orientation, body type or ethnicity are rare—aliens would think the only people having sex are skinny white heterosexuals. And don't expect to find explicit photographs (regardless of gender or orientation) illustrating the text; recent legislation has targeted graphic images in any and all contexts. So we get books featuring air-brushed photographs of couples demonstrating sexual positions with not a genital in sight! Today's manuals are whitewashed, pure and simple.

The backlash against feminism gave rise to a resurgence of "pleasing your man" advice in mainstream sex manuals. Women are bombarded with suggestions for improving personal appearance, avoiding or "masking a pungent smell around the genital area" (The Magic of Sex), catching a dominant man, and tips for stripping off sexy black lingerie. Instead of emphasizing individual preferences, or pointing out that lots of women like black lingerie and wear it because it's a turn-on for them as much as for their partners, modern sex manuals frequently relegate women's sexual desires to the back seat in the interests of "what men like." The stereotypes about women wanting romance while men want sex have come flying back out of the closet where they should have perished long ago. God help the woman who wants to find out if anyone else likes to dress up in black lingerie and anally penetrate her boyfriend!

Even the most well-intentioned sex books have a tendency to abuse statistics. People frequently use statistics as a means of determining whether they're "normal"—are they having the right kind of sex, the right amount of sex? Yet surveys are just as vulnerable to cultural biases and trends as any

other popular literature. For example, in 1994 sociologists from the University of Chicago published findings from a survey of over 3400 men and women which basically concluded that not only were Americans having sex less frequently and less imaginatively than all prior research had shown, but that less than three percent of the general population is gay. Serious flaws were found with the researchers' methodology, but the damage had already been done—hundreds of people were questioning whether they were nymphomaniacs for wanting sex more than the "norm." These results, published in the book Sex in America, will probably be cited as fact for years to come.

We won't be able to say it enough throughout this book: Everyone's different. This book is not about keeping up with the Joneses or judging the Joneses. It's about finding out what the Joneses—and everyone else on the block—are really doing, so you can try it if it strikes your fancy. While we cop to citing a statistic now and then, it's usually to counter a stereotype. No matter how many times you ask, we won't tell you how many vibrators it would take to satisfy the staff at the White House.

The good news about sex books is—the times they are a changin'. Since the first edition of this book went to press in the early nineties, several manuals have appeared that buck at least some of the unfortunate trends we've just discussed. Although most mainstream manuals still presume a white heterosexual readership, at least now you can find good manuals for gay, lesbian, disabled and multi-partnered individuals. Some books also try to tailor their language to be more inclusive. Graphic representations of different ethnicities are still very rare in sex manuals, however, a variety of ethnic and cultural perspectives are popping up in erotic art and literature. Positive references to sex toys can now be found in mainstream sex manuals such as The Ultimate Sex Guide, 101 Nights of Great Sex, Mindblowing Sex in the Real World and Hot Monogamy, as well as in books targeted to specific audiences such as Sex: A Man's Guide and Women Who Love Sex. We hope that these trailblazers signal a trend toward honest, inclusive books about sex, and we've noted our favorites in the bibliography.

What's Between These Covers

Good Vibrations customers come from a wide range of cultural, religious and political backgrounds; they are all ages and all sexual preferences. We supply sexual resources to urban professionals, bikers, suburban newlyweds, mobile-home-dwelling retirees, college-age lesbians, transsexuals, stroller-pushing moms, therapists and nuns. We hope to reach a similarly wide range of people with this book—gay, straight, bisexual, young, old, novices, old-timers, singles, partnered, multi-partnered, the physically challenged, the transgendered, the hip and the sexually jaded, to name a few. And we dream that this book will wind up in the hands of folks too shy to enter the Good Vibrations stores or to ring up our mail-order department. We may not always succeed, but we try, through our language, illustrations and attitude, to reflect and be respectful of a variety of interests.

It's our experience that people from a wide range of backgrounds share certain traits: They crave accurate, practical, nonjudgmental information about sex, and they relish the opportunity to speak frankly about sexual activities. Furthermore, people of all sexual preferences take pleasure in many of the same toys and activities and have similar questions about what toys to play with and how to play with them. The teen looking for ways to enjoy safer sex and the transsexual looking for alternatives to intercourse may discover identical solutions in one of our chapters.

We've arranged the chapters according to types of sexual activities that can be practiced by one, two, or sometimes more people. For example, whereas most sex books will discuss penetration in a male/female intercourse section—usually billed as the ultimate sexual experience—we describe the variety of ways to penetrate a partner of either sex (vaginally, anally, with toys, fingers, etc.) and as only one of many enjoyable sexual activities. Where physical limitations might hinder an individual's enjoyment of some of the techniques or toys described, we've tried to suggest adaptations that might prove helpful.

You won't find chapters entitled "How Monogamous Heterosexuals Can Spice Up Their Love Lives" or "What Lesbians Do in Bed." We like to think that the contents of every chapter are relevant to women and men of all sexualities. To this end, we speak to our readers directly in the second person, as this seems to us the most graceful way to avoid any presumptions about sex or sexuality. Furthermore, this is how we're accustomed to addressing our customers. You'll notice that we tend to describe sexual activities from the point of view of the active partner. We've done so in order to keep the descriptions simple and the language clear. We certainly don't mean to imply that the experience of the passive partner is of less worth.

One of the most exciting aspects of our job is bearing witness to the breadth and variety of human sexual response and encouraging people to trust their own experiences and to respect their own unique responses. The single most frustrating question Good Vibrations' clerks field every day is "What's the best vibrator (or lubricant or massage oil or erotic video)?" The myth that there's one sure-fire sexual silver bullet that will guarantee orgasm for one and all dies hard. Yet, you wouldn't dream of asking the clerk at a record store, "What's the best CD you've got in here?"

The beautiful and fascinating thing about sexual taste is its variety. We all have the same basic body parts, and our bodies undergo the same basic sexual responses, yet the range in kinds of stimulation people enjoy and how they subjectively experience arousal and orgasm is breathtaking.

You'll doubtlessly consider some of the activities described in this book old hat. Some activities will strike you as intriguing, others will seem completely unappealing, and some will make you want to rush right out and try them for yourselves. We'd just like to point out that this diversity of experience is not only completely "normal" but it's one of the many things that inspires Good Vibrations staffers to get out of bed and go to work every day!

Our Contributors

When we set out to write this book, we knew it wouldn't be complete without input from the people from whom we've learned so much over the years, our customers. Resources describing sex toys and sexual activities that are somewhat off the beaten track are few and far between. At Good Vibrations, we rely heavily on the pooled knowledge of our entire community—vendors, coworkers, peer educators and, above all, the customers whose honest, unabridged feedback we disseminate back through the community.

In order to tease out information we thought would be helpful, we composed a brief questionnaire asking respondents to describe their experiences of orgasm, masturbation, partner sex, sex toys and fantasy, and we distributed these questionnaires in our store and in mail-order packages. We made a conscious decision not to ask our respondents to identify their sexuality, as the issue of whether someone is gay, lesbian, bisexual or heterosexual has very little to do with what she or he enjoys doing in bed. Our goal was not to compile statistics, but simply to get first-person quotes as to what kinds of sexual activities our customers are enjoying and why.

We received over one hundred fifty responses, and reading these completed questionnaires was the best part of writing this book. The responses were sincere, enthusiastic, open, funny, poignant and arousing. We feel privileged to have been entrusted with such honest and forthcoming feedback, and we've included numerous quotes from these questionnaire respondents in the following pages. In some cases, it's impossible to know, not only the sexuality, but even the sex of the person quoted. How does this affect your reaction to the quote? Perhaps you'll want to read the same quote several times over, imagining a different identity for the subject each time. If this exercise should happen to subvert some of your assumptions about gender and sexuality, so much the better.

We've included a copy of our questionnaire in the Appendix in case you'd like to fill one out yourself—many of our respondents told us they enjoyed having the opportunity to think and write about their sex lives, and you may find the process enlightening and enjoyable as well.

Who We Are

In exchange for the intimate personal details our customers shared in their questionnaire responses, we thought it only fair to introduce ourselves and to tell the stories of how we each came to work in a vibrator store.

CATHY I wound up working for a vibrator store because vibrators wound up working so well for me. You could say we have a certain affinity, which dates back to my college years. While debates about feminism, pornography and censorship raged about me, I was in single-minded pursuit of "the big O," the elusive orgasm that always seemed just out of reach. Thorough student that I was, I did extensive research on the subject: reading "The Playboy Advisor" column religiously, combing through *Penthouse Forum* articles for possible techniques, quizzing all my girlfriends about what "it" felt like, and gamely tackling a variety of sexual positions and activities, to no avail.

Finally, after reading the classic texts, *For Yourself* and *Becoming Orgasmic,* I decided to buy myself a vibrator and see what would come of it. Off I went to the Pink Pussycat Boutique in Greenwich Village, where I purchased a battery vibrator made of gleaming gold plastic. Sure enough, reliable, consistent stimulation did the trick for me—I still have sentimental memories of the long summer evenings I spent with that vibrator, enjoying the first orgasms of my life.

My first vibrator got quite a workout, and its motor died within a couple of months. The thought of facing the smirking clerks at the Pink Pussycat again was just too intimidating, so from then on I made my vibrator purchases from mail-order catalogs and drugstores. When I moved home to San Francisco and heard about Good Vibrations, a women-run sex-toy store, it sounded too good to be true. On my first visit to Good Vibes, I was struck by the low-key, living-room atmosphere of the place—the worn carpet, homemade bookshelves and the friendly librarian-type behind the counter were in sharp contrast to the garish walls of the Pink Pussycat and the sterile aisles of a drugstore. Both the store and the electric vibrator I walked out of there with made a lasting impression.

Over the next couple of years, the image of that cozy, hospitable storefront stayed with me, and when I decided that I wanted to give up temporary office jobs in favor of retail work, I took a trip to Good Vibrations to see if they were hiring. Lo and behold, they were, and before I had much chance to wonder just what I was getting myself into, I had a new job.

Customer Snapshots

Over the years our customers have brought us great joy. Imagine waiting on two women in their sixties who are sporting corsages and buying each other a vibrator as part of their day on the town. Imagine getting a thank-you letter from a woman who had never had an orgasm before purchasing her vibrator. Or the woman who feared that the trauma from a violent rape might permanently interfere with her ability to feel sensations during sex, but who shared sex toys with her husband as a way of overcoming her fear and inhibition. She told us, "I have shared many triumphs with your products—without your company, I would never be as far along on my path to sexual freedom as I am today."

Imagine a friendly conversation between two lesbians helping a nervous husband decide which dildo to buy his wife. Or our sympathy when a self-described "sex-starving female from a forgotten land" wrote us from Iran asking if we could smuggle in some lesbian magazines. "Here there is no explicity, and everything about sex is forbidden, especially for female creatures," she confided. We consider ourselves honored to have access to the confidences and concerns of all the curious, courageous folks who come into our stores or write to our mail-order department. Several years ago, a rural mail-order customer wrote to thank us for rushing her order and to say that she was going to dedicate her next vibrator orgasm to the staff of Good Vibrations. How could we help but feel a vicarious glow of sexual pleasure? We feel extremely privileged to have contributed in our own humble way to so many people's pursuit of happiness.

I started out with a part-time sales job, and eventually became store manager and toy buyer. For a period of several years, I worked full time in the store, and there was hardly anyone who came through our doors whom I didn't wait on. Sometimes, I'd have trouble understanding why complete strangers blushed or smiled broadly when they saw me on the street, and then I'd realize they were customers identifying me as "the girl from the vibrator store."

Working at Good Vibrations proved to be both an empowering and entertaining experience. A sex-toy salesperson is sort of a cross between a stand-up comic and an advice columnist. My job as a store clerk was to try to make people comfortable with highly charged subject matter and to offer accurate sex information without judgment or personal bias. I learned how to coax people into handling the display vibrators rather than eyeing them nervously from five feet away. I learned the dildo and harness rap—my personal favorite—backwards and forwards. I learned how to diplomatically insist that someone buying an anal toy buy some lubricant as well. I negotiated the treacherous shoals of whether our books were "erotica" or "pornography." The fact that I'm the hopelessly respectable, wholesome-looking product of girls' schools finally

seemed to serve a purpose—many customers' worst fears about entering a sex store dissolve when they see a "nice girl" behind the counter.

I loved the wide variety of people I met, and the way my own preconceptions were constantly challenged. The hippest leftie was likely to walk out of the store in a panic of shyness. The most Republican of military men was likely to display complete familiarity and affection for our product line. I couldn't guess customers' sexualities, and they couldn't guess mine. It was very liberating to be forced to toss out assumptions and start from square one with each new customer.

In the decade I worked at Good Vibrations, our staff expanded from four to sixty people; we launched a nationwide mail-order business; opened a second store; and became a democratically-managed worker-owned cooperative. There's no way the company could have become as successful as it has if there weren't thousands of people across the country who appreciate sexual products and yearn for sex information. And why should it be otherwise? In a healthy society, shops like Good Vibrations would be like bakeries or hardware stores, with one in every urban neighborhood, suburban mall or small town square. Working at Good Vibrations changed my life, not merely because I took pride in our thriving business and our sociopolitical agenda, but because it was so much fun. After all, selling sex toys is the next best thing to playing with sex toys, and I'm happy I got to do both for a living.

ANNE Vibrators first entered my consciousness in ninth-grade English class. Two girlfriends and I staged a sixties' version of *Romeo and Juliet* that featured Lady Capulet draped over her chaise lounge reading *The Sensuous Woman* (on loan without permission from my friend's mother). Desperate for any and all sex information, we devoured this book in which the mysterious "J" extolled the virtues of vibrators, revealing that these devices could help women have orgasms. After eight years of Catholic school and no real sex education, I barely knew what an orgasm was, but I was quite certain I hadn't had one. I knew I simply had to learn how, but turning to this machine seemed so daring and risqué. I traveled to the next town to buy birth control for fear of being discovered; there was absolutely no way I'd risk being seen purchasing a vibrator!

Somewhere in those high-school years I became best friends with my best friend's shower massager. I experienced long sessions of self-pleasuring in that tiny shower; I would emerge certain that my prunelike skin and rosy glow would be a dead giveaway to her parents and brothers. I know now, of course, that they were none the wiser, but that fear of being caught or discovered acted as a powerful aphrodisiac. While I was busy wasting one of California's precious resources, a friend from English class had gone out and bought herself a vibrator. On a trip we took together I tried it while she was out shopping. What bliss! I came instantly and powerfully. I paused for a few seconds and then went for broke—three or four more orgasms later I was a convert. After we got back from our trip, I headed straight for the nearest drugstore. I didn't care who saw me; no one was going to keep me from such intense pleasure! Selecting my little Oster Coil was easy—it was the only one on the shelf—but that little gem lasted me ten years. Not only that, it serviced many of my roommates and lovers along the way.

During college, the teacher in one of my women's classes arranged a field trip to San Francisco to visit the Women's Building, the women's bookstore and her favorite taqueria. Someone casually mentioned a vibrator store in the neighborhood, but to my disappointment no one suggested we visit. I snuck away from the group that day and crossed the threshold of Good Vibrations for the first time.

I, like so many others before and after, walked through the door, stopped and just gazed, with equal parts wonder, embarrassment and terror. I headed straight for the bookshelves, picked up a book of illustrations of women's genitals and gasped. I picked up a magazine full of lesbians having sex and gasped again. I walked over to the vibrator section, started to gasp and then laughed—sitting next to the modern vibrators were a dozen or so antique vibrators. Everything clicked for me then—people long before me were using these things for more than just massage; there was a historical precedent for my activity. There I was standing in a store devoted to, and not ashamed of, getting people off! My sexual self-esteem soared through the roof.

My euphoria was interrupted by a cheery sales clerk asking if I needed help, which of course rendered me completely mute and sent waves of color up to my roots. I stammered something and stumbled out of the store, only to come back a week later and buy my roommate a vibrator. Since then, I've supplied many of my pals with toys from Good Vibrations—showers, birthdays and weddings are all perfect excuses to slip that little pleasure box discreetly in with the other gifts with a note saying "open in private."

During my post-college job search, a feminist publisher unexpectedly referred me to the owner of Good Vibrations. Much to my astonishment and delight, I soon found myself answering questions about vibrator speed and dildo size for an adoring and curious bunch of customers. Having been raised believing sex was something you didn't talk about, you just "knew," speaking frankly about it to strangers was awkward at first, but eventually became as effortless as giving directions to lost tourists. I have learned an incredible amount from these interactions, and the thought that I may have been responsible for a few customers' sexual enlightenment—as they were for mine—makes me proud. Sure we all blush and stammer, but the payoff is the glee in the eyes of a customer about to purchase a new vibrator, or the hungry anticipation of one who can't wait to leave the store and try out new toys.

There are other things to appreciate about working at Good Vibrations—the sight of a store clerk restocking the shelves with a basket overflowing with sex toys conjures up images of a naughty Little Red Riding Hood. It's a joy to visit the warehouse every afternoon, marvel at the five-foot wall of packages and imagine each customer opening a box and touching his or her toy for the first time. Working with a bunch of people who talk about sex like other employees talk about the football pool is a perspective I'll never take for granted. And having recently been pregnant and experienced a sex life held hostage to the whims of raging hormones, I feel a renewed gratitude for the privilege of easy access to good sexual resources.

How to Use This Book

In our fantasies, we dream of this book with its cracked spine and well-thumbed pages lying on your nightstand next to your vibrator, lube, massage oil and condoms. In reality, we hope you'll use this book to explore your own sexuality in whatever way you see fit. Whether you're interested in a particular practice or are searching for some fresh ideas, we encourage you to read the entire book—you never know what might spark your imagination!

The other advantage to reading this book in its entirety is that you increase your comfort level, not only with your own sexuality, but with that of others as well. Our book is about exposing yourself to and exploring a range of sexual activities. We certainly don't expect you to like them all; we don't even expect you to try them all. But if your sex life or your feelings about your sexuality improve one millimeter thanks to something you read here, we'll have been successful.

The New Good Vibrations Guide to Sex is not a program or an exercise book. For example, we won't promise you twenty-four hours of ecstasy in exchange for using six toys four times a day. This sort of goal-oriented approach only serves to make people more self-conscious about performance at the expense of enjoying them-

selves in the moment. We merely offer you a menu; it's up to you to sample the entrées.

You will notice that we've chosen not to write about subjects we felt were out of our league. While we expect that individuals with sexual dysfunctions will benefit from much of the information in this book, we are not qualified to explore them in depth, and we direct you to the resource listings for referrals. Whether you're looking for the sex-toy outlet nearest you, a good sex-information line or a sex therapist, we think you'll find our resource listings helpful. We've also compiled a bibliography and videography, which should provide you with some excellent self-help and fantasy material.

Finally, we hope all of you think of sex as something to enjoy throughout your lifetime. Many of the activities and toys we describe can be enjoyed at any age and regardless of whether or not you have a partner (we plan to masturbate from the cradle to the grave). It might be too much to hope that teenagers will get their hands on this book, but should you find yourself reading this line, congratulations! We like to think this book could contribute to your evolution as a sexually healthy, responsible adult. There are too many people telling you that sex is evil and dirty (yet who can't deny their own sexual urges), so let us point out your many sexual options and cheer you along the way! Similarly, society tends to label older adults as sexless, but there's no reason we can't enjoy sex for many years. If you're experiencing some physical constraints, sex toys and fantasies are among the many options at your disposal—all it takes is the time and desire.

More than anything, this book is a celebration of the sexual nature of every living and breathing individual, regardless of how you choose to express it. A healthy sex life is your birthright, and no one should be deprived of either the information or the tools to pursue it. By reading this book, you're taking responsibility for your sexual self, thereby becoming part of the celebration. While we recognize that AIDS has affected many peoples' experience of sex, our enthusiasm for sex is not diminished, and we hope yours is not either. It is not only possible, it's exciting to have great sex safely. We'll offer our suggestions throughout the book—but it's up to you to put them into practice.

Sexual Self-Image

A healthy sense of self-esteem can improve your sex life, just as a healthy sex life can improve your self-esteem. Allow us to illustrate this maxim with a few examples. If you feel good enough about your body and your sexual desires to masturbate, the act of masturbating will make you feel even better about your body and your desires. Or try this one on for size: Confidence in your beliefs about safer sex will contribute to an erotic, safe sexual encounter with a new partner, resulting in increased confidence in yourself.

Clearly, self-esteem is an integral part of your sexuality. Self-acceptance is a prerequisite for any intimate relationship—especially the one with yourself. Whether you're gathering the nerve to try a new sex toy or preparing to negotiate a sexual scene with a partner, the more confidence you bring to a sexual encounter the more likely you are to meet with success. At Good Vibrations, we've been able to witness first hand the impact that sexual information and tools can have on self-esteem, as evidenced by these two customers:

> *I was non-orgasmic for years, but with a little advice/assistance from your store and a vibrator, I am now orgasmic. I can't tell you how happy this has made me. Tapping into this sexual energy has vitalized me and improved my life in every way!*

> *The anal toy I bought from your company three years ago was the most wonderful thing I ever purchased!*

We are about to describe a myriad of activities you can try alone or with other people, and we recognize that nothing is ever as easy as it sounds on paper. Experimenting requires that you assert yourself and take a few risks. Part of jumping this hurdle requires admitting that you deserve sexual pleasure. Two things tend to dampen self-esteem when it comes to claiming your pleasure: One is body image, and the other involves the messages we receive about what kind of sex we should be having. We may experience these messages differently, but each of us can benefit from an increased awareness of how they affect our sex lives.

We hope you'll use this chapter to explore your own sexual self-image. Self-love doesn't refer just to masturbation; it encompasses the physical, psychological and subconscious relationship we have with ourselves. The more familiar you are with your own sexual profile (including past and current attitudes, roadblocks, battles won and those being waged), the more confident you'll be in your approach to sex. We recognize that everyone suffers from poor sexual self-esteem occasionally—there are times when we simply don't feel attractive, loved or satisfied with ourselves. It's normal! But being in a perpetual state of dissatisfaction might indicate some more ingrained problems. Hopefully this discussion will help you to identify any problem areas, to uncover an endless list of reasons to love yourself and, ultimately, to emerge with a happier, healthier self-image.

Body Image

Physical Appearance

You're probably familiar with the statistics revealing that only a very small number of people (at least in the United States) are satisfied with their bodies. While most of us continue to have sex despite wishing we had better hair or thinner thighs, the extent to which these anxieties about appearance erode our sexual self-esteem is painfully disproportionate. Almost everyone has experienced, in some form, the effects negative body image can have on one's sex life, whether you're feeling unattractive and plan to put more energy into your sex life after you've lost ten pounds or you're having trouble enjoying sex because you're embarrassed by some physical attribute.

Even though we may know better, it's not easy to steel ourselves against the (often sexualized) media images of perfect body-types that bombard us daily. Whether you're a woman trying not to envy the curves on the latest *Cosmopolitan* models or a man who notices he doesn't fill out his briefs like the athletes in the underwear ads, the images can be depressing at best and damaging at worst (as when taken to extremes in the case of eating disorders):

I much prefer watching videos of "normal people." We don't all have to be Cindy Crawford or Richard Gere to be sexy, sensual people.

Given that you can't very well close your eyes to the media, you can keep a few things in perspective. Remember, these images reflect a small segment of the population, the young and thin; there are folks of all ages, sizes, physical abilities, ethnicities and proclivities enjoying sex. Real diversity is visible right outside your door—take a walk or ride the bus; what you see is far more representative of America's sexual jigsaw puzzle than what's plastered up on a billboard. These people are all having sex with each other, which simply proves that all kinds of bodies enjoy all kinds of sex with all kinds of other bodies. Maybe you prefer burying your nose in soft flesh to bouncing off hard muscle. Maybe that bald head heats you up at night whereas those golden locks leave you cold. Maybe you're the only one who even cares about the size of your feet. The point is, trying to live up to a glorified ideal in hopes that it will bring you better sex is a waste of time and energy because sexual chemistry is not that formulaic. What's more, society's definition of beauty changes with the wind—by the time you've lost twenty pounds, thin might be out and Rubenesque in. We encourage you to scoff at the societal ideal and celebrate your body's uniqueness.

While we wish we could just tell you to "accept your body unconditionally," and you'd do it, we know that's not very realistic. Some of us have been harboring new visions of ourselves for our entire lives and can't just wish them away. But questioning whether your vision is necessary, productive and realistic might give you some answers that will alleviate the pressure. You could try a few of the following suggestions to work on improving your self-esteem:

♦ Start a list of all the attributes you like about your body. Keep it somewhere and add to it. Share it with a partner.

♦ Strip down to your birthday suit, stand in front of the mirror and get used to looking at your body. Tell yourself what you like—appreciate your body's uniqueness. If you get good at this, you may end up with some hot erotica!

♦ Listen to compliments people give you and try to accept and believe them.

♦ Expose yourself to images of different types of people being sexual. There are plenty of magazines that do show other body types—visit a large newsstand or the library and check some out. More and more collections of erotica are devoted to specific groups. For example, *Fat Girl* is a fat women's sex 'zine, *Erotique Noire* is by black men and women, and *Pleasure in the Word* is by Latin American women.

♦ Join a support group. Just finding out you're not alone can boost your self-esteem.

♦ Talk to a close friend—share your anxieties as well as what you admire about yourselves and each other. Try exploring where some of your attitudes originated.

♦ Change something about your physical appearance that will boost self-esteem—new clothes, hairstyle, glasses. If you're bound and determined to diet, be realistic. Set reasonable goals, eat nutritiously and get plenty of exercise.

♦ Learn how to give and receive massage. This can enhance your appreciation and enjoyment of your body and of others.

♦ Read some self-help books about body image and self-esteem.

Genitals

Few of us were given permission, let alone encouraged, to familiarize ourselves with our genitals. Any self-discovery we experienced as kids was usually accidental and nearly always secretive. This manifests itself in adulthood, particularly for some women, as a tendency to ignore our genitals and/or consider them dirty or off limits. The women's health movement in the early seventies sought to put women "in touch" with their genitals by teaching self-examination. Some women who had never seen other women's genitals expressed private fears that theirs were ugly or deformed. A few publications have sought to remedy this lack of visual representation: *A New View of a Woman's Body* and *Femalia* feature full-color photographs of women's vulvas, while *Sex For One* and *The Cunt Coloring Book* contain black-and-white illustrations.

Men, too, can harbor less than enthusiastic feelings about their genitals. Obsession over penis size is wasted energy since the stereotype equating sexual satisfaction with penis size is a ridiculous myth. Not only are people's orifices different sizes (meaning that the likelihood of a "perfect fit" is slim), but sexual gratification in a relationship comes from countless other things, from full body pleasuring to good communication.

If you feel negative or ambivalent about your genitals, ask yourself why. Perhaps you too just need to familiarize yourself with your own anatomy. Sit down in the nude with a mirror and the following chapter on anatomy and learn the names for each part of your genitals. Masturbate—this is an excellent way to appreciate your genitals; it feels great and has a direct impact on self-esteem!

Attitudes about Sex and Pleasure

Just as we should question media messages about body type, so too should we question the messages we receive about sex and pleasure. Whether it's a politician telling you to "just say no" to sex, a support group warning you that you are a "sex addict," or a sex researcher telling you you're sexually illiterate, you've got to stay on your toes if you want your sexual self-esteem to emerge intact. When internalized, some of these messages can damage self-esteem because they leave you feeling—depending on the script—inadequate, oversexed, presumptuous, promiscuous or ignorant. We pick up these messages all over the place—from parents, church, friends, media, sex "experts," medical professionals, lovers. When it comes to sex, their favorite stomping grounds have to do with quantity and quality.

How Much? As Much as You Want!

We live in a society founded on certain Puritan notions of abstinence and self-control. Throughout this book you'll see examples of the ways society has attempted to regulate the amount of pleasure we should have—from "masturbation will give you hairy palms," to "keep up that pace and you'll get an STD for sure." As a result, we sometimes question whether we even deserve pleasure. If we answer yes, the next question is how much do we deserve? Won't too much lead to dependency? Disease? A bad reputation? This fear can play itself out in our sex lives in many ways—perhaps we don't masturbate as often as we'd like, perhaps we feel selfish having more than one orgasm, maybe we don't ask for what we really want to avoid risking sounding greedy. Even if you have all the facts and sexual resources you need, you may still find it a bit overwhelming to confront the sheer amount of pleasure you're capable of having. You may unconsciously find an abundance of pleasure intimidating and wonder if there must not be something wrong with feeling so good.

We can't wave a magic wand and erase centuries of social conditioning, but we would urge you to be conscious of these underlying influences. A lot of our customers are so accustomed to the notion of sexual deprivation that they become alarmed at how easy it is to feel good with sex toys. A common concern is, "If I buy this vibrator, won't it ruin me for regular sex?" What an interesting concern! After all, no one refuses to bake a chocolate mousse cake on the grounds that it might "ruin" them for apple pie—more likely, you'd leap at the chance to expand your dessert repertoire. Our experience suggests that increased sexual pleasure doesn't lead to anarchy, the destruction of your relationship or the degradation of family values. Instead, the more pleasure you have, the more pleasure you're capable of having.

On the Road to a Soaring Self-Image

Obviously, not everyone has the same self-image issues. Some of us are the products of loving and understanding parents whose example fostered healthy self-esteem in their children, like this man:

I ordered one of your Magic Wands because I have vivid memories of my parents' now eleven-year-old model (my first orgasm at age thirteen).

It has been a reliable tool and toy for them, so I want it to start us off on the right foot, too.

For many of us, developing strong sexual self-esteem may become an even greater challenge because of present difficulties or past experiences. Perhaps you're a lesbian coming out to conservative parents in a small town; you're recovering from some sexual trauma; you're having questions about gender identity; or you're simply going through puberty. You are taking a huge step towards sexual self-assertion simply by reading this book, and we hope that you, like this customer, will benefit from the honesty, acceptance and encouragement you find within these pages:

As a survivor actively healing from childhood sexual abuse, I want to tell you what an important place your products, catalog and philosophy hold in my life. It is incredibly validating to me as I continue my healing journey to realize that sexuality chosen and desired by consenting adults is not only okay but fun. Thanks for being a part of my healthy and whole sexuality in a powerful way.

We realize there are other important issues, relevant to your experience, that we are not qualified to address here. We've provided resource listings in the back of the book that we hope you'll utilize along with the bibliography.

Finally, we suspect that all of you have a fairly positive sexual self-image or you wouldn't be reading this! We applaud your initiative and hope this book will give you the tools and motivation to pursue your sexual dreams.

CHAPTER 3

Sexual Anatomy 101

Although there's a lot more involved in sexual pleasure than focusing on what's "down there" between your legs, it's also true that many men and women could be experiencing more sexual pleasure if they were better informed about their own and each other's genitals:

> *I'm always shocked at how few of my partners—women or men—know anything about female anatomy. I've had girlfriends who thought their urethras were in their vaginas. People act like it's all just blurred together "down there."*

> *I wish I had a dollar for every time I've asked a woman to grab hold of my penis more firmly. They always act like it's so delicate and they're afraid they might hurt me if they take off the kid gloves.*

So before we go any further, we'd like to offer you a brief tour of human genital anatomy. Why not get undressed, get comfortable, grab a hand mirror and follow along on this guided tour of your own genital landscape?

On the surface, women's and men's genitals don't seem to have a whole lot in common. But a closer look reveals that they are two very similar structures. Every part of the vulva has its counterpart in the penis—and vice versa.

Female Anatomy

The female external genitals are generally referred to as the *vulva.* Your vulva includes the outer lips or *labia majora,* the inner lips or *labia minora,* the tip of the clitoris and the vaginal opening. Women's labia vary greatly in size, shape and coloration. Similarly, the clitoral tip or glans of the clitoris can vary in size, shape, color and the extent to which it protrudes from under the clitoral hood.

> *When I took Betty Dodson's Bodysex workshop, my favorite part was the genital show-and-tell. We each took turns sitting in front of a hand mirror and displayed*

our vulvas to each other, while Betty extolled their virtues and variety. It was amazing to hear the sighs of awe as we each unveiled ourselves. One woman had a blue clitoris; another, black feathered lips contrasted against a rosy interior; another, rich layers of folds; and another had labia that folded right up like a heart-shaped ziplock.

The Clitoris

You can easily locate your clitoris, the most sensitive spot in your pubic area, tucked under the folds of skin where the top of your labia meet. Pull back the hood of skin over the clitoris to reveal the clitoral glans. You may be surprised at how much it resembles a miniature penis—or how much a penis resembles a large clitoris. If you move your fingers above your glans and press into your body, you should be able to locate something that feels like a short rod of cartilage directly beneath the skin and extending up to your pubic bone. This is your clitoral shaft.

Until fairly recently, the clitoris was defined as a visible, highly sensitive glans connected to the short clitoral shaft under the skin. Since the early eighties, feminist health clinicians and educators—most notably Suzann Gage, in *A New View of a Woman's Body*—have pointed out that the clitoral glans is actually only the tip of the proverbial iceberg. Beneath the skin the clitoral shaft separates into two legs (or *crura*) which extend in a wishbone fashion for about three inches on either side of the vaginal opening. The entire clitoris consists of erectile tissue made up of blood vessels, spongy tissue and nerves, just like the erectile tissue of the penis. During sexual stimulation this tissue fills with blood, and the clitoral glans, shaft and legs swell and become firmer. Since the clitoral legs run beneath the labia, when you stimulate the urethra, vagina or anus, you indirectly stimulate the clitoris as well.

The clitoris is the only organ in the human body whose sole function is to transmit sexual sensation. Despite the constant outpouring of sex "information" in popular culture, thousands of men and women still have no idea that the clitoris exists. At the same time, many women who know the clitoris exists and who regularly enjoy orgasms from clitoral stimulation are convinced that "vagi-

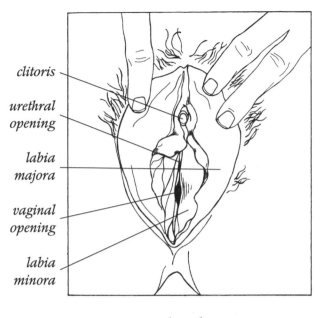

The vulva

clitoris

urethral opening

labia majora

vaginal opening

labia minora

nal orgasms" are somehow superior. Yet it's impossible for a woman to stimulate her vagina without simultaneously stimulating her clitoris. Some women do experience different types of orgasm, which they identify with either clitoral or vaginal stimulation:

I feel there is a difference between clitoral orgasms and orgasms I have without clitoral stimulation.

In my experience, there are clitoral orgasms and G-spot orgasms.

If these kind of distinctions fit your own experience, feel free to make them. If reading these quotes makes you worry that you're missing out on another "kind" of orgasm, remember that orgasm is a subjective experience. After all, the clitoris and vagina don't inhabit separate postal codes, and the sexual pleasure each provides is completely interconnected.

The Urethral Sponge (A.k.a. the G-Spot)

As you move your attention down from your clitoris toward your vaginal opening, you should be able to locate the opening of the urethra, the tube that conducts urine from the bladder out of the body. The urethral opening is more visible in some women than others. You may have to spread your labia and bear down with your pelvic muscles to get a good look at this area. The spongy acorn-shaped protrusion around the urethral opening is loaded with nerve endings and is an erogenous zone for many women. For others, stimulation of this area may be irritating and unpleasant.

Inside your body, the urethra runs parallel to and above the vagina, so that the ceiling of the vagina is closest to the floor of the urethra. The urethra is surrounded by spongy tissue dense with blood vessels and containing glands similar in their makeup and in the fluids they produce to the male prostate gland. These glands are most densely concentrated in an area equivalent to the outer third of the vagina. This urethral sponge is what has come to be called the *G-spot,* or female prostate, named after Ernst Grafenberg, a gynecologist who first published research on the erotic pleasure potential of the urethra in the 1940s and 1950s. Some women greatly enjoy stimulating the urethral sponge, and some women experience an ejaculation of fluids through the urethra as a result. This experience has come to be termed *female ejaculation.*

So You Want to Find Your G-Spot

We've chosen to use the somewhat arbitrary term *G-spot* throughout this book because it's made its way into popular usage, thanks to the publication of a book by the same name in 1982. Unfortunately, this terminology plays into a common sexual misconception that specific physiological buttons need only be located and pressed to produce mind-blowing pleasure. The G-spot has variously been described as a dime-sized, quarter-sized or half-dollar-sized raised area located in the front wall of the vagina. Many women are understandably confused by this notion of the vagina as piggy bank and fret that they "don't have" or "can't find" the G-spot. The G-spot is not a vaginal ecstasy button—it's simply a cushion of tissue wrapped around the urethra. Your urethral sponge can be stimulated through the front wall of your vagina in the same way that a man's prostate gland can be stimulated through the front wall of his anus. While every woman has a urethral sponge, not everyone has the same response to its stimulation— your reaction could range from pleasure to indifference to irritation:

I've never had an orgasm through intercourse or stimulation of the G-spot. I can't seem to find it!

G-spot stimulation to me simply feels good; it does not generate an orgasm.

The only orgasm I have ever experienced was elicited by intense penetration and stimulation of my G-spot by my partner, using her fingers.

We certainly encourage you to explore G-spot stimulation either with your own or a partner's fingers, with dildos or through intercourse. Many women find that G-spot stimulation is only pleasant after a certain level of sexual arousal has been reached. If you are tense or insufficiently aroused, prodding your urethral sponge will probably only irritate your bladder. Choose the position that best enables you or your partner to reach the front wall of your vagina—squatting, lying on your stomach or rear-entry intercourse are all good bets. Dildos are also particularly handy helpers, as they can reach farther than most people's fingers, and they afford the firm pressure that many G-spot-sensitive women find most arousing. Numerous G-spot vibrators and vibrator attachments, curved to hit the front wall of the vagina, have come on the market since the early eighties. You may or may not find these long enough or curved just right to hit your individual G-spot.

Doggy-style sex seems to provide a highly pleasurable form of G-spot stimulation.

I often hit what I believe is my G-spot with the aid of a pillow and my legs in the air. It produces an almost painful orgasm that's great.

I found my G-spot with a vibrator. I have to angle it towards my belly and put it on high. Intense.

Female Ejaculation

Continuous stimulation of the urethral sponge can cause the paraurethral glands to fill up with a clear, odorless fluid which is sometimes expelled from the body through the urethra. This ejaculation can either accompany orgasm or simply be part of arousal. Ejaculation and orgasm are two distinct physiological phenomena in both women

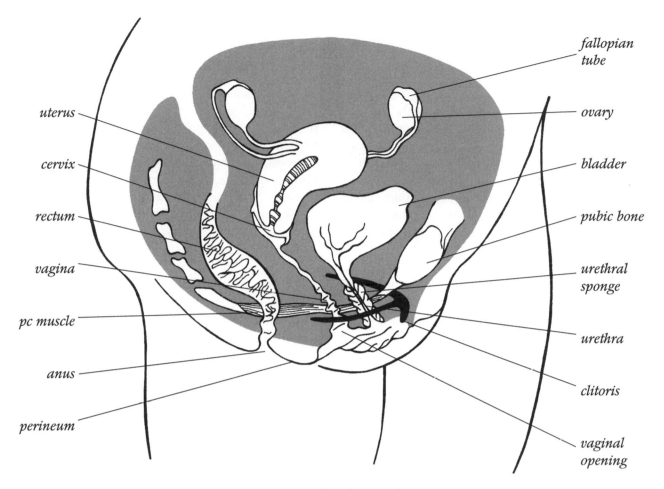

uterus

cervix

rectum

vagina

pc muscle

anus

perineum

fallopian
tube

ovary

bladder

pubic bone

urethral
sponge

urethra

clitoris

vaginal
opening

Female genitals

and men. Female ejaculation has been around as long as females have been around. Until recently, however, medical literature dismissed anecdotal evidence, suggesting instead that ejaculation was urinary incontinence:

> *I had never experienced ejaculation before I was with a woman. I have always had orgasms, but never like those I have now. At first I would love the wet sensations but seconds later feel guilty, thinking maybe it was pee. It smells like pee, and there aren't too many documents supporting the female ejaculation theory. I wish I wasn't so uptight, because it is a very enjoyable experience.*

In recent years, female ejaculate has been chemically analyzed and determined to be distinct from urine in its composition, although the ejaculate of some women has been found to be more similar to urine than that of other women. In either case, ejaculation is a perfectly normal phenomenon, and if you've ever felt embarrassed or intimidated by the fear that you're peeing in bed, we hope the following quotes will inspire you to go ahead and do what comes naturally:

> *I've found that ejaculation happens when I've been slowly aroused and teased maximally (clitorally speaking) by a patient partner, as this can take one to two hours. It's wonderful and very intense! At first I thought I peed, but then I thought, "Who cares?"*

> *I've ejaculated many times, especially during pregnancy when I'm particularly juicy anyway. Has made me nervous partner reaction-wise, but it feels goo-oo-ood.*

> *I ejaculated the first time when I was twenty-five and was on top during intercourse with a man.*

The next time I ejaculated was recently during G-spot stimulation by my girlfriend's hand. I just realized that urination anxiety was holding back my ejaculate, so I let it go, and I did ejaculate!

If you've never experienced ejaculation and would like to, try incorporating G-spot stimulation into your usual masturbation techniques. As your urethral sponge grows more swollen and sensitive, bear down with your pelvic muscles. Women's experiences of ejaculation can range from simply feeling more wet than usual to shooting jets of fluid. Of course, plenty of women may never ejaculate and may never want to. We are pleased that female ejaculation is now acknowledged as a genuine sexual response, but we don't like to see it promoted as a new goal that every woman should strive to achieve. Ideally, you'll undertake your explorations in a spirit of fun and curiosity, rather than one of grim determination. Whether or not you "find" your G-spot, you're certain to learn new things about your sexual responses:

Discovering my G-spot, actually seeking it out rather than just having occasional, accidental stimulation of it, has totally increased my sexual pleasure—whether alone with a dildo or with a partner. I never knew what was producing the giant wet spot underneath me until then. I love the feeling that I might be about to pee...

I still haven't found the G-spot yet, but I'm enjoying the search. The longest, most intense multi-orgasm I had was with a man stimulating my clit while thrusting my new G-spot vibrator in. Whoa. I didn't realize how much fun that G-spot vibrator was until I put someone else behind the wheel.

I was so blown away the one time I climaxed with G-spot stimulation that I didn't notice if I ejaculated, though I wouldn't be surprised if it happened. I definitely ejaculated verbally!

The Vagina

You'll notice that the vaginal opening appears as folds of skin, rather than as an open space. The vagina is extremely expandable—think childbirth—yet most of the time the vaginal walls rest against

each other. The vagina is about four inches long. After the initial bulge over the urethral sponge, the vaginal canal curves back to the cervix, the neck of the uterus. The outer third of the vaginal walls consists of ridges and folds of tissue, has more nerve endings, and is more sensitive than the rest of the vagina. The inner two-thirds of the vaginal walls are smoother and contain few nerve endings—therefore, the inner part of the vagina is more responsive to pressure than to light touch, friction or vibration. The cervix has no nerve endings on its surface, but, like the inner vagina, can be quite sensitive to pressure. Every woman's vaginal geography is unique, and we encourage you to explore your own to discover any "hot spots" or particularly pleasurable areas inside your vagina. Some women have no interest in pursuing vaginal stimulation during sex, while others find that penetration enhances a sexual experience:

I've definitely noticed a difference between coming with penetration and coming without. With penetration, there's more of a total body sensation, whereas without (i.e., with finger, tongue or vibrator on my clitoris), sensation is more localized. Both are great.

I differentiate between the intense clit-centered climaxes I have during oral sex or manual stimulation and the wave of full-body climaxes I experience during vaginal penetration. They are both equally desirable, and I usually experience both.

Male Anatomy

External Organs

While most of us are familiar with what the penis and scrotum look like externally, there's a surprising amount of mystification around what's beneath the surface. There are no bones and no muscles inside the penis. Instead, two long cylinders containing spongy erectile tissue and blood vessels run down the length of the penis. These cylinders are called the *corpus cavernosa* and are analogous to the clitoral legs in women. The urethra runs along the bottom of the penis, surrounded by a third cylinder of spongy tissue, the

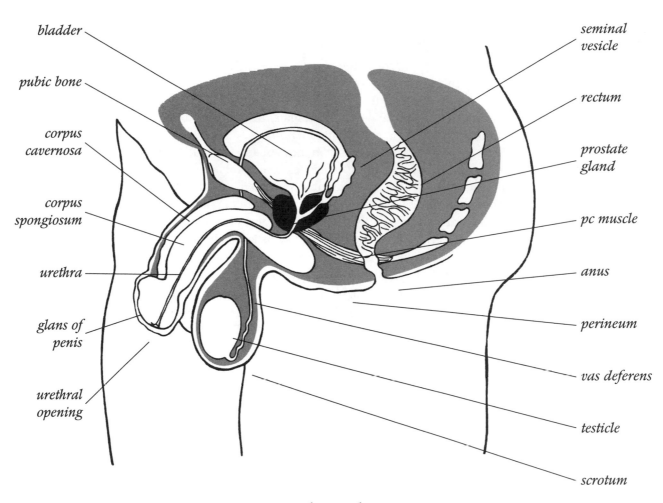

bladder

pubic bone

corpus
cavernosa

corpus
spongiosum

urethra

glans of
penis

urethral
opening

seminal
vesicle

rectum

prostate
gland

pc muscle

anus

perineum

vas deferens

testicle

scrotum

Male genitals

corpus spongiosum, which is connected to the glans or head of the penis. The urethral opening is in the glans. The head of the penis is generally the most sensitive part, particularly around the coronal ridge at the base of the glans, and is analogous to the tip of the clitoris. However, nerve endings are not as densely concentrated on the head of the penis as they are on the clitoral tip, so the glans of the penis is considerably less sensitive than the clitoral glans.

If you hold your penis in your hand, you'll notice that the skin covering the penis slides easily over the shaft. All men are born with a foreskin, a retractable extension of the skin of the penis, which covers the glans. When boys or men are circumcised, this loose skin is cut off. Since the glans of an uncircumcised man is protected by his foreskin, it is usually more sensitive when exposed

than the glans of a circumcised man. Try stroking all around your glans and coronal ridge to see what spots feel particularly pleasurable. Some men find stimulation of the urethral opening pleasant while others find it irritating. The frenulum, the piece of skin on the underside of the coronal ridge between the shaft of the penis and the glans, is another area rich in nerve endings. As you move your hand down the shaft of your penis, pay attention to the hump of skin running along the underside of your penis—you are feeling the *corpus spongiosum,* which lies just beneath the skin. This ridge, known as the raphe, runs from the frenulum all the way down the shaft of the penis, along the middle of the scrotum, to the anus and is particularly sensitive to touch.

The scrotum is the loose sac of skin, hanging below the penis, which contains the testicles.

A Word About Circumcision

The foreskin, nature's way of keeping the glans of the penis protected and lubricated, is a sheath of skin lined with mucous membrane. Not only is the foreskin itself packed with sensory tissue, rich with blood vessels and nerve endings, but it serves to enhance the sensitivity of the glans of the penis and to provide natural lubrication. This has led many men and women in recent years to question the American social norm of circumcising infant boys.

While circumcision is a religious, cultural ritual in Judaism and Islam, it's a purely secular, medical tradition for the majority of American families, one which is arguably out-moded and unnecessary. Circumcision became widespread in twentieth-century America in part due to a legacy from the Victorian era, in which circumcision was seen as a method of controlling masturbation, and in part due to post-World War II standards of hygiene. By the sixties, doctors routinely circumcised between eighty to ninety percent of American boys, as it was widely believed that circumcision would reduce chances of fungal infections, urinary tract infections, cancer of the penis and cervical cancer.

Recent research has proven that good hygiene (a simple daily washing with soap and water under the foreskin), rather than circumcision, is the key to avoiding infections, and that circumcised American men don't have lower rates of penile cancer than uncircumcised Europeans, nor do American women have lower rates of cervical cancer than the female partners of uncircumcised men. Consequently, American circumcision rates have dropped below sixty percent and are steadily decreasing. If you're an expectant parent, we strongly advise you to research and come to your own decision before the birth of your child, so you'll be prepared to communicate your wishes to doctors after delivery.

They say you should circumcise your son if his father is circumcised, so the kid doesn't worry about his penis looking different. Well I'm a lesbian who's not planning to circumcise her son, so I guess I'll have to go out and buy some uncircumcised dildos and leave them lying around the bathroom.

The majority of circumcised men in America experience the penis as a great source of pleasure. There are, however, men who experience desensitization of the glans and mourn the loss of the foreskin to such an extent that they seek "uncircumcision" or "foreskin restoration." If you're interested in pursuing the nonsurgical methods of restoration, all of which involve gradually stretching the skin of the penile shaft until it covers the glans, more power to you. However, we'd strongly advise against surgical intervention, which frequently results in problematic scarring.

Testicles are two glands involved in the production of both testosterone and sperm. They can vary greatly in size, from grape-sized to egg-sized. The scrotum serves to protect the testicles from injury and from extremes of temperature, which would inhibit sperm production. You've probably noticed that when you're cold, physically active or sexually excited, the muscles in your scrotum contract, thereby pulling your testicles protectively closer to your body. It's common that one testicle will hang lower than the other. As we're sure you're aware, most men's testicles are extremely sensitive to pain and require gentle treatment.

Although even light tapping on the testicles can be painful, firm pressure or steady pulling on the scrotum can feel good. Many men enjoy having their scrotums stroked, squeezed and tugged on. This is a principle behind the numerous cock-and-ball toys on the market. Cock-and-ball toys, which resemble harnesses for the male genitals, are variously designed to snap around the base of the penis and scrotum, lift and separate the testicles, or stretch the scrotum. Some men enjoy hanging light weights off their scrotums to create a sensation of steady pulling. And some men crave more vigorous treatment:

*I like lots of strong stimulation of my balls.
Squeeze them, smack them, twist them, pull them
apart from side to side, slap them on the steering
wheel of my car—I don't care. I love it all!!!*

Internal Organs

There's more to the male genitals than what's visible outside your body. The base of the penis extends into the body—in fact, there's enough room in the pelvic cavity that the entire penis and testicles can be tucked inside the body when soft. If you press your fingers against your perineum—the area between your testicles and anus—you can feel this root, or bulb, of your penis. The root of the penis is sensitive and can be stimulated through the perineum or the rectum—one reason anal penetration feels pleasurable to many men.

The urethra passes into the body and through the prostate gland to the bladder. The prostate gland, an internal organ that produces ejaculatory fluid, is situated behind the pubic bone and just below the bladder. The prostate is a source of sexual pleasure for many men. Tucked close to the root of the penis, the prostate lies along nerve pathways to the penis and the brain, and is exceptionally well situated to pick up pleasurable signals both coming and going. Many men can have orgasms purely from prostate stimulation. Prostate massage also enhances genital stimulation, as it produces pressure against the root of the penis that feels like an internal erotic massage. The prostate is analogous to the G-spot in women—the decision as to whether to name the G-spot the "female prostate" or the prostate the "male G-spot" is up to you.

You can massage your prostate by inserting a finger about three inches into your anus and stroking toward the front of your body through the walls of your rectum. You'll feel the prostate as a firm bulge about the size of a walnut (it may be larger in men over forty). Given the angles you're working with, you may find it difficult to reach your prostate with your own fingers, but a partner's fingers, a vibrator or a dildo can come in handy. As with G-spot stimulation in women, men are more likely to enjoy prostate stimulation once they're already aroused, and responses to prostate stimulation can range from extreme pleasure to irritation:

*Prostate stimulation? Love it! I often find myself
kneading that area when I read or talk on the
telephone. I love to play with myself.*

*Too much prostate stimulation makes me lose the
desire to orgasm. Is this common, I wonder?
Perhaps it "oversatisfies" me.*

*One of the most wonderful sensations I've
learned to enjoy is prostate massage, which when
combined with oral sex is out of this world.*

Erection

Erections are usually inspired by sexual stimulation. In response to this stimulation, your brain sends signals through your nervous system, which trigger increased blood flow into the penis. As blood flows into both *corpus cavernosa,* the spongy erectile tissues fill up with blood. The cylinders become engorged with blood and expand against the protective membrane that surrounds them, thereby compressing shut the walls of the veins that normally carry blood away. This reduces blood flow out of the penis, which, combined with the pressure of the increased blood flow into the penis, produces an erection. An erect penis can hold eight times as much blood as a non-erect penis. Erect penises don't, however, expand in direct proportion to their non-erect size. Some penises increase in size more during erection than others; there's actually a smaller range of sizes among erect penises than among non-erect penises.

Ejaculation

Although they tend to be inseparably linked in many folks' minds, ejaculation and orgasm are two distinct physiological phenomena, controlled by different nerve groups in the spine. Ejaculation is the result of a build-up of sexual tension that causes muscles near the prostate gland to contract, sending fluids from the prostate gland and seminal vesicles into the urethra. This produces the sensation referred to medically as "ejaculatory inevitability" and popularly as "ohmigod, I'm about to come!" Seconds later, intricately timed signals from the brain close off the valve between the bladder and the urethra and propel the ejaculate down the urethra and out the penis. Generally, ejaculation is accompanied by the involuntary, rhythmic contraction of the pelvic muscles, which is experienced as orgasm. However, it's possible to pass over the neurological point of no return and ejaculate without having yet reached orgasm:

I don't remember having an orgasm without ejaculation, but I have ejaculated without an orgasm—a disappointing experience!

It's also possible for a man to reach orgasm without ever ejaculating. Orgasm without ejaculation can be the result of retrograde ejaculation, which occurs when the valve between your bladder and urethra doesn't close, and ejaculate is forced back into the bladder, rather than out the urethra. Retrograde ejaculation sometimes happens in men with spinal injuries or in men who have had prostate or bladder surgery—it should not adversely affect the pleasure you experience during orgasm. Orgasm without ejaculation can also be a conscious technique in men who train themselves to bypass the expulsion of semen and to experience the pleasurable full-body sensations and muscular contractions of orgasm without ejaculating. We'll discuss the phenomenon of orgasm without ejaculation in the "multiple orgasm" section later in this chapter.

Male and Female Anatomy

Anal Eroticism

The anus is an erogenous zone that doesn't always receive the acknowledgment it so richly deserves. For many people, the anus is the seat of a lot of physical tension and is associated with uncleanliness, discomfort and pain. Anal eroticism is all too frequently dismissed as "unnatural." Yet if you can get past societal taboos and personal fears, you may be pleasantly surprised by the erotic possibilities of anal play.

After all, the anus is not only loaded with blood vessels and nerve endings, but also shares in the genital engorgement of arousal and the muscular contractions of orgasm. Many women and men find that direct stimulation of the anal opening enhances sex. The perineum, the area between the vaginal opening and the anus in women and between the base of the scrotum and the anus in men, is another potential erogenous zone.

The anal opening is controlled by two sphincter muscles, which you can learn to relax and contract at will. The anus is only about one inch long and leads into the rectum, a five to nine inches long, highly expandable canal lined with smooth tissue. Many men and women enjoy the feeling of fullness and pressure in the rectum resulting from anal penetration. Since rectal tissue is not as sturdy as vaginal tissue, and since the rectum takes a sort of S-shaped curve, you should never insert anything rectally that isn't smooth, flexible and well-lubricated. The rectum leads into the colon, so you shouldn't insert anything anally that doesn't have a flared base, to prevent its slipping into your body.

Pelvic Muscles

The pelvic organs are supported by a complex muscle system that lies just beneath the surface of the pelvic floor. The pubococcygeus muscle group—known as the PC muscle, for short—runs from the pubic bone to the coccyx or tailbone and surrounds the genitals in a figure eight. The PC muscle contracts involuntarily during arousal and orgasm. Learning to contract it voluntarily can be a great sexual enhancer.

The easiest way to locate your PC muscle is to practice stopping the flow of urine—the muscle you use to do this is your PC. Once you've found it, you can exercise your PC muscle in a variety of ways. It's helpful to try to coordinate your breathing with these exercises. For example, inhale and contract your PC at the same time. Hold both your breath and your contraction for a few seconds, then exhale and relax your muscle. Or try inhaling slowly while rapidly tightening and releasing your PC as many times as you can before exhaling and relaxing the muscle. Another exercise that involves abdominal muscles as well as pelvic muscles is to inhale and pull up your pelvic muscles as though you were sucking water into your anus and/or vagina, then exhale and bear down as though you were pushing the water out.

These exercises are sometimes referred to as Kegel exercises, in honor of the gynecologist who first popularized them. The benefits of "doing your Kegels" are numerous. You'll gain greater aware-

Beyond Anatomy

Our discussion in this chapter focuses on the anatomy and sexual response of people who are born genetically female or male. In the modern world, we tend to assume that a clear distinction between two biological sexes is not only absolute but integral to defining identity. Yet the distinction isn't so clear. Certain individuals, born with genetic variations in the number and mix of their sex chromosomes, have genitals and hormonal patterns that combine aspects of both sexes. And intersexed people have both male and female genitalia. It's estimated that one to two people out of every thousand are born intersexed, but these figures are hard to confirm, since most intersex babies are surgically altered at birth to be assigned one sex (usually female).

Other individuals realize that the bodies they were born with don't accurately reflect who they are and choose to live as a member of the opposite sex and possibly to pursue hormone therapy and sex-reassignment surgery. Given how expensive and difficult it is to obtain surgery, many transsexuals live as the sex that feels right to them without undergoing surgery.

The surgery for male-to-female transsexuals is more common than that for female-to-male transsexuals. It's been argued that it's less threatening for the medical establishment to surgically create a vagina than to surgically create a penis—but it's only fair to note that it's also less complicated to do the former. In penile-inversion surgery, the penis is turned inside out, so that the skin of the former penis shaft becomes the walls of the new vagina, and part of the *corpus spongiosum* is used to create a clitoris.

Female-to-male transsexuals can choose between phalloplasty—in which a penis is surgically constructed from skin grafts—and metoidioplasty—which involves releasing the testosterone-enlarged clitoris from its hood and creating a scrotum out of the labia majora. The resulting penis is smaller than one "built" through phalloplasty and can't necessarily be used for penetration, but it has full sensitivity, unlike a penis created through skin grafts. In phalloplasty, the clitoris is left at the base of the newly constructed penis, above the scrotum, to allow for sexual sensation.

A thorough discussion of the varieties of pre-operative and surgical procedures available to transsexuals is beyond the scope of this book, but we include referrals in our resource listings. At this time, sex-reassignment surgery is far from perfect. Post-op transsexuals may suffer genital nerve damage, have limited ability to reach orgasm or have reduced sex drives. Others, however, draw on the rich variety of sensations available from erogenous zones other than the penis and vagina: Anal eroticism, dildo play or nonpenetrative activities such as tribadism or intercrural intercourse are among the many options.

Some transsexuals identify exclusively as their post-transition sex and embrace traditional gender roles. Others use the term *transgendered* to identify as someone who blurs the cultural and physiological boundaries between male and female. The transgendered movement includes transsexuals, cross-dressers, intersexed people and anyone who feels the terms *male* or *female* are inadequate to describe their experience. In recent years, an increasing number of transgendered organizations have come forward to draw attention to the fact that our society is oppressively phobic of any blurring of gender lines—transsexuals face hostile and violent discrimination simply for being who they are. The existence and growing strength of the transgendered movement reveals the fluid nature of sexual experience and the futility of limiting our definition of what's sexually "normal."

ness of sensation in your pelvic region. Exercise increases blood flow to the area, which is pleasurable in and of itself. Toned muscles are more flexible and better able to transmit sensation. You may well experience increased vaginal lubrication or easier, stronger erections thanks to a well-toned PC muscle. Techniques of controlling ejaculation and experiencing male multiple orgasm are based on learning to voluntarily contract and relax your PC muscle. Many people report increased sexual sensitivity and stronger orgasms as a result of exercising the PC muscle. And, of course, there are no expensive gym memberships to worry about—you can do your Kegels anytime and anywhere.

For a long time, I thought that feeling a penis inside my vagina would make my otherwise "superficial" orgasms feel more intense and deep. But I was wrong. I started exercising my PC muscle, and from then on whenever I was close to orgasm, I would squeeze my PC muscle, and the orgasm would go straight to my core.

Sexual Response

The Sexual Response Cycle

The *sexual response cycle* is the term used to refer to the physiological changes our bodies go through during arousal and orgasm. Masters and Johnson can be credited with popularizing this phrase. Their laboratory studies of thousands of men and women engaging in a variety of sexual activities led them to develop the concept of a four-stage cycle of sexual response. These four stages are: excitement, plateau, orgasm and resolution.

According to the Masters and Johnson model, the excitement phase in both men and women is characterized by an increase in heart rate, muscle tension and blood flow. Increased blood flow results in engorgement of the genitals, lips and breasts; general body warmth and flushed skin. Women's responses include vaginal lubrication, swelling of the clitoris and vaginal lips, and a lifting up or ballooning of the back of the vagina and the uterus. Men's responses include erection, contraction of the scrotum and elevation of the testicles. Many men and women also experience nipple erection. The entire body experiences muscular tension and warmth. Arousal frequently produces increased sensitivity to stimulation and reduced sensitivity to pain.

The plateau phase is a continuation and heightening of the excitement phase. In women, the clitoris retracts under the clitoral hood; the outer third of the vagina becomes even more congested with blood; and the uterus becomes fully elevated, creating a tenting effect in the inner vagina. Men often secrete a clear glandular fluid, which may contain some stray sperm. Often referred to as "pre-come," this fluid is the reason withdrawal before ejaculation is an ineffective method of birth control.

Orgasm is the discharge of sexual tension through involuntary muscular contractions. These contractions take place in the outer third of the vagina and the uterus in women and in muscles throughout the pelvic region in men and women. Anywhere from three to fifteen contractions occur, at intervals of eight-tenths of a second. Orgasm releases the blood from engorged genital tissue.

During resolution, the body returns to an unaroused state. Heart rate, breathing and blood pressure return to normal; the body flush subsides; and genitals return to their usual size, shape and color. If you've been aroused but haven't had an orgasm, it will take somewhat longer for the blood to ebb out of your congested genitals and for resolution to be completed.

The physiological changes our bodies go through during excitement and orgasm are distinctive and measurable. Your body is undergoing these same changes regardless of what kind of stimulation you are receiving or how subjectively different your arousal and orgasm may feel. Please don't despair, however, if you've never noticed your skin flush during arousal, if you find it hard to conceive of eight-tenths of a second, or if you're not sure if you've ever experienced "the plateau phase." Masters and Johnson's sexual response cycle is a fairly arbitrary construct. They interpreted their data somewhat selectively in order to create a model that could be applied to men and women alike. In fact, few of us experience sexual arousal as though our bodies were spaceships moving inexorably from one discrete launching phase to another as we lift off toward orgasm.

Masters and Johnson's emphasis on the physiology of sexual response has influenced sex therapy and the treatment of people's sexual dysfunctions since the sixties. The idea that sexual response is not only natural, but quantifiable, is appealing. Who wouldn't be tempted by the notion that if we're just taught to push the right physiological buttons, sexual pleasure will automatically follow? The trouble with this mechanical approach to sex is that it doesn't take into account the huge influence that subjective conditions, social factors and psychological readiness have on one's experience of sex. Furthermore, physiological arousal doesn't necessarily indicate a readiness to have sex. Just because a woman is lubricating or a man has an erection doesn't mean he or she feels like being sexual.

Recent years have seen more professional acknowledgment of the power of subjective, immeasurable components in sex. In the seventies, sex therapist Helen Singer Kaplan theorized that desire is a fundamental component of sexual arousal and proposed a three-phase sexual response cycle: desire, excitement and orgasm. Yet, as the lesbian sex therapist JoAnn Loulan points out, even desire isn't a necessary prerequisite to a sexual experience. If you enter into sex with willingness, desire may follow. Kaplan's model has also been challenged by therapists such as David Schnarch, who argues that desire and arousal are each on a different continuum, varying independently of each other. Desire doesn't necessarily begin with sexual stimulation or come to an end upon orgasm. Perhaps the only absolute truth about sexual response is how fundamentally fluid it is. One can move from arousal to desire, from excitement to indifference, from boredom to passion, from orgasm to arousal and back again.

Orgasm

There are many reasons to enjoy sex: It's a celebration of the human body; it's relaxing; it's entertaining; it promotes intimacy; you can do it alone, with a friend or in a crowd. And you can have orgasms as a result. Orgasms are a simple pleasure, which we'd all benefit from taking less seriously. Orgasm generates more anxiety than any other single topic in our line of work. Men worry that they're coming "too quickly"; women worry that they're taking "too long" to come, and everyone worries that they're not having good enough, strong enough or simply enough orgasms. We live in a competitive society, and we need encouragement before we can appreciate our own unique responses, without looking over our shoulders to see if somebody else out there is having an even better—or more "normal"—time. If you had never heard another person describe an orgasm, never read a bodice-ripping novel or never seen a romantic movie, how would you describe your own experience of orgasm?

Some are just a quick hard rush that shoots through my body like a bolt of lightning. Others feel like a slow burn, they build up over time, they tease me, floating up and down my body—spreading out like concentric circles, and then there will be a burst of release.

Orgasms at different times involve different parts of my body—back, buttocks, different parts of my legs down to the calves, feet, shoulders, neck. I must be moving my legs in order to come.

Orgasm feels like water shooting up through the top of a fountain, tickling all the way, then shooting out of the top in electric vibrations through my body.

Orgasm is often for me this very still point; there's lots of movement as I'm getting increasingly excited, but when I come everything is tight and intense and still.

Well, orgasm is the most intensely pleasurable physical sensation I have ever experienced. It can vary from a simple but too-quickly-ended ejaculation, on up the scale to a full-body rush.

Orgasm feels good. Sometimes it's very concentrated, and sometimes it's totally diffuse throughout my body. Sometimes, if I'm very stressed out, it just feels like a release. When I'm relaxed, I feel like I'm floating in a place where there is no time or space.

EXPECTATIONS   Orgasm, in the most pragmatic sense of the word, is an involuntary muscular contraction, which signifies the release of sexual tension. Yet, as the plum in the pudding of sex, this simple physiological reflex inspires a wide range of emotional, psychological and even spiritual responses:

I leave everything. I'm conscious only of ecstatic sensation, a universal sensation, warmth and vibrance coursing through me. Freedom from everything mundane rips through me, and I float on the breath of god—so to speak.

I experience orgasm as a mini-death, approaching black out. Psychologically, I have an approach/avoidance conflict. The closer I get, the more afraid I am. My partner has to reassure me.

My orgasms aren't completely reliable, and I often feel like I need more. Maybe I'm afraid of them. Afraid of the intensity or of being so far away from myself.

Before you read any further in this book, you might want to take the time to consider your own internalized expectations of orgasm. Do you share either of the following viewpoints?

Orgasm is always the ultimate point of any sexual experience. Sex without orgasm is like a cheeseburger without the cheese...missing something.

I enjoy having orgasms, but they're not my goal of sexual activity.

We propose that you consider treating orgasm as a possible, even probable, outcome of any sexual experience, but that you try to avoid focusing on it as a goal. When you focus on the end result of any sexual experience, you run the risk of rushing past or even denying yourself some of the more subtle pleasures to be enjoyed along the way. If you're reluctant to embark on a sexual experience unless satisfaction is guaranteed, you're cheating yourself out of the joys of the unexpected. New toys and techniques may not set you on a tried-and-true path to orgasm, but they will open up entirely new horizons of sensation. We hope that you'll approach the techniques described in this book with pleasure, rather than orgasm, as your goal.

Orgasm leaves me feeling energized, refreshed and beautiful. Sometimes it's a very quick experience, and other times the build-up is so great that it becomes almost like an orgasm itself.

I like reveling in the last minute or two before surrender to orgasm. Often I will tense up all over my body, rise up and let my partner know how good I feel.

Your expectations of orgasm may manifest as anxiety about what type of physiological response truly "counts" as orgasm. This is more of an issue for women than men, as women are more likely than men to have never experienced an orgasm or to feel a discrepancy between their own physiological experiences and a hazy, romantic ideal of orgasm as an earth-shaking event:

I was around ten or twelve, and would lie in bed and rub myself until I shook. I read my mom's Cosmo *magazines and—because I didn't understand what was happening—kept thinking that if I only could get past these spasms, I'd find out what an orgasm was.*

If you are someone who's never experienced an orgasm, many of the toys and techniques described in this book may be of use to you in exploring your sexual responses. Vibrators, which provide sustained, consistent stimulation, are particularly helpful for those women who have not yet been able to move beyond arousal to orgasm. If you're someone who's not sure if she's experienced orgasm, take note of the range of sensations described throughout this book. Do any of the experiences you read about echo your own?

SOLO OR PARTNERED It's quite possible you'll find that your experience of orgasm shifts depending on whether you're alone or with a partner. You may find more freedom in solitude:

I enjoy coming by myself best because I can float uninterrupted from intensely screeching pleasure into blissful relaxation without worrying about pleasuring my partner.

Orgasm is pretty hard to come by for me. It's easily attainable when I'm alone, but a lot harder with a partner. When I'm alone I can go as fast or slow as I want—I guess I don't feel as much pressure to come right away—I can spend as much time on myself as I want.

Or you may find the presence of a companion gives you more satisfaction:

Orgasm with a partner rocks my whole body, and then there's a wonderful release. By myself, it builds to a height of pleasure and then release, not as intense as with a partner.

In the best of sexual relationships, you'll each feel secure in your unique responses, and you can honestly share each other's pleasure, however it's taken:

I find that since I have been with my husband these past five years I can slow down and truly enjoy orgasm. We like to share each other's orgasm, watching the other person come. Coming together is not a necessity, and it's also okay that I do not choose to come during intercourse. Because of this I feel more free about my orgasm. I use a vibrator, dildo and vibrator, my hands, his hand or mouth—and sometimes I do come during intercourse.

MULTIPLE ORGASM *Multiple orgasm* is the term used to describe the experience of having more than one orgasm in quick succession. We do hope you won't translate the fact that some folks experience multiple orgasm into a performance hoop to jump through in bed. However, if you're intrigued by the idea of expanding the parameters of your sexual responses, read on. Whether or not you experience more than one orgasm in a single session, you can certainly have a good time practicing!

Men. Multiple orgasms are more common in women than in men, as men tend to experience what's known as a "refractory period" after ejaculation, during which they're temporarily unable to achieve another erection. This refractory period can last anywhere from a few minutes to a few hours. There are, however, men who have reported experiences of consecutive ejaculatory orgasms with only brief refractory periods between each ejaculation. You may have experienced this yourself in adolescence—it occurs fairly infrequently in men over thirty. More commonly, men who achieve multiple orgasm have trained themselves to orgasm without ejaculating, thereby sidestepping the "draining" effects of ejaculation and the need for a refractory period.

As noted previously, ejaculation and orgasm are two distinct physiological phenomena, and it's possible to train yourself to experience the latter separately from the former. You might undertake this training in the spirit of Taoist sexual practitioners, with the goal of preserving the "vital energy" of your semen. Or you might undertake this training to expand the timing and nature of your sexual experience.

How do you train yourself to orgasm without ejaculating? The key is to consciously play with your level of arousal in order to learn that responses you may have experienced as "inevitable" do fall under your control. Stimulate yourself until you reach the point where you feel an impending orgasm, then stop for up to twenty seconds and wait for the urge to ebb: It's helpful to hold still, breathe slowly and deeply and relax your pelvic muscles. Then start up again. Continue to tease yourself, backing off from the verge of orgasm several times.

My technique is partial orgasms. This is when I jack off for a while, and then when it's getting so good that I have to come, I let go of the pressure from my hand, and just let my cum drip out. This gives me about ninety percent of the pleasure of a complete orgasm, but since there isn't a full release of energy, I can continue this cycle of jacking off endlessly.

I sometimes come without orgasm, and often orgasm without coming. The longer intercourse lasts for me before ejaculation, the greater the chance of orgasm without ejaculation.

Experts on male multiple orgasm fall into two slightly different camps when it comes to coming. Both emphasize the importance of cultivating PC muscle tone and awareness. One school of thought advises men to contract the PC muscle at moments of high arousal as a way of "putting on the brakes" to prevent ejaculation—this squeezing should be followed by holding still, breathing deeply and relaxing all the muscles of the pelvis and butt in order to back off from orgasm. In this school, men are taught to gradually build arousal until reaching the brink of orgasm, at which point, if they squeeze the PC muscle long and hard, they can launch themselves into orgasm without ejaculation. The second school of thought holds that contracting the PC muscle will inspire, rather than delay, ejaculation, and that the trick to orgasm without ejaculation is to keep the PC muscle completely relaxed. Whichever techniques you employ, the bottom line is that voluntary control of the PC muscle can be a great sexual enhancer, so start doing your Kegel exercises today.

Ready for a few final tips? Taoist sexual teachers advocate pressing an acupuncture point located in your perineum when you feel yourself close to ejaculating. This is supposed to halt the passage of prostatic and seminal fluids to the urethra, and to allow you to experience orgasm without any expulsion of fluids. If you're having intercourse with a partner, you may also find it useful to adopt a position that generates minimal muscle tension in your body (such as partner on top), so you can focus on and control your PC muscle more easily. Whichever of these tips you adopt, if you take the time to build your level of arousal, you'll doubtlessly be rewarded with at least one powerful orgasm—and maybe many more.

When I was about to climax, my girlfriend took her middle finger and placed the tip of it on my anus, with the rest of her finger resting behind my scrotum, pressed hard against the skin, while she cupped my balls in her hand. I don't know what she did but it took me FOREVER TO CUM! I remember jumping out of bed and screaming, "What the hell did you do to me, and can we do it again!!!"

Orgasm without ejaculation is tough to achieve for me, but well worth the extra effort. I have nearly the same feelings as orgasm with ejaculation, but all the sensitivity remains, and I remain horny. This makes sex last longer.

Women. Although every woman theoretically has the physiological capacity to experience multiple orgasm, not every woman will particularly want to have or enjoy having more than one orgasm at a time:

Usually I feel satisfied and very relaxed after my one orgasm.

I'm lucky if I can manage two orgasms in twenty-four hours, let alone in a row. Never had multiple orgasms happen. After I've come once, it's just too sensitive, and I'm not interested enough.

I come fairly easily with masturbation, a vibrator or water from the bathtub faucets. Once per session is plenty.

I experience multiple orgasms. They eventually decrease in intensity for me, and rubbing myself raw isn't really that pleasurable. Quality is more important than quantity.

Of course, if your curiosity is piqued, there's no reason not to explore the possibility of having more than one orgasm in a sex session. The three basic rules of multiple orgasm are: back off, breathe and move. After your first orgasm, your clitoris may be too sensitive to take any more direct stimulation. Continue stimulating yourself indirectly—switch to a lighter touch. If you're using a vibrator, you might want to move the vibrator to another part of your genitals, or to the back of your hand, while you continue to touch yourself with your hand. Take deep, panting breaths, and rock your pelvis in time with your breathing. Let the energy build back up in your genitals. Within a few minutes, excruciating overstimulation may well give way to excruciating pleasure and you'll find yourself sailing off into another orgasm. Some people find that their second or third orgasms feel more powerful than the first, and some find that their orgasms become progressively less intense:

Multiple orgasms are fantastic, but sometimes I feel my body doesn't know when to quit!

During masturbation, I generally enjoy four to five orgasms—though they diminish in intensity after that. Several times, more out of curiosity than anything else, I have gone out for marathon sessions—between one to two hours long—and continued to orgasm (stopped counting at fifteen to twenty). Hands and fingers finally worn out, but clit still obliging.

When I do have a second orgasm, it is more intense than the first, though a lot harder to achieve. In these cases, my partner brings me off the first time, and I bring myself off the second time (usually manually). When I am alone and masturbating, I normally stop after just one orgasm.

Some people trained in breath work and meditative techniques report experiences of orgasms lasting five or more minutes long. One explanation is that these individuals are riding an extended, intense plateau of arousal and subjectively interpreting this experience as extended orgasm. Another explanation is that these individuals are pioneers of envelope-pushing sexual exploration. There's no scientific study on the topic as yet, and really no need to demand an explanation. Orgasm may be a quantifiable response in a laboratory setting, but it's a highly subjective response in a human being.

I have to work at orgasms, but once they arrive I keep coming, i.e., my clit keeps throbbing, especially with firm pressure.

I used to have something more like multiple orgasms, which occurred after the second or third when they would all blend together into a continuous extremely high state which was almost torturous (but great).

SPONTANEOUS ORGASM *Spontaneous orgasm* is the term applied to the phenomenon of reaching orgasm without touch. A fair number of women report that they can reach orgasm purely through mental stimulation, breathing techniques and contracting the PC muscle. In Gina Ogden's *Women Who Love Sex*, she coins the term *thinking off* to describe the sexual pleasure some women achieve courtesy of a well-developed imagination. Wet dreams are better documented in men than women, but both sexes can attest to having orgasms in their sleep. Women and men with no genital sensation due to spinal cord injuries have also been documented experiencing orgasms while sleeping. People with nerve damage can often learn to have orgasmic sensations in other parts of the body. The long and short of it is,

there's plenty of proof to the adage that the brain is the biggest sex organ.

One of Good Vibrations' most popular workshops in recent years has been a "Breathe into Orgasm" class taught by Jwala, an internationally renowned Tantra teacher. While a "don't-touch-me-there" approach to sexual pleasure might strike you as somewhat suspect (what's so bad about touching your genitals anyway?), it can teach you the power of the sexual imagination and the value of full-body experience.

THE BIG O We realize it may seem a bit contradictory to follow our assertion that orgasms are but one of many reasons to have sex with several pages full of orgasm tales. We do believe that orgasms aren't the be-all and end-all of sexual experience, and we know that many people have great, pleasurable sex without orgasms. But orgasm strikes us as a fascinating and revealing topic because in many ways people's feelings about orgasm serve as microcosms of their feelings about sex in general. If you were asked the question "How are you feeling about your orgasms?" your response would doubtless include, not only the sensations and the emotions you experience during sex, but your feelings about your body, your genitals, your relationships and your desires. Try answering this question, and see what you learn about yourself.

Since learning to masturbate, my response cycle has evolved so that I will come and then shortly after (less than one minute) my crotch will be begging me to do it again. These days I will come once or twice, but for a while nothing less than twice would do! It was an amazing feeling to have the need be beyond my control or creation in a way. I have had trouble coming with partners and being able to sexually respond well, so there is something special about this.

Orgasm is my elusive best friend. I've been sexually active since about thirteen, and I only started having orgasms a few months ago, at the tender age of twenty-three. That's when I started to use my vibrator. I really enjoy my orgasms, demure and non-earth shattering though they may be. That warm, warm feeling is just terrific. I try not to think about having one while I'm masturbating, because I think it lessens their intensity. When I'm not masturbating, I do think about them. I remember how my temperature goes up, how I lose sense of time, how these waves pulse through my insides and hips up through my stomach. I like the noises I make.

Changes over a Lifetime

Your experience of sexual response and orgasm is bound to go through some changes over the course of your life. You're far more likely to benefit from these changes if you go with the flow, rather than assuming that one pattern of sexual response developed in adolescence should remain static throughout your lifetime.

Pregnancy and Postpartum

Pregnant women frequently experience decreased desire, due to the overwhelming changes going on in their bodies and to simple physical discomfort.

I thought both morning sickness and my low sex drive could be conquered by mind over matter. Well guess what? You can't fool Mother Nature!

When I was pregnant I was never "in the mood" to have sex. But I did spend a lot of time resting and snuggling with my partner, which was very relaxing and soothing. This helped me be more receptive to his caresses, and occasionally led to some powerful erotic encounters.

Others may be surprised to find themselves experiencing increased sexual desire, given that medical and anecdotal references tend to focus on the probability of decreased desire. The hormonal and physiological changes your body is going through can make you feel a heightened sensual or sexual consciousness. After the first trimester, your vagina and labia become blood-engorged and your vaginal lubrication increases, just as in sexual arousal. Your genitals and breasts swell along with your belly. These physical changes can be arousing, especially if you're willing to experiment with the new methods of stimulation your temporarily

"new" genitals might require. Whether you're interested in discovering more comfortable alternatives to intercourse or exploring the erotic possibilities of your changing body, you're bound to end up with a richer sex life.

One of the benefits to being pregnant was being forced to discover new ways to have sex. We tried out an inflatable pillow, which we still use, to keep pressure off my back. When I wasn't in the mood for intercourse, we'd strike provocative poses and masturbate for each other. And often just having my partner stroke my body while we kissed was a welcome form of erotic intimacy.

My breasts went from a size 36B to a 38EE. We joked about my porn-star boobs, but boy were they fun to play with. Suddenly they were everywhere—I could drag them all over my lover's body. I didn't have to bend over so far to get them in his mouth and he loved fucking them with his cock.

You may also have different emotional demands during pregnancy:

When I was pregnant, having sex with the baby's father felt like the most romantic, fulfilling thing I could do. It was kind of embarrassing—I didn't even want to masturbate any more, I just wanted to be with him.

Whatever your level of desire during pregnancy, you should feel free to be sexual as often or as seldom as you please. There's no possibility of harming a fetus during sex or from orgasm. The sole exception is if you're at risk for premature labor. In this case, doctors will probably advise that you avoid orgasm late in your pregnancy, as there's a slight chance the uterine contractions of orgasm could induce labor.

After your baby is born, your doctor will caution you to abstain from "sex" for six weeks to allow the tissues inside the vagina to heal and to avoid possible bacterial infection. The waiting period may be longer if you've had a cesarean birth or complications with your vaginal delivery. Even after you've healed from the delivery, intercourse may be somewhat painful the first few times.

Sex and the New Parent

Here are some helpful hints for rediscovering sex once your baby arrives:

Give yourself a break. Your life just changed completely—don't beat yourself up if sex is the last thing on your mind. New mothers may find that breast-feeding, getting used to a new routine and pressure from a partner to have sex inhibit their sex drive. Respect your feelings, take your time and do what feels best for you. The less you worry about sex, the more likely you are to want and enjoy it.

Plan for sex. With much of your day dictated by your baby's needs, it's important to plan time for sex. You may look back fondly on the days when you could drop everything and get nasty whenever the spirit moved you, but the reality is that these days you'll probably have to plan ahead. The anticipation, however, can add a nice thrill to your upcoming encounter. If you've got babysitters, you may try scheduling a regular time during the week for sex. If you can't find someone to babysit, plan around your baby's schedule. If he or she takes a regular nap, use that time—just make sure you're relaxed and rested too or sex may feel like a chore. If your baby's schedule is unpredictable and you're up for it, grab your partner the minute the baby falls asleep—you may rediscover some spontaneity after all.

Get help. Call on family, friends and neighbors to babysit so you can spend some time with your lover. If your budget permits, consider ordering prepared meals, hiring a housekeeper or having the bank pay your bills directly. Every minute saved is one you could be spending with a partner.

Respect your health. Your sex drive will stay on permanent hiatus if you run yourself ragged. Try to get plenty of sleep, eat well and exercise. This will boost your self-esteem and probably make you feel more desirable. And the more energy you have, the more likely you are to want a good roll in the hay. New mothers should do Kegel exercises; strengthening your PC muscle will improve your experience of sex.

Relax. You may not realize how tense you are until you make a conscious effort to relax. Take a warm bath, ask your lover for a massage or have a glass of wine. Easing the tension can make room for arousal.

Be patient. Once the baby is born, many women are surprised, not only to find that their bodies don't instantly revert back to normal, but that vaginal intercourse can hurt for some time. Experiment with different positions—side-by-side and woman-on-top allow you to take more control. Use plenty of lubricant—your fluctuating hormone levels can dry up your natural lubrication. If you want to try easing back into intercourse, try using lube and a small dildo. Don't feel you have to rush back into intercourse, even if your doctor says you're ready. Experiment with other ways of expressing sexual intimacy.

Be creative. If you're too tired to get hot and heavy but want to feel sexual, try a quickie masturbation session. If one of you is in the mood but the other is not, maybe it's a good time to enjoy a little voyeurism. Rent an X-rated movie instead of the latest blockbuster and watch it from bed. If you want to have sex but don't want to make any decisions, play an erotic board game. Have a meal of finger foods delivered to your house. If orgasm is harder to achieve, use a vibrator. Anal intercourse can be a satisfying alternative to vaginal intercourse.

Get away. Sometimes just getting away from it all does wonders for the libido. Go to a romantic inn, take a camping trip, offer to house-sit for someone, just do something to get out of your own environment. If you can, bring someone along to watch the baby or find a sitter.

Communicate. As always, communication is vital. You and your partner are going through so many changes, it's important that you share your feelings. Talk about your concerns, your desires, your needs, your preferences and your expectations.

Use resources. Whatever you're feeling or experiencing, you're not alone. Connect with other parents to get advice, suggestions or just a friendly ear.

Obviously, there are plenty of ways of being sexual that don't involve penis/vagina intercourse, and we would encourage you to follow your desires wherever they lead you—surveys show that up to sixty percent of couples ignore the six-week waiting period in favor of enjoying some form of sexual intimacy.

On the other hand, it's also common for women to feel reduced desire for a couple of months to a year after birth. The healing of an episiotomy, the low estrogen (and consequently low vaginal lubrication) levels caused by breast-feeding, the slow process of regaining a sense of ownership of your body, and the major changes in your lifestyle can all contribute to make sexual activity seem less than compelling. Many women also report that their orgasms become temporarily harder to attain for a few weeks to a few months following birth, which can have libido-dampening effects.

Unfortunately, doctors aren't trained to be forthcoming with information about this, as in so many sexual matters, and your OB/GYN probably won't provide you with much guidance about the possibilities for sexual activities or the vagaries of sexual desire. We encourage you to compare notes with other postpartum women and/or midwives, as grassroots information-sharing will probably yield a more reassuring range of responses than checking in with your HMO.

I talk about sex with strangers for a living, but when it came time to ask my nurse practitioner—who had been very motherly during my prenatal visits—questions about sex, I procrastinated and conveniently "forgot." My partner would come along and prod me to ask the questions we both wanted answered.

I don't know where I'd be without my mothers' group. Five of us got together when we had our first kids and we're still fast friends seven years later. We share all kinds of information and can talk about things we're too embarrassed to bring up even with our partners.

I found incredible resources for expectant moms and parents on the World Wide Web. I located a group of women who were all expecting the same month as me. Being able to ask questions and

share experiences was incredibly enlightening and reassuring.

Sex and Aging

With increasing age, most men find that they require direct physical stimulation to attain an erection and that mental arousal will no longer suffice. Many men report softer, shorter-lasting erections than in their youth and that there's a longer time-lapse between erections. Women may find that decreased vaginal lubrication and the natural thinning of their vaginal walls after menopause affects what sexual activities they find pleasurable. You may experience reduced sensitivity of the clitoris or glans of the penis, and your orgasms may seem qualitatively less intense.

Both men and women may have health concerns that affect their experiences of sex and orgasm. The debilitating pain of arthritis or even the simple discomfort of stiffening joints can make sex seem unappealing. Take the time to warm up your joints with a warm bath, a massage or gentle stretching, and experiment with different positions to find those that are more comfortable.

A heart condition may make you leery of sexual activity—the good news is that if you can handle normal physical exertion, such as climbing stairs, it's perfectly safe to have sex. The vast majority of cardiac patients can resume their sex life. High blood pressure (and the accompanying medications) and adult-onset diabetes can produce erection problems—we address some recommended coping mechanisms in our chapter on penetration. Abdominal surgery, such as hysterectomies, may affect women's physiological experience of orgasm:

My orgasms are less intense than prior to a hysterectomy, but they still are intense.

Yet physical changes from aging or from illness need not slam the door on your sex life, and in fact if you listen to your body, it may *open* the door to a whole range of new pleasures. Most likely, as you age, you'll grow in self-awareness, and your repertoire of physical responses will expand.

You can explore sensual massage and a range of techniques that aren't strictly goal-oriented. Masturbation provides an excellent tool to explore how your body and its responses are changing. You may switch to having sex in the morning if you're less energetic at night, or to having sex in the afternoon if your arthritis is more painful in the morning.

After menopause, you may feel liberated from the fear of unwanted pregnancy. After retirement, you may delight in having your days free for long leisurely sexual escapades, alone or with a partner. We ourselves cherish the dream of retiring from our labors at sixty-five and moving to a community house by the seashore, where we'll sit on the porch in our rocking chairs, surrounded by friends, with our vibrators and lubricants close at hand.

Sex and Your Doctor

In an ideal world, members of the medical community would be a valuable resource should you have further questions about sexual anatomy and response. Despite the fact that we count on doctors for accurate physiological information, at least as many people have been alarmed, misinformed or intimidated about sex in their doctor's office as have received useful, reassuring advice. It's understandably challenging both for laypeople to bring up sexual matters to medical professionals, and for medical professionals to address these matters. Consider the following limitations and our suggested coping mechanisms:

♦ Medical schools offer no standardized program of training in human sexuality, and state licensing requirements are hardly strenuous (for instance, in the state of California, medical students are only required to have a total of twelve hours of human sexuality training). There's a growing movement to provide better sex training for doctors, but the effects of this could take decades to trickle down.

Many grassroots organizations can fill in the gaps left by mainstream medical ignorance. Sex-information hotlines (see our resource listings for referrals) offer far more extensive human sexuality training to their volunteers than medical schools do to students. Subscription newsletters, such as *Men's Confidential* or *Sex Over Forty,* provide up-to-date, accurate information for laypeople on a host of medical issues. If you have access to the Internet, you can find a wide range of information on-line.

♦ Doctors operate from a disease-based model, and are more likely to be able to diagnose medical conditions than to discuss behavioral guidelines. Furthermore, they're raised in the same sex-negative society as the rest of us and aren't any better equipped to discuss sex than the average person.

Don't expect your doctor to be the one to raise the topic of sex. You'll need to be proactive in requesting information. Come to your appointment with a clear idea of what specific questions you'd like answered—it can be helpful to write these down beforehand just to identify what it is you want to know. Even if doctors can't answer your questions right then and there (remember, they may not know the answers), they should either schedule a follow-up appointment or refer you to a nurse or social worker who can help you.

♦ Doctors tend to have very specific areas of expertise and knowledge.

If you're experiencing a specific sexual problem, discuss it with the appropriate specialist. Take your erectile concerns to a urologist. Discuss your vaginismus with an OB/GYN. If your concerns aren't primarily physiological, you may find that a sex therapist is best equipped to help you. If you're seeking advice on sexual practices, rather than information on sexual problems, you may find a family practitioner has a more holistic, better-informed approach than a specialist. As noted above, nurse practitioners and social workers can be valuable resources. The staff at women's clinics are frequently well-informed about sexual matters, thanks largely to advances made by the feminist health movement.

♦ You may have qualms about approaching the doctor with whom you have or hope to have a long and trusting relationship with a question that might embarrass one or both of you. For example, "You've told me I shouldn't have vaginal intercourse until six weeks after childbirth, but what about anal intercourse?" or "After my heart attack, is it more dangerous to masturbate or to have sex with my wife?"

Well, the choice is up to you. You can ask the question and assume that your doctor will either have a good answer or will have to research the answer, in which case you'll have made a valuable contribution to sexual consciousness-raising in the medical community. If your embarrassment might prevent you from clearly communicating what it is you want to know, you can take advantage of some of the more anonymous resource options mentioned above.

♦ There's an inherent power dynamic in the doctor-patient relationship. Not only is the doctor an authority figure, but whatever he or she puts into your medical records will be easily accessible to other doctors and insurance companies.

Here again, you can either go public with your concerns for the sake of increasing the general pool of medical knowledge, or you can opt for anonymity (for example, most free clinics offer anonymous HIV testing). In medical emergencies, you need to get to a doctor regardless of what will or won't show up in your patient files. Be aware that there's nothing new under the sun, and that emergency staff won't blink twice at situations that might strike a layperson as unusual.

The bottom line is that doctors are people, too, and you're going to find some who are excellent, sensitive communicators about sexual matters and others who aren't. You deserve access to accurate sex information, and if you can't get this from a doctor, please don't assume you've exhausted all of your resources.

Regardless of the response you may get, we do encourage everyone who feels comfortable doing so to bring up sexual questions and concerns to their doctors. We encourage you to identify, support and refer others to the sex-positive doctors you find. And we encourage you to talk with friends and family about the sexual repercussions of medical and physiological events throughout your life. Bringing sexual topics out into the open is a crucial step toward normalizing sex, which leads in turn to a freer exchange of accurate information. Changing the status quo demands everyone's proactive participation, and you can make an invaluable contribution to raising the sexual IQ of everyone in your community simply by sharing your experiences.

CHAPTER 4

Communication

Communication is the key to any successful sexual relationship. We know you've heard it before, but if some of the activities described in this book tempt you to expand your sexual repertoire, we hope you'll take the time to make sure your communication skills are in good shape. After all, you can acquire all the toys, lotions and manuals in the world, but they're useless in a relationship unless you can talk about what you want to do with them. You can study your anatomy, learn one hundred and one different positions and read about new techniques, but if you're unable to describe where it feels good and why, you're headed for disappointment and frustration.

And since communication is a two-way street, your years of sexual experience or open-mindedness won't do any good if you aren't attuned to your partner's needs. Discovering her or his needs, anxieties and desires, as well as learning to share your own, will open doors to understanding, experimentation and healing, ultimately leading to overall greater sexual intimacy.

Unfortunately, there are a million and one things that get in the way of effective communication. In this chapter we'll examine some of these barriers and suggest ways to move beyond them.

Why So Difficult?

Our primary goal as sex-toy saleswomen is to get people to articulate their sexual needs. Without this information, we are unable to help a customer find something that will satisfy her or his particular need. This crucial first step, however, is also the most difficult one, simply because so many of us are too embarrassed to talk about sex, either with lovers or total strangers.

Our discomfort with sex is ironic. Although we live in a society where we are bombarded daily by sexual images and references to sex, speaking intimately with someone about our sexuality is extremely challenging. At Good Vibrations, we routinely discuss strangers' sexual needs with them without ever raising an eyebrow, yet when it came to interviewing our friends about their sex lives for this book, we balked and procrastinated, imagining our combined embarrassment.

We are all motivated by an intense curiosity about sex but thwarted by our inability to discuss it. We seek information, elucidation, titillation—note the commercial success of the daily talk shows, sex manuals, advice columns and the *Sports Illustrated* swimsuit edition—but our curiosity is far more restrained when it comes to discovering a partner's needs or sharing our own.

You don't have to look very hard to uncover reasons for this behavior. From the attitudes and morals instilled in us at a young age to the conflicting messages about sex society imposes on us as adults, it's no wonder we're a tad repressed. Here are just a few examples of communication inhibitors:

Social Conditioning

Think about your intimate relationships. Is it true that one of you usually wants to talk about sex and "the relationship" more than the other? There's an automatic imbalance when you begin a relationship, simply because you've each developed your own approach to communication. Many things influence individual communication patterns: gender differences, family dynamics, traumatic experiences—figuring out which ones are relevant to you can be a starting point if you want to change something.

Inadequate Sex Education

No one teaches us about sex when we're kids because we're not supposed to have it, yet when we reach adulthood (some arbitrary age), we're expected to magically know how to expertly please ourselves and our partners. After a certain age, our curiosity and inquisitiveness become a liability—a sure sign that we're inexperienced, poor lovers, virgins (take your pick), so we quit asking and start faking.

What we do learn about sex as kids comes sporadically from parents, school, friends and the media. Depending on the accuracy or depth of the information, we may end up more confused, misinformed or intimidated by our discoveries. Formal sex education in school is usually about prevention of disease and pregnancy—downbeat lectures emphasizing danger and disaster. How do we learn sexual self-esteem and respect, let alone how to talk about sex, when we're taught to fear the consequences of our libidos?

Beliefs, Attitudes, Stereotypes

Each one of us was raised with a unique set of moral beliefs about sex, usually informed by myriad cultural stereotypes and/or religious doctrines. How we incorporate these into our adult sex lives is directly related to how, what and even whether we communicate. Guided by whatever we have come to view individually as "acceptable sexual behavior," we're bound to run into a few problems exploring or experimenting with someone holding even slightly different views. Take these few examples:

♦ Perhaps you don't want to tell your partner you masturbate because you think it's wrong and you're trying to quit—remember when the priest told you masturbation would lead to blindness?
♦ Maybe you're really intrigued by anal sex, but you've always heard that anal sex is a gay practice and you don't want anyone, including yourself, to think you might be homosexual, so you never explore this activity.
♦ Maybe you're a gay man who feels that his erotic dreams about women are inconsistent with his practices, so you keep this a secret from your lover.

We deny ourselves and our lovers access to different facets of our sexual personalities when we practice this kind of self-censorship. Getting at the root of some of these attitudes can help you overcome the inhibiting ones or clarify those that are very important to you.

Fear

Fear of rejection or of the embarrassment that comes from revealing our ignorance or beliefs is an enormous communication deterrent. Our fragile egos often prevent us from making a simple inquiry or confession, one which might lead to greater sexual self-awareness.

It's not uncommon at Good Vibrations for a clerk to approach every individual in the store and offer to answer questions, yet be turned down by each one. But should she start explaining the differences in vibrators or dildos to just one customer in the store, those very same people will gather around to eavesdrop on the rest of the instruction. Remember your schoolteachers telling you that "there's no such thing as a dumb question"? You still didn't ask because you thought everyone else probably already knew, and you weren't about to make a fool of yourself. The fear seems even greater when it comes to questions about sex.

Many customers confide in us because they're afraid to tell their partners what they want, certain they'll sound kinky or stupid or demanding. We act as a sounding board, reassuring them their curiosity is natural and encouraging them to talk to their partners.

People also worry about deflating their partners' egos by suggesting a change. Perfectly harmless suggestions can be misinterpreted as dissatisfaction with previous performance:

When I was married, my husband hated it when I masturbated—he couldn't understand why I needed to do that when he was around.

This woman probably deprived herself (or masturbated on the sly) instead of attempting to disabuse her husband of the notion that her solitary enjoyment was a poor reflection on their sex life. She could have explained why she enjoyed it, perhaps even suggesting they try it together.

Goal-Oriented Sex

Many of us have specific requirements for a satisfying sexual encounter. For some it might be a minimum of two orgasms each, for others it might be hour-long foreplay or a new position. How rigidly we adhere to these requirements can increase our own and our partner's performance anxiety.

The more proscriptive and goal-oriented we make our sexual activity, the more we set ourselves up for anxiety and frustration. Talking with a partner about our expectations can help relieve the pressure, while allowing us to push back the boundaries we've set up around our sex lives:

I like to negotiate beforehand, clearly state each person's limits. My husband and I talk about what we feel we want to do on any given night. It doesn't deter spontaneity, just keeps us in synch.

Language Considerations

The differences in our relative comfort or discomfort around sexual terminology can affect the way we communicate. While one person might say, "I'm dying for you to plunge two wet fingers in my juicy cunt and pump," another might say, "Please put two fingers in my vagina" and hope for the best, while yet another may hate having to spell out what she wants, perhaps spreading her legs and raising her hips to encourage the activity. Finding a common, comfortable vocabulary to share, including clear nonverbal signals, can minimize this confusion and add an erotic edge to your sex play.

If you need a little assistance developing a sexual vocabulary, there are several options available to you. Make a list of words you like or find particularly hot (flip through a sexual slang dictionary if you need help with words). While you're alone, practice saying them aloud and using them in sentences—after a while they won't sound so foreign coming out of your mouth and you can start reciting them more dramatically. When you masturbate, try imagining the words you'd like to say to heighten arousal. You and your partner can create separate lists of preferred words or phrases and then compare them to see what turn-of-phrase works for each of you. You can also build a shared language by reading a variety of erotic stories out loud and discussing which turn you on most— some folks favor Victorian euphemisms, others prefer urban slang, while some employ flowery prose. Similarly, watching X-rated or educational sex videos can show you how others use sexual vocabulary. For more on talking dirty, refer to the chapter on fantasy or pick up a copy of *Talk Sexy to the One You Love* or *Exhibitionism for the Shy*.

Prerequisites to Good Communication

"I know what I like."

Something often overlooked in discussions of sexual communication is the importance of articulating our needs to ourselves. While this may sound a little obvious, it's actually a crucial first step in the communication process. We don't expect people to go supermarket shopping without first having some idea of what they want—and if they can't find something, they must be able to describe it to someone who can assist them.

The same goes for our sexual needs. It's going to be pretty hard to tell a partner what we want if we aren't sure ourselves. Ask yourself a few questions about what you want to change: Is your partner touching you in a way that is unpleasant? Is it the motion or the spot? Would you prefer being touched somewhere else or in a different way? If you aren't sure, you could do a little homework—are you confused about anatomy, sexual response, certain fantasies? Try reading, chatting with a friend, calling a sex-information line, talking to a therapist or visiting a sex-toy store.

The very best way to pinpoint what you like is to concentrate while masturbating. Pay attention to what does or does not feel good so you can show your partner.

"I know what I need."

Your commitment to pursuing what you like in a sexual relationship is just as important. We all have specific sexual needs, so it does no one any good to assume that there is a standard way to have sex. The chance that your lover will know instinctively what you like is slim, so expect that you're going to have to get vocal at some point. You might want to practice alone first, saying out loud, with specifics, what you want. Imagine different scenarios and practice how you would introduce your concerns. If you've got very specific physical or emotional needs that your partner may not be aware of, don't assume that he or she will figure them out—be up front and honest, and you'll both be more comfortable negotiating sex.

When I was pregnant for the first time, my sexual desire dropped off drastically, but my need to be held, caressed and spoken to lovingly increased dramatically. My partner was incredibly understanding—I got to dictate the terms of our sex life and there was never, ever any pressure from him. In the end, we discovered a new way of being sexual.

This self-assertion is especially vital when orchestrating new sexual relationships, particularly when it comes to issues like safer sex and contraception:

I'll admit when I have a new partner I have to negotiate safer sex because most of the women I've slept with aren't used to latex.

If you have familiarized yourself with safer sex practices and have decided ahead of time what

activities will or will not be included in your sexual encounters, you are much more likely to get what you want.

Improving Communication

You know what you want, now how do you tell your partners? It sounds so much easier than it is. There's always some reason, in the heat of passion, that you decide to keep it to yourself: You don't want to hurt your partners' feelings; you don't want to seem greedy; you're afraid your partners won't want to do what you want; you don't want to shock someone you just met; you don't want to shock someone you've been lovers with for fifteen years. The excuses are endless! But the alternatives to being honest are grim—frustration, boredom, resentment, irritation and so on.

Some people find it easier to communicate their sexual desires to strangers because their desires aren't enmeshed with the emotional intimacy experienced with a long-term partner. Others may not feel comfortable sharing the same information until they've known someone for a while. Whatever your experience, we hope you'll benefit from the following suggestions.

In the Bedroom

If you're fond of the relatively direct, but often misunderstood, nonverbal method, make sure your partner understands what you're trying to convey. Your lover is rubbing your clit and you moan. Is it a moan of pleasure or irritation? Your lover continues, and you moan louder. Are you signaling encouragement or annoyance? Obviously, moans are not universally understood. Lend a hand to this confusing situation—literally. If your lover is not pleasing you the right way, take your hand and guide your lover's. If this still doesn't do the trick, show your lover just how you like it by masturbating while she or he watches, and then have her or him try it again.

During sex I often masturbate and let my partner "help." This works well and is very satisfying and intimate without the performance anxiety I get when trying to come for somebody else.

Speaking of Sex

Many communication barriers would cease to exist if we were more comfortable talking about sex. One way to increase our comfort level is to practice discussing sex with a partner when we're in a nonsexual setting. This removes sex from the impassioned, volatile setting of the bedroom. Here are a few ways you could introduce the topic:

News commentary: "I read the most interesting editorial today about condom distribution in public schools." A news item can lead into discussions of safer sex, sex education, your sex history, etc. Or, "Today on Oprah, she interviewed female pornographers." A TV talk show might create an opportunity to exchange views on women's sexuality, erotica and porn.

Fantasy and imagination: "I had the most incredible erotic dream about Captain Kirk and Spock and some aliens." Your dreams can spark discussions of fantasies, taboo behaviors or secret desires.

Fact finding: Conduct sexual histories of your partners. Pretend you're from the Kinsey Institute, and you want to know what your respondents think about masturbation: When did they start? How did they feel? Were they ever discovered? How often do they masturbate? Don't judge, just listen. Make up your own questions, or use Kinsey's.

Read a sex book: You could agree to read a self-help book together and discuss the issues it raises. Or try some erotic fiction, sharing your reactions to the passages. You could read a book of sexual biographies to see how other folks talk about their sex lives. Any of these will expose you to the language of sex and help you find a comfortable sexual vocabulary.

Correspondence: Several of our customers cited letter writing as an informative and erotic way for partners to share their thoughts with each other.

Leaving judgment and dogma behind will make it easier and safer for you and your partner to talk honestly about sex. Once you find yourself tossing around sex terms, expressing yourself and your needs may come more naturally. And in addition to being good practice, the background information you gather will be helpful when you or your partner wants to try something different.

Remember that communication also means letting your partner know when the stimulation is oh-so-perfect. Try cheerleading—a simple, one-word exclamation goes a long way. Use your body to convey appreciation in a clear way—arching your back, breathing hard, grabbing hair!

The alternative verbal route is more direct, though often more difficult for people. We're afraid to add to our lover's already intense performance anxiety or to appear too demanding. But remember, your partner wants to please you, so your suggestions will most likely be met with enthusiasm. And expressing your needs doesn't have to be done in a critical way. Compliment your lover on her or his performance of the activity you like, and then ask for more: "Your mouth on my penis feels great, and I'd really love it if you sucked on it a little harder." If it's an activity that just doesn't feel good at all, gently guide your lover's hand or head somewhere else and say what does feel nice:

I hate to say anything that could sound critical or unappreciative to a woman who is trying so hard to give me pleasure, but it is important to just say "softer," "slower," "harder" or "let's do something else for a while." I've learned that simple words like these are real easy and effective ways of communicating; they can be used either as a request or as a question. I learned this from a woman who liked to know she was doing it right.

If your partner is not very responsive to your ministrations, ask for feedback or signs of encouragement. Give your lover options, moving from one body part to another, varying pressure or movement, asking what feels good, great or bad.

AURAL INHIBITIONS
I would like to use my voice more—to allow moans, sighs and cries to come out naturally rather than suppress them because I'm embarrassed.

You may share this person's concern. Are you afraid your roommates or neighbors might hear you? Just turn up the volume on your stereo. Are you afraid your partner will think you're odd if you make noise? If your lover emits pleasurable sounds, chances are he or she will be turned on by yours. To practice, try giving free reign to your vocal chords while masturbating. Have your partner watch if you like and then describe to you afterwards how it felt to watch you. Or during your next lovemaking session, follow your partner's moans with your own sighs of passion. This can be good practice for you and the duet effect can increase excitement for both of you. If your partner is also the silent type, you may discover you're both suppressing sound for fear of what the other will think—try addressing the subject in a nonsexual setting. You might also watch a porn video (or a sexy mainstream movie) together. Watch the love scenes with the sound on and then hit the mute button—once you discover how much those sighs of pleasure enhance your viewing, you may be inspired to incorporate them into your personal X-rated moments!

Outside the Bedroom

Of course, there's far more to sexual communication than just lying in bed and moaning loudly when something feels good or flinching when something annoys you.

Discussing change and introducing new sexual activity can be difficult for couples, yet the rewards are obvious: variety, experimentation, growth, self-discovery—all of which can contribute to a more satisfying relationship. This book is all about exploring new kinds of sexual activity, but it is essential for you to think carefully about the hows and whys behind your desire to change. Here are a few things to consider:

MOTIVATION Why are you contemplating a change in your sexual repertoire? Are you dissatisfied with something? Why do you feel the need to upset your routine? Are you trying to save your relationship? Does your lover feel the same way? Are you trying to change something about your partner? How will your partner react to this suggestion? Are you hot for this activity because everyone else on the block is doing it?

It's very important to consider the effect your suggestion might have on your partner's sexual self-image or how you might be adding to his or her performance anxiety. Are you buying your girlfriend a G-spot vibrator because you want her to learn how to have orgasms during intercourse? How does she feel about this? Does it diminish the value or importance of the clitoral orgasms she has? Encourage her to tell you what she thinks about the activity. What do each of you expect to get out of it? Clarifying what you're really after and why should help you figure out the best way to approach your partner.

I tried using a vibrator with a longtime girlfriend. However, she was very shy about it and couldn't really get into it. It was very awkward introducing it. I think it began by us talking about masturbating and I asked her if she ever used a vibrator. She said no, so I brought one out. We fooled around with it for a while, but it didn't seem natural.

It sounds like these two were off to a good start, but their embarrassment got the better of them. Perhaps they could have acknowledged their mutual discomfort and talked about what was causing them to feel shy. Perhaps the girlfriend felt intimidated or pressured by the focus on her arousal. It also sounds like the vibrator was a surprise, which might have taken her aback. If they'd been able to clarify their expectations for the vibrator, they might not have approached the experiment so halfheartedly.

INTRODUCING THE SUBJECT Unless you're absolutely certain that your lover adores the element of surprise, it's best to bring the subject up when you're not in a sexual setting. Just because you think something sounds fun doesn't necessarily mean your partner will.

Take the example of a woman buying a dildo to use on her girlfriend. She's been penetrating her lover for years with her fingers, and she figures her girlfriend will love the feeling of a dildo. Plus, if she buys a dildo harness to go with it, her fingers will be freed up to explore other areas of her girlfriend's body. However, when she dons her new garb that special night, her girlfriend recoils in horror, saying she doesn't want to be fucked by a man.

Had they talked about it first, our intrepid shopper might have explained to her lover that it didn't even occur to her to impersonate a man; she just wanted to free up her hands, and at the same time please her lover the way she likes. They could have discussed the dildo/penis association and what to do about it, possibly avoiding the whole misunderstanding and ending up with a great new sex toy.

When you do bring up your ideas in conversation, try not to be confrontational or demanding. You might introduce the subject by making an observation: "I noticed that you really like having me hold your wrists down during sex. Do you think you might want to be tied up?" Or take the playful approach: "I had this terrific fantasy about the outdoors, some trees, some rope, you...me." If you're trying to change a pattern, you might just inquire how it got to be a pattern: "I dreamed about doing it in the stairway, which made me wonder why we always have sex in the same place." Listen carefully to your partner's reactions; try to get to the bottom of any reservations or feelings your suggestion may have elicited.

Of course there are times when surprising your partner can pave the way for an explosive sexual encounter. If you've discussed the desired activity before and ascertained that it's something your partner is interested in, by all means, take the initiative and plan the event. Just make sure your partner likes surprises, and that you're planning something he or she might actually enjoy experiencing, not something that's best kept a fantasy.

You don't always have the opportunity or the desire to discuss your sex concerns with a partner. If you just met someone and aren't planning on seeing her or him after an afternoon or evening of sex, you obviously won't know that much about the person. While it's still in your best interests to be as direct and specific about your desires as possible, you obviously can't follow our advice to find out how your partner feels about sex toys before whipping one out from under your bed. There's certainly nothing to stop you from suggesting the toy or technique to your partner, but obviously if he or she is not receptive, you're more likely to enjoy the encounter if you're willing to compromise. You could ask what the reservation is, which might be something you could alleviate quickly with a thorough explanation or reassurance. For example, someone's eyes might bulge when he or she sees the Magic Wand vibrator, but assurance that it's not meant for penetration might elicit a sigh of relief.

BE SPECIFIC It can never hurt, and is usually infinitely more helpful, to be specific about what you want from your partner. Avoid saying "I want you to pay more attention to me," if what you really want is for your partner's lips to linger lovingly on your breasts.

If you find yourself dissatisfied with a routine—perhaps you would like your partner to initiate sex more—offer some suggestions: "I'd devour you on the spot if you ever propositioned me in a public place." Or create a nonverbal vocabulary that you can both use—a signal or a modification in your dress, for example.

FOLLOW UP If you try something new, by all means talk about your experience afterwards. If you both had a great time, tell your partner in detail what you found so exhilarating. It may have been more fun for one of you, and this will give you an opportunity to acknowledge that and fine-tune your sex play so neither of you feels left out or shortchanged next time. This couple could have benefited from such a discussion:

> When I first got the Wahl two-speed, I got the guy I was dating to consent to include it in our lovemaking once. It was, for me, EXCELLENT: I mounted him from the top and used the vibe on my clit, and it was one of the most pleasurable experiences I remember. He, however, never wanted to use it again—threatened? I don't know.

Troubleshooting Problem Areas

Negotiating Differences, Compromising

If you suggest something to your partner and meet with total resistance, you have a few options. If you're with someone you aren't planning on seeing again, you're better off not pushing. If you're new to the relationship and would like it to continue, you could wait until you're a bit more familiar with each other before exploring your suggestions. In either case, if the activity you're proposing is necessary to your satisfaction, and your partner is unobliging, you probably ought to find another place to hang your hat.

If you're interested in trying something but your partner isn't, try talking together—examine the reasons behind your curiosity and your partner's resistance. Talking about it might break down some attitudes, stereotypes, fears or anxieties. You might also find a way to compromise. You can evaluate how important it is for you to pursue this particular sexual activity. Is it worth jeopardizing the relationship?

A textbook example is the man who wants his wife to perform fellatio on him, but she's not interested. Once he explains how much pleasure it would give him—perhaps offering to reciprocate something she desires—they can explore the reasons she's hesitant, and perhaps reach a compromise. Does she think it's a dirty practice? Maybe he can shower first, or use a condom. If she doesn't like him coming in her mouth, he can tell her when he's about to come, and she can finish with her hand. Or he can wear a flavored condom on his penis. If she doesn't like the feeling of having her mouth filled with penis, perhaps she can take just the tip of the penis in her mouth, and stimulate the length of his penis with her hand.

Your partner might be resisting your suggestion merely because the activity is unfamiliar. Try reading some self-help or erotic literature together. Give it time; sometimes all one needs is a little time and space to get used to a new idea.

Desire Discrepancies

One of the most common sexual concerns expressed by couples today is something sexologists refer to as "desire disorder" or "desire discrepancy." In short, your sex life feels out of synch because one of you wants sex more or less frequently than the other does.

Here's a simple example: When asked how often they'd each like to have sex, Bill claims he's comfortable with once a month, but Ted would prefer twice a week. Ted is always initiating; Bill starts feeling pressured. Bill may also feel like the one with the problem; he may eventually lose any desire to have sex. Both just get more frustrated.

If this situation sounds familiar, it's in your best interest to start talking. Here are some things you and your partner can discuss:

Share your definitions of desire and sex. What does sex mean to you? Is it intercourse, orgasm, genital stimulation? Perhaps one of you has a broader definition of sex—more touching or emphasis on the sensual side of sex, role-playing or experimentation. Use this as a basis for negotiating sex play.

Maybe one of you defines sexual desire as the urge to have intercourse, while the other associates desire with any sort of erotic feeling. The latter might actually be experiencing greater sexual desire than either of you think; she or he just needs practice channeling it into partner sex. It might even come as a relief to realize one of you hasn't lost desire—it's just being experienced differently.

What are your expectations? Where do they come from? Is there some statistical average you and your partner are aspiring to? Are you trying to keep up with the mythical Joneses or the leads in the latest romantic movie? It will help to examine your expectations about frequency of sexual desire, and whether you as an individual are comfortable with that.

Unfortunately, it's not uncommon for the person with less sexual desire to feel like the one with the problem. It's good to remind ourselves that there is no standard for sexual frequency. It's about as absurd to expect two people to have the same desire for sex as it is to expect them to have the same craving for chocolate or exercise or reading material. But since sex for so many of us is integral to our primary relationships, it makes sense that we'd have to work on negotiating our differences (just as we would other lifestyle conflicts, like how to raise kids, religious differences, different cultural tastes, etc.).

When desire discrepancies trouble a relationship, it's crucial that *both* partners work toward an acceptable middle ground.

Talk to your partner about what affects your desire. Exploring the various elements—both positive and negative—that affect sexual desire can help both of you understand and work with these issues. Stress at home or work, sexual trauma, pressure from a partner—these are a few of the many things that can inhibit us. If you are the partner who wants sex more frequently, you might ask yourself whether you use sex to satisfy other needs (for example, gaining attention, seeking acceptance, relieving job stress).

It's just as important to discover, share and explore those things that enhance our sexual desire. Visual imagery, a certain smell or a particular fantasy may activate your desire. By identifying these stimuli, you can learn how to access, cultivate and channel them into partner sex.

Use this shared information to reach a compromise. Fueled by the information you gather through these discussions, you and your partner can begin to explore your options toward mutually satisfying sexual encounters.

Let's use our original example. Perhaps after discussing their views on sex and desire, Ted learns that Bill is annoyed by their goal-oriented, orgasms-required lovemaking routine. Bill would rather do without the performance anxiety or sexual acrobatics. Ted might agree to expand their routine to one more inclusive of sensual touching or verbal gymnastics.

Bill may also have felt that since he was never going to want sex as much as Ted, there was no point in trying at all. Perhaps he stops initiating because he knows Ted will do it eventually, or he's afraid if he shows interest, he and Ted will be having sex all the time. The two could agree to exchange roles for a period of time, so that only Bill will initiate. This may take some of the pressure off Bill and give Ted something to anticipate.

Maybe Ted confesses that he sees each sexual encounter with Bill as a confirmation of Bill's love for him. They might explore this further and devise substitute ways for Bill to express his love for Ted, thereby reducing the sexual demands on Bill.

The two can work toward being more accepting of their desire discrepancies, adapting their sexual activity in order to accommodate them. For example, Ted could masturbate while lying in Bill's arms or Ted could massage Bill with no sexual expectations.

Obviously, depending on the specific circumstances, there are numerous ways to work on desire discrepancy. The only requirement is your willingness to discuss it with your partner. You may be able to work out quite a few things yourselves. Should you require further counseling, there are some excellent self-help books available, or you may find it helpful to work with a sex therapist.

Keeping the Flame Alive

If you've ever been or are in a sexual relationship that's lasted longer than a year or two, you're probably well aware that one of the biggest challenges facing any couple once they walk off into the sunset together is attempting to sustain a hot and happy sex life. In the first flush of a relationship, effortless passion is just a kiss away as the two of you revel in the excitement of getting to know each other, uncovering secrets and sharing confidences. That you aren't yet secure in your relationship adds an element of dramatic tension that heightens arousal, and can lead you to seize every erotic opportunity with abandon, for fear that it might be your last with this partner. If you settle into a long-term relationship, you may find that once the first wave of erotic exploration subsides, you and the person who's now your domestic partner are having sex less and less often.

Studies have shown that the frequency of sex drops over time for couples of all sexual orientations, a phenomenon sometimes ominously labeled "bed death." One popular theory holds that couples who "merge" together, sharing every aspect of their lives in a cozy cocoon, aren't getting the distance required for sexual sparks to fly. While it's true that settling into a predictable shared routine can dampen your libido, some therapists are beginning to point out that "bed death" is hardly the result of two people knowing each other too well. In fact, hot sex with a long-term partner requires both intimacy and self-disclosure, and many couples would rather maintain a boring, but nonthreatening, status quo than expose their sexual selves. "Merged" couples may be intertwined in the practical, emotional details of each other's daily lives, but they often stop well short of sharing their sexual hopes, dreams and aspirations.

In the early days of a relationship, you may trust your partner less, but you also have less to lose if he or she lets you down. Many of us find it easier to take sexual risks—to assume the active role of seducer, to explore brand-new sexual activities and to share fantasies—during the heady time when everything's slightly off-kilter and we feel powerfully attractive. As the dust settles, we not only become habituated to each other, but habituated to certain assumptions about each other: "Oh, I'm sure he doesn't really like going down on me," or "She wouldn't want to watch porn with me—it would offend her political sensibilities."

For every assumption we make about the other, there's an accompanying fear: "Maybe it really turns him off to get close to my genitals, and he just doesn't want to tell me," or "Maybe she'll think that real lesbians shouldn't even *like* watching porn." Being open about sexual desires and fears doesn't necessarily get easier the longer you're in a relationship—it can be harder to expose yourself, because you risk offending, disgusting or disappointing the person you care about most. It's natural to have the unconscious fear: What if the scales fall from my lover's eyes and she or he discovers what a pervert I really am and stops loving me? All the sexual shame that melted away in the heat of your first combustion comes creeping back in to silence you. And in the hustle-bustle of domestic living, it's easy to think: I'm sure we'd be having sex if only her in-laws weren't coming to dinner, or the dog didn't need walking, or he hadn't had such a long day at the office.

Of course, being in a long-term relationship doesn't mean you have to settle for infrequent, routine sex. But if you want to get yourselves out of a rut, you will need to take some risks. Your first step will be to communicate: Address your fears, regrets, sorrows and longings head on, and share these with your partner. Keeping the spark alive takes a certain amount of initiative. We sometimes fall into the trap of assuming that if our partner hasn't requested a certain activity by now, it must mean he or she is not interested in it. But if you're both thinking this, imagine what fun you could be missing out on!

Consider some of the suggestions in this chapter on improving your self-awareness and your awareness of your partner's preferences. A couple of recent books flesh out these ideas in greater detail and are particularly useful to people in long-term relationships. *Hot Monogamy,* primarily geared toward heterosexual couples, offers exercises designed to help you and your partner identify your individual emotional and sexual needs

and effectively communicate what you want. Jack Morin's *The Erotic Mind* provides unexpected insights into the sources of sexual passion and offers a road map of ways to inject dynamic excitement into an intimate relationship. His book is valuable reading for individuals of all sexual orientations, whether partnered or not. It addresses the complex nature of sexual arousal and guides the reader toward a better understanding of what it is that turns him or her on, and why. With this information under your belt, you'll be well-equipped to keep the home fires burning.

Initiating Sex

Communicating your desire to be sexual with another person, whether a complete stranger, a new acquaintance, an old friend or a long-time partner can be challenging. You're risking possible rejection while trying to satisfy a sex drive. Whether you're successful depends, of course, on whether the person is interested, but you can improve your prospects by tuning in to your partner's preferred approach. If you are with a new lover, you can either ask what approach pleases or go with your instincts. In longer relationships, you'll eventually become familiar with each other's preferences.

It's not unusual in most couples for one person to initiate sex more often than the other. If this is a dynamic that works well for you, great. If it's a source of frustration, you may be experiencing the desire discrepancy discussed above and now have an idea of what areas need work. If you've simply fallen into a rut, talk about it and see if you can't find a way to break the routine. Perhaps one partner just needs encouragement that he or she won't be rejected, or the partner who normally initiates just needs to practice taking turns. Maybe you'll recognize that you like sex initiated in different ways, and sharing your requirements will give you each a better understanding of what will please the other.

You're not always going to get the response you hope for when you initiate sex. If someone turns down a sexual proposition, rather than perceiving it as a blow to your self-esteem, why not congratulate yourself for having had the courage to pursue your desire? Celebrate your sexual feelings in a different way—masturbate. If your lover simply isn't "in the mood," respect that and find an alternative way to be sexual. You can't expect to be sexually in synch with a partner all the time.

We thought you'd enjoy seeing the many unique ways people enjoy having sex initiated. For some it can vary with their moods; for others, the requirements are quite specific. We asked customers to describe their favorite ways to have sex initiated, and their responses varied immensely. Maybe you'll come up with a few new ideas the next time you've got sex on your mind!

Many people are fond of the nonverbal method:

If I'm really driven, I like to communicate physically—just reaching over or coming up from behind and grabbing. Not talking is much sexier.

A lustful look and touching. Lots of words are unnecessary. I like a certain look that says, "I wanna fuck you."

I like my partner to initiate by slowly undressing me or turning baths for two into a lovemaking session.

Others prefer the verbal approach:

I like to express that I want this or that in a way that's friendly, loving and HOT.

With a new partner, it needs to be verbalized. I initiated my most recent encounter by saying, "Can I touch you? Can I kiss you?"

Double entendre is big with me; wit and a quick mind are a turn-on.

Some enjoy planning ahead so the anticipation can enhance the sex:

I like to talk about it long before we actually get down to it. It's wonderful to spend an afternoon or evening together knowing that it's going to happen.

I love to whisper and tease my partner along, often for hours, over dinner.

I like some very intentional setting up like, "I want to make love tonight, why don't you put on perfume only and I'll be over later."

While others relish the element of surprise:

I like them to be spontaneous. If I'm sitting in a chair reading, I want the book taken from me and my glasses removed and my mouth covered with wet lips.

I like to be caught off guard, for my partner to start massaging, fondling, stripping or teasing me while on the phone.

I like my lover to come up from behind, grab my breasts and bite my neck while I'm doing something boring like the dishes.

Some respond better to force:

I like to be grabbed in a darkly lit club and dragged outside for a good time!

Since I'm a pretty aggressive female, sometimes I like my partner to be forceful with me so I can be passive for once!

Others are partial to a slower or gentler approach:

I like to start with a kiss, then get into heavier and heavier groping to the point where I feel like I'm going to die; then I like for my partner to undress me slowly. I like to be teased into a frenzy.

Others have their own methods of initiating!

More often than not, when I initiate it's either by kissing or stroking or sometimes by just fellating my partner as a way of saying hi.

In the past I would initiate sexual encounters by reading someone's palm and telling them some great sex was in their future!

Usually I grab him by the balls and growl!

One Last Example

As a way to illustrate some classic communication pitfalls, here's a description of a not-uncommon transaction at Good Vibrations:

A woman shyly enters the store and looks around surreptitiously. She heads over to the vibrator section, where she gazes in bewilderment at the many sizes and shapes. A clerk approaches her:

"Is there anything I can help you with?"

"Oh no, no. I'm just looking," she says, clutching her purse, visibly embarrassed.

"Do you have any questions about the vibrators?" the clerk persists.

"No. I'll let you know if I do. Thanks."

The clerk retreats. After some time and consideration, the woman selects a large, very realistic-looking penis-shaped battery vibrator, makes her purchase as quickly and discreetly as possible, and makes a hurried exit.

The next day the woman returns. She whispers to the clerk that she'd like to return her vibrator, perhaps saying something like. "It didn't work out," or "My husband didn't like it." She's disappointed; at this point she'll either elaborate on the problem, and perhaps the clerk can help her choose a more appropriate toy or, being too embarrassed or defeated, she'll give up on sex toys for good.

Here's What Probably Happened

At some point this woman (let's call her Ellen) decided she wanted to try a vibrator. Maybe while talking to a friend about her difficulty having orgasms, Ellen learned of the wonders of vibrators. Maybe Ellen read about vibrators in a book or a magazine and decided it was worth a try. So, she pays a visit to Good Vibrations.

It's the first time Ellen's ever been in a sex shop and, like most newcomers, she's embarrassed. Once she finds the vibrator section, she is overwhelmed by the variety of sizes and shapes. Understandably, her brain is firing questions: "What does that do?" "Where does this go?" "Do women really like that?" She probably begins questioning what she plans to do with her vibrator once she buys it.

When the clerk approaches to offer help, Ellen's shyness and embarrassment render her speech-less, so she doesn't ask her questions. Maybe she's not sure what she should ask. Eventually she purchases a vibrator that looks vaguely familiar to her—the penis-shaped battery toy.

That night during lovemaking, she pulls the toy out from under her bed to surprise her husband. He's shocked, confused, threatened, defensive. He questions his performance. "Don't I satisfy you?" He questions her need for him. "Won't that fake penis eventually replace my real one in your affections?" She might try to explain, to express her needs, but most likely the toy goes back under the bed, and both of them give up.

What Went Wrong?

How could this have been avoided? When Ellen decided she wanted a vibrator, she could have asked herself, "What specifically do I want it for? To stimulate my clitoris or to use as a vibrating dildo?" Ellen could have talked with her friend about how she uses her vibrator. Maybe she could have even borrowed her friend's vibrator. Then Ellen could have talked to her husband, perhaps saying, "I have a friend who uses a vibrator, and she says her orgasms are really different. I'd love to try one; would you like to help me experiment?" This might have opened up a discussion on what her orgasms were like at the time, whether the vibrator would complement their sex play or be used solely by her. If either of them felt uncomfortable about toys, they could have talked about that. Discussing their issues in a nonsexual, nonthreatening setting might have provided Ellen the opportunity to reassure her husband about his performance and her affection for him.

But instead, Ellen set out for Good Vibrations with the vague notion that she wanted a vibrator for something. When she walked in the door and was instantly overwhelmed by the variety, she began to wonder what she really was going to do with the thing. She felt foolish, ignorant, and just plain embarrassed. She became increasingly uncomfortable, but since she came on a mission, she purchased the phallic model that looked most like a vibrator to her.

Had Ellen talked about her sexual needs with her friend or her partner, she might have been able to articulate what might satisfy those needs. Perhaps she could have conveyed her questions to the clerk, who could then steer her in the right direction. She might have seized the moment to ask the clerk for feedback or information on any of the issues that came up during her conversation with her husband.

Since Ellen never let her husband know that she was at all interested in vibrators, he was shocked by the abrupt change in their routine and figured she was trying to tell him something about his performance. His defensiveness, combined with her confusion over the sex toy, ultimately killed any enthusiasm Ellen had for trying something new. If they had discussed it first, or if at any point along the way Ellen had figured out what she wanted out of that vibrator, she might have been able to explain it to someone: herself, her friend, her husband, or the store clerk, who could

have offered some useful information and some much-needed encouragement.

Benefits

The benefits of good communication are infinite. New relationships can prosper from early sharing of likes and dislikes, not to mention discussions on safer sex and contraception. People in longer relationships can troubleshoot problem areas if they're able to discuss sex comfortably. And people at all stages of a relationship can benefit from the chance to experiment with new kinds of sexual activity. Talking about sex enables us to break old patterns, eliminate archaic attitudes, and explore the many sides to our sexual selves.

CHAPTER 5

Masturbation

You would be hard-pressed to find a group of people more enthusiastic about masturbation than the employees of Good Vibrations. Every time we talk to a customer about sex toys we're inwardly cheering, "Go home! Masturbate! You can do it! You'll love it, we promise!"

Why sing the praises of an activity most people can't even admit doing?

We think masturbation should be the national pastime: It feels good; it's healthy; it's natural; it's free; it's legal; it's your birthright; it's easy to do; it's convenient; it's voluntary; you can do it alone; you can do it with someone; it's educational; it's a unique form of self-expression; it's relaxing; it's invigorating; it builds self-confidence and self-esteem; it's creative; it's ageless, colorless, genderless—the list could go on for pages.

These days, masturbation is often referred to as solo sex or self-loving. While we appreciate the existence of a larger sexual vocabulary, and we will use these words for variety's sake, we're standing up for the word *masturbate!* Enough of those clinicians or authors who find the word dry, technical or tainted by a sordid past. We're liberating it from its oppressive history and embracing it in word as well as practice!

To Know Me Is to Love Me

Here are just a few excellent reasons to masturbate regularly:

Masturbation Is Natural

Despite a wide range of cultural taboos, there is nothing unnatural about masturbation. You're born with all the equipment. Ultrasound images have shown a fetus masturbating (touching his genitals with fingers) in the womb. Children, those little barometers of all things biological, i.e., unlearned, do it with no instruction and often before they're even talking. They touch their genitals because it brings them physical pleasure, just as scratching an itch would:

My earliest memory of touching myself is when I was still in a crib, on my stomach, with a blanket rolled between my legs—rocking myself with my hand underneath me on my genitalia through the blanket. My mom said she caught me doing this at six months old!

At age five I discovered this great way to feel good. I called it "tickling" myself.

My sister who is five years my senior taught me to masturbate when I was around five. I had no concept of sex at the time and used to masturbate to the alphabet!

Instead of denying kids pleasure, parents could try simply stressing the difference between things done in privacy (like going to the bathroom or picking your nose) versus those done in public. Unfortunately, even well-intentioned parents can project their own embarrassment or discomfort onto a child, resulting in the child associating masturbation with something bad. Discussing masturbation with your child in a direct, permissive manner lays the groundwork for a healthy sense of sexual self-esteem:

I don't have any anxieties about masturbating. My mom encouraged me to masturbate when I was younger. She said it would help me learn what I liked sexually.

When I was little (six or eight), I was sure there was something terribly wrong with me for having what I now know were orgasms. I finally gathered my courage and asked my mother about them, and she was fantastic. My fears died down after that. In reaction to the turmoil I felt then, I have fought inside myself and in the community to foster good feelings and clear consciences about self-pleasuring.

Our ancestors left us a legacy of misinformation, guilt and pleasure-phobic attitudes about masturbation. As adults, we'd do well to note childhood experience (either by affirming our own children's practice and/or by conjuring up memories of our own) in our efforts to embrace masturbation. Our survey question that resulted in the most voluminous, as well as the most colorful, enlightening and humorous responses, asked people to recount their earliest memories of self-pleasuring. Because there are too many to list here, we've ended the chapter with some of them, and we expect you'll be as moved as we were by these anecdotes.

If you are still not convinced that masturbation is natural, remember that in 1972 the American Medical Association declared masturbation a normal sexual activity.

Masturbation Is the Basis for Good Sex

What better way to learn about your anatomy and sexual responsiveness than by masturbating? We are all unique sexual beings, and masturbation will teach you just what type of stimulation feels good to you. In fact, sex therapists and other health professionals often prescribe masturbation to women and men who want to increase their sexual awareness, break through sexual barriers or who may be experiencing some type of sexual dysfunction. Preorgasmic women are encouraged to masturbate regularly in order to experiment with various types of stimulation. Masturbation allows women who are unaccustomed to paying attention to their own sexual responses the time to explore their unique sexual rhythms. Men can gain control over the timing of ejaculation with masturbation methods such as the squeeze technique and the stop/start technique.

You can improve your own sexual awareness by experimenting with masturbation. Many of the techniques and toys we discuss relate in some way to masturbation. Adding Kegel exercises to your masturbatory ritual will have positive effects on both solo and partner sex. Women pursuing multiple orgasms and men trying to orgasm without ejaculating may enjoy experimenting alone free of performance anxiety. In Betty Dodson's masturbation training video for women, *Celebrating Orgasm,* she sagely notes "to get really good at sex, we need to practice for a couple of hours at least once a week."

Almost all the toys we discuss can enhance or add a new dimension to solo sex. If you're planning to introduce a toy into partner sex, you might increase your chances of success by playing with it alone first. If you're buying a toy for a partner, you should encourage her or him to play with it alone as well as with you.

By playing with a toy or practicing a new technique alone first, you spare yourself performance anxiety, frustration or disappointment when your fondest expectations aren't fulfilled. One woman's first masturbation story confirms this:

In my twenties a man friend/lover bought me a battery-operated vibrator and wanted to teach me how to masturbate. He went very slowly and was very patient, but I was embarrassed. Once I relaxed and practiced on my own, I loved it.

Alone, you're responsible only for your own pleasure, so you're free to go as slowly or as quickly as you like. You're more likely to give yourself the time and permission to practice until something works for you. Once you've discovered the secrets of success, you can approach partner sex with more confidence.

For instance, let's say you're the proud new owner of a Hitachi Magic Wand and would like to use it with your partner, but you're not quite sure how. Play hooky from work to try your toy out alone (how liberating to take a day off to masturbate!). Use it as many ways as your imagination permits, but wait to use it on your clitoris or penis last. Press it against different parts of your body and notice where you get an erotic charge: maybe the back of your neck, the inside of your thigh or your nipples. Vary the speed and pressure, stop and start the vibrator, lie on top of it. When you place the vibrator on your genitals, pay as much attention to what doesn't feel good as to what does.

After you've had a delightful afternoon (or several) with your new toy, you're in a better position to orchestrate a fun toy tango with your partner. You can begin by describing all the ways you like to play with the toy. Let your partner maneuver the vibrator while watching your reactions, or vice versa. Try exploring the unique ways two bodies can enjoy a vibrator. Two women can nestle the vibrator between them. A man can enjoy indirect vibrations if he uses the vibrator to stimulate his partner's clitoris while he is penetrating her. Are you catching on?

Here's another example: Perhaps you've always wanted to dress your penis up in one of those sexy leather cock-and-ball toys, but you're not sure whether you'd be comfortable showing it off to your partner. Plant yourself somewhere comfortable and try it out. Practice putting it on and removing it so it becomes second nature; if it's adjustable try out the different options till you discover the right fit. Admire yourself in front of the mirror, don't be afraid to strut your stuff! Use a variety of touches, caresses and strokes on your penis and testicles, so you can share these with your partner later. You're discovering the pleasure potential of your new toy and gaining confidence using it, so you're in a much better position to introduce the new you to your partner.

Are you ready to call in sick? Well, if that doesn't seem likely, remember that another advantage of masturbation, as one woman reminds us, is that you can do it discreetly almost anywhere:

My only anxiety about masturbation is that someone will catch me in the restroom at work. It doesn't stop me!

Masturbation: Freedom of Sexual Expression

I like to be sexual every day, either with myself or someone else.

When I'm in a relationship I masturbate regularly as a gift to myself.

Every time you masturbate you're asserting your identity as a sexual person. Masturbation is sex. If you believe you're only being sexual when you're with a partner, you're missing out on an entirely satisfying, fulfilling aspect of your sexual self.

Every time you masturbate you actively cast off those repressive attitudes about sex instilled in you by parents, teachers, friends, priests, aunts, uncles, counselors, therapists, politicians and the media. You're not going to go blind; you aren't "wasting your seed"; you're not frigid; you aren't being punished; you won't get a disease. You're celebrating your sexuality and practicing safe sex. Give yourself a hand! For many of us, it was a strong sex drive and a sense of humor that helped us survive those formative years:

During my elementary-school years, I was in Catholic school, and comments made by the nuns made me feel I was committing a sin. So I prayed for God to forgive me while I rocked and rubbed!

I went to a Catholic school where the only sex education we ever received came from a nun one afternoon during the eighth grade. She advised us to try and distract ourselves when we were experiencing "impure" thoughts. Her suggestion (which she admitted worked for her), was to picture, in great detail, a juicy hamburger with all the trimmings! For years, every time I saw a hamburger I got turned on, and every time I got turned on I got hungry!

Masturbation Is Healthy

Don't you wonder why we never see newspaper headlines about the health benefits of masturbation? Every other month you hear of a study proving that a daily glass of wine or a brisk walk through the park is good for the heart. Considering how the media loves sex, it's surprising that we haven't seen the headline "Study Shows Daily Masturbation Reduces Stress, Invigorates Heart and Prolongs Life." It's just another example of the taboo shrouding this simple sexual activity, because all of that is true!

Masturbation Is Popular and Creative Sex

When you masturbate you disprove the myth that heterosexual sex in the missionary position is the most widely practiced sexual activity. Far more people regularly masturbate than engage in sex under that narrow definition.

As you will see later in the chapter, there are hundreds of ways to indulge in this exciting recreation. You can spice up partner sex with masturbation or choreograph a slow self-loving ritual:

Masturbation

- relieves stress and tension
- releases endorphins
- relieves menstrual cramps
- fights yeast infections by increasing the blood flow into the pelvis
- exercises and flushes the prostate gland, reducing the risk of prostate infections
- strengthens pelvic muscles
- is a good cardiovascular workout and burns up calories
- improves sexual self-esteem and self-confidence
- allows you to remain sexually active throughout your entire life

I make a double-handed fist and lie on my front on top of my partner with the pressure indirectly on my clit, directly on hers. I move in a familiar rhythmic pattern; the pace picks up and I usually come in less than three minutes. I have nice arm muscles because of it.

I used to be a quick and dirty gal but now I've learned to take my time. I like to come home before my housemate gets off work and grab a few various erotica books and flip to all the really hot parts. I like to get myself as aroused as possible just using one hand on my clit and then at the last moment toss the book aside and insert my left middle finger into my vagina to feel the pulsing. I love that!

Pregnant women and people with physical limitations can enjoy sex through mutual or solo masturbation:

When I was pregnant I wasn't that keen on the high energy, participatory demands of sex with my lover. Masturbating gave me a welcome sexual outlet that was relaxing and soothing at the same time.

Historical Perspectives

Why do we need to give you all these fantastic reasons to masturbate when the Kinsey Institute's statistics reveal that ninety-four percent of men and at least seventy percent of women already indulge in this marvelous pastime? Because most won't admit it!

Part of the reason comes from masturbation's legacy as a taboo activity, so we'd like to impart a little of its infamous history.

Masturbation in the Bible

In the Western world we often assume that all sexual proscriptions have their basis in the Bible. In fact, the Bible adopts no particular stand on masturbation. However, the story of Onan, which is found in the book of Genesis, is frequently interpreted as an injunction against masturbation. The story relates how Onan's brother died childless. According to the customs of the time, if a married man died childless, it was the duty of the male next-of-kin to attempt to impregnate the dead man's wife in order to ensure the continuity of the family name and property rights. Any child born this way would be considered the offspring of the deceased. Onan was not inspired by this idea "...so whenever he slept with his brother's wife, he spilled his seed on the ground so as not to raise up issue for his brother. What he did was wicked in the Lord's sight, and the Lord took his life" (Genesis 38:9-38:10). Onan's spilling of seed (semen) has been interpreted as either masturbation or *coitus interruptus*, and just to be on the safe side, the Christian church has condemned both activities for centuries as sins against God.

The Economics of Ejaculation

The taboo against masturbation has roots in the socioreligious rejection of any sexual activity that is nonprocreative. It's bolstered by a time-honored tendency to apply an economic metaphor to the "spending" of bodily fluids. The notion that men have a predetermined, fixed allotment of sperm, and that every ejaculation depletes a finite store of this precious fluid, is astonishingly widespread over time and across cultures. Chinese Taoist sexual practices are based on the notion that female Yin energy is inexhaustible, while male Yang energy must be hoarded. Therefore, Taoist sexual techniques involve men controlling ejaculation and channeling semen back up to the brain. Aristotle wrote that semen is a valuable nutrient and that the loss of even a little of this nutrient results in exhaustion and weakness. This philosophy lives on in the modern superstition that male athletes shouldn't weaken themselves by having sex the night before a big game.

The classic tract against masturbation, and one that influenced popular thinking on the subject for over one hundred years, was published by a Swiss doctor, S. A. Tissot, in 1758. His *Onanism: Treatise on the Diseases Produced by Masturbation* argued that the loss of a single ounce of semen was more debilitating than the loss of forty ounces of blood. Following this logic, a man who masturbated consistently gradually depleted his life force, becoming enfeebled, ill and mentally deranged—ultimately, the madman could masturbate himself to death.

Despite the obvious fact that they do not produce semen, women were not exempt from Tissot's theory of the destructive forces unleashed by masturbation. Tissot argued that masturbating women developed symptoms ranging from hysteria to lengthened clitorises, and were ultimately driven to uterine fury, "which deprives them at once of modesty and reason and puts them on the level of the lewdest brutes, until a despairing death snatches them away from pain and infamy."

Nineteenth-Century "Cures"

Tissot's work was first translated into English in 1832, and during the second half of the nineteenth century, Europe and America saw an explosion of treatments designed to curb masturbation in children, men and women. Doctors designated masturbation as the cause of most ailments that could not otherwise be explained or cured. Masturbation was blamed for mental illness and consumption. In a stunning display of circular logic, masturbation was blamed for the constitutional invalidism of Victorian women (who, had men allowed them to get out of the house and out of their corsets, would doubtless have been in excellent health).

Treatments for preventing masturbation ranged from the pathologically violent to the absurd. Turn-of-the-century magazines featured advertisements for penile rings that were spiked on the inside so that any boy who experienced an erection during the course of the night would be woken in pain. Bondage belts, restraints, straitjackets, cauterizing irons and even clitoridectomy (the surgical excision of the clitoris) were all methods used to dissuade young women from masturbating. These methods lived on into the twentieth century in the more benign form of mittens put on children at bedtime so that they couldn't easily play with themselves during the night.

American health reformers of the nineteenth century tackled masturbation as part of a larger problem of excessive excitation of the senses. Radical reformers felt that physical excitement of any kind—even the seemingly innocent pleasure of spicy food—was a dangerous drain, robbing one of the energy necessary for productive labor. Sylvester Graham assured young men that they would be capable of self-restraint if they followed a course of cold baths, fresh air and bland, vegetarian food (such as the whole-grain cracker named after him). John Kellogg treated visitors to his Battle Creek Sanitarium with continence-inspiring cereals, and lectured that masturbation was "the vilest, the basest and the most degrading act that a human being can commit." However Graham and Kellogg were at the extreme end of a continuum of medical literature. By the beginning of the twentieth century, attitudes were beginning to shift to an acceptance of sexuality as a force that needed only to be properly channeled, rather than totally reined in.

Twentieth-Century Acceptance

Sigmund Freud has had a tremendous influence on sexual attitudes in the modern world. On one hand, Freud normalized the varieties of sexual experience with his theory that every human being goes through homosexual, oral, anal and narcissistic phases during childhood development. And yet, by decreeing penis-in-vagina sexuality to be the ultimate goal of sexual maturation, he effectively dismissed the enjoyment of all other sexual activities as proof of immaturity and inhibited development. The interpretation of masturbation as an immature activity lives on today, as does the equally unfounded Freudian theory that arousal from clitoral stimulation is somehow less mature than arousal from vaginal stimulation.

It was Alfred C. Kinsey, the trailblazer of sex researchers, who contributed the most to a destigmatization of masturbation. In interviews with thousands of men and women, Kinsey focused on gathering data as to what sexual activities his subjects were actually engaging in. He was unique for his time and ours in treating all sexual activities with equal respect. Kinsey noted that masturbation was the activity most likely to result in orgasm for women, and spoke out against the Freudian notion of masturbation as an immature activity.

Yet even with the statistics to prove the ubiquity, and therefore presumably the "normalcy," of masturbating, a stigma remains to this day. This isn't surprising—despite the fact that there are countless excellent reasons to masturbate, there are just as many widespread fears and anxieties around doing so.

Why Is *Masturbation* Still a Four-Letter Word?

While it's true that some people still believe the masturbation-leads-to-insanity myths just discussed, most are aware that these claims are untrue, serving only as a reminder that science and "morality" make dangerous bedfellows. What then is it that keeps masturbation, even today, cloaked in secrecy and denial?

A Tenacious Taboo

In many ways the taboo against masturbation is the most long-standing and tenacious of sex taboos. We see this every day in our store. Individuals who are comfortable with the idea of buying sex toys to share with their partners become skittish, embarrassed or downright irritable when it comes to buying a toy for solo use. The notion that masturbation is an immature activity or a second-rate substitute for partner sex has a powerful hold on the popular imagination. "If I were having enough partner sex or good enough partner sex," the myth seems to go, "I wouldn't need to masturbate."

Apparently, the pure self-interest implicit in masturbation makes many people uncomfortable. Countless sex manuals acknowledge the universal practice of masturbation, but it is often presented as a useful tool in the building of a better sex life, rather than as a pleasurable end in itself. It's certainly true that masturbation provides valuable information about an individual's sexual responses and preferences, and this information can enhance sex with a partner. However, we question the notion that masturbation is, at best, a necessary means to the exalted end of better partner sex. A lot of people who consider themselves free of sexual hang-ups have simply rewritten the equation: "Sex is only good if it involves procreation," to "Sex is only good if it involves two loving people." This myth gets exploited by authors, not just of sex books (though they can be the worst) but by novelists, advice columnists and screenwriters—think of the sex scene in the last movie you saw.

The philosophy that motivates us is that sexual pleasure, whether arrived at alone or in a crowded room, is a perfectly valid end in itself. After all, it's delightful to take a bath alone, eat a good meal alone, go for a bike ride alone or listen to music alone. It's equally delightful to have sex alone. We like to think that there's not a person alive whose life wouldn't be greatly enhanced by masturbation.

Addiction Fears

You know that popular cliché, "You can never have too much of a good thing"? That about sums up our feelings regarding masturbation and addiction. If you do it and you like it, keep doing it, with our blessing and encouragement. It's true that if you masturbate, and you enjoy it, you're probably going to come back for more, which conceivably qualifies you as an "addict." It's the negative connotation behind the word *addiction* when used in the same sentence with *masturbation* that causes our hair to stand on end.

Some people maintain that it's bad or unhealthy to rely on one activity or behavior as the primary source of one's pleasure. But if this were true, couldn't we just as easily be adversely addicted to our hobbies: reading, fishing, traveling, jogging? Can you imagine the mind boggling array of recovery groups that would spawn? Masturbation is natural, healthy and brings us pleasure—why deny ourselves? As long as you are not hurting yourself or anyone else (which is difficult to imagine with a solitary habit), you can get off till the cows come home for all we have to say in the matter. We suspect that, behind folks' fear of masturbation, there are a few other factors at work, which are often disguised as addiction anxieties.

Guilty Pleasures

Many of us have a long association of sexual pleasure and guilt. We feel guilt because we're doing something we were told was bad throughout our youth, or we feel selfish or greedy for putting our sexual needs first:

I feel a little guilt when I masturbate that I should be having an orgasm with my husband.

I feel guilty about having more than one orgasm.

Once my grandmother caught me masturbating and slapped my bare ass that was sticking up in the air. That was awfully traumatic for me as an eight-year-old. I'm living in a dorm room now with a very light sleeper and my self-love life has dwindled. I'd be embarrassed if she slapped me on the ass.

Because it's difficult for many of us to enjoy our pleasures guilt-free, we tend to look for something that might be "wrong" with them. For example, if you eat too much chocolate you'll get acne; if you jog too much you'll get overly fond of the endorphin high. In reality, these fears function as unnecessarily negative ways to control or moderate our pleasures. Some people might not "give in" to the temptation to masturbate because they fear that once they try it, they'll quit their jobs and stop seeing friends just so they can stay home and masturbate all day. In fact, once people "give in" they'll probably start going to work with a better attitude!

Sometimes we just need a reminder or reassurance that what we're doing is okay. For the gentleman who won a Good Vibrations contest asking folks to submit their top ten reasons for masturbating, all it took was a pat on the back to liberate his guilty conscience.

Thank you for picking my list as the "most universal" ten best reasons to masturbate. I think this means that I am now completely able to leave behind any left-over guilt I might have felt about masturbating when I was an adolescent. I am no longer a pervert! I am a normal, masturbating person! Yahoo!

Frequency

People are constantly questioning whether they are masturbating "too much."

Too much for whom or what? There's no magic number measuring "normal" frequency. Some folks masturbate several times a day and feel just fine about it, while others masturbate once a week and are wracked with guilt. If you fall into the latter category, try to determine what questions or attitudes are fueling your concern. You might seek answers or support from a friend, book or professional. Sometimes hearing or reading about the habits of other people is all the reassurance we need that we're "normal":

I got the good news early on that masturbation was okay! Liberating Masturbation *by Betty Dodson and the original* Our Bodies, Ourselves *were important texts. Rita Mae Brown helped me think more outrageously about the right to jack off!*

I used to wonder if my masturbation methods were sick, but books by Betty Dodson, Shere Hite and Lonnie Barbach reassured me that many other women had my orgasmic patterns.

Perceived Danger

Masturbation is not dangerous as long as you exercise good judgment and use common sense. When it comes to masturbation, there are lots of "dos" but only one "don't." Don't endanger yourself. We've all heard stories about boys inserting their penises into vacuum-cleaner hoses with gruesome results. And while we're constantly assuring people they can't electrocute themselves with a vibrator, we're assuming they aren't planning to use it in the bathtub.

Some people express concern over their rapid heart rate when they become increasingly sexually excited. One woman even joked about it:

My only anxiety now is having a heart attack and being found with all my delightful toys!

Let us assure you this is extremely unlikely. The *Journal of the American Medical Association* reports that men with heart disease are at a lower risk of having a heart attack after sex (1%) than they are upon waking up (10%), exerting themselves (4%) and getting angry (2%). Those movie scenes of men having heart attacks during sex are convenient plot devices so the young wife can inherit all the money!

Hang-Ups

People incorporate a variety of anxieties about sex into their masturbation practices, either consciously or unconsciously. Folks who find their genitals "dirty" might only masturbate through clothing. Those afraid of "getting caught" might wait until they're alone in the house, or have learned to masturbate without making a sound. One of our most common requests at Good Vibra-

tions is for a quiet vibrator, "one that can't be heard through the walls in my apartment." Still others might turn these limitations into necessary ingredients for their arousal; many people enjoy masturbating in situations where there is a greater possibility of getting caught. There's nothing wrong with any of this; it's helpful to be aware simply in case you come face to face with an anxiety that's limiting your enjoyment.

Masturbation and Partners

Many of us may feel fine about masturbating in private, but when it comes to divulging this practice to a partner or—heaven forbid—actually masturbating in front of him or her, we'd sooner stop altogether. An interesting statistic comes from the Kinsey Institute citing a small study in which twenty-four couples were asked individually if they masturbated regularly. All forty-eight individuals responded yes. Ninety-two percent of the husbands, however, did not know their wives masturbated, while only six percent of the wives thought their husbands did not. While we won't go into what this says about gender stereotypes, what's startling is how common it is to conceal one's masturbatory habits from a partner.

An overwhelming number of the respondents to our questionnaire confessed to changing their masturbation habits when partnered versus single. Of those who elaborated, some explained that they got so much satisfaction from partner sex that they no longer wanted (or needed) to masturbate. Others cut down on masturbating because they didn't want their partners to know they did it. In either case, there seems to be a general belief that masturbation should not be part of partner sex.

These are some of the anxieties that were expressed, along with our suggestions for overcoming them:

When a lover walks in, I feel caught and have to work to overcome that feeling.

This may be triggered by your own ancient associations of masturbation with shame. If your partner is making you feel bad for masturbating, try to find out what's really causing his or her resentments. Only by discussing your anxieties about masturbation can you hope to overcome them. It may be a fear of rejection:

I once masturbated while kissing a woman, but when I finished she started crying. She took it as a personal rejection.

When I masturbate he asks plaintively, "Ain't I enough?" and seems to be in competition with my toys.

Try describing your solo sex as a complementary sexual activity, not a replacement for partner sex. Invite your partner to participate if you like. Perhaps simply sharing the act will supplant the feeling of rejection with one of adventurous experimentation.

People expressed concern that masturbation would reduce their desire to have sex with a partner:

I'm afraid if I masturbate too much, I won't get turned on by my partner.

If you're worried that you'll "spend" all your sexual energy masturbating and have little left for a partner, you should try it first. Many people find the opposite is true:

If I'm getting a lot of sex I tend to masturbate more—I get greedy.

Now that I'm married I sometimes masturbate when my sex drive is flagging—to get myself more in the mood.

You could also try to stop thinking of masturbation and partner sex as an either/or choice. Either I have sex with myself, or I have it with a partner. As you probably surmised from the preceding section, we want you to have it both ways! If you enjoy masturbating, do it in front of or with your partner periodically. This adds a new twist to partner sex and satisfies your lusty masturbation urges.

Masturbation can also come in handy if you and your partner have different sexual schedules. Maybe your sex drive is strongest in the morning,

Reasons to Masturbate

As part of our celebration of National Masturbation Month, we invite our customers to submit their top ten reasons to masturbate. We've printed a few of our favorites here.

♦ You never have to tell yourself, "A little to the left, a little higher and a whole lot harder."
♦ It's a really good "pick-me-up" in the middle of the day when decaf is all that's available in the office coffee room.
♦ Every time you do it you're part of the world's largest simultaneous experiment proving that masturbation does not cause blindness.
♦ What better way to have fun, keep the birth rate down and reduce stress...all in just minutes a day.
♦ It's a great way to sound animated on the phone while the parents are telling you about the latest goings-on in "the old neighborhood."
♦ Self-serve is always cheaper.
♦ It's less embarrassing if you call out the wrong name.
♦ Gets you into the mile-high club without too much hassle.
♦ You'd go insane if you didn't do it.
♦ It's always there when you need it.

but hers peaks at night. In fact, no two people will always be in the mood at the same time, so if you're both comfortable with masturbation you won't have to keep taking cold showers.

Sometimes I get so good at self-pleasuring, I worry that a partner will never be able to offer the same perfect stimulation.

Sometimes I think that if my sole sexual release is through masturbation, I will not be able to orgasm with other kinds of stimulation. I notice that I need a lot of stimulation on my cock to keep it hard.

If your partner aims to please, he or she will make a very attentive student. Masturbating is an excellent way to instruct a lover in the finer points of pleasure. We expect people to know intuitively how to please us, but unless we're willing to show them, we may indeed be disappointed.

Sometimes I'm afraid I will become a hermit and not look for partners anymore because reaching orgasm and enjoying self-stimulation is so satisfying and simple.

It's true that the beauty of masturbation is that it is an easy and extremely rewarding activity, but it doesn't satisfy our need for human interaction. Whispering "I love you" to yourself is a most respectable practice, but it won't necessarily have the same effect it would coming from a lover's lips.

Mutual Masturbation

Watching him masturbate is just incredibly sexy because I can see what he's feeling in ways that I can't when I'm involved. It's so clear that he is intensely inside himself and his desire. It makes me jealous in this really neat way. I could swallow him whole, I think. Masturbating in front of him is great because I really enjoy my reactions—how wet I get, my sounds, my smell, how freely I can move—and I know that I am completely turning him on.

Throughout this chapter we've made references to the benefits of masturbating with a partner, otherwise known as mutual masturbation. Considering the difficulty people have sharing their masturbation practices with a partner, we'd like to summarize a few of the benefits of this practice, in the hopes that it will inspire you to give it a try:
♦ It's an ideal form of safe sex for new lovers.
♦ Seasoned lovers can enjoy incorporating their previously "secret practice" into sex play.
♦ You both don't have to be "in the mood" to enjoy this activity.
♦ It brings out the voyeur in you.
♦ It brings out the exhibitionist in you.
♦ It alleviates performance anxiety for your partner or for both of you.
♦ You get exactly the kind of stimulation you like best.
♦ Your lover learns first hand (no pun intended) what kind of stimulation you like best.

Mutual masturbation can take any form you'd like. You can masturbate yourselves at the same time while watching each other. You can each masturbate with your eyes closed and try to come when the other is ready. You can masturbate yourself while your lover attends to other parts of your body. You can masturbate yourself while lying in your lover's arms. You can masturbate yourself with one hand and jerk your partner off with your other hand. Are you getting the picture? Here's what a few fans of mutual masturbation have to say about it:

My lover and I discovered hot mutual masturbation when I was pregnant and wanted to try non-intercourse sex play. I was on my back (with lots of pillows) with a vibrator between my legs while he stood over me stroking his cock right in my line of vision.

My lover likes watching me when I masturbate. She'll pick up on my lead and soon we're rubbing our clits in synch!

When I masturbate with a partner I'm louder— for dramatic effect!

I like to masturbate with a partner because I can use the pressure of the other person's body to get off.

I don't prefer solo experience but am very enthused when my wife orders it for her viewing pleasure.

I like to be fingered by my partner when rubbing my clit.

Mutual masturbation is used as foreplay or as a joint adventure. I thoroughly enjoy watching my partner masturbate.

Mutual masturbation can be an incredibly intimate experience—it really requires you to let your guard down if it's to be highly pleasurable. It demands openness, trust and caring.

How Do I Love Me?
Let Me Count the Ways...

So you've made it this far in a chapter on masturbation, and now you're ready for a little action. Before we describe the most common ways folks masturbate, we'd like to encourage everyone—whether you're a seasoned masturbator or new to the activity—to spend a lazy afternoon exploring your body. The following section is geared toward women who need a little practice masturbating, but we invite you all to participate!

If You're Preorgasmic

Preorgasmic is the word used to describe women who have never had an orgasm before. Sex therapists generally prescribe a series of masturbation exercises, which, if performed regularly, succeed in teaching most women how to achieve orgasm. The best and most thorough do-it-yourself book is *For Yourself* by Lonnie Barbach. Most programs suggest that you set aside at least an hour a day for several weeks for a masturbation session. During each session your goal is to free yourself from distractions and to focus your attention solely on your body and how you're making it feel good.

You should be completely alone during your session. It's important to relax as much as you can. Let go of all those distracting worries about work or family. If you've got any guilt feelings about masturbating, try to check them at the door. Let your mind wander to images or thoughts that you find arousing. You may want to replay an exciting past sexual encounter. Perhaps you have a favorite fantasy, or even an image of yourself in some erotic environment. If watching yourself in a mirror turns you on, try that. If music, videos or reading material help, try those. Remove your clothes if you like, and explore the sensations of sun, soft sheets or water against your skin. Run your hands along parts of your body, noticing which areas are more sensitive than others. Try a variety of touches: tickling, stroking, pinching or massaging.

When you feel ready, touch your genitals, using the same variety of touch that you did on the rest of your body. Explore the inner and outer lips, the clitoris, the vagina. Try one finger or many, the palm of your hand, knuckles, anything to elicit a number of sensations. (If you are a man, alternate lighter and heavier pressure on parts of your penis and your testicles.) Stroke or squeeze, fast or slow, use fingers, knuckles, the palm of your hand or both hands.

Masturbating with fingers

I like to lie on my back and stroke my breasts, squeeze my nipples gently and stroke my thighs. Sometimes I use lotion. I then massage the lips of my vagina with my first two fingers, insert fingers into my vagina, and then when I feel really excited I put my two first fingers on either side of my clitoris and squeeze, and move them up and down—so the clitoris slides in its hood.

Lying back on my bed, I get excited touching my breasts, my stomach, my vulva, bringing the clit smell up to my nose—I love the wetness and moving my hips in a rocking motion. I can fantasize myself coming or pick a book with arousing material and allow the words to guide my thoughts and my body.

The important thing is to experiment with these sensations, repeating the ones that feel especially good. Let your mind pursue erotic thoughts as your arousal heightens. Continue in this manner until you feel like stopping or until you orgasm. If you don't orgasm, that's okay—what's important is your discovery of what feels good. You can build on this the next time you masturbate.

Try not to get too fixated on the orgasm or else "trying too hard" might kill your arousal. It's not unusual for it to take an hour of stimulation to bring you to the edge, so remaining patient and focused is important. If you find you're easily distracted, try reading some erotica or looking at a video to maintain your state of arousal. Take little breaks if you start to get frustrated. When you resume the stimulation you'll find your place again. If you find you get really aroused but are having difficulty letting go into an orgasm, reduce the intensity of your stimulation and build back up. Try to relax other parts of your body and concentrate on your genitals. Try doing some Kegels (see the chapter on anatomy) or teasing yourself by stopping and starting the stimulation. Experiment with your breathing—for some women taking deep breaths increases the buildup, for others holding the breath enhances arousal.

You can also try adding some toys for a little variety. Vibrators are ideal for women whose hands tire easily or who need more intense stimulation, and many have the added attraction of more than one speed. A stream of water from the tub or a shower hose can be a welcome alternative, offering variation in temperature and pressure. The first orgasm you have may be somewhat mild, even disappointing. Don't worry, once you've learned how to do it, there are plenty of ways to play with or enhance your experience of orgasm. The important thing to remember with whatever method you try is that practice makes perfect!

Changing Your Style

Perhaps you have no difficulty orgasming but would like to change your routine. Most of us have one tried and true method of masturbating—which is perfectly fine—but you may want to experiment with a little variation at some point. Masturbating with a variety of methods has several advantages.

One, you increase your options for pleasure and learn more about your sexual responses. A vibrator-induced orgasm will feel different than one brought about by your finger. A penis positioned under a flow of water will experience different sensations than one thrusting in and out of your hand. This, in turn, will allow you more freedom when it comes to deciding where and how you want to indulge in solo sex. It might be hard to masturbate on the roofdeck of your apartment if you only know how to come in the bathtub.

Secondly, masturbation can have some pretty nice ramifications for partner sex. As a boy you may have had to masturbate on the sly, so coming quickly was key. While there's nothing wrong with coming quickly as an adult, you might want a little more control over timing so you're not always beating your partner to the punch. Similarly, if you're able to get off from a variety of methods, it'll probably be easier for your partner to please you in many different ways.

How to go about altering your pattern? It's important to get in the mood, go slow, vary the stimulation and practice! Hard as it sounds, you might try depriving yourself of your favorite technique. This will help your desire build, which could make you more receptive to different kinds of stimulation.

How To

There is no single "right" or "best" way to masturbate. Really, can you imagine someone telling you you're masturbating the wrong way? A lot of people have a favorite method, but this changes from person to person, and your favorite way today might be old hat tomorrow. During one of our continuing education nights at Good Vibrations, eighteen of us went around in a circle and described our favorite way to masturbate. It was astonishing, because although many of us used the same toy, or stimulated the same general area, no one masturbated in exactly the same way. Think about all the things that can vary from person to person, like position: sitting, squatting, standing up, lying down on your stomach, back or side, knees up or down, legs open or closed; or pressure: fast or slow, stop and start or continuous, hard or soft. Toss in a variety of toys or different locales, and you've got endless possibilities for a good time.

Sitting naked, watching gay pornos, right hand "jacking," left hand on the remote, fast forwarding to the good parts. I enjoy a basic up-and-down motion—basic but beautiful.

My favorite method is a toss-up between hand or vibrator on my clit, either in a car or in the dark. I also like to masturbate in a pool with the water from the jet hitting my clit.

I strip naked, lie on the bed, then warm myself up by playing with my nipples, rubbing my thighs and fingering myself till wet. Once excited, I use a dildo to fill me up and, at the same time, use a battery-operated vibrator to play with my clit.

I like manual stimulation (my first two fingers moving in circles over my clitoris) while I'm kneeling. Sometimes I put a finger inside me and use my thumb on my clit. My girlfriend rubs her clit while she's driving and has an orgasm with her pants on!

I enjoy using a vibrator and sometimes a dildo or candlestick at the same time. I also like oral stimulation: eating a banana or Vienna sausages while masturbating. I am very oral, used to smoke while doing it, but have quit for health.

We can't emphasize enough the individual, experimental approach to masturbation. Unfortunately, in all the hoopla over the clitoral-versus-vaginal orgasm and the endless quest for the G-spot, we tend to lose sight of the fact that any way you come is the best way! What follows are brief descriptions of a few different methods, with quotes from people telling it like it is for them!

Women

Studies reveal that at least seventy percent of women masturbate. Many women like to combine a variety of activities as part of their solo sex ritual. Use one hand to stimulate yourself while caressing your body with the other. Alternate or combine clitoral, vaginal or anal stimulation. Try doing Kegel exercises, taking deep breaths and rocking your pelvis in time with your breathing to see how this enhances your arousal. Add a little lube for a different sensation but especially if you'll be inserting your toys. Get off on a good fantasy or enjoy some porn as you play with yourself.

CLITORAL STIMULATION *Hand, fingers:* This involves stimulation (rubbing, stroking, pinching) of the clitoris with one or more fingers or the palm of your hand. Some find direct contact with the clitoris too intense. You may prefer stimulation near or around the clitoris. Others prefer to have a layer of clothing or some other fabric between the hand and clit.

I prefer manual stimulation with the flat of my hand and fingers inside my vagina.

I love fingering my clitoris with my index finger and thumb while reading or watching porn.

I lubricate my vulva with baby oil and rub my clit with two fingers until it gets hard. I often use a dildo in my vagina or a butt plug.

The middle finger of my right hand rubs my clit. I start rubbing just to the right of my clit, then quickly move to the left side where it remains for most of the session. My left hand is holding the wrist of my right hand. I'm lying on my back, with my legs spread, but sometimes I prefer raising my knees to my head.

Lying on my back with my legs as tightly together as possible. Tickling my clitoris with one finger kind of bent-up very lightly.

Water: A shower massage with a hose attachment will render any tubless shower a masturbation den. The added attraction of the shower massage is the versatile control that switches the water from a steady stream to a pulsating jet spray. Keep one hand free and adjust the temperature or water pressure for even more variety. Hot-tub jets work, too. Avoid sending strong streams of water into the vagina; this can cause a fatal air embolism.

Using a detachable shower-head or shower massager, I stimulate myself by varying the water pressure on my clit. It's particularly interesting at the YWCA, where the only shower-head is in a stall with no curtain, so I try to be surreptitious and stop when someone comes by. This tends to prolong my buildup in a good way!

Lying on my back with legs spread far apart, I "skootch" down to position myself under the flow of water from the tub faucet.

Rubbing against an object: Press against some object to stimulate the clitoris. Many discovered this pleasure by lying on top of a pillow or a piece of furniture, others found it by pressing against the washing machine during the spin cycle or rubbing against the crotch seam in a pair of jeans!

I love to balance myself on a corner of the ottoman in our living room. I rub my clit on the corner and periodically lift my hands and my feet off the ground. This gives me an exquisite feeling of flying when I come.

Riding on a pillow, the end of the pillow twisted into a hard knot and pressed against my clit. I loved it at seven and it's still my favorite.

Vibrators: Vibrators are used primarily for clitoral stimulation, though many women also use these electric or battery-powered toys for vaginal or anal stimulation. They can be combined with different toys and used in any number of positions:

I prefer lying in bed with sexy music, rubbing my body with scented oil, fingering my nipples and using the Hitachi Magic Wand on my clit.

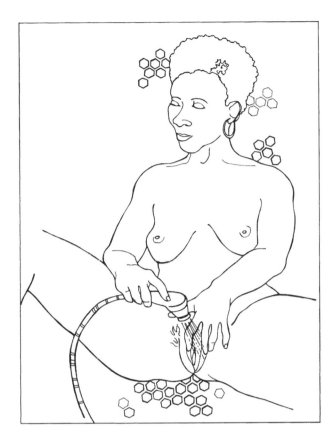

Masturbating with water

I enjoy lying on top of my vibrator and whacking myself on the butt.

I most enjoy vaginal penetration with firm, fast strokes, usually using a vibrator. I like to have one hand playing with my nipples.

G-SPOT STIMULATION Inserting a vibrator or dildo into the vagina can help you locate and stimulate your G-spot and offers a feeling of fullness in the vagina. Try this independently or in conjunction with clitoral or anal stimulation. You can locate your G-spot with your fingers, but it's difficult to provide adequate stimulation through manual masturbation. Women who enjoy this method usually use toys.

I insert a smooth, curved table-knife handle (a particularly nice shape of flatware for G-spot stimulation) in my vagina—and wiggle it with one hand while stimulating my clit with the other.

ANAL STIMULATION The anus is quite sensitive to touch. Many women enjoy stimulation of this area during masturbation or partner sex play. You can experiment with your fingers or anal toys either by themselves or in conjunction with clitoral or vaginal stimulation. Use plenty of lubricant!

I push a lubed-up dildo in and out with one hand, and either rub my clitoris or use a vibrator on my clitoris with the other hand. If using a vibrator, I'll also hold the vibrator against the dildo and up against my anus. Yeow!

Depending on your mood or your level of arousal, you may not always come from similar kinds of stimulation, but you can still enjoy the feelings they induce. Try to ignore the performance aspect and just enjoy the sensations elicited by the activity.

Men

Approximately ninety-four percent of all men masturbate, many by the time they reach puberty. The penis, being a prominent, external organ, practically begs to be handled. You can heighten your pleasure by using a bit of lubricant (or saliva). One new product on the market is designed specifically for male masturbation. Developed by a concert pianist (what busy hands he must have), Men's Cream is an oil-based cream that lasts a long time, heightens sensation and cleans up easily. Men who've tried it rave about it. Look for it in sex-toy catalogs and stores.

You might also like to combine a variety of activities as part of your solo sex play. Use one hand to stimulate yourself while caressing your body with the other. A lot of men like to massage or tug on the testicles while masturbating. Experiment with pinching your nipples or inserting an anal plug while masturbating. Try doing Kegel exercises, taking deep breaths and rocking your pelvis in time with your breathing to see how this enhances your arousal. Get off on a good fantasy or enjoy some porn as you play with yourself.

PENILE STIMULATION *Stroking:* Place one or both hands around the penis, and stroke up and down along the shaft. Variations include using a few fingers, using just your palms, changing your hand position, limiting your stroking to a certain section of the shaft or glans (particularly the frenulum), stroking in a specific direction, or encircling the head of the penis with each stroke. Another variation involves pressing your hand against your penis so it rubs against your stomach as you stroke it. Or you could try wrapping your penis in a piece of clothing or fabric:

I often like to wrap my cock in a soft cloth to stroke it.

I like to be up on my haunches so I can pull on my balls while stroking my cock gently. Most men like to stroke vigorously, in my experience, but I like it slow.

I lie in a recliner and apply some lotion. I use one hand on the shaft and rub the head, testes and the area towards my anus with the other hand.

I love to tie off or stretch out my balls and look in the mirror at myself while I lube the head of my dick.

I much prefer to lie on my back and use my right hand to stroke the entire shaft of my penis. I may masturbate as much as an hour before orgasm.

I use a little shampoo or lube around the head and prefer straight wrist-pumping on my cock shaft. I also like a little nipple rubbing and a little fingering of my butthole.

Slapping, beating: This involves a steady slapping of the penis back and forth between two hands, or against the stomach or another object.

Rubbing against an object: This is similar to women who like to rub their genitals against pillows or furniture. Try rolling over onto your stomach and rubbing your penis against the mattress, a pillow, clothes or whatever you find does the trick!

I enjoy reading a dirty book and lying on my stomach pushing my cock against the surface I'm lying on.

I use a pillow underneath my stomach, thrusting between the pillow and sheets.

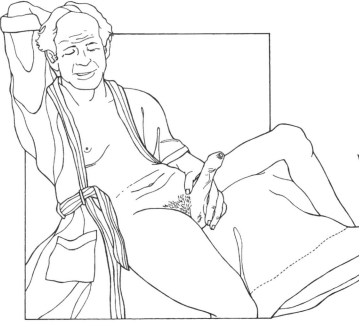

Masturbating with hand

A pillow, a porn movie and a couch. I usually fast forward the porn tape to a section where entry and penetration of a woman is graphically shot. Next, I'll fold the pillow so that it engulfs my penis and with sufficient pressure, match the porn stars in the movie "stroke for stroke." I'll either come on my stomach or towel off if I choose not to wear a condom.

Inserting or thrusting: Just as women have appropriated many a household appliance for insertion, so have men found a variety of things and places into which a penis can be inserted—socks, watermelons, warm banana skins, toilet paper rolls, eyeglass cases and plastic blow-up dolls to name just a few. Just remember to exercise caution and avoid sticking it somewhere that it might get stuck!

Men with intact foreskins know that they are highly sensitive and may enjoy pulling the foreskin over the glans, so it serves as a type of sleeve through which the penis can slide. The foreskin reduces friction between the glans and the hand as it thrusts into the hand.

One of the nicest toys for masturbation consists of a very soft latex sleeve, open at both ends, looser than a condom, but tight enough to stay on my erect penis even in the presence of lubricants.

I slick up my hand with water-soluble lubricant, grasp my penis and try to simulate the feeling of a wet cunt, thrusting and caressing.

I sometimes put tissue around a knot hole in the floor and fuck through the floor.

Penis pumps: Pumps have long been popular with men as masturbation devices. These consist of a long cylinder that fits over the penis and is attached to a pump. The pump creates a vacuum around the penis and pulls in blood to temporarily enlarge it, a feeling many men find pleasurable. Men who enjoy this type of stimulation play with varying degrees of pressure and suction. You should be sure to follow the recommendations for proper use and avoid using the pump at high pressure for longer than fifteen minutes. Use ample amounts of a water-based lubricant inside the cylinder, as well as around the base of the penis, as this helps create a seal. Attachments for nipples are available for some pumps. Penis pumps vary drastically in quality; if you're in the market, it pays to shop around for the good ones, which start at about one hundred dollars.

My husband LOVES his pump! He likes it the best for masturbation, but we also get off on admiring his ample member.

Vibrators: A variety of vibrators provide penile or anal stimulation. Back of the hand models, vibrating sleeves, spot vibrators, and cylindrical and anal vibrators can all provide intense stimulation:

I like to slide my wife's battery vibrator along the shaft of my penis.

When I use a dildo inside me, I usually stimulate my penis with the other hand or with a powerful vibrator.

Water: Women aren't the only ones who can spend suspiciously long periods of time in the bathtub! Many men have discovered the joys of placing the penis under a steady stream of water. Jacuzzi jets, pulsating shower-head attachments, or the stream from the tub faucet can all do the trick. Experiment with different areas on the penis. Many men report enjoying water-stimulation the most when they are about two-thirds erect and often prefer a direct spray on or below the glans. Some uncircumcised men enjoy directing the stream of water underneath the foreskin.

Masturbating at fourteen involved bathing in a tub and stimulating myself using a hand-held shower-head, directing the spray at the glans of my penis to give me curiously pleasurable and powerful sensations. I would lie on my back in the tub and hold the shower-head over me. Then I found that the shower-head was removable. I would remove the shower-head, turn over, belly down, squeeze the stream of water exiting the hose to make it stronger, and then direct this stream against the glans of my cock. This was astoundingly pleasurable.

ANAL AND PROSTATE STIMULATION The anus is quite sensitive to touch and the prostate gland can be stimulated by inserting fingers or a toy into the rectum. Many men enjoy stimulation of this area during masturbation or partner sex play. You can experiment with your fingers or anal toys either by themselves or in conjunction with penile stimulation.

I like to jack myself off slowly—keeping the excitement low grade for about an hour or so. When I come after one of these sessions, it's usually very intense. This sort of jacking off is usually accompanied by the insertion of one or two fingers into my anus toward the climax.

Masturbators Unite!

Although that may sound like a call for a circle jerk (and if it inspires you, go for it), it's actually our humble plea for all you masturbators to stand up and be counted. We know there are thousands of you happily engaged in this pursuit of pleasure, but public awareness of masturbation as a powerful and accessible source of sexual pleasure is fleeting at best. As we approach the end of the twentieth century, we've seen numerous TV sitcoms address the subject with humor and affection, magazines pop up devoted to the subject, and celebrities admit to doing it. But we've also seen a Surgeon General dismissed for acknowledging its existence, and we wouldn't be surprised if public admission to the act was used to malign someone in an election year. As one TV dad tells his masturbating, adolescent son, "Everyone does it, but no one talks about it."

If you're like us, you're fed up with masturbation's bad reputation. Would you like to take matters into your own hands? Join in the celebration of National Masturbation Month, which Good Vibrations instituted in 1996. Every May, friends, customers, businesses, politicians, celebrities and anyone who's ever twanged the wire or tiptoed through the two lips are invited to celebrate this popular pastime. We know many of you can't join us in San Francisco, but there are plenty of ways to pay tribute to masturbation, both publicly and privately, in your own hometown.

◆ Choose one day to honor as National Masturbation Day by indulging in your own private celebration. Call in late for work so you can take an extra hour enjoying a bit of self-pleasure. Convince your coworkers to do the same, then fantasize about business as usual coming to a halt while everyone is home playing with themselves! We dare you to put a message on your answering machine telling callers why you're indisposed.

◆ Send a proclamation to your mayor asking her or him to officially sanction May as National Masturbation Month. Our mayor didn't endorse our proclamation—maybe he was too busy with a little one-handed business of his own.

◆ Engage in a bit of healthy voyeurism—watch others masturbate. We held a screening at a local theater and showed masturbation clips from X-rated videos to two sold-out audiences. If you can't make it to San Francisco, and your local theater would rather show Disney movies, do a little at-home viewing. Check the videography for some notable masturbation movies and cue them up with your friends, your partner or by yourself. If porn doesn't inspire, try the real thing—dedicate an evening to watching your partner masturbate, and vice versa.

◆ Start a Masturbation Hall of Fame. Know someone who has come out of the masturbators' closet in a public way? Send them a note of appreciation and tell them they've been inducted into the Masturbation Hall of Fame. We wrote biographies of famous folks who've spoken publicly about masturbation and pioneers who've devoted their lives to its liberation. We displayed these in our stores much to our customers' delight.

♦ Come up with your top ten reasons to masturbate. We held a contest that drew hundreds of entries. Many participants said simply composing their lists was very empowering. Our favorite entry won the "most universal" prize: "fingers, freedom, fantasies, convenience, nostalgia, pleasure, love, hope, self-esteem and fun."

♦ Spread the word! Phone up your friends, family and coworkers or start your own letter-writing campaign. Announce it on your web page, post it to a newsgroup or e-mail all your acquaintances.

♦ Start your own celebration. We were tickled to discover the formation of The Masturbation Society at Miami University, whose stated purpose is to promote safer sex, to challenge stereotypes and to "strive toward manual dexterity and hand-eye coordination!" We also learned we were not alone in hoping to honor masturbation with its own month; one men's group advocates creation of "Monkey Spank Month" on their web page.

The sky's the limit, depending on your imagination. A Good Vibrations customer wrote a letter to Hallmark chastising them for producing dozens of cards for Secretary's Day but not a single sentiment for Masturbation Day! With grassroots support like that, it won't be long before government employees get the day off.

What's Your Earliest Memory of Masturbating?

To conclude this chapter, here are a few of our favorite questionnaire responses:

I was lying on my stomach on my parents' bumpy comforter. Before I knew it, I was rubbing back and forth, and I felt this terrific tightening of my muscles and a feeling of euphoria. I was thirteen.

I recall at age twelve trying (unsuccessfully) to stimulate myself using a plastic object for vaginal penetration. At about the same age I inadvertently discovered pleasurable sensations from stimulating my belly with the base of an electric toothbrush.

It was my sixteenth birthday. I was playing with my clitoris and I ejaculated all over the bed. I squirted an easy eighteen inches.

Preschool "playing with myself" was pleasurable from an early age. I remember it well as a "secret" diversion that brightened many a happy hour by age three or four.

I was in my grade-school classroom. Everyone in the class was sitting on their desks, and I was wiggling back and forth rubbing my crotch on the hard surface while we watched some educational film.

I was eleven and used to sneak around in the woods by our house naked. It felt very exciting to be exposed like that!

I remember taking one of my mom's maxi-pads and placing it between my legs and peeing in it. The warmth as it spread through the pad and toward my clit was quite a turn-on.

Around eleven (after learning about the birds and bees), I tried inserting a Lindy brand ballpoint pen in my vagina, round end first, to see how deep it was. Also around twelve, I engaged in heavy petting with boys and discovered I could reach orgasm alone by two methods, with water from the shower and an inner-thigh exercise I found in a book.

I was around eleven or twelve. I remember wanting to put things between my legs. Then I discovered I could take out the blade of my electric shaver and there was a tiny vibrating piece which brought me to my first orgasm.

At about five I felt this "feeling" climbing a rope. I referred to it as "my feeling" and would secretly climb bars or ropes—flapping my legs together.

Age four, playing with plastic animal figurines.

Around five. My friend and I would spend a good deal of time playing with our "poes." We would open the outer labia, put tiny smoothly rounded creek pebbles next to our clitorises, carefully close the labia and walk around for what seemed like hours feeling too damned good!

I was thirteen or fourteen. My balls and cock were itching. I started scratching them and it felt like nothing I had ever experienced. I started rubbing myself harder—pretty soon I was having an orgasm.

I started at thirteen, and my earliest memory is of being caught by my mother—I was lying on my stomach in the living room, and I told her I was "swimming."

When I was six. I remember climbing the "No Parking" sign pole outside our house over and over.

When I was little my mother made us kids wear long nightgowns and underwear. So when I felt sexual, I would take off my clothes under the bedding and just lie there feeling naked and nasty (we're Catholic).

Around six or seven. Lying in bed before falling asleep. Not with my hands. With objects: bobby pins, pencils and other helpful tools. Not inside, outside. Over my underwear, which was stretched out tight across my clit. I felt an extreme sense of "criminal discovery" and erupted into the most incredibly sharp rippling orgasm that stunned my face into masks of frozen ecstasy, until I gently fell off into slumberland. (I did this every night. I eventually weaned myself off things and used my hands.)

Leaning against the washing machine when it's in the "spin" cycle. Sticking my toe in the bathtub spigot and letting warm water trickle up to my crotch. I had my first orgasm at about ten when a kitten was purring on my neck.

We lived near a medium-sized lake in Michigan. I used to swim, hang out near the end of our dock. I was thirteen, wearing cut-off jeans. There were small fish in the water. I can remember getting an erection that was uncomfortable. I decided to try to remove my jeans, thinking that nobody watching on the shore would notice. The liberated feeling when I did this was fantastic and wonderful. I touched myself without knowing why I was doing so, and stroked my penis gently, and waved water toward it, loving the feeling. I never came this way, but I used to do this often during that summer.

I recall stimulating myself at five years old. My favorite thing to do was to rub my penis against the cushions of the couch whenever I saw a couple kissing on television. I probably had my first orgasm this way when I was ten or eleven. When I was eleven, a priest gave me a book called Safeguards to Chastity, which said masturbation was a mortal sin. So I stopped for about a year. I remember when I started back up again, I was reading the novel Twins. The premise of two twin boys being hot for each other was too much for me, priest or no priest.

Ten years old. I masturbated with a male friend, then we masturbated each other. Later we sucked each other, but it seemed very innocent.

I was six, playing with a stuffed bunny—I liked to hold the bunny's ears and rub my vulva on it.

I was five, playing with my penis when I got my first boner. I showed my female cousin (six) and my sister, who in turn showed me how they could make pencils "disappear."

I remember once running a comb through my pubic hair and being shocked by the spasm it provoked.

My earliest experience was pressing doll-house furniture to my clitoris at age seven or eight.

At age fourteen, I was wearing jeans and discovered that wonderful seam in the crotch of Levi's 501s.

I acted out fantasies by myself when I was somewhere around nine or ten. They involved sprinkling powder, scented with lily of the valley, that belonged to my grandma, in my underpants.

Being about seven and having orgy-type sessions with one or two other little girls. We'd touch ourselves and rub on the side of the bed until orgasm. I don't know if that's possible, but I distinctly remember seeing my girlfriend "finish" when I didn't feel finished. Once I was done, I no longer wanted to continue. We were also having oral sex at this age (with each other).

I was twelve and had just stepped out of the shower when I began to "rub myself the wrong way" as I was drying off. The orgasm was so intense it knocked me off my feet (I fell, shivering, onto the bed). I also remember it as being an absolutely horrifying experience. I thought I somehow damaged my body and spent the whole night worrying that I'd be dead in the morning! Needless to say, I lived and have the hairy palms to prove it!

Lubrication

Who Needs a Lubricant?

At Good Vibrations, we consider lubricant one of life's more enjoyable essentials, right up there with bread, wine and a decent cup of coffee. Every time a customer approaches the front counter at our stores, preparing to purchase a dildo, butt plug or insertable vibrator, we ask politely, "Do you have some lubricant to go with that?" The responses we get frequently include blank looks or even hostile glares. A lot of people have been led to believe that their own bodies should generate enough lubrication to keep any sexual situation slippery, and they take the suggestion that this might not be the case as an insult to their sexual prowess. Of course, men are aware that their penises produce only a small amount of "pre-come" fluid when they're aroused, but many women and men believe that vaginal lubrication is an automatic physical result of a woman's sexual arousal and that lack of lubrication is an indication of lack of sincere enthusiasm:

> I occasionally use lube when I have trouble getting wet. But I feel better when I get wet enough on my own—that usually means I'm into it more.

> I don't generally use lube—I want to do it on my own. It feels like admitting that my body is abnormal or dysfunctional. I don't know. I'm trying to get over it.

In fact, vaginal lubrication doesn't automatically follow sexual arousal and doesn't automatically indicate sexual arousal. Lubricating is influenced by hormonal fluctuations and can vary dramatically depending on where a woman is in her menstrual cycle. Women who have reached menopause, have had a hysterectomy, have just given birth or are breast feeding will experience a decrease in their natural lubrication and a thinning of vaginal tissues due to reduced estrogen levels:

> I used lubricant following the birth of my child, when my tissues were tender and dry.

> I use lubricant when on my own and occasionally with a partner. There's less lubrication from me as I grow older.

Hormones aren't the only influences on vaginal lubrication. Alcohol, marijuana and over-the-counter cold medications dry up all mucous membranes—those in your head and those between your legs. And, of course, stress can throw almost any "natural" physical response off kilter.

Besides, even those situations in which a woman is lubricating heavily can be enhanced by the addition of artificial lubricants. Vaginal secretions don't necessarily make their way up to the clitoris, and most women enjoy direct stimulation of the clitoris far more when the touch is smooth and moist. Lubricant makes any kind of vaginal penetration more pleasurable—it's always more comfortable to have two wet surfaces sliding against each other—and is crucial for anal penetration.

I use lube for extended sex play when I tend to lubricate less toward the end.

I use lube to avoid pain or soreness during and after penetration. I also use it when masturbating with my vibrator.

Whenever a customer returns from a first encounter with a new dildo or plug confessing that it was just "too big," we double check that she or he took plenty of time to relax and used lots of lube. Lubes are a crucial accompaniment to anal insertion, as the anus and rectum don't produce any natural lubrication, and they're invaluable for vaginal insertion as well—many dildos have a sort of velvety surface texture that will absorb your natural juices, resulting in an unpleasant friction that only a lubricant can tame.

What's in a Lube?

But why worry? If all of life's minor inconveniences could be solved as cheaply, easily and enjoyably as the insufficiency of natural lubrication, the world would be a wonderful place. There's a dazzling array of options when it comes to artificial lubricants. We've been told that egg whites make a fabulous organic lube—when your roommates ask where all the eggs have gone, just tell them you're perfecting your meringue recipe!

Oils

Oils have been used as lubricants for hundreds of years, but there are some facts you should bear in mind to have the best possible experience when anointing yourself for sex. Genital tissue is sensitive and easily irritated, so you should stay away from scented oils. Stick to pure, light-weight vegetable or mineral oils. Lotions and creams are absorbed into the skin too quickly to make very effective lubricants. Oils, which stay slippery indefinitely, are very popular for male genital massage, a.k.a. hand-jobs. Men who enjoy using oils for masturbation often develop passionate preferences, from the classic Albolene hand cream, to coconut oil, to the latest and greatest Men's Cream. This petroleum and Vitamin E-based formula boasts an enthusiastic fan club.

While women can also enjoy using oils for masturbation, we do entreat you not to use Vaseline or any petroleum product as a vaginal lubricant. This stuff is extremely hard to wash out of your body. Vaseline is likely to remain coating the walls of your or your loved one's vagina for days, welcoming all kinds of bacteria and creating an environment that promotes yeast infections. In fact, all oils will linger in your vagina longer than you might wish, as there is no way for them to be flushed out of your body. And oils of any kind will destroy latex condoms, dental dams, gloves or diaphragms, so oils are completely incompatible with practicing safer sex. Your best bet would be to restrict your genital use of oils to solo sex activities.

Water-Based Lubricants

The safest type of all-purpose lubricant is the water-based lubricant. Water-based lubricants are especially formulated to be taste-free, nonstaining, non-irritating to genital tissue, and they will easily wash out of your body. These lubricants contain deionized (i.e., purified) water, long-chain polymers (biologically inert plastics commonly found in foods and cosmetics) and some kind of preservative to prevent contamination by viruses or bacteria (such as methyl paraben or propyl paraben). Many water-based lubes also contain glycerine, a syrupy-sweet byproduct of fats, which adds a slippery quality. Like many fine things in life, water-based lubes are an acquired taste, and people's initial responses to them can be less than positive:

Space-Age Serendipity

A revolutionary lube formula can have its genesis in the most unexpected places. Slippery Stuff was originally designed to make it easier to slide in and out of rubber wet suits. The manufacturers didn't take long to figure out that any liquid that remained slippery under water could be equally handy on dry land.

Astroglide, an enduringly popular lube, was developed by a gentleman who had worked at NASA. When a female relative complained about post-menopausal loss of lubrication, he turned his attention to cooking up a useful aid. His final recipe was inspired by the fluid used to lubricate O-rings on space shuttles.

Using lubricant makes me feel like a frog swimming in a pond.

I don't use lube if I can help it—I hate it. Sticky, messy, yuck!

The sticky quality folks find disturbing about lube results when the friction of your activities causes water to evaporate, leaving only the poly-mer and glycerine ingredients on the surface of your skin. Customers frequently complain that water-based lube gets used up too quickly and that they have to keep applying more. Actually, you can reconstitute and reactivate the lube by simply adding some water or saliva to your geni-tals. We recommend keeping a glass of water or, for the playful, a water gun, by the bed. One good squirt with a plant mister, and your lube will be flowing again. Lubricant is specifically designed for use on moist membranes, where it should stay slippery. When applied to the rest of your body, it will dry, leaving a sticky residue, which makes it completely undesirable as a massage product. Glycerine-free lubes tend to be less sticky and are more likely to just absorb into the skin like a lotion. Lots of people like to wipe the lube off

themselves with a warm washcloth after sex in order to avoid the experience of hopping into the shower the next morning only to slide off their feet when water hits skin and reactivates the lube residue. (Keep this in mind if you're romping around a hot tub, and watch your step!)

For some people, the problem with lubricants is not that they generate too little but too much moisture:

Sometimes I don't want lubricant because it takes away a certain friction that is good when I have my vulva touched/rubbed. Without that friction, it doesn't feel as good.

I hate when I can't get the traction I need. I also hate the cat-hair factor.

If you too crave more friction, by all means scrub that lubricant off your genitals with a wash-cloth, and you'll be back to your natural state in seconds. Whenever you feel "too wet," you should consider incorporating safer sex supplies such as condoms, latex gloves or dental dams into your activities—latex requires a lot of lubrication before it will get slippery.

As for the argument that water-based lubri-cants are too "messy," we have to wonder why anyone would want a sexual encounter to be tidy. Nobody refuses a massage on the grounds that it is "messy," and in fact, water-based lubes are much easier to wash off both your body and your bed sheets than massage oils. It's true that some water-based lubricants are stringier than others and may form long, sticky strands that land on your sheets or in your hair on their journey from the bottle to your genitals, but a little practice will enable you to show the lube who's boss. The decision as to whether to apply a discreet dab or a big sloppy handful is entirely yours.

I like the feeling of lube—that it is increasing the sexy wetness/messiness of sex.

I use lube because, while I'm always quite wet, I think wet is very, very sexy. It makes me happy.

Buying a Lubricant

Name-brand and generic water-based lubricants produced by major pharmaceutical companies can be found in drugstores across the country. These lubricants, such as K-Y Jelly, were originally formulated for use during medical exams, so they don't have the slippery properties of lubes specifically designed for sex. They tend to get tacky and pill up with extended use. For low cost and wide distribution, however, these over-the-counter lubricants can't be beat. Public health campaigns stressing the importance of using latex barriers in conjunction with water-based lubes to prevent disease transmission have greatly expanded the market for sensual lubes. In a notable recent development, Johnson and Johnson has come out with a newly formulated K-Y Liquid, which they're marketing explicitly as a sexual lubricant with ads in women's magazines promising "another good night's sleep, lost."

By and large, sexual lubricants are produced by small manufacturers and sold through adult bookstores, sex boutiques and adult mail-order companies. Here in San Francisco, brands such as Aqua-Lube, Astroglide, ForPlay, Probe, Slip and Slippery Stuff share space on drugstore shelves with K-Y Jelly. Our mail-order lubricant sales, however, suggest that sensual lubes aren't as readily available in the rest of the country. What's the advantage of these lubes? They tend to stay slippery longer than pharmaceutical lubes, and they come in user-friendly flip-top bottles or pump dispensers, rather than fiddly little tube containers. You can expect to pay anywhere from fifty cents to four dollars per ounce of lube, depending on how concentrated a brand you're buying.

Lubricants are a "personal care" product about which folks can develop almost fanatical brand loyalty. This loyalty can result from specific preferences regarding texture or from purely sentimental associations.

Astroglide doesn't get sticky as fast as other things I've used.

My first girlfriend turned me on to Probe, and now I can't imagine using any other brand.

LUBE SHOPPING CHECKLIST

✓ *Purpose.* Will you be using the lube with latex or for vaginal intercourse? Then look for water-based lubes. Anal sex? Try a thicker lube. Oral sex? Avoid lubes containing nonoxynol-9.

✓ *Sensitivities.* Do you have sensitive skin? Check that your lube doesn't contain methyl or propyl paraben or nonoxynol-9. Are you prone to yeast infections? You may want to avoid lubes containing glycerine.

✓ *Taste.* Do you want a lube with the least possible taste? Avoid lubes containing nonoxynol-9. Try Probe or Slippery Stuff.

✓ *Texture.* If you'd prefer a thinner lube, try Astroglide, ID Lube, Slip or AquaLube. If you'd prefer a thicker lube, try Embrace, Slippery Stuff Gel, Probe or K-Y. If you're looking for a lube that won't get sticky, try Liquid Silk.

For every customer who turns trustingly to one of our store clerks and asks which one of our lubricants is "the best," there are always two or three customers clustered around the lube shelf ready to jump into the discussion with conflicting advice:

"Get Astroglide. A little bit goes a long way, and it's not stringy, like Probe."

"Probe is the best: it isn't too sticky, doesn't irritate me and is similar to human lubrication."

"I like ForPlay because it's nice and thick."

"Good old K-Y Jelly works fine for me."

What's a lube novice to do? If possible, get sample packs or small bottles of several different brands and experiment to determine your own preference. Water-based lubes all have basically the same ingredients—the main distinction between them is in their consistency. Some folks prefer thin and watery lubes—close to saliva in texture—while others prefer thick and jellylike lubes.

People with very sensitive skin should try applying the lube to the insides of their wrists and waiting a day to see if any irritation develops before trying the lube on their genitals. Individual reactions can vary greatly. If you have environmental or dermatological sensitivities, you might want to avoid lubes that contain the preservatives methyl paraben or propyl paraben—some folks report allergic reactions to parabens. Probe, ID Lube and Slip are all good paraben-free options. Some women look for lubes that are glycerine-free, out of concern that the sweetness of the glycerine promotes yeast or bladder infections. Glycerine, however, is completely non-irritating to the vast majority of people and is used widely in everything from lubes to liquid soaps to cosmetics. You may choose to avoid glycerine because you object to its stickiness—Liquid Silk, a glycerine-free lube with a creamy texture, is one of the most popular new lubes on the market.

If you expect to encounter the lube during oral sex, its taste will matter to you. All water-based lubes are advertised as being taste-free; most containing glycerine, though, have a slightly sweet taste. Some will have a slight citrus flavor due to natural acids (like grapefruit seed extract) added as preservatives. And any lubricant containing detergent ingredients such as nonoxynol-9 will have a somewhat soapy, medicinal flavor and may even briefly numb your tongue.

Detergents such as nonoxynol-9 are added to lubricants primarily as a safer sex precaution; these detergents have been shown to kill viruses (including the HIV and herpes viruses) in a laboratory setting. While nonoxynol-9 is a common ingredient found in everything from contraceptive foams to baby wipes, it can be irritating to people with sensitive skin, and we do recommend that you test your own sensitivity before investing in a case of lubricant containing nonoxynol-9. Since these detergent ingredients also function as spermicides, and since the preservative ingredients in lubricants are all capable of killing sperm, you should stay away from lubricants if you're attempting to get pregnant. We hasten to add that lubricants, in and of themselves, are not effective contraceptives.

Anne Learns That Lube Makes the World Go Round

G V T A L E S

Several years ago, a friend and I were traveling through Egypt. Tired of self-guided tours, we decided to splurge and hire a tour guide for our day trip to the Valley of the Kings, the burial ground for ancient royalty. Much to our delight, our guide was a woman. Although women rarely hold public jobs in Egypt, our guide explained that she'd been lucky enough to get a university education, which enabled her to land one of the coveted tourist-industry jobs.

She reminded me of an Egyptian Oprah Winfrey—full of confidence, style, humor and showmanship. During a pause in the tour, while she and I waited for the rest of the group to catch up, our guide asked me what I did for a living. Without thinking, I blurted out that I worked for a women-run sex shop in San Francisco. She looked puzzled but before we could talk further the rest of the group arrived and she slipped back into her routine. Since all of the treasures from King Tut's tomb are now in museums, I stayed behind with her while the others went off to explore the tomb.

As soon as we were alone, the guide began to discuss her sexual problems with me! She said sex with her husband was very painful because there was too much dryness and friction. Her doctor, who was uncomfortable discussing sex, simply told her to get used to the pain. As a result, she was losing interest in sex. I told her all about lubricant and asked whether she could get some in Egypt; she said it would be difficult. I asked for her business card and told her I'd send some lube along with a catalog. She specifically requested that I send the package to her office so her husband wouldn't open it first! Too soon our group returned, and the two of us reverted to a conversation about the unbearable heat.

I hope that bottle of Astroglide reached its destination and that my wonderful guide was able to slip back into a happy sex life. As for me, nothing inside Tut's tomb could have thrilled me as much as our conversation that day.

Lubes and Anal Play

There aren't many places in this book where you'll find us making an absolute statement or insisting that there's only one way to go about sexual play, but this is one of them: Never try any anal penetration without using a lubricant. While the anal canal produces some protective mucus, the anus and the rectum don't produce any natural lubrication. Please don't ever insert so much as a finger inside your anus without the aid of some form of lubricant. Anal tissue is thinner and more delicate than vaginal tissue and can be easily damaged by a rough, dry approach.

You do have plenty of options as to what kind of lube you can use anally. Since your anus naturally flushes itself out during defecation, it's not as problematic to use heavy oils anally as vaginally. Many people prefer oils for extended anal play, as they don't dry up the way that water-based lubes do. However, for the vast majority of people who should be observing safer sex precautions, oils are out of the question for partner play, as any type of oil will destroy latex barriers. Consider using the thicker varieties of water-based lubricant such as Embrace, ForPlay and K-Y Jelly. While lubes containing nonoxynol-9 are frequently recommended for safer sex, there's considerable support for the idea that detergents are too harsh for tender anal and rectal tissue and may do more damage than good.

If you've shopped in adult bookstores or with adult mail-order companies, you may have come across products marketed as "anal lubes." These products usually contain desensitizing ingredients such as lidocaine or benzocaine, and their existence is based on the false premise that anal play always hurts and that you need to anesthetize yourself before you can be receptive to anal penetration. In fact, with sufficient relaxation and patience, anal play need never be the slightest bit uncomfortable. If you experience pain upon penetration, your body is warning you to stop what you're doing. Rather than anesthetizing yourself in order to deaden sensation, you should be learning to voluntarily relax your anal sphincter muscles and to bring a heightened awareness to bear on all the sensations you're experiencing.

Lubes and Latex

We have one more absolute statement to make in this chapter that is critical for your health and safety: Never use any oil whatsoever with latex products. Oils destroy latex—this means that even the lightest-weight massage oil, Albolene cream, hand lotion, baby oil or Vaseline will eat into a condom or diaphragm and produce microscopic holes in the latex within sixty seconds of contact. Although many condom manufacturers have begun labeling condoms with warnings against using them with oils, we need consumer education on an even broader scale. Please take the time to read the label on any lubricant you are considering for purchase. Don't be taken in by lubes that advertise themselves as "water-soluble"—these frequently contain oils.

On the bright side, water-based lubes and latex make ideal companions. A dab of lubricant on the inside tip of a condom increases sensation for the wearer—just be careful to use only a drop or two, so that the condom doesn't slide off the wearer's penis. Lube on the outside of a condom minimizes uncomfortable friction for the receptive partner and reduces stress on the condom. Lubes also help transform latex gloves and dental dams into sleek, slippery instruments of pleasure:

Since I use condoms and gloves, I always use lubricant, and why not? It feels nice, and it kinda adds to the whole experience.

Despite the advent of polyurethane safer sex products such as the Avanti condom and the Reality female condom, which can be used with oils, water-based lubes and latex remain preferred safer sex accessories due to their versatility and affordability. Given the importance of using water-based lubes with latex, there is an extensive range of water-based products on the market. Lubes now come in a variety of textures, bottle sizes, prices and flavors. Trimensa, the manufacturer of the popular lubricants Slip and ForPlay, has a line of flavored lubricants called Sensual Succulents, while several companies manufacture edible gels geared towards jazzing up safer oral sex. Yes, now that condom-covered penis or those dental-dam-clad labia can be transformed into a fruit-flavored taste treat. If you have particularly sensitive genital tissue, you may feel that these edible balms contain too many artificial colors and flavors to be appropriate for internal use as lubricants, but they are fun safer sex enhancers.

In closing, we'll leave you with the following enthusiastic endorsement from our kind of lube fan:

Once I started using lube, my sex life improved one million percent. It just makes everything easier and feels better all around.

CHAPTER

7

Creative Touching

Sometimes an accidental touch by a stranger can hold a sexual charge. Maybe it's because I'm tuned into the eroticism of my whole body, I adore overall body stimulation with hands, tongues, lips, toys—you name it!

In our touch-deprived culture, even the most casual physical contact communicates a message of intimacy. Whether you're extending your hand in greeting to a new acquaintance, placing your hand on a coworker's shoulder, or brushing up against someone in a crowded subway, you're establishing familiarity (whether acknowledged or not) by the physical contact. When you stop to think about it, that's some powerful stimulus.

Many people do not take full advantage of the erotic potential of touch. Sure, you can wax ecstatic about the first time you pressed your naked body against your lover's, but can you describe the sensations evoked when the back of the knee or the small of the back is lovingly caressed? Your entire body is capable of being aroused—not just the buttons you push "down there." Awakening your body to its pleasure potential can boost your self-esteem, expand your definition of sex and improve intimacy with a partner. In this chapter, we encourage you to explore the tactile delights of the entire body, not just the genital area, through activities we've dubbed "creative touching." This includes the basics of massage as well as our suggestions for other activities and toys with which to experiment.

I like a lot of stimulation and find that in "real" life people get fixated on one body part or activity (oral or anal sex, for example) and don't have the imagination to view the entire body as an erogenous zone. So many of my fantasies involve getting and giving whole body stimulation with at least one partner—preferably stimulating a number of body parts at any one time.

Erotic Massage

I love massage. Giving and receiving it are terrific ways to stimulate your partner.

Massage can be used for many different reasons: to soothe aches and pains, to reduce stress or relieve tension, to improve circulation, to heighten physical

Setting

♦ Temperature is most important. The surest recipe for disaster is to try to give a massage to a lover covered in goose bumps. An excellent way to warm up prior to the massage is to take a hot bath. Not only does it raise your body temperature, but it's exceptionally relaxing.

♦ If it helps your partner feel warmer and more secure, cover her or his body (except for the portion you're massaging) with a sheet, light blanket or towel.

♦ If you've got a dryer, throw in some bath towels. Your lover can lie on these during the massage or be wrapped in them upon emerging from the bath.

♦ Use a bed, a padded table, or thick blankets on the floor. If you're using a bed, position your partner diagonally so you have a bit more room. If you're using oil or lubricant, place easily washable towels or sheets under your partner.

♦ Find out if your partner has specific physical needs or special requests and prepare your massage area accordingly. A pregnant women might find lying on her side most comfortable, or she might like to use cushions to help support her stomach.

♦ Warm oils ahead of time. Microwave your bottle, or immerse it for a few minutes in warm water.

♦ If you're planning to use other toys, have them nearby.

♦ Unplug the phone, put the kids and the pets to bed, play some music if you like. Your goal is to relax as much as possible.

sensations. All of these can affect your sex life. Many people discover the erotic possibilities of massage by accident. Have you ever been turned on during a professional massage? Or been surprised when a friendly massage given by someone you had no sexual interest in left you aroused? It's perfectly natural for the body to respond this way—after all, the skin, like the brain, is also a sex organ.

I get off on giving my partner massage—great foreplay.

I love just holding and being held, caressing and spending long hours in bed.

Many folks enjoy massage as a warm-up to a sexual encounter, while others experience the eroticism of the massage as an end in itself. Whatever your preference, you can benefit from going slowly and learning how to give and receive pleasure. Too often we're in a hurry to move on to some other activity and don't take enough time to appreciate the intensified sensations of lingering over different parts of the body. Pregnant women and people with chronic pain or disabilities are among those who speak enthusiastically of the rewards of massage:

I have partial feeling from my waist down, but my face and head have become incredibly sensitized to any form of touch—a kiss, a caress, a cheek upon mine is incredibly exciting.

During pregnancy, massage helped alleviate some of my back pain, but also helped me stay in touch with my ever-changing body. The massage was sometimes relaxing and at other times profoundly erotic.

You don't necessarily have to be aroused to want a massage—many folks find the massage itself is what triggers their excitement:

I'm usually stressed and unable to relax, so massage is needed as kind of a foreplay to foreplay!

Although massage professionals may describe their specialties differently, we've chosen to include any type of touching in this category. Whether it be a light touch, a tickle or a firmer stroke, the goal is to discover new sensations. And massage by no means has to involve a partner—you can incorporate many of these techniques and toys into your solo sex play.

Your attitude about giving and receiving pleasure can affect performance, often to the detriment of your own satisfaction. In order to enjoy a massage, both the giver and the receiver need to let go of expectations and simply enjoy the physical sensations. Embrace the concept of selfishness and indulgence when it comes to giving and receiving pleasure. If it's not clearly understood beforehand, you might want to discuss the nature of the massage. Are you both interested in an erotic massage? Is the massage meant to ease tension and induce sleep, or to arouse? Are orgasms expected or will you explore heightened sensation by denying yourself an orgasm?

I like massage that moves into mutual masturbation.

Massage is great but seldom sexual for me. It's relaxing and comforting but not really a turn-on.

The person giving the massage should try to be as comfortable as possible. Anticipate what positions you'd like to avoid and set up your massage area accordingly. If you prefer standing, set up a foam pad or cushion on a table. During the massage, remember to change positions often so you don't get sore—try kneeling, sitting or straddling your partner. It's just as important for you to enjoy the massage as it is for your lover.

Try to avoid conversation during the massage. This allows both people to focus their attention on the physical sensations and eliminates any distractions. It's fine to communicate what does and doesn't feel good, but remember, you can convey pleasure or satisfaction with a moan or a smile!

Tips and Techniques

With the preparations completed, you now have your delectable, nude lover awaiting your ministrations.

If you've agreed on a genital massage, consider saving the genital area for last in order to heighten the anticipation. You may want to experiment with avoiding the genitals altogether to see how it affects your experience of other body parts.

If you're giving a full body massage, here's a suggested itinerary. With your lover face down, start with the back, shoulders, arms and hands, then move on to the butt, legs and feet. Turn your partner over. Begin with a scalp and face massage, move on to the abdomen, chest, arms, legs and feet, and end with the genitals.

There are numerous books about sensual massage offering detailed descriptions and illustrations of dozens of strokes. Since most folks just want to know where and how to begin, we'll explain some very simple, pleasant strokes, which can be adapted to suit your needs. Let your imagination run wild. Take any one of the following strokes and modify it slightly, using your fingertips, fingernails, palms, backs of your hands, knuckles, heels of your hands and thumbs; or try varying the pressure, speed or direction of your stroke—each will evoke a different sensation. The point is to discover what movements feel best so you can use them to please your partner in the future.

Full Body

I love my whole body being stroked gently. I love being teased.

Here is a superb way to begin and end your massage: With your partner face down, arms at her or his sides, position yourself at your partner's feet. Place one of your hands on each of your partner's hands and travel lightly up the arms, around the shoulders and then straight down the body all the way down to the feet, ending at the toes. Don't remove your hands, but follow the same path now in the opposite direction. Try this stroke several times, gradually adding more pressure. When it's time for your partner to turn over, repeat the same stroke on her or his front side.

Fanning

Place palms face down and side by side on the skin. Simultaneously fan each hand out about ninety degrees, then slide them gently up or down; bring hands back together and repeat the motion. The pressure should come from the heel of your hand and/or the thumb, and your fingers will feel great grazing over the skin on the back, butt, abdomen, thighs and breasts.

Pulling

Place your hands next to each other along your partner's side (fingers pointing toward bed) and pull them up toward your partner's spine (or belly, if partner is on back), alternating each hand. As one hand pulls, the other slides back down. Try this on a woman who's on her back; you're moving up from the stomach toward the armpit. As your hands approach the breast, slide lightly over the nipple with your palm. This is also an excellent stroke for the thighs, starting at the knees and moving away from the feet. As you work up the inside of the thigh, approaching the butt, the pulling motion tugs on the genitals, which can be quite arousing.

Thumbs

With your thumb at a right angle to your fingers, place your hands at the base of the spine with your thumbs pointing at each other. Press down with your thumbs and glide slowly up the spine. Try this on the arms and legs as well. Modify this stroke by pressing each thumb in turn, or by rotating them in a circular motion. The focused, direct pressure afforded by thumbs makes them ideal for hand, foot and face massages. When massaging the face, apply gentle pressure, starting in the middle of the face and sliding toward the outside. For example, place your thumbs where your partner's eyebrows connect and move toward the temples, or start on the nose bridge and travel down under the eyes toward the ears.

I love massage that includes having my hair and face stroked.

Butt

Seated at your partner's feet, place one hand on each butt cheek and slide your hands up and down in opposite directions. Kneading or dragging your fingers lightly across the butt can also feel good, as can light slapping.

Breasts

Don't ignore the breasts if you are doing a full body massage (unless, of course, your partner asks you to avoid them). If you're seated at your partner's head, place your hands next to each other on the stomach and slide up between the breasts. Circle around the breasts as you come back down the outside. Repeat this motion several times, allowing your palm or thumb to cover more of the breast area each time.

Place a hand over each breast so that the nipple touches the center of your palm. Spread your fingers as if they were the spokes of a wheel, and as you pull your hand up and off the breast, let your fingers graze the skin until they approach the nipple. You may want to finish the stroke with a light pinch.

I think massage is great as long as I get my nipples played with.

I enjoy stroking my partner all over her belly, breasts, ass and mons. I love fat women and enjoy kneading and sucking my lover's heavy, soft breasts and large belly.

I like massage as extended foreplay—a lot of breast fondling, pinching, light slapping and touching.

This was one of the most wonderful sexual experiences I've had in my life. I had stupidly gone without a bra all day and my nipples were sore by the time my lover and I got home. He massaged them with moisturizer and then moved on to a full body massage. It was great because it was much slower and more gentle than usual.

Genitals

If you've ever watched closely when your partner masturbates, you've had the best instruction for genital massage. You've seen what kind of stimulation feels good on certain areas. Use this as the starting point from which to further explore other pleasurable sensations.

While you may wish to continue using oil during genital massage, please note that some oils, particularly scented ones, can cause an allergic reaction when they come into contact with mucous membranes. If you are sensitive, try testing a small amount first or consider using a water-based lubricant instead. Also, a note about safer sex massage: While massage in general is considered a very low risk activity, the risk increases if there's a chance that blood, vaginal secretions or semen will come in contact with broken skin or mucous membranes. You may want to use a latex glove or condom during a genital massage along with a water-based lubricant (oil will break down rubber).

Here are a few areas you'd do well to include:

ON WOMEN *The labia:* With your partner on her back, place a well-oiled (or lubed) hand over her labia, fingers pointing toward her anus. Pull up toward the navel and alternate hands, always keeping one hand on the body.

Explore the inner and outer lips with your fingers. Pull gently on one and then the other and work your way down the right side, then switch to the left. Rub the outer lips gently between your forefinger and thumb, then the inner lips while applying varying degrees of pressure and asking your partner which feels the best. Starting at the perineum, place your forefinger between the inner and outer labia and trace a clockwise pattern up and around the clitoris.

The clitoris: Encircle the head of the clitoris during a stroke that takes you up the length of the inner lip and around the head of the clitoris. Try not to touch the clitoris directly (as most women find this too intense), but run your fingers over the clitoral hood. Remember to maintain a fluid, continuous motion and repeat these strokes several times.

The vagina: Circle around the outer edge of the vagina several times and then pop in a finger or two and let it rest a moment. Then explore the vaginal walls by stroking or applying pressure, asking for your partner's feedback.

The anus: Lightly circle the rim of the anus.

The perineum: Lightly massage or apply pressure to the area between the anus and the vagina with one hand while you explore her vulva with the other.

ON MEN *The penis and scrotum:* With your partner on his back, place a well-oiled (or lubed) hand over his penis and scrotum, fingers pointing toward the anus. Work your palm up toward the navel, sliding along the penis and gently pressing the penis against his stomach. Try alternating hands with each stroke and slowly massaging the penis around the body in a clockwise motion. Another technique involves forming a ring around the scrotum with your forefinger and thumb and gently pulling his balls away from the body while stroking the penis in an upward motion. You can also leave the penis for a while and gently massage the testicles in this position.

The shaft: Try anchoring the skin at the base of the penis with two fingers of one hand and stroking upward with the other hand. Or cup one hand around the base of the penis and begin to slowly slide upward. When you reach the head, finish the stroke with a twisting motion. As your hand gets near the head of the penis, place your other hand at the base of the penis and begin the same motion. You can also reverse the direction of this stroke. Another stroke often referred to as the "twister" involves cupping both hands around the penis and then gently twisting in opposite directions. If you think your partner would like spot stimulation of the frenulum, clasp the penis between both hands and interlock your fingers together with the thumbs pointing toward the glans and massage using your thumbs.

Massage Basics:

Never given a massage before and feeling a little intimidated? Not to worry, you're certain to meet with undying gratitude if you remember four basic tips:

♦ *Go slowly.* You know that feeling of disappointment when you race through a delicious meal, devouring it so fast you barely taste it? Don't race through the massage! Linger over each part of your lover's body so she or he can savor the sensations.

♦ *Repeat strokes.* Repeat a stroke anywhere from several to a dozen times. The consistency soothes, relaxes and allows your lover to luxuriate in the skin contact with one area.

♦ *Don't break contact with the skin.* Once you've started the massage, stay connected. If you're using oil, squeeze some into your hands before applying it to avoid shocking the skin. When you need to apply more oil during the massage, turn your hand over while it's still resting on your lover's skin, cup it and pour some more oil into it.

♦ *Pay attention to your partner's reactions.* If you see goose bumps, turn up the heat. If you see a grimace, don't press so hard, or ask what caused the reaction. If you see a smile, continue with that stroke. If you're uncertain, ask. You might both agree on some signs beforehand to communicate pleasure or discomfort.

The glans: In a move known as the "juicer," wrap one hand around the penis while you place your palm on top of the glans and rotate, repeating this motion just as if you were juicing an orange. Another version of this would utilize just your fingers in a motion similar to unscrewing a jar.

The anus: Lightly circle the rim of the anus.

The perineum: Apply firm pressure or stroke the section of skin between the base of the scrotum and the penis. Many men find stimulation of this area particularly pleasurable when they're approaching orgasm as it puts pressure on the prostate.

Variations

So far we've discussed just one way of tickling someone's tactile fancy—with your hands—but there are other, playful and just-as-pleasurable means to this end.

Other Body Parts

Your mouth is an incredibly versatile and intimate sex toy. Think of all the possibilities—trace a path on your lover's body with your tongue; kiss, suck, nibble, bite or blow on the skin—all of these can evoke pleasurable sensations. If kissing isn't very erotic for you, you and your partner may need to practice your lip chemistry. You may prefer deep kisses while he prefers soft, light ones. You don't need to assume there's only one way to kiss—experiment so you can find kisses that work for both of you.

Kissing turns me on—my neck, shoulders and arms especially. I love to be sucked and licked all over from fingers to nipples.

You've got quite a number of nerve endings under your arms, which is why many folks find this area erotic as well as ticklish. Try different strokes to see what elicits the best response.

I really like to have my armpits licked.

The nipples are particularly responsive to stimulation. Some folks claim to orgasm from nipple stimulation alone. Sadly, men's nipples are often overlooked as an erogenous zone.

I got my nipple pierced just so my partners would play with this sensitive part of my body.

Experiment orally with sucking, licking, blowing on the nipples or try pinching, flicking or tickling the nipples. A woman's breasts can be very responsive to stimulation, though you should check in with her since their tenderness can vary depending on where she is in her menstrual cycle. Try some of the techniques we described earlier.

A woman's breasts can also be a wonderful tactile tool, both for her and her partner. Drag your breasts over your partner's body. Vary the pressure from just lightly grazing your nipples over the skin, to pressing firmly against it. Rub your breasts against your partner's genitals.

Hair can create a pleasing sensation when dragged across the skin, and it certainly holds a fetishistic appeal for many. Running your hand through someone's hair, gently tugging on it, giving someone a scalp massage or an erotic shampoo can also be pleasant.

I like it when a partner starts massaging my scalp and using her voice to seduce me.

I always find my visits to the hair salon slightly embarrassing because the shampoo sequence is such a turn-on. I love having a stranger's hands gently scrubbing my scalp and pulling on my hair slightly during the rinse.

We encourage you to linger over every part of your lover's body, but there are some particular places you may want to give special attention. Your hands can be skilled instruments of pleasure, but don't forget they should be worshipped as well. We use our hands so much we usually take their sensitivity for granted. Whether you're giving a massage or sitting next to your sweetheart in front of the TV, take the time to gently and lightly explore the intricacies of your lover's hands. Explore the surface of the skin, each finger, the nails and the knuckles:

Out of the blue, my girlfriend will take my hand and start running her fingers along it while we're chatting away. Sometimes it gets me really excited.

The feet are also tremendously sensitive—toe sucking did not originate as an alternative to bathing! The toes and soles of the feet are full of nerve endings, so take some time to discover them. Bathing your partner's feet in warm water and toweling them off can be a sensual experience. Applying powder or oiling the feet can evoke a range of pleasant sensations. If your partner is ticklish, try applying a firmer stroke. If that doesn't work, move to another part of the foot.

Playing with a partner's ears can be arousing and intimate. Those who orgasm from ear play can thank a phenomenon known as "auriculogenital reflex," which traces your orgasm to a nerve found in the ear canal. You might try lightly exploring the ear's folds and creases with a finger or lips. Touch or nibble on the lobe. Don't probe too deeply into the ear cavity, and remember how loud it sounds to your partner if you're sucking, blowing or smacking your lips. Some folks find ear play incredibly erotic and others find it a sure-fire turn-off, so attend to your partner's desires and responses.

I like to initiate sex with a little gentle touching, neck kissing and ear blowing.

The nape of the neck is another fun spot—it lends itself well to continuous smooth strokes, kisses and licks. Try blowing on it. You may want to continue up the scalp and stroke the hair.

Pour me wine, kiss my neck and finger me.

I love to be touched everywhere with her fingertips as gently as possible. I especially love to be caressed from my shoulder to the nape of my neck. My hot spots include my ass, feet, hands and outside my breasts.

I like to be kissed gently on my neck and shoulders to turn me on.

The backs of the knees and inner thighs can be highly pleasurable spots in both men and women. Try a light licking on the back of the knee, vary a soft caress with a firmer stroke on the inner thighs.

Food

Folks are endlessly creative about what they like to lick off another's body—you can turn yourself into an ice-cream sundae or a tropical fruit platter.

My girlfriend and I love licking small dabs of yogurt off each others' nipples. The shock of the coldness on my nipple sends ripples to my cunt, and when her warm, wet mouth starts to suck it off, I nearly lose consciousness.

Food can be a creative way to camouflage the taste of bodily fluids, if you're not fond of them. Chocolate, whipped cream, jellies, spreads and honey are all popular.

Water

I really like mutual masturbation in the shower.

Baths, Jacuzzis, saunas, hot springs—not only do they relax, they awaken desire. There's no denying that warm water feels exquisite on skin, so immerse yourself in it! The Romans had this pastime down to an art form; their bathhouses were luxurious and ornate—the epitome of sensual decadence. While those grand days may be gone, most people do have a bathtub at home. If you don't, hot-tub rentals are usually as close as the nearest phone book. You might also enjoy late-night skinny-dipping in a cool lake, pool or ocean, or sharing a Jacuzzi with friends or a lover. Bath accessories like shower massagers, sponges and brushes can also enhance bath time.

Toys and Accessories

Feathers: Try lightly running a feather over your partner's body for a sensation that even the lightest fingertips can't approximate. Ostrich feathers, which are about two feet long and exquisitely soft, are harvested from farms where the birds shed them. If you aren't up for hunting down your own feather, you can sometimes find these in sex-toy or lotion stores. Be careful not to let massage oil gum up your feather!

Fur: It may be a cliché today, but sex on the bear-skin rug originated somewhere! Soft fur on naked skin is luxurious, but if you're short on

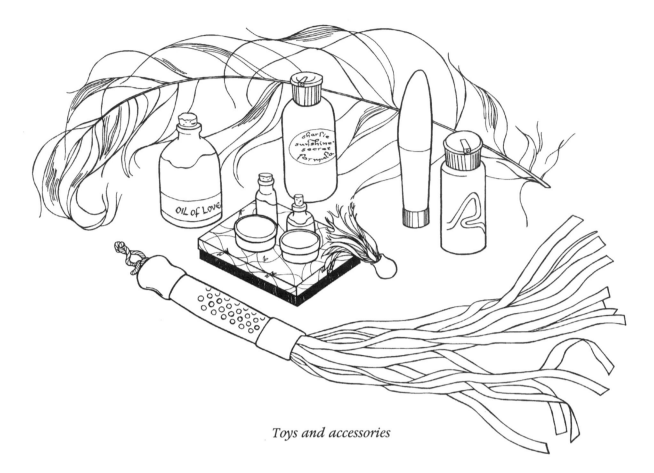

Toys and accessories

rugs or fireplaces, you can invest in a fur mitt for a similar feel. Fake fur has made it possible for everyone to appreciate this sensation.

Fabrics: Satin, velvet, silk, suede, latex and who-knows-how-many other fabrics feel terrific against the skin. While satin sheets have been commercially available (and popular) for decades, other fabrics may be a little harder to play with, unless you're willing to do a bit of sewing ahead of time or to shop around in sex boutiques. Blindfolds, fur-lined restraints and a variety of other leather and latex accessories can be found at specialty shops.

Textured mitts: These are usually large rectangular gloves that fit over the hand so you can use them on a lover's body. Mitts can be made out of any of the fabrics listed above. The adult-toy industry's version is made out of soft rubber with tiny nubs on the glove.

Whips, paddles and S/M gear: Whips and paddles can offer you a range of sensations—from a light slap to a hair-raising sting. Bonds can add an element of restraint to your massage.

Powders, gels, edible items: Rub 'em on and lick 'em off. These appeal to folks' desire to eat something off a lover. Flavor selections rival that of ice cream these days—passion fruit, cappuccino, hot chocolate—but beware: These products run the gamut from sweet-as-honey to tasty-as-motor-oil. Almost all have some kind of preservative in them, but a few boast natural ingredients and really do taste authentic. We questioned customers about their most disappointing toys and a large percentage cited some kind of edible lotion. Most shops have samples open for you to taste—it's definitely worth the time to try them before you buy.

These edible gels do not double as massage lotions since they contain no oil and won't spread easily—imagine using grape jelly for a full body massage. However, many of these contain no oil and they're safe to use with latex, so next time you complain about the taste of latex, flavor it with strawberry. Some of these gels heat up upon application or when you blow on them, which can be a nice sensation, and can offer some interesting possibilities for oral sex.

Body paints: That's right, your canvas is your lover's body and you can "express yourself" with these colorful, washable paints. They tickle when applied, and the edible variety offers you the unique opportunity to eat your work of art and your lover at the same time.

Oils: Massage oils are intended for external use but can be used for genital lubrication, as long as you don't combine them with latex. Oil will break down the latex, rendering any safer sex barrier completely useless. If you intend to practice safer sex during your erotic massage, use water-based lubricant for genital massage.

Massage oils come in a few textures and dozens of scents, but if smelling like a flower or citrus doesn't appeal to you, you can use the unscented kind. It's nice to have a variety of oils on hand, but bear in mind that vegetable oils will go bad after a period of time. To maximize their life span, store them in the refrigerator. It's not too difficult today to find massage oils that are made exclusively from natural ingredients, most commonly almond and safflower vegetable oils, which are completely hypoallergenic. They are safe to ingest, though they're not designed as edible treats, like the gels above. Some women are allergic to scented oils if used on the genitals, so experiment first with a small amount or use water-based lubricant instead. Remember to warm them up before applying.

I like massage lotion all over, moving into erotic touching focusing on cunt/clit/anus.

Vibrators: Vibrators are usually packaged as "massagers" so why not try them during your next massage? They provide an intense stimulation that can work wonders on sore muscles or merely offer a pleasant alternative to one's hands. If you're trying out a variety of sensations on your partner's body, a vibrator—especially one with several attachments like the coil vibrator—is a must. Experiment on the scalp, the feet, the inner thighs, the neck and face.

Latex and Lube: The smoothness of a lubricated latex glove or condom can offer a unique sensation for both the giver and the receiver during a genital massage. Lubricants are an especially appealing option for genital massage since you'll get the slipperiness of oil without the risks of getting any oil inside you (which can be hard for your body to break down and jeopardizes any latex condoms you may introduce later). If your lubricant starts to dry out, reactivate it by spraying on a bit of water.

Sensate Focus

If you find you don't enjoy these activities because you're easily distracted or anxious, you might want to pursue something known as "sensate focus" exercises. These are designed to help you focus your attention solely on your physical sensations and to expand awareness of your body and its surrounding environment. Sensate focus exercises involve coordinating your breathing and your mental state with your body's physical responses to a variety of caresses. Several good books outline self-help programs of this nature, and many sex therapists prescribe these exercises to individuals who experience performance or desire problems.

Reach Out

By now you're envisioning hands running along your body, light feathers tickling your skin, or lips working their way up the back of your neck. The tips you've learned in this chapter complement many others in this book very nicely, so try out combinations to discover which ones bring you the most pleasure. And remember, touch is a universal language, so go out there and improve your vocabulary!

CHAPTER 8

Oral Sex

When we asked our questionnaire respondents to describe their favorite sexual activities, oral sex topped the list. Oral sexperts are upbeat, enthusiastic cheerleaders for this art form.

Fellatio is one of my favorite activities, both giving and receiving.

I feel much more coordinated with my mouth than with my hands.

There's nothing that beats a warm, soft, wet tongue and lips just delicately slurping away on my clit.

I love cunnilingus, especially receiving. I could do it all day (well, I wish I could anyway). It's so warm....

I don't just think about physical sensation. I think about the intimacy and giving involved in oral sex. That's what I enjoy almost as much as the wonderfully subtle sensations oral sex can provide.

Like masturbation, oral sex is one of those "crimes against nature" that the majority of sexually active adults engage in, but few talk about. As a nonprocreative sex act, oral-genital sex is included in the legal definition of "sodomy" in many states. Twenty-one states have criminal laws prohibiting consenting adults of the same gender from engaging in oral sex; fourteen states prohibit consenting adults of the opposite gender from engaging in oral sex; and nine states prohibit consensual oral sex between married people, even in the privacy of their home. Although anywhere from fifty to ninety percent of adults engage in oral sex, many people are embarrassed, uncomfortable or downright repulsed by the idea of mouth-to-genital contact.

What makes oral sex so arousing and unnerving at the same time? Perhaps it's that oral sex, by definition, brings you face to face with your partner's genitals and the sights, smells and sounds of his or her sexual arousal. The arms-length detachment of manual stimulation or the lights-out decorum of intercourse can't be maintained when you've got your nose, lips and tongue soaked in your partner's juices. There's a unique intimacy and vulnerability involved, whether you're exposing yourself to your partner's tongue or savoring your partner's genitals. Since sucking is a powerfully infantile pleasure with an unavoidably primal appeal, you've got a potent blend of physiological, emotional and mental stimulants.

I could suck cock twenty-four hours a day. I love the feeling of it in my mouth, the smell, the taste. And I love to make men writhe in ecstasy.

I go down on my wife every chance I can get. I enjoy observing her enjoyment and the intensity and volume of her response to my pleasuring her.

Many people build a versatile and satisfying sex life around oral sex. Oral sex is a gratifying technique for women and men, old and young, disabled and able-bodied alike. It's a time-honored activity for adolescents who want to be sexual without grappling with the risks and complications of intercourse. Women who find that the physiological changes of menopause make penetration less appealing, and men who find that their erections are less predictable with age often rediscover the joys of oral sex. People with spinal-cord injuries that limit physical mobility or sensation frequently develop a rich sexuality based on oral play:

I'm spinal-cord injured and have limited sensation below my nipples. I can still get erections, but I get a lot more pleasure from my hands and tongue than from my penis.

I'm in my late seventies and still active sexually, especially orally, which is beautiful.

Inhibitors

Body Odor

Probably the most common factor inhibiting people from experimenting with oral sex is the fear that their own or their partner's genitals will smell or taste bad. After all, in our culture, an entire industry exists to mask, erase or transmute natural body odors into scented wonderlands of "spring rain" or "pine forest." Yet, there's nothing inherently "dirty" or unpleasant about genital odors and secretions (except in the case of certain vaginal infections, which can result in an unpleasant smell). Plenty of people find natural body odors much more arousing than the smells of soaps and deodorants.

I've always delighted in female scents, especially when a woman is aroused.

It's exciting to kiss someone who tastes like my pussy.

I like immersing my face in someone's cunt, getting her juice all over my mouth and face and her scent up my nose.

I love the way penises taste and feel in my mouth. I like to masturbate while taking a man in my mouth.

However, if you feel that a little body odor goes a long way, you might be more comfortable bathing or showering with your partner before sex. When it comes to oral sex, cleanliness is next to confidence for a lot of people. Another option is to experiment with the latest latex technology, namely flavored condoms and dams. You may consider a penis clad in a chocolate condom irresistible, or enjoy tonguing your partner's labia through a berry-flavored dam.

We don't want to drop the topic of hygiene without encouraging everyone who hasn't already done so to try tasting and smelling their own sexual secretions. In order to enjoy sex, you have to enjoy your sex organs—this means appreciating everything about them. Take the time while masturbating to raise your fingers from your genitals to your lips and nose. Women can compare how the odor and consistency of their vaginal secretions change with different phases of their cycle or with different levels of arousal. Men can compare the taste of pre-ejaculate with that of ejaculate. The natural salty, musky tastes and smells of sexual secretions are biochemically designed to arouse, delight and inspire us to sex. Why not take conscious pleasure in them?

I let a little cum drip into my hand and lick a little bit, just enough for a powerful taste. Believe me, this is an aphrodisiac, even for a heterosexual. I don't do this all the time, but when I do it's a real turn-on.

The Gag Reflex

The fear of gagging or choking during oral sex is generally more an issue for those performing oral sex on men than on women. The gag reflex is a natural one, and it takes a bit of practice to get to the point where the sensation of a penis at the back of your throat won't make you gag a bit. Your best recourse is to wrap your hand around your partner's penis while you suck—not only will this enhance sensation for your partner, but you'll be able to control the depth of his thrusting. We've read that the military once claimed it was easy to identify gay recruits by applying a "Gay Reflex Test." Any man who didn't gag when a large tongue depressor was inserted in his mouth was considered unfit for military service. If, by some chance, you're worried about gagging or choking while performing oral sex on a woman, just remember to breathe through your nose, and you'll be fine.

Sexual Fluids

Sexually transmitted diseases can certainly be transmitted through oral sex, and we'll discuss safer oral sex and risk management in depth below. However, there's nothing inherently harmful in semen, female ejaculate or vaginal secretions, and if your partner is not carrying sexually transmissible diseases, there's no reason to feel you shouldn't swallow your partner's sexual fluids. Swallowing semen cannot make you pregnant, nor is it fattening. The average amount of semen a man ejaculates contains about five calories. We don't know the number of calories in female ejaculate or vaginal secretions.

By the same token, there's no reason to feel you should swallow your partner's fluids if you don't want to. Plenty of sincerely enthusiastic fellatrixes simply may not find the taste or texture of male ejaculate pleasing enough to go that extra mile. If you don't want to swallow semen, you can ask your partner to let you know when he's about to come. At this point you can remove your mouth from his penis and continue stimulating him by hand. Or your partner can wear a condom during oral sex, in which case his ejaculate will be contained and swallowing won't be an issue. If your partner is an ejaculating female and you don't particularly want to be flooded by her fluids, you can

arrange some sort of signal as to when you should move your mouth away and continue stimulating her by hand.

Boundaries

The same intimacy and sense of vulnerability that make oral sex so arousing to some make it frightening to others. Respect your partner's feelings, and let her or him set the pace of your explorations.

I like fellatio, but I've never felt comfortable with cunnilingus. I was sexually abused for ten years, and that seems to be one lingering after-effect. I've not had the opportunity to surmount that fear with a partner yet, but I look forward to it.

Oral sex may offer a kind of physical stimulation not to everyone's taste. Some men find that fellatio doesn't provide sufficiently intense stimulation to reach orgasm, and some women find cunnilingus more irritating than pleasurable.

The truth is, I don't really care for blow jobs. I believe I give good ones, but I rarely ever come close to ejaculating when I'm being blown.

Cunnilingus doesn't arouse me as much as I'd like it to. It makes me tense. Sometimes a lover puts too much pressure on my clit that way (I'm sensitive).

If oral sex makes you anxious or uncomfortable, you can certainly enjoy a satisfying sex life without it. But if you've never explored this simple sexual technique, we do hope you'll give it a chance—many people find oral sex a uniquely pleasurable and fulfilling activity.

Cunnilingus

Techniques

The word *cunnilingus* comes from the Latin *cunnus* meaning "vulva" and *lingere* meaning "to lick." But licking is only one of the pleasures involved in cunnilingus. Your moist lips and mouth are capable of creating a uniquely subtle range of sensations. Sucking your partner's clitoris, nuzzling her labia and penetrating her vagina with your tongue or fingers can all enhance the experience of oral sex. As with any sexual activity, the same strokes won't work for all folks, and the same woman might prefer different types of stimulation depending on how aroused she is. Start by finding out what kind of clitoral stimulation your partner prefers: She might like you to lick or suck directly on the tip of her clitoris, to approach it from the underside or to concentrate on the less-sensitive hooded side. She might favor a slow, gentle tonguing, or she might crave a ferocious licking. She might prefer feeling the tip of your tongue, the flat of your tongue, a circular motion, a lapping motion, even a slight scraping of teeth.

Tongues are usually soft enough and slick enough to feel good directly on my clit.

I found that I simply needed the courage to grind into him, to get a more forceful touch from his tongue, in order to come completely. I overcame my shyness and really got off!

The softness and delicacy of a tongue on my clitoris is heavenly. I love an indirect approach with lots of teasing—coming close, backing off, returning, etc.

If I'm being eaten-out, it's a total turn-on to have him pull me against him by wrapping his arms around my thighs and holding me tight as he licks me hard and fast.

Many women enjoy having the whole vulva licked, from pubic bone to perineum. Pay attention to the sensitive area around the urethra. You can insert your tongue in your partner's vagina, though obviously the average tongue will only go so deep. Most women would much rather have their external genitalia tongued. Generally, it's easier to use a finger or a dildo for penetration during oral sex.

Cunnilingus

I enjoy the combined effect of sitting on my girlfriend's face while she has her finger inside me stimulating my G-spot and is licking my clit.

Bear in mind that as your partner approaches orgasm, she'll probably appreciate it if you maintain a steady stimulation up to and through her orgasm. Many women need consistent, reliable stimulation to put them "over the top," and if you test-drive a brand-new tongue stroke right before she's about to come, it may not go over too well.

I like cunnilingus because it calls on me to be more subtle and adventurous in determining where the locations of pleasure could be for my lover. The searching and ingesting quality is very exciting—especially if she comes.

If you'd like to see the kind of activities we're talking about, check out the video *Nina Hartley's Guide to Better Cunnilingus*. After years of viewing and selling adult videos that feature seemingly endless scenes of fervent fellatio, it's thrilling to find an educational porn film that dispenses accurate anatomical information along with hot depictions of cunnilingus. And nobody's better-equipped to dish out the advice and the tongue-lashings than America's Porn Sweetheart, the versatile Nina Hartley.

Positions

Experiment with different positions to see which are most comfortable and pleasurable for the two of you. You may enjoy simply lying between your partner's legs, facing her vagina, while she lies on her back–this position allows you to reach her upper body with your hands. You can try kneeling on the floor between her legs while she lies back on the bed (or the sofa or the kitchen table) or stands over you. Or you can lie on your back while your partner straddles your face–she'll be free to move her pelvis and control the rhythm of movement. This straddling position is popular both with those women whose arousal is enhanced by watching their partner perform oral sex and those cunnilinguists who enjoy the sensation of being surrounded by their partner's vulva:

I love having my lover sit over my face, feeling her lose control.

In any event, there are more possible positions for cunnilingus than we could ever name–you're limited only by your imagination.

My fondest oral sex memory is of the time I made my girlfriend go down on me while I was standing in a phone booth in our hotel lobby. No one passing by could see her kneeling between my legs, but I must have looked like I was having the most exciting phone call of my life!

Enhancers

There's truly no limit to the variations you can come up with when you're eye-level with your partner's vulva. Your hands are free to wield a dildo on your partner and/or on yourself. You can slip a finger in her vagina or anus or both. Women who find their orgasms are more intense when the vagina is full may particularly enjoy having a dildo inserted during oral sex.

My fantasy involves having my partner give me oral sex while his penis is inside me–but that seems impossible. My partner surprised me once by inserting a vibrator in my vagina and his fingers in my anus while licking my clitoris. This gave me one of the most memorable orgasms I've had, and I think this is as close to my fantasy as I will be able to get.

Try playing a vibrator across her labia while you suck on her clitoris. Or try holding a battery vibrator against the underside of your tongue while you're licking, and transform your mouth into a sex toy. If that last idea makes your teeth hurt to even think about, bear in mind that sound creates vibration, so you can create a similar, slightly less dramatic effect by humming and purring while you lick. An innovative oral sex toy is a harness designed to strap over the head and hold a dildo over the wearer's mouth or over the wearer's chin. Anyone willing to transform themselves into a cross between a sex toy and a unicorn is rewarded with a whole new perspective on penetrating their partner.

Before we leave this topic, we should admit to a bit of a bias. We like to think that every woman and every lover of women should experience the pleasure of cunnilingus. That women's genitals are more hidden than men's has led to an exaggerated sense of mystery and, in some cases, a certain fear and disgust towards what's "down there" between a woman's legs. When you go down on a woman, you're bringing all your senses to bear on an appreciation and admiration of her genitals. When you invite someone to go down on you, you're affirming that your entire body is worthy of tender attention.

I'm a huge fan of cunnilingus. Sometimes it takes a while for me to really let go and get into it, but wow! It's so cool to feel like someone's worshipping my cunt.

Fellatio

The word *fellatio* derives from the Latin verb *fellare*, "to suck." Where would our sex vocabulary be without the Latin language? One of the best-selling videotapes we carry is the half-hour educational porn video *How to Perform Fellatio*–proof-positive that good cocksuckers are made, not born. *Nina Hartley's Guide to Better Fellatio* is another excellent video that includes specific anatomical information and tips you won't find in *How to Perform Fellatio*. The common-sense advice dispensed in both these videos is to take your cues

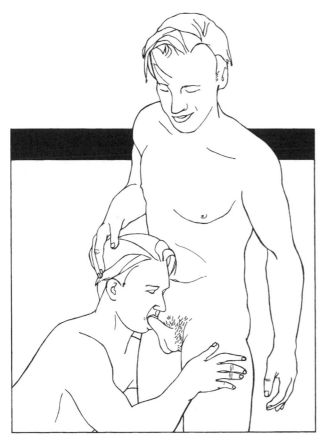

Fellatio

from your male partner's body language and to respect that different men will have different preferences when it comes to oral stimulation. Find out whether your partner prefers firm or gentle pressure, attention lavished on the head of his penis or the base, a vacuum-style suck or rhythmic flicking of the tongue. Of course, your partner might be perfectly happy with a variety of approaches:

I love fellatio, from teasing licks to deep sucking.

My favorite kind of orgasm these days is squatting over another man's face and having him kiss and chew my nuts with his snorting nose tickling my asshole.

The one rule-of-thumb that you can safely apply to most men is: no teeth. Do make sure not to scrape your teeth across your partner's genitals, as this could be quite anti-erotic. If your partner happens to enjoy a little nibbling on his penis, he'll probably let you know.

What I don't like is if I'm sore, or a woman nicks me with her teeth or uses too much pressure.

Techniques

Generally speaking, there's more to giving head than bobbing your mouth up and down over the shaft of the penis. Of course, you can simply open your mouth and let it be a passive receptacle for a thrusting penis. There's even a specific term for this technique, *irrumation,* but this kind of fellatio is not as popular—or as fun for the fellator—as that in which the sucking partner is in charge of the action. As with cunnilingus, your best bet is to put your mouth to work on those areas of greatest sensitivity, namely the glans, or head, of the penis, the coronal ridge around the base of the glans and the raphe, which is the seam running down the underside of the penis. With the exception of the raphe, the shaft of the penis is not particularly sensitive, so licking away at the shaft as though it were a popsicle won't necessarily generate a great deal of sensation. Instead, concentrate on working your mouth around the glans and coronal ridge—you can wrap your hand around the shaft as a sort of continuation of your mouth. Your partner may enjoy you sucking the head of his penis while stroking up and down on the shaft.

She would move very slowly, taking me in her mouth and using very soft, light touches with her lips and tongue. What I liked best about her technique, besides the slow and deliberate use of her mouth, was that she always kept her hand on my body, stroking the lower part of my shaft. As I got closer to orgasm, she would pick up a steady rhythm, moving her whole head up and down in a long then short, slow then fast, milking motion.

One technique I very much enjoy is when my partner opens her mouth and, with her hand on the base of my shaft, rapidly shakes or wiggles my cock about in her mouth. It makes a wonderful sound, which I find exciting.

Positions

Frequently, a man will lie on his back to receive oral sex while his partner lies, crouches or kneels between his legs. If you're sucking your partner's penis while facing his head, you'll be able to rub your chest against his penis and scrotum and to reach your hands up to stroke his body. If you're facing his feet, you'll be at a better angle to take more of his penis in your mouth, although you won't be as well-positioned to lick the sensitive underside of his penis. You may want to kneel on the floor to suck his penis while he stands or lies back on a bed. Or you may prefer to lie on your back with your head well-supported by pillows while your partner kneels over you, straddles your face and penetrates your mouth from above. Basically, any position in which you both feel comfortable is a good position.

With one woman, we would gaze into each other's eyes when we were doing one another. I found that really mesmerizing and erotic. I think it can be easy to lose eye contact during oral sex, but she would lie down on her back and have me straddle her. This is a great position for fellatio and prostate massage.

Enhancers

In your attentiveness to your partner's penis, don't forget the rest of his body. You can reach a hand up to play with his nipples, or massage his butt and thighs while you suck. Many men enjoy anal stimulation—either with a tongue, finger, dildo or vibrating butt plug—as an accompaniment to oral sex.

Gentle prostate simulation complements cocksucking. I like to have my nipples bitten and sucked. Simple thumbing of my anal opening is nice.

You may want to hold a vibrator against your partner's perineum, or you may want to play with a vibrator yourself. There's no law that says only one of you at a time is entitled to sexual stimulation. Many heterosexual couples enjoy incorporating breast play into fellatio—tit-fucking is a popular alternative to intercourse, and it can easily be combined with oral sex.

I used a vibrator once while performing fellatio—it was great! It's the only toy experience I've had with a partner.

I like fellatio if it's preceded by my partner

alternately fucking my breasts and then my mouth while doing a lot of sex talk. When he's at the point of coming, I like him to take control of his cock with one hand and move my head with the other. This frees up my hands so I can start rubbing my breasts and touch myself so that we can come together.

Giving head provides you with a great opportunity to explore your partner's genitals. You can massage his perineum with your fingers, gather his scrotum together using your hand as a cock ring, lick or mouth his testicles and otherwise lavish attention on his entire genitals. As with cunnilingus, fellatio allows you an intimate view of your partner's arousal and an almost unparalleled sense of control over his sexual pleasure.

Actually performing fellatio on my partner is one of the most wonderful pleasures. I've gotten it down to such an art of sweet torture, ending in an outrageous orgasm for him and an inability for him to move for the next thirty minutes or so. The most recent time, I almost came just from going down on him.

What I like about fellatio is feeling the slow approach to orgasm. Often I'm just lying there, maybe moving slowly, just feeling the nerve stimulation building and building and knowing it's going to keep building until I come.

Deep Throat

Deep throat is the term commonly used for the technique of taking an entire penis into your mouth. What this technique lacks in finesse—you won't be able to lick, suck or do anything more than hold your lips around his shaft—it makes up for in terms of impressing your friends and loved ones. Relaxation and positioning are both key to performing this technique. You either have to be kneeling over your partner's penis facing his feet, so that your mouth and throat will be at the right angle to accommodate a whole penis, or you should be lying on your back with your head off the side of a bed so that your mouth and throat are in a line. Basically, you'll be taking his penis all the way into your throat, which means you need to work on relaxing your gag reflex. Keep your hand at the base of his penis with the understanding that you can push the penis out of your mouth in a hurry without any hard feelings between you. Gagging is a natural response to having any object blocking your throat. Practice and trust will make it easier to relax this reflex. Of course, you can be an excellent fellator without ever swallowing more than a couple of inches of penis.

Sixty-Nine

Sixty-nine is the popular term for simultaneous mutual oral sex. The term derives from the fact that a six looks like an upside-down nine and vice versa. In a sixty-nine position, you and your partner would either lie side by side facing each other's feet or one of you would lie on your back with the other kneeling above facing the prone partner's feet. The notion of arranging yourself in an unbroken circle with your mouth on your partner's genitals and his/her mouth on yours is unquestionably an appealing one.

I like to fantasize about sixty-nine a lot if a particular guy has hold of my heartstrings…that always seems so loving and mutually giving and incredibly intimate.

It's wonderful to be falling into someone else's cunt while my own is also being stimulated.

Sixty-nine is my absolute favorite. Being eaten while returning the favor with two naked bodies touching is the most intimate and intense experience.

Sixty-nine all the way—mmm-mm-mmm. I prefer it over just having my man or woman go down on me. My partner is most often on top of me, and I am underneath with his luscious dick in my mouth. It makes me twitch even thinking about it.

My number-one favorite activity is sixty-nine—it fills a lot of cravings all at once, i.e., to suck cock, to be sucked, and to be in close physical coupling with my partner. It's wonderful as a mutually narcissistic circuit of oral nurturing and trusting masculinity.

For every individual who swears by sixty-nine, there's one who finds this technique overrated. It's difficult to concentrate on orally teasing and tantalizing your partner while your own genitals are flooded with pleasurable sensations. Most of us find that sexual arousal is accompanied by a certain amount of heavy breathing and increased muscle tension. It's hard to maintain a rhythmic tonguing of your partner's clitoris or to refrain from scraping your teeth across your partner's penis if you're trembling on the brink of orgasm yourself.

Sixty-nine is too confusing for me…I forget to hold up my end of the bargain.

Sixty-nine is, for me, overrated, since one or the other is distracted.

Sixty-nine is all right once in a while for variety, but I like taking turns better than doing oral sex simultaneously. I either like to focus on pleasing my partner or on being pleased.

But by all means, don't let this discourage you from experimenting with mutual oral pleasuring. You may well wish to incorporate sixty-nine as part of your sex play without focusing on it as a means of reaching orgasm.

I prefer to either receive or give oral sex, not both simultaneously, but I also don't turn down an offer of sixty-nine!

Tips and Techniques

Playing with temperature is a tried-and-true method of enhancing oral sex. You might want to try holding a small ice cube in your mouth while you run your tongue up and down your partner's penis. Or you could apply ice to your partner's clitoris and then warm her back up with your mouth. Similarly some folks drink hot fluids before wrapping their mouths around their partner's penis or clitoris. Blowing on your partner's genitals up close creates a warm rush of sensation, while blowing or fanning the genitals from six inches away creates a cool, tingling sensation.

Making the Grade

One day a heterosexual couple approached the counter of our San Francisco store requesting books and videos related to cunnilingus. The man explained that his wife currently gave him a grade of C+ for his oral sex skills and that they were both interested in raising his grade to at least an A- as soon as possible. After browsing our library, this enterprising couple decided that lesbian erotic videos would be the most effective training tools, and left the store with a stack of rentals in tow. When they returned their rental videos a couple of days later, they proudly announced that he'd already graduated to a B+. Given this couple's open, good-humored attitude, we're sure it wasn't long before he was pulling straight A's.

Many sex-toy businesses, including ours, sell a variety of flavored gels for enhancing oral sex. These gels usually break down into two varieties: those that generate heat and those that numb sensation. The former usually contain either glycerine or essential oils such as cinnamon, peppermint or clove oil. When you apply these gels to the surface of your skin and blow softly, warmth spreads over the skin. The latter frequently contain benzocaine or other mild anesthetics. The pleasure of using these numbing gels lies in feeling sensation flood back into your genitals as the anesthetic wears off. While these gels can be safely applied and licked off a penis or clitoris, women should be careful not to get these products inside the vagina. Essential oils and anesthetics are potentially irritating to delicate mucous membranes. The licker should also bear in mind that his or her mouth will get quite numb.

Those people who'd rather stick to food and drink, which don't contain artificial ingredients, may enjoy licking whipped cream, chocolate sauce or berries off each other's bodies. (If you're using latex barriers for safer sex, do abstain from using food products containing oils, which destroy latex.) Whether you prefer your oral sex au natural or à la mode is entirely up to you.

I once had a banana inserted and eaten out of me—fabulous!

One of my best lovemaking memories is of the time I had jam licked off my clit, a full wine bottle inserted in my cunt, wine poured in, and then my lover drank the wine out of my cunt.

Rimming

Rimming is the popular term for oral/anal stimulation. Licking, kissing and tonguing the anus are also referred to as "analingus." The whole notion of rimming is highly charged for many people, and even those who are comfortable with oral/genital sex can find themselves repelled by oral/anal sex. The opposing points of view about rimming can basically be summed up as: "Why would I want to lick the orifice that feces come out of?" and "Why wouldn't I want my anus to get the same loving attention as any other erogenous zone?" The anus is highly sensitive and loaded with nerve endings, and there is no question that, physiologically speaking, it feels as good to have your anus kissed as to have your mouth kissed.

Rimming is a special treat and only happens once in a while by "accident." My current partner thought it was disgusting until I did her and she came big time. She refuses to talk about it.

If you follow basic hygienic precautions, you should feel free to enjoy the pleasures of rimming. The risks involved in ingesting feces include contracting hepatitis or intestinal parasites. While early AIDS researchers grouped rimming under high-risk activities for transmission of HIV, this classification is now considered debatable. Given that feces are stored in the colon, and do not pass through the rectum or anus until just before defecation, it's unlikely you'd encounter more than traces of feces in your partner's anus. You may be inspired to bathe together before embarking on a rimming episode, but bath or no bath, you should seriously consider using a barrier of some sort between the mouth and anus. Dental dams (small squares of latex), cut-open condoms or latex gloves, and Saran Wrap are all considered acceptable barriers. If you aren't using a barrier, you should never lick your partner's anus and then move to kiss her vagina or his mouth. Licking from the anus to the vagina or from the anus to the mouth can transmit feces–and therefore infection–from one orifice to another.

Once you've taken the hygienic precautions you feel necessary, and your tongue is poised over your partner's anus, what shall you do? You can circle the anus with your tongue, flutter your tongue against the anal opening, lick, suck or slip your tongue into the anus. Our anuses are the seat of so much tension that any kind of tender tonguing will doubtless feel extremely relaxing and pleasurable to your partner.

I love being on my knees, ass held high, while she works my ass with her tongue. Not so much thrusting, but teasing, flicking, licking. Luckily all of my girlfriends, save for one, liked to eat my ass.

Safer Sex

While we've made several mentions of safer sex precautions throughout this chapter, we cannot close without a more detailed summary of current opinions regarding risk management in oral sex. Currently oral sex is considered to be a fairly low-risk activity with regard to the transmission of HIV, the AIDS virus. In June 1996, a widely publicized study of rhesus monkeys reported oral transmission of a virus analogous to HIV, yet most AIDS organizations continue to point out that there have only been a handful of human AIDS cases in which oral sex was the proven means of transmission. There is, however, simply no such thing as absolutely safe sex, and we hope you will weigh carefully all the relevant information to decide what precautions are appropriate to take.

STDs

It is possible to transmit yeast, hepatitis B and herpes through unprotected oral/genital contact. Oral herpes (cold sores) can be transmitted to the genitals, and genital herpes can be transmitted to the mouth. You should never have unprotected oral sex if you or your partner are having an outbreak. Furthermore, it's possible to transmit herpes

asymptotically, that is to say, even when you aren't experiencing an active outbreak. Consider using a dental dam, a cut-open condom or latex glove, or Saran Wrap as a barrier during oral/vaginal or oral/anal sex. Use condoms during fellatio. It would probably be a good idea to forego fellatio during a herpes outbreak, as herpes sores can cluster at the base of the penis or on the testicles, where a condom would not cover them.

HIV

HIV is contained in the semen, blood and vaginal fluids of those infected with the virus. While it's present in trace quantities in sweat, saliva, urine and tears, there's no evidence that it can be transmitted by these fluids. Blood, including menstrual blood, contains HIV in much higher concentration than vaginal fluids, and therefore it is riskier to come into contact with your female partner's menstrual blood than it is to contact her vaginal secretions. There's some debate as to whether an HIV-infected woman has ever transmitted the virus to a partner through oral sex alone. Enzymes in the mouth of healthy people are known to kill viruses as delicate as HIV. However, if you have open sores in your mouth or even small cuts in your gums from brushing your teeth or flossing, and you go down on a person with HIV, it's conceivable that the virus could enter your bloodstream. Save your dental hygiene routine for after sex. Allowing your male partner to ejaculate in your mouth is a higher-risk activity than his withdrawing before ejaculating. The risk that an HIV-infected individual could transmit the virus by going down on a partner is slight.

What to Do

None of the above information need stop you from enjoying safe and pleasurable oral sex. A variety of latex and plastic barriers are available to protect the mucous membranes of one partner's mouth from contacting the mucous membranes of the other partner's genitals. Dental dams are one type of latex barrier that can be used during oral/vaginal or oral/anal sex. On the plus side, dams are available in different flavors: bubble gum, vanilla or wintergreen, and creative people have been known to wear them in place over their genitals using a leather harness or a garter belt.

On the minus side, dams are only six inches square, thick and unwieldy—after all, they were designed for use during oral surgery, not for use in the bedroom.

Look for Glyde Lollyes dams distributed by the Australian company Kia-Ora. Lollyes are designed explicitly for oral sex—they're larger (six by eight inches) and thinner than dental dams, yet equally strong. They come in vanilla and wildberry flavors. Lixx dams are also designed especially for oral sex and come in vanilla and strawberry. Other options include cutting open a condom or latex glove or using large sheets of Saran Wrap. Condoms, gloves and Saran Wrap are thinner and transmit sensation better than dental dams do. In 1993, the FDA tested Saran Wrap for its permeability and found that it was effective in halting the transmission of virus-sized particles.

Whatever barrier method you use, be sure to put some lubricant on the side of the barrier pressed against your partner's genitals. This will enhance the sensations received through the latex or plastic. Many cunnilinguists have found that using barriers during oral sex has added a whole new array of tricks to their repertoires. If you stretch a dam tightly across your partner's genitals, pucker your lips, and suck in a little bubble of rubber directly over her clit, you can create a stimulating vacuum-suction effect. Needless to say, it's also extremely liberating to lick freely back and forth between your partner's vagina and anus without feeling restricted by hygienic considerations.

Many people have already made the adjustment to using condoms during oral sex. You'll probably want to use unlubricated condoms, as standard lubricating gels aren't known for their great taste. There are several flavored condoms on the market: mint, banana, chocolate, licorice and tutti-frutti, or you can flavor a plain condom with a water-based edible gel. Then again, you may be someone who prefers plain latex flavor to disguised latex flavor. The condoms manufactured these days are so thin as to be almost like a second skin. Your partner may be surprised to find that latex transmits sensation and temperature with arousing intensity and that being sucked through latex feels just as good as being sucked without.

The Avanti polyurethane condom hit the U.S. market with great fanfare in 1995. Polyurethane is a clear, odorless plastic that is considerably stronger than latex, so polyurethane condoms can be made thinner to allow for greater sensitivity than latex condoms. It has the further advantage of not breaking down upon exposure to oil and not smelling or tasting like latex. It has the disadvantage of being considerably more expensive and considerably less elastic than latex. The Avanti's lack of elasticity has resulted in high slippage and breakage rates, so the FDA and *Consumer Reports* currently recommend this condom only for the estimated two to four percent of the population with allergies to latex. If you're someone who is allergic to latex or who wants to experiment with a thinner condom for oral sex, you may want to check out the Avanti.

CHAPTER 9

All About Vibrators

I love waking up in the morning with a jolting orgasm from my beloved vibrator. Better than a cup of coffee!

Vibrators may well go down in history as the best-kept secret of the twentieth century. We have waited on hundreds of people curious about vibrators who, up until their visit to Good Vibrations, were unable to find out much about them. If you've ever gotten up the nerve to visit an adult toy store, you probably encountered piles of vibrating novelties but received little assistance or information about them from the clerk. Not surprisingly, many of you described disappointing experiences with toys like the Throbbing Ten-Inch or the Fantasy Joystick purchased on such trips.

Trying to find answers in sex books can be hit or miss. Since the first edition of this book was published, several other manuals have begun to enthusiastically endorse vibrator use, in addition to offering accurate information about them. Many mainstream sex manuals, however, still treat the vibrator as a woman's masturbatory tool at best, an evil addictive device at worst. Vibrators often merit little more than a paragraph; it's usually a not altogether accurate description of one or two models, and perhaps a few words reinforcing or dismissing the anxiety they generate. (Will I get addicted? Electrocuted? Will it replace my partner?) Take this classic example from Alex Comfort's *The New Joy of Sex*:

> *Vibrators are no substitute for a penis—some women prefer them to a finger for masturbation, or put one in the vagina while working manually on the clitoris.... Careful vibratory massage of the whole body surface is a better bet than over-concentration on the penis or clitoris.*

Let's dissect what's wrong with this paragraph. First, by suggesting that women might prefer vibrators as "penis substitutes," Dr. Comfort reinforces the prevailing myth that most women orgasm by using them vaginally (we also detect a bit of insecurity here, Doc). He then correctly relates that women use them both clitorally and vaginally. In his last statement, however, he mysteriously hints that there may be something evil or dangerous about using the vibrator solely for genital stimulation and that we should concentrate on giving equal time to the rest of the body.

This lack of accurate information about vibrators prompted Good Vibrations' founder Joani Blank to write the vibrator history and how-to manual *Good Vibrations*. This remains the only book ever written on the subject, but most general bookstores deem the content too scandalous, choosing instead to stock books like *The New Joy of Sex*.

In this chapter we enthusiastically bring vibrators out into the light of day. There are thousands of people out there plugging in and turning on, and it's not because they're dysfunctional, single, man-hating, sex-crazed, sex-starved, frustrated, preorgasmic or disappointed with a partner—it's because vibrators feel great. There are a million ways to have fun with a vibrator—you're limited only by your imagination. We'll give you the who, what, when, where and why of vibrators, but it's up to you to play with your toys in order to discover what brings you the most pleasure.

A Brief History of Vibrators

The illustrious history of the electric vibrator begins in 1869 with the invention of a steam-powered massager, patented by an American doctor. This device was designed as a labor-saving medical tool for use in the treatment of "female disorders." Within twenty years, a British doctor followed up with a more portable battery-operated model, and by 1900, dozens of styles of electric vibrators were available to the discriminating medical professional.

Treating Hysteria

What, you must ask, were these esteemed physicians doing with their vibrators? They were treating hysteria—the most common health complaint among women of the day. While the existence of hysteria as a disease was debunked in the 1950s, medical experts from the time of Hippocrates up to the twentieth century believed that hysteria expressed the womb's revolt against sexual deprivation. A woman's display of mental or emotional distress was a clear indication of her need for sexual release. Genital massage was a standard treatment for hysteria; its objective was to induce "hysterical paroxysm" (better known today as orgasm) in the patient. Obviously, such treatment demanded both manual dexterity and a fair amount of time, so turn-of-the-century physicians were delighted with the efficiency, convenience and reliability of portable vibrators.

Health, Vigor and Beauty

Ours being a consumer society, the vibrator was soon marketed as a home appliance in women's magazines and mail-order catalogs. Ads proffering "health, vigor and beauty" promoted the vibrator as an aid to health. By the 1920s, doctors had abandoned hands-on physical treatments for hysteria in favor of psycho-therapeutic techniques. But vibrators continued to have an active commercial life in which they were marketed, much like patent medicines, as cure-alls for illnesses ranging from headaches and asthma to "fading beauty" and even tuberculosis!

Ad copy for these vibrators was coy and ambiguous. "Be a glow getter," one package insert suggests. And who wouldn't be tempted to experience "that delicious, thrilling, health-restoring sensation called vibration," when assured that "it makes you fairly tingle with the joy of living!" The vibrator's usefulness for masturbation was never acknowledged; however, as vibrators began appearing in stag films of the 1920s, it became difficult to ignore their sexual function. Probably as a result, advertisements for vibrators gradually disappeared from respectable publications.

A Superior Sex Toy

To this day, electric vibrators are marketed solely as massagers, and their sexual benefits are steadfastly ignored by manufacturers. Vibrators are a big business; they are sold through drugstores, department stores and popular catalogs, yet their true talents remain unsung. We dream of the day when electric vibrators are proudly promoted as the superior sex toys they are. After all, as an early advertisement points out, "almost like a miracle is the healing force of massage when rightly applied."

When I first got my vibrator and learned how to incorporate it into my self-loving, I found it to be the best thing for a girl to have in her house.

Why Would I Use a Vibrator?

If you're asking this question, you might be inclined to skip the entire vibrator section. Perhaps you're thinking "I'm a man and vibrators are only for women," or "My orgasms are perfect and I don't need additional stimulation," or "I'm in a relationship where I'm completely satisfied," or "Vibrators just seem so unnatural." If any of these rings a bell, or if you're deterred by any reason short of "I've tried them all and none please me," we encourage you to read on. Just about anyone can enjoy a vibrator, but the charms of these versatile instruments of pleasure are often obscured by a cloud of misconception, stereotypes and sex negativity.

Allow us to clarify a few main areas of confusion:

Vibrators Can Be Enjoyed by Everyone

Vibrators have traditionally been associated with women because so many learned how to orgasm— or at least how to orgasm more easily—using a vibrator. Most women require consistent, intense stimulation of the clitoris in order to achieve orgasm, which a hand or a tongue isn't always able to give:

> I used to masturbate with my hand, but it would get so tired. Just as I was about to come, my hand would start to cramp up and sometimes it just froze before those crucial last strokes.

Since most men learn how to masturbate to orgasm during adolescence, they're less likely to seek "outside" assistance. This shouldn't mean, however, that vibrators are exclusively girls' toys. As Joani Blank points out in *Good Vibrations:* "If men, like women, enjoy a wide range of stimuli (and we know they do), then why shouldn't a vibrator be another potential source of sexually arousing stimulation?"

In fact, many men are happily discovering vibrating sleeves, cock rings and anal toys, as well as inventing ways to adapt and enjoy more traditional massagers:

> I remember one time staying at a hotel in Aspen, and there was a powerful foot massager in the room. I used it on my dick and balls at the same time and had a memorably intense orgasm.

People with disabilities have also discovered the sexual appeal of vibrators. If you're experiencing reduced sensitivity, you may find that the intense stimulation offered by a vibrator can be felt when the stimulation offered by a hand cannot. If your mobility is impaired, you may enjoy lying on top of some of the larger vibrators, or wearing styles that don't require the use of your hands. If you have difficulty grasping smaller toys, slip the battery vibrator inside a cloth mitt or insert the base into a Nerf ball with a hole cut out of the center to give you a greater surface area to grasp. Velcro, adhesive tape and certain types of everyday hardware can assist you in modifying your toys. The mail-order company Lawrence Research has a special catalog full of suggestions like these; see the resource listings for their address.

During the later stages of pregnancy you may find that vibrators help alleviate soreness or pain as well as provide convenient genital stimulation if your mobility is reduced. In *Susie Bright's Sexual Reality*, Susie describes using her vibrator as her focus object during labor:

> I have a great photograph of me, dilated to six centimeters, with a blissful look on my face and my vibrator nestled against my pubic bone. I had no thought of climaxing, but the pleasure of the sweet rhythm on my clit was like sweet icing on the deep, thick contractions in my womb.

In *Good Vibrations*, Joani Blank offers this additional tip for new parents:

> Keep a battery vibrator handy for the first few months of your baby's life. Parents report that some fussy babies can be calmed with a gentle back massage à la vibrator, or by placing the vibrator, wrapped, in the crib.

Finally, for those of you who eschew vibrators because you're completely satisfied with your orgasms, we'd like to remind you that variety is the spice of life! Just as your taste in food can change, so can your experience of orgasm. Many women report vibrators make them come more quickly as well as

Lost and Found

When it comes to toys, the practice of "finders keepers" knows no age or nationality.

We hear many tales of vibrators discovered under Grannie's bed or relationship breakups that result in the loss of a precious toy. But one of our favorite lost-and-found stories is related in the following letter that was faxed to Good Vibrations by some customers who received it from an Italian hotel attendant who discovered the vibrator they left behind in their hotel room.

Signora,

I write to thank you for changing my life. I found the object precioso *which you left in room. I do not know that such objects like yours exist and am so happy now I know. Now when me* sposato *is away I am not so lonely* e moroso.

America must be wonderful land! So many happy objects. Have all women in America ones such as these? I have been showing my women friends all this and they now wanting also. Molto grazie da via tutta!

I have not much money to pay because this thing must cost much, certamente. *Here inside this* busta *is what I can send. Perhaps now you have got another object but please accept* con tutti respetti e molto grazie.

From your thanking friend.

make their orgasms feel more intense. Others find vibrator orgasms less intense. Some men claim vibrators allow them to orgasm quickly, while others find the stimulation too overwhelming. Some use vibrators to create a powerful buildup for an orgasm that they then finish by some other method.

Vibrators Can Enhance Partner Sex

The belief that masturbation and vibrators are just a temporary substitute until a real live body comes along is a prevalent one. As you read through this book we hope you're struck by the number of men and women who reject this notion by happily incorporating masturbation and sex toys into their partner sex play. Sometimes we just need to be reminded that it's worth taking a little risk now and then—remember Mom telling you to share your toys? Take her advice—sharing your sex toys can add an exciting new dimension to your sex life. Chances are, if your partner knows something brings you that much pleasure, she or he will want in on the action. Seize the opportunity to expand your sexual repertoire, rather than confine it. Instead of assuming that your partner will be threatened or disinterested, take the time to find out how she or he feels. Vibrators may be just the thing to help you break out of a dull routine. You can enjoy the added visual charge, the new sensa-

tions and the undeniable fantasy component that come with playing with all kinds of toys. We hope our suggestions later in this chapter, concerning how to introduce toys into partner sex, pique your curiosity and spur you into action.

Vibrators Come in All Sizes and Shapes

The penis-shaped, plastic vibrator is probably the most well-known model, yet it is also the source of endless confusion and frustration for women hoping to use one to vibrate to orgasm. The dildo shape suggests insertion, but most women orgasm from pressing a vibrator against the clitoris, not thrusting it in and out of the vagina. We could weep for the scores of misled women who have pumped and thrusted in vain—searching for that elusive orgasm they heard came so easily with a vibrator. By learning about various vibrator sizes, shapes and uses, as well as experimenting to find out what kind of stimulation you like, you're bound to find a vibrator (or several) with your name on it.

Vibrators Are Natural Pleasers

Many people feel sex should only involve the body parts we were born with, but why? We could make the argument that humans were put on this earth naked, therefore we should have no need for clothing. But none would disagree that we have adapted to our environment, donning clothes in the process. We maintain that we've also evolved sexually, earning the right to play with toys.

Vibrators complement our natural sexual impulses by allowing us to explore a variety of sensations. If vibrators are too artificial to incorporate into "natural" sex, what sensual pleasers aren't? What about lingerie, satin sheets, massage oils, furry mitts and feathers? The enjoyment of tactile stimulation is as natural as it gets, and we object to anyone drawing an arbitrary line in the sand over vibrators simply because they're powered by electricity.

If you're in a relationship with someone who has an ingrained aversion to the artificial aspect of sex toys, you can try offering some of the arguments we just proposed. Be flexible—you may work out a compromise where you both agree to use the vibrator some of the time. Perhaps in time, after watching it bring you so much pleasure, your partner will grant your toy a place in his or her heart (or between his or her sheets).

Styles and Sources

Vibrators—also commonly referred to as "massagers"—come in all sizes and shapes. Some look like eggs, some like hand-held mixers, some like

---

Playing with Vibrators

Vibrators can be enjoyed in a number of ways by both men and women. Although vibrators are most commonly associated with women seeking vaginal and clitoral stimulation, many men rhapsodize over the penile or testicular stimulation they afford, and both sexes can use vibrators to tap into anal eroticism. Whatever your preference, take a tip from the many people who employ more than one toy, and try out several different models, either singly or in unison. You never know what pleasures await you behind door number three! Here are a few basic tips for anyone interested in playing with a vibrator:

♦ Get yourself in the mood. Read a dirty book, walk around the house naked, explore a favorite fantasy.

♦ Try different positions. Lie on top of the vibrator, lie on your back with the vibrator on top of you, grasp it between your thighs. Run the vibrator over different parts of your body.

♦ Try moving the vibrator around different parts of your genitals. If you're a woman, you can press it against your clitoris, the clitoral hood, the mons, labia, vaginal opening and anus, or insert a vibrator into your vagina or anus. If you're a man, you can run the vibrator along the shaft of your penis, press it against the base, the scrotum, the perineum and around or into your anus. Try pressing below the glans on the bottom side of your penis. You can also press your penis against your abdomen with the vibrator to disseminate the vibrations.

♦ Vary the pressure and speed. Experiment with a steady, direct pressure, alternate between a hard and light pressure, or try stopping and starting. Many vibrators come with more than one speed or a variable-speed control, so you can switch gears any time.

♦ If the vibration is too intense, don't place the vibrator directly against your genitals, but move it slightly, so the vibration is diffused. Or place your hand, clothing or a thick towel between the vibrator and your clitoris or penis to absorb some of the vibration.

♦ Enhance your vibrator play by teasing yourself. Pay attention to your arousal level and turn your vibrator off intermittently, so you can build arousal gradually.

♦ Incorporate other types of stimulation—touch other parts of your body, add deep breathing and Kegal exercises, use some other toys, watch a porn movie, or talk to yourself.

♦ If the vibrator doesn't make you come, don't worry—just play with it for fun. It might make you come too fast or it might numb you out so you're unable to come. Only by experimenting can you figure out your own ways of getting maximum pleasure.

penises. Depending on what kind of stimulation you like, you might find one style, or a combination of several styles, to be your favorite. In this section we'll describe a multitude of different models along with suggestions for incorporating them into your sex play. Keep in mind that while this may look like an exhaustive list, it isn't—there are enough different vibrators on the market to fill a dozen toy chests. Since we don't want to overload your circuits with too much information, we've limited our selection to the most popular, well-made and best-known.

Many people confuse vibrators and dildos. What distinguishes a vibrator from a dildo or another type of sex toy is that it vibrates. The vibrator is powered either by electricity or batteries (no solar-powered toys yet!). Phallic-shaped vibrators can be used as vibrating dildos (i.e., they can be inserted vaginally or anally), but if you want something penislike that does not vibrate, you're looking for a dildo or plug.

We debated whether to list prices for the different models in this book. Obviously, any prices we list today will be outdated next year, one reason why we chose not to include them. And depending on where you buy them, the prices vary drastically. We used to tell people that, in general, electric vibrators are more expensive than battery vibrators. But these days you can buy an inexpensive electric vibrator at most department stores, then turn around and pay twice as much for a novelty battery vibrator purchased from an adult bookstore or mail-order catalog. We have included the names and addresses of our favorite sex boutiques and mail-order catalogs at the end of this book and we encourage you to shop around!

Electric Vibrators

These vibrators run off the standard one hundred twenty volts. The body of the vibrator is attached to a plug-in cord. Most commonly marketed by major appliance manufacturers like Sunbeam, Panasonic and Hitachi as "personal massagers," they are well-made (most come with a one-year warranty) and are widely available—you can almost always find a brand or two in drugstores or department stores, shelved as beauty-care products or sports massagers. Because they are not marketed as sex toys, you are less likely to find electric massagers in adult bookstores. What you will find are cheap electric knock-offs from adult-industry manufacturers, which don't compare in quality with brand-name manufacturers' vibrators.

Besides being well-made with long life expectancies, electric vibrators are great for other reasons. Most feature a couple of different speeds or a rheostat so you can adjust the vibration to your liking. Because they run on electricity, you won't experience the frustration of your batteries running out at the crucial climax. (Although there is the chance of a power outage or a blown fuse!) Electric vibrators tend to be more powerful than their battery brethren, something you may or may not prefer for sexual purposes, but which makes them far superior for muscle or body massage.

In countries with different electric currents, it is possible to use your electric vibrator with an adapter. Pay careful attention—the vibrator may heat up more quickly than usual.

WAND VIBRATORS *What they look like:* Dubbed "wand" vibrators because they are long and fairly slender in shape, this type of vibrator is the most popular at Good Vibrations. Wand vibrators are usually about a foot long, with a tennis-ball-sized head attached to one end. The long handle is made out of plastic and the vibrator runs on a motor. Most wands have either a high and a low speed or a rheostat. When the vibrator is on it emits a low whirring noise. Hitachi, Wahl, Panasonic, Sunbeam and Pollenex make quality wands. Because of the rising popularity of wand vibrators in the last decade, you may see cheaper, generic versions of them. These are not as well-made and you'll get more bang for your buck in the long run if you stick to the name brands.

Variations: The length of the body, the size of the head, the weight, the noise and the intensity of the vibrations vary somewhat between brands. Some also have angled bodies for "hard to reach" places. There are rechargeable versions of some wand vibrators, so you don't have to be connected to the nearest outlet. The charge usually lasts from thirty to sixty minutes, then takes eight to twelve hours to recharge. One wand vibrator marketed as a sports massager comes with a flat vinyl attachment that you can fill with warm or cold water—that ought to heat up your sex play!

How to use: Women can try pressing the side of the head against or near the clitoris. The shape of the wand lends itself well to numerous positions—lie down on top of it, prop it up against your clit while on your side, hold it between your legs while on your back.

I like to lie on my side with the head of the wand gripped firmly between my thighs—keeping it snug against my clit. This frees up my hands to do other things.

I lie on my stomach, on top of a pillow or blankets or something high with the wand against my crotch, so the pillow beneath it pushes it into my body.

I prop my Hitachi up on a pillow and lean forward onto it while I'm squatting on a vibrating dildo (the kind that rotates and vibrates). I orgasm to my heart's content.

The large head spreads the vibrations out over a greater surface area when it's pressed against the skin, which many experience as a more penetrating vibration. Because the vibrations are diffused by the large head, not all the intensity is focused solely on one spot.

Where was I before my Magic Wand? The level of stimulation is just great.

Men can try pressing the wand directly against the base of the penis, running it along the shaft, touching the head, or resting the penis on top of the head. If this is too intense, try cupping the penis with one hand and holding the vibrator against the back of your hand. You may also enjoy the indirect vibrations provided when your penis is inside the vagina of a woman using the wand on her clitoris:

The first time she turned on her wand when I was inside her, I came in thirty seconds. Once I got used to the stimulation of the vibrator, I would often use it on myself, resting my soft penis

Masturbating with wand vibrator

on top of the vibrator head. I found the vibration was more numbing than stimulating though, once I got hard.

The straight body and large head allow the wand to be easily positioned between face to face partners. This dual stimulation is the reason one customer describes this vibrator as her favorite sex toy:

During intercourse my wand vibrates the base of his penis and my clit at the same time, which gets us both off.

Because the vibrating head is fairly large, people with limited mobility may find it easier to lie on top of the wand or to clutch it between their thighs. Finally, wand vibrators can't be beat for full-body massage—they feel particularly good run along either side of the spine, across the shoulders or on the lower back.

Attachments: To date, there are only three specifically sexual attachments designed to fit over the head of a wand (and they will only fit the Hitachi and the Sunbeam Stick). These can be purchased separately from sex boutiques or mail-order catalogs. The Wonder Wand and G-Spotter are two lightweight, vinyl caps, which can be pushed all the way down over the head of the vibrator. The Wonder Wand has a seamless four-inch straight tip and is about three-quarters inch in diameter. The G-Spotter is the same size, but curved to vibrate against the G-spot area in the front wall of the vagina. When you insert the tip, the area of the cap below the tip will vibrate against your clitoris, offering you glorious simultaneous clitoral and vaginal vibrations! There have been countless requests over the years to make attachments with larger insertable portions, but so far none have materialized. Entrepreneurs, are you listening? These attachments also provide very focused clitoral stimulation, which some customers find an enjoyable alternative to the larger head.

A wand with the G-spot attachment provides perfect, direct stimulation of my clitoris.

My plug-in massager lets me change attachments when I need stronger or gentler massage on my clitoris.

The G-spot stimulator on the Hitachi Wand is my favorite sex toy. Wow! Now there's an intense orgasm. It also makes the vibration against my clit less intense, which is better for me since my clit is very sensitive.

These attachments are also ideal for anal insertion, since the insertable portion has no chance of slipping off and getting lost in the rectum.

The third attachment, called the Magic Connection, fits over the head of a wand vibrator like the other two. It has a small black protrusion, which is used to adapt attachments from coil vibrators to a wand. The Magic Connection is used most commonly to adapt the Come Cup, a tulip-shaped attachment designed to stimulate the head of the penis (see the discussion of attachments in the following section).

COIL-OPERATED VIBRATORS *What they look like:* These vibrators resemble small hand-held mixers or hair brushes. They're usually about six or seven inches long with a handle; the attachments fit over a small round metal nub (about one-half inch) that sticks out at a right angle from the body. The term *coil-operated* refers to the electromagnetic coil

inside the body that creates the vibration (and is also responsible for the relative heaviness of this type of vibrator). These vibrators are practically silent, making them very appealing to folks who want to masturbate quietly. They are always packaged with a variety of attachments (see below). Most models have a high and a low speed, but never an adjustable speed. This type of vibrator has been on the market the longest, which is why you may recognize one that looks like your grandmother's! Sunbeam, Prelude, Wahl and Pollenex are the most famous brands—one of them can almost always be found in drugstores, usually in the beauty-aid aisle.

Variations: The shape of the handle, color, attachments, weight and speed vary only slightly between models. Most are packaged with either four or six attachments—the shape and size of these may vary by manufacturer.

I distinctly remember visiting several different drugstores in search of the perfect vibrator to give our friend in high school. We couldn't rest until we had purchased the Wahl vibrator for her so she could be as happy as we were.

I have a Wahl two-speed from 1989, which has been a faithful partner. I love it.

How to use: Place the desired attachment over the metal nub on the body. When you turn it on, it should be practically inaudible (without an attachment, the vibrator may make a loud rattling noise). Grasp the handle and place the vibrating tip on your genitals.

Because the attachment is relatively small, the vibrations are quite focused when placed against the skin, creating a very intense, localized vibration. It is a markedly different sensation than that produced by the larger-headed wand vibrators previously described, and the reason why some people remain true to one type or the other for their entire lives. Remember that you can experiment—stop and start the vibrator, switch the speeds, or place a towel between you and the vibrator.

I've had the coil massager for four years. I enjoy the stimulation through cotton or something like a sheet or underwear.

I'm giving him massages with the Sunbeam, and he likes it on "high" on his genitals.

I masturbate propped up on two pillows in bed, with a silicone dildo and Sunbeam massager, aromatic lotions and an X-rated movie featuring well-hung guys who are tender lovers.

Attachments: Coil-operated vibrators are usually packaged with four to six attachments. For clitoral stimulation, most women prefer the small, rounded attachment we call a Clitickler (sometimes referred to on the box as the "spot massager"). Some models come with a modified version of this that resembles three concentric rings in the shape of a small pyramid. Try different attachments; one woman told us her favorite attachment was the spiky one advertised as the "scalp massager." Another intrepid customer discovered that the concave attachment will form a tight seal when attached to the bottom of a silicone dildo or plug, thus creating a powerful vibrating dildo.

I love my plug-in Wahl vibrator with clit attachment. I use it as much on myself as I do on my partner (on his butt, or during intercourse so it hits the base of his penis and also my clit).

I've gotten off from holding the vibrator with the scalp massager attachment gently against the underside of my testicles. Also lightly running the clit attachment along either side of my penis.

I love the suction-cup attachment to my vibrator—I rub its side along my clit. After an orgasm on the light speed I can switch to the heavy, feel the rumble on my G-spot and come forever.

Other attachments designed specifically for sexual purposes can be purchased separately from sex boutiques or mail-order catalogs. These are long, insertable attachments, but as in the case of the wand attachments, they're currently only available in one size (about four inches long by about one-half inch in diameter). You can choose between a straight or curved attachment—the straight one will maneuver more comfortably inside

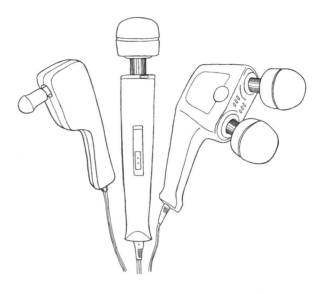

Coil-operated, wand and double-headed vibrators

your vagina if you're using the vibrator in different positions, the curved one is designed to stimulate the G-spot. These are not safe for anal use.

An attachment we call the Twig, with two finger-width branches set at a forty-five degree angle, provides both clitoral and vaginal vibrations. If the angle isn't perfect for you, try pressing down on the clitoral branch with your free hand. This attachment is the only coil attachment that's safe to use anally, because the branch prevents it from disappearing into the rectum if it should pop off the short shaft of the vibrator.

The Come Cup, an attachment just for men, is designed to vibrate the head of the penis. The attachment is tulip-shaped (about one and a half inches deep) and is expandable, though we do recommend placing ample lube inside the attachment to prevent pinching.

I have to be in the right mood for it because the vibration on the head of the penis is pretty intense, but when I am, that Come Cup attachment feels great. I alternate stroking my penis and vibrating the tip.

DOUBLE-HEADED *What they look like:* These powerful vibrators boast two tennis-ball-sized heads that protrude several inches apart at an angle from the vibrator body. They are motor-driven, usually have a high and a low speed, are fairly loud and quite heavy.

Variations: There aren't too many of these on the market, but the couple we've seen vary in size—both the body and the size of the heads—and subsequently in weight. The speed of the vibrations can vary noticeably between models.

How to use: The heads on these personal massagers are placed just far enough apart so that an individual can enjoy simultaneous vibrations on the genitals and the anus. The Hitachi heads will accommodate the wand attachments described above, so you can experiment with multiple vibration and penetration. A man's penis will fit nicely between the two vibrating heads—but hold on to your hat—this is a powerful vibration. The angle of two heads makes this perfect for two people who want simultaneous vibrations. You may argue over which of you has to hold it in place though; some models are heavy and cumbersome. Don't forget to use this for massage—moving the double heads slowly down the spine has turned scores of our customers into jelly.

SWEDISH MASSAGER *What they look like:* Many of you will recognize these back-of-the-hand, one-speed models as the contraptions barbers used to massage your scalp. Slip your hand through the wire straps so that the black vibrating box sits on top of your knuckles.

How to use: These vibrators enable you to maintain skin-to-skin contact since the vibration is transmitted through your hand. Many men find these pleasant to use while stroking the penis. They also make nice massage tools, since your hand remains in contact with your partner's skin. The main com-

plaints about this model are that the vibrations can numb the user's hand pretty quickly and the springlike straps occasionally snag a hair or two.

EROSCILLATOR This vibrator resembles an electric toothbrush and creates a sensation somewhat like a subdued coil vibrator. Why then, at a retail price of nearly ninety dollars, does it cost more than three times as much as a coil vibrator? According to the product packaging, seven years of research and state-of-the-art Swiss engineering have gone into the design of the "oscillating" Eroscillator head, which moves side to side "thirty-six hundred times per minute" with "pinpoint intensity" that "provides easier, faster, better orgasms." It's great that a decent quality toy is finally being openly promoted for sexual use, but it's depressing to us that the toy comes with an inflated price tag and irresponsible hype.

Battery Vibrators

If we conducted a poll asking people to name their most pleasure-giving portable toys, we know battery vibrators would rate right up there with cell phones and camcorders.

Battery vibrators come in a mind boggling variety of shapes, sizes and colors. Most run on the common C or AA batteries, but there are some that run on other kinds as well. The batteries are inserted either into the body of the vibrator or into a battery pack that is attached to the body by a cord. Battery vibrators have always been marketed as sex toys, which means you will always find them in adult bookstores, sex boutiques and mail-order catalogs but, sadly, seldom in department or drugstores.

Overall, battery vibrators emit gentler vibrations than electric vibrators. However, the intensity of any given battery vibrator can vary based on the type of battery and the number required. In other words, a vibrator that runs on one AA battery will be significantly weaker than one that runs on three C batteries. Many of the battery vibrators have a variable speed control at the base, but considering the overall vibrations are fairly gentle, the difference between the high and the low speeds is usually minimal.

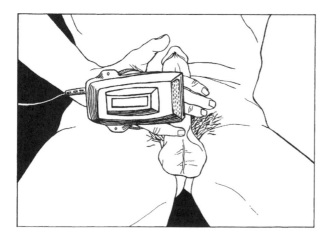

Swedish massager

Battery-operated vibrators are my only deities!

This customer is not alone; battery vibrators boast a large and faithful following. The charm of this style lies primarily in its portability, its versatility and its low cost. Because it does not run on electricity, your vibrator can accompany you anywhere—on a trek through the woods, across international borders or to a play party. In general, battery vibrators are usually fairly lightweight and compact, making them ideal for tucking into an overnight bag or a purse.

I like my tiny battery vibrator, which I use in traffic (only in still traffic). Because I have so much time, it usually does really get me going and I have come occasionally on the road.

I like to be prepared for any sexual encounter, and along with condoms, battery vibrators are a key item in my portable bag of tricks.

The adult industry has flooded the market with a million variations on a couple of themes. A typical cylindrical vibrator can be used externally to stimulate the clitoris, or internally for vaginal or anal vibrations. There are vibrating sleeves for the penis, gadgets to simultaneously vibrate the penis and the clitoris during intercourse, vibrators you can sit on, strap on, clip on, and so on.

While battery vibrators are generally pretty inexpensive, expect the price to go up for every new and unusual feature. It bears repeating that it's worth shopping around; prices can fluctuate as much as twenty dollars for similar models sold by different companies.

Of course, the flip side of the low price (and you knew there was one) is that quality is not usually a consideration in the manufacturing of these toys. If there is a warranty at all, it's for one month, tops. Most battery vibrators are poorly made; they can break easily or poop out for no apparent reason. Even with proper care and a supply of fresh batteries, history has proven their life span to be as unpredictable as the timing of the next earthquake:

My battery-operated vibrator broke at the screw-on part and every time I use it, it loses its contact with the battery and dies. I end up having to whack it to get it to work. Sometimes it stops tragically right before I come.

Finally, keep in mind when reading about these vibrators that although many styles sound similar, they are often packaged and sold under a variety of different names. We're using the names we're familiar with, but in general, you're usually better off trying to hunt down a battery vibrator by description (size, shape, color and any special features) rather than by name.

CYLINDRICAL VIBRATORS *What they look like:* These are the toys that come to many people's minds when you say the word *vibrator*. There are two basic versions of this style, one is designed to resemble a penis, while the other is smooth and usually straight. They are usually made of either hard plastic, pliable vinyl, or jelly rubber. In general, the vinyl and rubber models' vibrations are not as strong as their hard plastic counterparts, primarily because the material is thicker and absorbs a lot of the vibration.

They range in size from about four to eight inches, an average size being about seven inches long by one-and-a-quarter inches wide. Most of them have a variable speed control at the base, though some are attached to a battery pack by a cord. These vibrators are available individually or can be found packaged as kits, with an assortment of attachments (see below).

Variations: The design, size, color, texture and type of battery vary between models. Here are four common versions of this type of vibrator.

♦ Realistic: This is designed to look and feel like a real penis. While the mold attempts to capture the look of a real penis (veins and all), no one has ever mistaken the color or texture for actual flesh. It is usually about seven inches long and available in pink, black, peach—the color the adult industry thinks resembles Caucasian skin tone—and even a glow-in-the-dark vinyl! This style is also available in jelly rubber, which comes in a wide range of bright colors.

♦ Smoothie: Long, cylindrical and smooth, made out of hard plastic. This is also about seven inches long and has the strongest vibrations of the cylindrical vibrators. Smoothies come in a mind-boggling array of colors, from pastel to metallic to pearlescent hues, as well in a transparent waterproof version. This makes them the ideal choice for someone who wants a vibrator to match every outfit, every room, every car, not to mention a spare for the swimming pool!

♦ Softer Smoothie: This is a vinyl or jelly rubber version of the Smoothie, which means the vibrations are gentler. It's also available in assorted colors—the jelly rubber models come in the most beautiful jewel tones we've ever seen in a sex toy. Some jelly rubber models are also slightly rippled, and are attached to a battery pack by a cord.

♦ Mini Smoothie: This is simply a smaller version of the Smoothie, usually about five inches long by one inch wide, also available in many different colors. A slight variation on the Mini, called the Twig, features a short branch at the base that can be used for clitoral stimulation when the dildo portion is inserted. This model can also be used safely for anal insertion.

How to use: We can't reiterate this enough. Despite the myth and marketing of this style as a "penis substitute," most women don't orgasm from inserting these without some accompanying clitoral stimulation. They can, however, be easily pressed into service as very effective clitoral stimulators:

I come using a dildoesque battery-operated vibrator. It was only six dollars when I bought it, but it's brought me tons of pleasure. I like to read erotica while I place it on my clit.

These vibrators in particular offer fairly gentle vibrations, which makes them ideal for men who find electric vibrators overwhelming when placed on the genitals. For women who prefer mild stimulation, this style offers a lot of variety. But if power is what you seek, these may not do the trick. If you enjoy the feeling of fullness in your vagina combined with vibrations, try placing one vibrator on your clitoris and another in your vagina. Or you can use this style—particularly the softer models—to explore prostate or G-spot stimulation.

Until recently I rubbed my clitoris with my fingers. Recently I purchased both vaginal (with clit stimulator) and anal vibrators and love them!

I like to steal my girlfriend's jelly jewel while she's on business trips and give my prostate a little buzz. I prefer the kind attached to a battery pack because I can easily reach and manipulate the speed control.

I like sex with a vibrator inside me while rubbing my clit on a pillow, which I've mounted. I love it while being held by my lover cooing in my ear and saying "oh yes, oh yes, uh huh..."

I like to use a vibrator vaginally while stimulating my clit manually and fantasizing about a hot woman or a dangerous place to masturbate.

I stuck my battery vibrator in the freezer once and got an intense thrill masturbating with a vibrating popsicle!

Attachments: Most of the standard cylindrical vibrators (about one-and-a-half inches in diameter) will accommodate a variety of attachments or "sleeves," which will allow you to change the shape and texture of the vibrator. Among the more functional is the "anal sleeve," a four-inch long, finger-width attachment. For the most part, these attachments feature a range of rubbery nubs or spikes, kind of like French Ticklers, that evoke little sensation when inserted vaginally, but might be worth experimenting with on the more sensitive clitoris. We'd advise you not to have high expectations of these attachments.

G-SPOT VIBRATORS *What they look like:* G-spot vibrators resemble the cylindrical vibrators except for a curve toward the end of the shaft. The angle of the curve is designed to vibrate against a woman's G-spot when inserted vaginally. These vibrators are made of soft vinyl or jelly rubber and are either smooth or resemble a penis.

Variations: We've seen a large (eight inches long by one-and-a-half inches in diameter) and a small (five-and-a-half inches long by one-and-five-eighths inches in diameter) version of this vibrator, as well as a water-proof model and one shaped like a banana. The vibrations are gentle and are controlled by a variable speed.

How to use: Some women can orgasm through stimulation of the G-spot, though not all women respond to this type of stimulation. If you're trying to locate your G-spot, you may want to explore it manually first and then sample the unique sensations offered by the G-spot vibrators. The most popular positions for G-spot stimulation are squatting or rear entry. Try inserting the vibrator a few

Ingenious Inventions

The more people discover what powerful tools of pleasure vibrators can be, the more people crave new and different ways for vibrators to please them. Fortunately toy manufacturers and entrepreneurs are listening, and some incredibly ingenious toys have recently hit the market.

♦ *Tongue Vibe:* You guessed it—the Tongue Vibe is designed to simulate cunnilingus. An undulating vinyl tip flickers in a remarkably lifelike and consistent manner. Unfortunately, the Tongue Vibe is noisy and has a high defective rate, so you take your chances ordering this product. The adult industry continues to produce variations on this theme—we've seen vibrating sleeves featuring internal tongues, and a "tonguing dildo" is in the works. None of these over-complicated toys live up to their billing as yet. Variations in genital anatomy being what they are, the best sex toys tend to be those that don't try to do too many things at once.

♦ *Auto Arouser:* Our name for a realistic vinyl dildo that attaches, via a cord, to the cigarette lighter in your car. Road trips, car camping and boring commutes just got a whole lot more exciting!

♦ *Octopus:* A battery vibrator with eight different attachments, including a cock ring, egg, twig and several sizes of anal plugs and dildos, which attach to a variable-speed battery pack. The bad news for you greedy folk—you can only plug in two attachments at a time.

♦ *Three-in-One Vibe:* A rechargeable dildo-shaped battery vibrator with a self-contained battery pack at the bottom. You can alternate between the three removable dildos, so have fun deciding whether you're in the mood for the G-spot, the realistic vinyl, or the rippled jelly dildo.

♦ *Venus Vibe:* Imagine a clam-shaped rubber shell about four inches long, with a clitoral stimulator and a short dildo attached to the inside of the shell. All of it hooks up to a variable-speed battery pack. A woman can insert the dildo vaginally and cozy up to the clitoral vibrations while the clam diffuses the vibrations around the vulva. Variations include ladybugs and turtles that vibrate the entire vulva.

---

inches, angled so the tip is pressing against the front wall of the vagina. Many women require vigorous stimulation of the G-spot, usually thrusting in addition to manipulating the vibrator. You might also want to simultaneously press down on your abdomen from the outside (around the pubic hair line) with your other hand. Sometimes arousal and orgasm triggered this way are accompanied by ejaculation of fluid through the urethra—this fluid is female ejaculate, not urine.

The curve on a G-spot vibrator also makes it a handy tool for stimulating the male prostate gland. Insert the vibrator about three inches into your rectum so that the tip is pointing up toward the front of your body. Experiment to find out what feels the most pleasurable—steady pressure, gentle movement or variations in the speed of the vibrator.

DUAL VIBRATORS *What they look like:* This variation on the cylindrical model has a branch protruding from the shaft of the vibrator, which is intended to stimulate the clitoris while the swiveling dildo portion is inserted in the vagina. There are separate variable-speed controls for each function; one controls the swiveling motion of the dildo, while the other controls the strength of the vibrating attachment. You decide whether you want to experience the rotation, the vibration, or both together.

This style originally hails from Japan, where it is against the law to make sex toys that resemble genitals. Consequently, manufacturers launched a tradition of creative alternatives. The rotating dildo portion of these toys often resembles a person or totem, while the vibrating clitoral branch resembles an animal—usually the animal's tongue or nose flicks the clitoris. If you've ever fantasized about an animal's tongue on your private parts, this is probably as close as you'll get. The sheer versatility and novelty of these toys renders them slightly more expensive than your typical battery toy. Until recently, the Japanese models have been far better quality than American knock-offs, and worth the extra expense. American manufacturers however, are beginning to use Japanese micro-chip technology in their dual vibrators, so you can expect prices on good quality models to go down.

My favorite vibrator is black rubber with two controls, one for the part that you insert and the other for the part which flicks at the clitoris, anus or whatever's handy. On mine, the flicking part is attached to this fetching little beaver. I really like masturbating with something that has a distinct personality.

Variations: The size of the dildo varies; a common size is about seven inches long by one-and-a-half inches in diameter (though the insertable portion is only about four inches long). The dildo portion on several models, such as the Rabbit Pearl, features rotating plastic balls in the center, adding yet another dimension to an already extraordinary experience! We've peddled a veritable menagerie of animals over the years—beavers, bears, cats and kangaroos, many of which are available in different colors. On some versions, the vibrator is attached to a battery pack by a cord, on others there is a self-contained battery pack in the vibrator's base.

Some models have no clitoral attachment, which you may prefer if you like the size and motion of the dildo, but prefer your own hand or another vibrator to the somewhat gentle clitoral vibrations offered by the animal tongue. Certain American models of this style are the most lifelike (in terms of mold, colors and texture) vibrating dildos we've run across:

My favorite toy is the Family Jewels battery-operated vibrator because I love the look and feel of a cock inside me while I play with my clit.

A further variation on this model is the dual vaginal/anal vibrator—instead of a clitoral branch, the other branch is a vibrating anal plug.

How to use: You've probably figured it out by now, but the beauty of this model is the explosive combination of internal and external vibrations. If you're using the vibrator vaginally and need more external stimulation, apply pressure to the clitoral branch to increase the vibrations against the clitoris. Whether you're using the vibrator vaginally or anally, try inserting the dildo portion while the vibrator is off and then turning it up slowly. The swiveling dildo alone may offer just the right stimulation of the G-spot or prostate gland. You may have to hold on to the base of the dildo with one hand in order to prevent it from sliding out, or from swiveling only at the protruding end. Another way to enjoy this toy is by kneeling or squatting and moving up and down on the dildo.

I love vibrators like the Great King, which has a clit stimulator–great invention. I used to take it in the bathroom when I was seventeen and fuck myself senseless while my family was in the other room.

The Rabbit Pearl vibrator is my favorite because I can fuck it to death and no one is there to see what a slut a nice lady can turn into.

EGG-SHAPED VIBRATORS *What they look like:* Slightly smaller than a real egg and attached to a battery pack by a cord, the egg is made of hard plastic or plastic covered in soft vinyl or jelly rubber. It is designed to be inserted vaginally, but can certainly be pressed against the clitoris. This style of vibrator is often referred to as a "pearl" or a "bullet." You can find these in almost any adult bookstore or sex boutique, but there's one Japanese model whose quality stands above the rest. It's often called the Pink Pearl (it is pink and shaped like a bullet) and is a little more expensive, but worth it. Here again, American manufacturers are slowly but surely catching up with Japanese sex-toy technology and producing ever-stronger, better quality vibrating eggs.

Variations: The dimensions of the egg can vary; sometimes the egg is shaped more like a large bullet (about two inches long by seven-eighths inch in diameter). We've seen these in a variety of colors. One model sports a vibrating egg and a vibrating anal plug attached by separate cords to one battery pack. The most ingenious variation on the egg vibrator to date is a remote-controlled, cordless version, which has obvious implications for tickling your lover's fancy from across a crowded room.

How to use: Grasp the egg between your fingers and insert it into the vagina as you would a tampon. The cord keeps the egg attached to the battery pack outside the body, which you use to control the vibration of the egg. Because the egg will stay secure up inside the vagina, you can literally wear this vibrator underneath your clothing and turn it on and off as you please! Just tuck the battery pack under your belt. When you're ready to remove the egg from your vagina, do not pull on the cord. Reach up inside your vagina and pull on the bottom of the egg. If you concentrate on relaxing your vaginal muscles and bear down a little, the egg will slide right out.

Women have mixed reactions to this type of vibrator. Some enjoy having their attention riveted to the vaginal sensations; others feel very little sensation, while still others find it downright annoying. One of the advantages of the egg-type vibrator is that it lends itself well to erotic combinations with other toys. Try using it with a clitoral vibrator to achieve sensations similar to that offered by the dual vibrators described above. The egg or pearl inserted into a little G-string with a pouch offers endless possibilities for no-hands clitoral stimulation (see next description). Or insert the egg into a hollowed out dildo or prosthesis to create a vibrating dildo. Its compact size also makes it a convenient masturbatory device for men; you can easily place it between your palm and your penis or rest your penis on top of it, like this gentleman:

My favorite masturbation method involves placing a vibrating egg underneath the tip of my penis and fantasizing. Though this tends to take longer to be successful, the orgasms are usually more powerful than with other methods.

Many customers have inquired about using these vibrators anally. We discourage folks from this practice because the cord can become detached from the egg once it's inside the anus, thus making it difficult to remove. Enterprising customers have told us, however, that by putting a condom around the egg and the cord and holding on to the condom while the egg is inserted, this threat is eliminated. You can always pull on the condom to remove the egg if the cord becomes detached. Employ this method vaginally as well if you have difficulty grasping the bottom of the egg once it's inside you.

NO-HANDS VIBRATORS *What they look like:* Leg and waist straps attach to a vibrator (powered by a battery pack) and strategically position the vibrator over the clitoris. This model is often requested by women who desire a vibrator that can offer clitoral stimulation during intercourse, yet doesn't require a hand to hold it in place. While the concept is ingenious, the product execution has suffered these common shortcomings: Flimsy elastic straps don't hold the vibrator in place, the vibrations are weak or the clitoral stimulator is poorly designed. There have, however, been some recent improvements.

Variations:
♦ Butterfly: The original, and probably the most well-known models are Joni's Butterfly and the Venus Butterfly. One newer model looks like a hummingbird. Elastic straps attach to a rather bulky pink plastic butterfly or hummingbird, which emits very gentle vibrations.
♦ Leather pouch and egg combination: This is the most recent and best attempt at the "no hands" vibrator. Leg straps attach to a leather pouch, into which you can insert a vibrating egg. The leg and waist straps are adjustable, and the whole ensemble sits firmly on the clitoris.
♦ The Scorpio: Elastic straps attach to the body of a scorpion, whose long, flexible tail curves around to offer anal stimulation.

How to use: Regardless of which model you use, the idea is to adjust the straps around your thighs and/or waist, and position the vibrator directly over your clitoris. If there's a battery pack, it can be tucked underneath one of the straps. This toy combination is particularly ideal for folks whose hands tire holding vibrators, or who have limited mobility. The adventurous report wearing this out underneath clothing to a nightclub or loud party where no one can hear the buzz!

Because the vibrator only covers the clitoris, you can enjoy penetration while wearing this vibrator. If you're wearing a cheaper model, you may have to apply some pressure to keep the vibrator in place (defeating the purpose of a no-hands vibrator).

VIBRATING SLEEVES *What they look like:* These are basically vibrating vinyl or jelly rubber sleeves into which you insert your penis. Inside the sleeve, there's usually a vibrating egg, tucked under the folds of the material, that creates the vibration. Some have little nubs inside for additional stimulation. Outwardly, these vibrators take on all manner of appearance. Some simply resemble long tubes, others look like a pair of sucking lips or a vagina.

Variations: Some of these simply vibrate; others also move up and down in a simulated sucking motion. Some are attached to pumps (like blood pressure pumps) which add suction. Some models are waterproof. If you like the Come Cup attachment for the coil vibrators, you'll enjoy the battery version of the same toy: a tulip-shaped vinyl sheath with a bullet at the tip intended to vibrate the head of the penis. Another clever toy consists simply of two inflatable vinyl sleeves attached together–slip your penis in one and a Smoothie vibrator in the other.

How to use: You can squirt a bit of lube inside the vibrator to make the sleeve more comfortable, particularly if you'll be thrusting in and out of it. Insert your penis and turn on the vibrator; most have a variable speed, so you can control the intensity of the vibrations.

VIBRATING COCK RING AND STIMULATOR *What it looks like:* This is a cock ring with a small bullet vibrator attached to one end. The vibrator is attached to a battery pack by a cord.

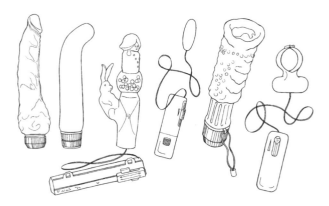

Realistic, G-spot, Rabbit Pearl, Pink Pearl, vibrating sleeve and vibrating cock ring

Variations:

♦ Classic: The original model is a plastic bullet vibrator attached to a cock ring. The plastic can pinch the penis, so use plenty of lube when playing with this model.

♦ Jelly rubber: In a slight variation on the classic, a jelly rubber cock ring is molded to a rubber ring into which you insert your own egg or bullet vibrator.

♦ Anal attachment: This version features a vibrating anal plug attached by a separate cord to the same battery pack as the cock ring and bullet vibrator.

♦ Latex: The cock ring is attached at the base to a pouch for your scrotum, which in turn is attached to a vibrating latex-covered bullet.

How to use: For solo sex, place the cock ring around the base of your penis with the bullet on the bottom to enjoy testicular vibrations. The newer latex model is designed especially for solo play; the snug feeling of the latex combined with the vibrations can be especially pleasurable. For vaginal intercourse, the man places the cock ring around the base of his penis with the bullet on top. This vibrates the penis, and in certain positions the bullet vibrates the woman's clitoris. During anal intercourse in certain positions, the vibrator can also provide stimulation for the receptive partner. The problem for some is that any thrusting results in a fleeting, start/stop vibration. If a woman requires more direct clitoral stimulation, both partners should remain somewhat motionless once the penis is inside her, or the man can try shallow rocking, rather than thrusting. You can also flip the cock ring around so the vibrator stimulates the testicles instead of the clitoris during partner sex.

Love the cock-ring vibrator–I swear I'm having a whipped cream ejaculation!

I have a battery-operated vibrating clamp that fits onto my cock. It adds zest to masturbation!

My lover and I recently used a cock-ring vibrator for the first time. We both loved it. Both of us were stimulated–it rubbed against my clit and definitely made his orgasm more intense.

This type of toy can also be adapted quite nicely for use with a dildo and harness. You can try it the same way (placing the cock ring around the dildo on the outside of the harness) so the receptive partner gets stimulation. Or a female harness-wearer can place the cock ring around the dildo, between the harness and her own clit for direct self-stimulation. Either way, you end up with a vibrating dildo!

VIBRATING STRAP-ON DILDOS *What they look like:* This is a vinyl or jelly rubber vibrating dildo (attached to a battery pack), which can be strapped on with elastic leg straps, enabling the wearer to penetrate a partner. There are usually nubby bits, on the bottom of the dildo portion, that the wearer is supposed to enjoy.

Variations: A slightly more secure variation has the vibrating dildo (attached to a battery pack) built into some latex briefs, but sizes can be problematic. Neither all-in-one toy holds a candle to the combination of a leather harness with a hollowed out silicone dildo and a Pink Pearl vibrator. You'll end up with a secure fit, a quality dildo and a stronger vibration. And you won't have to deal with any obnoxious nubs!

How to use: If you don your strap-on correctly, you can penetrate your partner with a vibrating dildo—definitely a unique sensation. However, the flimsy elastic leg straps will end up being mercilessly pulled out like a rubber band waiting to snap if your lover has a tight grip on the vibrating dildo! The vibrations are also focused primarily in the base of the vibrator, which is nice for the wearer, but essentially defeats the purpose for the penetratee. Using a vibrating dildo in a harness ensures the wearer a secure fit and enables much more control over the action. In addition, a silicone dildo will transmit the vibrations better than vinyl or jelly rubber, so both partners will feel them.

The newest variation in this product line combines a strap-on dildo with a vibrating cock ring and clitoral stimulator. A man can slip his penis through the cock ring, clitorally stimulate his female partner and penetrate her both vaginally and anally—all at the same time! Similarly, a woman could wear this toy in a dildo harness and do the same thing to her female partner. The dildo

portion of this toy is made of jelly rubber with a highly flexible spine, allowing you to mold it into the perfect position. Such ingenuity leaves us breathless!

VIBRATING DOUBLE DILDOS *What they look like:* Two dildos joined at the base are attached by a cord to a battery pack. There are usually two controls, one for each dildo so you can vibrate the dildos separately or simultaneously.

Variations: Length (typically fourteen inches) and diameter (one-and-a-quarter inches) may vary.

How to use: Lying in a scissors position, two women can accommodate each end of the dildo in their vaginas or a coupling of either sex can play with anus/anus or anus/vagina penetration. Once inserted, you can grasp the center of the dildo and move it in and out, or you can leave it in one place and focus solely on the vibrations. We recommend using lots of lube for anal play, and remember, don't switch ends or move your toy from anus to vagina unless you're using fresh condoms.

VIBRATING NIPPLE CLAMPS *What they look like:* Two little bullets attached to a variable-speed battery pack by a cord. The bullets attach to your nipples with adjustable, vinyl-padded clamps.

How to use: Use these for nipple stimulation if you want to free up your hands or if you want to experiment with a new sensation. Tug on them or turn them on and off for variation.

WATERPROOF VIBRATORS *What they look like:* The adult industry puts out a few waterproof battery toys, usually versions of the Smoothie or G-spot vibrators. Brand-name manufacturers occasionally get in on the action but do not market their waterproof vibrators as sex toys. Sizes and shapes vary tremendously. Pollenex makes a small, compact toy called the Aquassager, which includes three little attachments that look like dental aids. We've also seen vibrating shower brush massagers and nubby vibrating balls.

How to use: Well of course you ought to hop in the tub, the shower, the pool, the hot tub, the lake or the ocean to play with these! Aside from the cylindrical models, which can be used either internally or externally, most of the others are designed for external use.

What's In a Name?

When we receive battery vibrators named the "Hunk Multi-Speed" or the "Vibro Super-Cock" from our adult-industry vendors, we like to rebaptize these toys with more euphonious names before putting them out on our shelves. Over the years, our enthusiasm for catchy captions has landed us into some unexpected hot water.

For example, we thought nothing of listing all our dual-style vibrators under the heading "Double Your Pleasure" in our mail-order catalog—it seemed the obvious motto for vibrators that are designed to provide simultaneous clitoral and vaginal stimulation. We hadn't realized we were trespassing until we received a letter from the attorneys for the William Wrigley Jr. Company, requesting that we cease and desist employing their copyrighted slogan. While this was an eminently reasonable request, we bristled at the attorney's comments that "Our client cannot allow its trademark to be used in connection with vibrators and the other products you advertise because of the unwholesome associations." Our indignant publicist wrote back pointing out that vibrators are by no means unwholesome and that "a company that sells a tooth-decay promoting product with television advertisements that promise to 'double your pleasure' while prominently featuring images of comely young twins is not really in a position to criticize anyone for 'unwholesome associations'." We received the soothing response that "scientifically conducted tests indicate that Wrigley's chewing gum is not a tooth-decay promoting product."

But not all major corporations are sex-negative. In honor of Good Vibrations' fifteenth anniversary, we commissioned chocolates made in the shape of the Hitachi Magic Wand electric vibrator, our perennial bestseller. Not only did the sales executives at Hitachi's corporate headquarters contribute to the cost of casting the chocolate mold, but they ordered five hundred chocolates from us to distribute at their annual sales conference.

"Personal Massagers" There are a number of other battery-powered toys that have appeared in mainstream stores recently. These are marketed, much like their electric counterparts, as "personal massagers." You will not find any that are phallic-shaped, but you will find them in almost every other imaginable size and shape. Sharper Image carried one for a while that looked like a paperweight. The perfect desk accessory for the over-worked executive! Hitachi makes one with tiny attachments that look like dental tools. The smallest one we've seen looks like a spark plug—you've probably seen this advertised as the Pocket Rocket.

The good news is, these are often better-made than adult novelties, and for portable clitoral stimulation, many can't be beat. Most are quite small and innocuous-looking (though they pack a punch), so you won't be embarrassed when the X-ray machine picks them up at the airport. The bad news is, styles tend to come and go like the latest fashions, so the one you purchase today may not be around a few years from now.

We won't bother to list the many variations or manufacturers. Our advice is to try one if you're looking for a good quality, portable vibrator.

Anal Vibrators

A vibrating butt plug has brought the most enjoyable intensity to sex.

Partner used a vibrator in my anus. I thought I was going to pass out.

I was lying on my back. She put a well-lubed battery vibrator in me while stimulating my penis. I got instantly hard, approached orgasm very quickly and sprayed come all the way up my chest—which was common at sixteen, but not at forty-seven!

Anal vibrators are popular sex toys among both men and women who use them during masturbation as well as partner sex. Vibrators can stimulate the anal opening, the rectum and the prostate in men. You can use one to penetrate a partner, or an individual can "wear" one. As you probably noticed in the previous sections, many vibrators come with anal attachments—anal stimulation is a popular complement to other types of stimulation. Anal vibrators come in a variety of sizes and shapes. Most tend to be either long and slender, or shaped like a diamond. Some of the newer models come with a flexible spine, which allows you to mold the plug into any angle you desire. Others are set on handles, so you can reach yourself or a partner with ease. To date, there are no electric toys designed specifically for anal use (though you can adapt a coil vibrator—use suction to affix the concave attachment to the base of a plug). Most anal vibrators run on AA or C batteries, are attached to a battery pack and are made of vinyl or jelly rubber.

If you'd prefer to be free of the cord and battery pack, you can use a variety of cylindrical battery toys as anal vibrators, or slip more slender sleeve attachments over them. If you're going to use one of the vibrators described in the previous section anally, make sure it has a flared base or a branch on it so it won't slip into the rectum. If it doesn't have some kind of base, make sure it is at least seven inches long and keep a good grip on it. Also remember to change condoms on toys that go from anus to vagina.

Buying a Vibrator

You've made the decision to buy a vibrator, but you're not sure what the next step is. We suggest you answer the following questions to help ensure the success of your shopping expedition:

Do you want to stimulate the clitoris, vagina, anus, prostate or penis? If you have masturbated before, you probably have some idea which areas you'd like to try your vibrator on, and the information about styles in this book can help you make a selection. If you have never masturbated before, you might want a vibrator that's a bit more versatile so you can experiment. You might try a cylindrical model so you can experiment with insertion as well as external genital stimulation. Or you could try a massager with some attachments, which would offer the same options in addition to a good full-body massage.

Are you looking for one vibrator that will do it all, or a variety of vibrators? Maybe you'd like to stimulate several areas simultaneously. It's usually a better investment to combine a few different vibrators, each successfully stimulating one area, than to purchase some gizmo with lots of appendages. The other advantage to this is that you can pick and choose what you want stimulated and when, for those times when you'd rather not have everything going at once.

I love my Great King battery-operated dildo—using this with tit clamps is the best. A butt plug makes it absolutely beyond description.

Will you be inserting the vibrator? If you plan to insert a vibrator vaginally or anally, you will be concerned with size. Like Cinderella and that glass slipper, there's nothing better than the perfect fit. You can get a fair approximation of size if you know how many fingers fit comfortably in your vagina. Or, for even more accuracy, pare a cucumber down to a size you find accommodating and measure it. If you're planning to insert the vibrator anally, you can use the finger test to judge size. When purchasing an anal vibrator, make sure to invest in one with a flared base.

Is durability important? If you want a vibrator that will last for years, you'll want an electric vibrator.

I used my coil-operated Sunbeam almost every day for eight years and then gave it to my best friend. She says it's still going strong after three years. That is one loyal toy!

Do you want gentle vibrations or strong vibrations? If your clitoris or penis is very sensitive to touch and responds to light stimulation, you might be content with the gentler vibrations offered by a battery vibrator. If you prefer more intense stimulation, consider an electric vibrator or a stronger battery vibrator. If you want a vibrator that offers a range, invest in one with a rheostat or a variable-speed control.

Is portability important? If you travel a lot, or like sex in the great outdoors, you'll want a battery vibrator. You can use a rechargeable electric vibrator outdoors, but you still need to be near one hundred twenty volts to recharge it when it runs out of steam.

VIBRATOR SHOPPING CHECKLIST

✔ *Purpose.* Do you want to stimulate the clitoris, vagina, anus, penis, prostate, G-spot or a combination of any of these? Is it for solo play, partner sex or both?

✔ *Intensity.* Electric vibrators offer stronger vibrations than battery ones.

✔ *Durability.* Electric vibrators and brand-name battery vibrators last the longest.

✔ *Portability.* Battery vibrators or rechargeable electric models travel well.

✔ *Texture.* If you'll be inserting the toy, do you want hard plastic or a pliable vinyl or jelly rubber? Nonporous surfaces are easier to clean.

✔ *Shape.* Smooth? Rippled? Curved? Resembling a penis?

✔ *Color.* Flesh tones? Pastels? Metallics? Jewel tones? Glow-in-the-dark?

✔ *Noise.* Coil-operated electric vibes are the quietest; hard plastic battery vibrators and some large wand vibrators are the loudest.

✔ *Price.* Electric vibrators and dual battery vibrators are on the high end; basic battery vibrators are on the low end.

I already have a longtime plug-in vibrator but I needed a portable companion on my marathon treks along beaches and headlands. (What I call deep cuntry.) This battery vibrator has brought me to some lovely comes!

Is noise a factor? Some folks share apartments with thin walls and are embarrassed by noisy battery vibrators. The only virtually silent vibrators in existence are the coil-operated electric vibrators. You can also try vibrating under the covers, because the blankets muffle the noise quite a bit. And if keeping your vibrator a secret is important to you, please note that sometimes an electric vibrator plugged into the same circuit as a TV or radio can interfere with the reception!

Is price a factor? Electric vibrators tend to be more expensive than battery vibrators. However, you may go through so many battery vibrators during the life span of one electric vibrator, that the electric could turn out to be the better value in the long run.

Where to Buy Vibrators

The largest selection of vibrators is usually at adult bookstores or sex boutiques, if you're fortunate enough to live in a town that has one of these alternatives to adult bookstores. You may be reluctant to patronize a sex shop, but shopping at department stores can be awkward, too. We suggest asking for the "personal massagers"—you'll most likely get a clerk who feels sorry for your sore muscles. If they're wise to the fact that massagers are used for sexual purposes, it's probably because they have one, in which case they'll give you that secret "welcome to the club" smile.

If you aren't up for shopping at your neighborhood sex shop, or you're too shy to purchase a vibrator at Macy's, there are other ways to get satisfaction. The most convenient and discreet way to shop for sex toys is through a mail-order catalog—check our resource listings for our recommendations. In-home women's pleasure parties—the sex toy equivalent of Tupperware parties—were all the rage in the eighties, but these aren't as common any more. Of course we hope that on your next visit to Good Vibrations, you'll let one of our staff give you a tour in person!

Sharing Your Vibrator with a Partner

This is an area where success depends as much on your communication skills as it does on your positive attitude about sex toys. You might be excited about the introduction of vibrators into your sex life, but your partner may not necessarily be on the same wavelength. A few important things to remember are:

♦ Don't assume you want the same things; talk, listen and avoid judgment.

♦ A vibrator can never replace a partner.
♦ Vibrators bring pleasure. If it brings you pleasure, your partner will probably like it.

Sharing Your Own Toy

It's amazing how much easier it is for us to share our vibrators with friends or roommates than with our partners. It's as if there's a sign posted over the conjugal bed that says "No appliances allowed." Seriously, it's stunning how many people assume their partners won't like vibrators and don't even consider broaching the subject. No matter how many times we tell you how much fun two people can have with sex toys, unless you can raise the topic, the issue is moot. Here are a few common concerns people have cited for keeping vibrators out of their relationships, along with our suggestions for handling them:

He'll feel like he hasn't been pleasing me all these years. It's possible to be sensitive to a partner's ego without forgoing your own sexual pleasure. You can assure your partner that he has been pleasing you, otherwise you wouldn't have kept coming back for more! Introduce the vibrator as a way to increase pleasure for both of you, illustrating the many ways two people can enjoy it where one can not. For example, if your vibrator orgasms are more intense, the pressure on his penis will probably be more intense during penetration, allowing him to experience a new sensation. Offer him control of the vibrator so he

can learn how to use it on you and get comfortable handling it himself. Suggest, but don't insist, that he might like using it on himself.

She'll think I don't need her anymore. Again, reassure your partner that there are countless ways vibrators fall short as sex partners (they're predictable, humorless and make lousy kissers, to name a few). Treat your vibrator as an accessory to sex, not the main event. If vibrators are necessary for your orgasm, have her hold it, or encourage your partner to explore the rest of your body's infinite erotic terrain.

He thinks I shouldn't have to rely on something besides him for sex. Everyone employs something—in addition to a partner—during partner sex. For some people it's a certain fantasy, for others it's special clothing or a mood or setting. These components may not always be necessary for you to orgasm, but they do enhance your sexual experience. You can try to find out what sorts of stimuli he responds to and then draw a parallel between that and your desire to bring a vibrator into your sex play. If you haven't talked about it before, find out if he masturbates (odds are he does) and suggest that this is an example of his not relying on you for sex. If he feels he should be giving you orgasms during partner sex, teach him how to hold the vibrator.

Sharing your vibrator

One lover asked me, "Why would you want to use something mechanical?" to which I responded, "Wouldn't you rather machine wash than hand wash? Vibrators are quick, efficient and get the job done!"

Buying a Toy for Your Partner

Think about why you're buying a vibrator. Do you have some expectation around improving your sex life that your partner might not be aware of? Do you think her orgasms should be different? How will she react? Are you buying him a vibrator because you want to use it? What message will this send?

Talk to each other about your expectations beforehand (as opposed to whipping the toy out in the heat of passion). If your partner is feeling pressured or intimidated, don't push the issue. Try to get at the root of the anxieties, but don't pass judgment. In this example, it appears that the couple spoke about vibrators at some point, which may have contributed to the success of the surprise:

My lover knew I had never used a vibrator. I was blindfolded and tied up and she had been talking dirty to me. Then all of a sudden, I hear this buzzing and I felt the vibrator on my clit. Then she started fucking me in the ass with her fingers while she kept the vibrator on my clit. The fact that I couldn't see it, only hear it, made it exciting. I found out later that it was the Hitachi Magic Wand. From that day on, it was the only vibrator for me.

Common Questions about Vibrators

Which is the best vibrator? This question can usually be interpreted in two ways. Do you mean "Which is the best vibrator for reaching orgasm?" Only you can be the judge of that. People respond to all different kinds of stimulation, so what works best for one person may be completely irritating to someone else. The only way to find the best vibrator for *you* is to experiment.

The other way to interpret this question is, "Which is the most popular vibrator?" If you want to use popularity as a litmus test for which toys are more likely to please you, that's your preroga-

tive. At Good Vibrations, the Hitachi Magic Wand, the Wahl coil, the Smoothies, the Jelly Jewel vibes and the dual vibrators (like the Beaver and the Rabbit Pearl) have large and faithful fan clubs.

How long will my battery vibrator last? It's impossible for us to predict exactly how long any vibrator will last. Even if you take good care of the toy and change the batteries regularly, there's no guarantee that it won't poop out inexplicably in a month. We've heard reports from many customers whose vibrators buzzed happily for a couple of years, and just as many from frustrated customers whose toys died within a few months.

If you're seeking better-made battery vibrators, Japanese-made toys are somewhat higher quality than those manufactured in Hong Kong, and occasionally you'll run across brand-name battery vibrators (by Hitachi, Wahl, etc.), which almost always come with longer warranties.

Will I get addicted? There's absolutely no physiological basis for addiction to any form of sexual stimulation. It is true, however, that many of us become habituated to whatever stimulation reliably produces orgasms. Some of us prefer sex in a specific position, sex with a specific fantasy, or sex with a specific partner. It is equally possible to become habituated to sex with a vibrator. There's nothing wrong with it—what's wrong are the people or the voices inside our head saying we "should" have orgasms a certain way; therefore we "should" wean ourselves from our vibrators.

If you enjoy your vibrator, keep buzzing! If you want to learn other ways of orgasming, here are a few tips for breaking your sexual pattern with the vibrator. Set aside more time to explore alternative sexual activities. Try the "stop and start" method; bring yourself to the edge of orgasm in your usual way and then switch to another type of stimulation. You'll find it can be as much fun to go for heightened arousal as instant gratification. Experiment with different positions, fantasies and sensations.

Will my genitals get numb? Continuous use of the vibrator will not damage the nerve endings in the clitoris or the penis. You may experience a temporary numbness of your genitals caused by the vibrations, but your sensitivity always returns. You may be concerned that you build up a tolerance for the intense stimulation offered by a vibrator and question whether you'll ever be able to masturbate manually again. The answer is yes, you will build up a tolerance, and yes, you can masturbate manually again. Employ some of the suggestions above to break your pattern, and in time your clit or penis will be jumping for your hand like it used to.

What's that mysterious warning about calf pain? Vibrators and massagers sold in the United States are packaged with a label advising against using on unexplained calf pain because there's a risk of shaking loose a blood clot, which could cause serious heart damage or death.

Will I get electrocuted? Not unless you immerse your electric vibrator in the bath, the shower, the Jacuzzi or any other body of water. Some people have been concerned that bodily fluid in contact with vibrators is dangerous, but to date we've never heard of anyone receiving a shock from even the most copious lubrication or ejaculation.

Can vibrators be dangerous? If you apply common sense (don't leave your vibrator home alone and running when you leave for vacation, don't fall asleep with it on your stomach), there is no cause for concern. There are a few types of vibrators we try to warn people about, because of the potential for injury. Those electric vibrators that have a heating element can cause minor burns on tender genital tissue. There is also a dildo-type battery vibrator, which moves up and down like a slinky that has been known to pinch. Some vibrators have an uncovered metal rod in the center of the plastic, which can cause damage if it pokes through. Certain battery vibrators are much better-made than others. Check to make sure the material covering the motor is thick, strong and doesn't tear easily.

What about safer sex with a vibrator? If you're using your vibrator alone, you are engaging in safe sex. But you should avoid inserting a vibrator anally and then inserting it vaginally without cleaning it, as this will transmit bacteria that could cause infection. Remedy this by using condoms (or by having more than one sex toy within arm's reach).

If you're using a vibrator with a partner, you should clean the vibrator before sharing it. Many of the plastic attachments can be washed in hot soapy water; dildo-type plastic vibrators can be wiped with a wet cloth. You can avoid the inconvenience of interrupting sex play to bathe your toys if you use condoms—simply strip off the used condom and replace it with a fresh one between uses.

And They All Buzzed Happily Ever After!

Now that we've imparted practically every bit of information in our possession regarding vibrators, it's time for you to go play with them! Our dream is that one day vibrators will become as commonplace and acceptable as any other appliance in your house.

Thanksgiving dinner was at my house last year. My mom looked into my room and saw my vibrator peeking out from under the bed, then she went into my sister's room and saw hers. "You girls," she exclaimed, "aren't you even embarrassed that your guests will see?" I laughed. I don't even notice them anymore. I hope if my guests see my vibrator, they'll just smile and want one too.

CHAPTER 10

Penetration

In this chapter, we'll discuss the varieties of penetration you and your partners can enjoy and the ways in which we use our fingers, fists, dildos and penises to explore each other's bodies.

Vaginal Penetration

There are abundant physiological explanations as to why a woman would seek out vaginal penetration. As you recall from our discussion of the physiology of sexual response, when a woman is aroused, her outer vagina becomes congested with blood and the vaginal opening narrows, while the inner two-thirds of her vagina balloons open. The uterus and cervix become elevated, which accentuates the expanding space in the inner vagina. For many women, this ballooning sensation is accompanied by a desire to be filled. And many women find the experience of orgasm enhanced when the vagina contracts around something.

Dildos really improve orgasmic sensation.

I enjoy anything and everything vaginally, from a fist to a little finger. I love the feeling of being filled.

Sexual behavior is not dictated solely by physiological capacities, however, but must be inspired by desire, willingness and trust. We learn to trust our bodies' capacities only after repeated pleasurable experience. If a woman experiences penetration when she's not relaxed, aroused and lubricated, she certainly runs the risk of feeling pain and coming to associate penetration with pain.

I've noticed the more turned on I am, the more lubricated and open I am, the more I enjoy intercourse.

Penetration usually hurts at first, but lubrication helps. Then it stops hurting after I am aroused more.

Vaginismus is the term used to describe one extreme reaction in women who have had traumatic and painful experiences with penetration. The Kinsey Institute has estimated that anywhere from two to nine percent of women experience vaginismus, a psychological response to physical experiences such as rape, childbirth or painful intercourse. A woman with vaginismus will involuntarily and automatically contract her vaginal muscles whenever penetration is imminent. Treatment for vaginismus has a very high success rate and involves undertaking an exercise program in which the woman practices contracting and relaxing the muscles in her thighs and pelvis, and inserts progressively larger dilators (i.e., dildos) in her vagina over the course of several months. The process is one of relearning conscious control over voluntary muscles and regaining confidence in the capacity to experience pleasure.

Of course, many women are perfectly happy with a sex life that involves little or no penetration of any kind. One person's erogenous zone is another person's neutral zone, and everyone has different preferences as to which types of stimulation are most arousing. Assuming that all women find vaginal penetration pleasurable makes about as much sense as assuming that all men find anal penetration pleasurable. Furthermore, there's a psychological component to penetration that affects our responses. When you enter your partner's body, you're crossing a boundary emotionally as well as physically. For some people, this merging is profoundly erotic, for others it is profoundly invasive. We hope it goes without saying that you should always respect your partner's wishes in this matter.

To be honest, I could do without penetration. If a man just plays with my clit, I'm a happy camper. I don't like sticking things in my vagina.

Fingers

WHY USE YOUR FINGERS?   When an early sex therapist polled a group of men and women as to which part of their partners' bodies—fingers, tongues or genitals—gave them the most sexual pleasure, fingers took top honors. Hands are exceptionally sensitive, skillful instruments. The touch of your hand to your partner's genitals is an intimate communication, which creates a fine-tuned range of sensations.

Fingers are definitely the most sensual and loving—also most responsive.

I particularly enjoy penetration by a penis or fingers. They are warm and know where to go.

I like fingers before a penis to get me more excited and also just because fingers are nice.

I like fingers inside me. I like to feel my cunt squeeze them, and I like how warm they are when they're pulled out.

Of course, not every woman will have the same attitude toward digital penetration:

Don't like fingers in my vagina due to childhood sexual molestation experience.

Fingers are hard and dildos are cold. I like a penis.

HOW TO USE YOUR FINGERS   Before you dive in, take the time to remove any rings and bracelets, as these could scratch your partner. It's also a good idea to wear a latex glove. Latex gloves are not only a safer sex precaution, but they can enhance manual stimulation for both parties involved. We aren't suggesting that you approach your partner clad in thick, vinyl dishwashing gloves. Far from it. Latex surgical gloves are available from medical or dental supply houses—they come in a rainbow of colors, a wide range of skin-tight sizes and are extremely thin. If you or your partner are allergic to latex, there are synthetic alternatives that are just as thin as latex gloves. Either way, try to find unpowdered gloves, or if you can't, wash the potentially irritating powder off the gloves before use. You'll be able to feel every warm, moist inch of your partner's vagina, but you won't have to contend with the sting of her vaginal fluids, and she won't have to contend with your ragged cuticles, sharp nails and rough skin.

I like to use gloves because my hands are often irritated by the juices; also, I feel more comfortable probing a lover's vagina with gloves instead of worrying about scratching, even with the shortest of fingernails.

I like fingers very much, but one advantage of penises, by the way, is that they don't have fingernails.

Some folks prefer using finger cots—they are more commonly available in pharmacies and resemble the cut-off fingers of a glove. Finger cots are okay if you really are going to restrict your dabbling to one finger, but given the limited amount of surface area they cover, they aren't the most practical or versatile choice.

So you've got your gloves on, and you're wondering how best to let your fingers do the talking. Only your partner knows for sure. Tastes in finger-fucking vary just as much as tastes in any other sexual activity. Some women prefer to be penetrated with only one or two fingers and others prefer several. The same woman will have varying preferences as to how many fingers she wants inside her depending on her menstrual cycle and her level of arousal.

I'm crazy about finger stimulation, especially four or five fingers at once.

Occasionally, I like someone's finger inside me, generally when I'm ovulating and very wet. Sometimes after I come, I like someone's finger inside me—it feels very comforting.

Nobody likes being poked at or penetrated before she's turned on, so start by teasing your partner's clitoris, labia and vaginal opening until her genitals are swollen and warm. She may or may not lubricate heavily—it's always a good idea to add some water-based lubricant. If she's fairly aroused, your partner may slide right onto your finger(s) herself. Or you can start by inserting one finger and attend to her body language to see how to proceed from there.

You can either move your fingers straight in and out, twist them in a corkscrew motion or tap and press around the vaginal walls. Some women prefer no movement at all, others a gentle stroking and others a vigorous thrusting. If your partner enjoys G-spot stimulation, you can crook your fin-

gers up and stroke the front wall of her vagina under the pubic bone with what's aptly called a "come hither" motion. Some women enjoy massage of the perineal area between the vagina and anus. Some enjoy pressure against the cervix and would welcome deep strokes, while others find it painful to have the cervix jarred. Experiment by stroking and pressing all around her vagina to find her "hot spots," and ask her to let you know when your touch feels pleasant, neutral or irritating. Every woman has different responses, so the technique that puts one lover on cloud nine might put another lover to sleep.

Several fingers engaged in very specific ways (up under the bone) is really enjoyable.

A woman's fingers (a woman who knows my G-spot) do lead me to orgasm. But a lot of friction vaginally without G-spot stimulation is more annoying and painful than enjoyable.

Most women find the experience of penetration enhanced when their whole bodies are involved. You can both enjoy several kinds of stimulation at once—try rubbing your bodies together, sucking her nipples, licking her clitoris, fingering her anus, switching on a vibrator or kissing. And remember, latex gloves make it easy to move between vaginal and anal play. You can simply change your gloves rather than hopping up to wash your hands.

I like a tongue in my ear and on my neck; a hand lightly touching the small of my back; and clitoral and anal stimulation. In fact, in a perfect world, I could have all of that at the same time. Might overload my system, though.

Fingers that stroke my G-spot firmly are great, especially when accompanied by a tongue licking my clit.

I really like to kiss and do things orally while I'm being penetrated. I definitely like the rest of my body touched at the same time.

Vaginal Fisting

WHAT IS IT AND WHY DO IT? *Fisting* is the term used for inserting an entire hand in someone's vagina or anus. Although the word *fisting* sounds vaguely menacing and seems to suggest that the fister slams his or her clenched fist into the fistee's vagina, fisting is a downright tender sexual activity that requires great patience and trust on the part of its practitioners. With your hand planted deep inside your partner's body, you can expect to feel simultaneously humbled and all-powerful. With a hand filling your vagina, you can expect to feel sensations ranging from profound passion to meditative tranquillity. For some practitioners, fisting is an almost spiritual experience of union.

If your first reaction to the idea of fisting is to reject it as violent, painful and potentially dangerous, you might want to stop and review a few truths about female anatomy. The vagina is made of muscle, and nature has designed it so that it can expand to let a ten-pound baby come through. (In fact, the technique of "perineal massage," as taught in childbirth classes, is basically vaginal fisting.) It is certainly physiologically possible to get a human hand into a vagina without causing damage.

We're not suggesting that every woman try fisting simply because she's physically capable of it. But if you're someone who particularly fancies the sensation of being filled up vaginally, or if you've always enjoyed the subtleties of finger-fucking, you may be curious about what your partner's entire hand might feel like. What follows are some tips as to how to safely explore fisting. The only women who should never attempt vaginal fisting are male-to-female transsexuals, as a surgically created vagina is far less elastic than a biological vagina. Women who have had total hysterectomies—in which the cervix or the upper part of the vagina has been removed—may experience a loss of vaginal elasticity, which could make fisting painful and unappealing. The same is true for post-menopausal women.

Please do not ever embark on a fisting session if either you or your partner is drunk or in any chemically-induced, altered state. Fisting demands attentiveness and concentration on the part of both participants, and you would be foolish to choose this time to dull any of your senses. The first rule of penetration is: If it hurts, you're doing

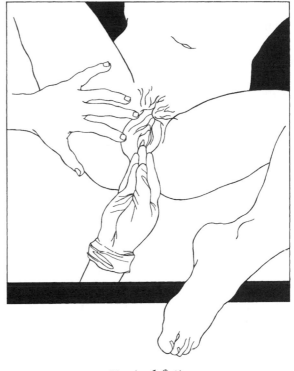

Vaginal fisting

something wrong. Alcohol and drugs can raise your pain threshold to the point where you're unaware you're causing damage until after the fact.

FISTING HOW-TOS First things first: Please take off all your rings and bracelets and put on a latex glove. For safer sex, you might want to wear a glove on each hand, as you'll be reapplying lube to your fisting hand at regular intervals. A well-lubricated glove not only protects your skin and your partner's vagina, but it also transforms your hand into a sleek and slippery surface. Furthermore, fisting is an activity that demands a slow buildup, and both you and your partner may discover unexpected benefits to instituting some preparatory rituals.

Before being fisted, watching my partner put on the glove and put lubricant all over it, very slowly and methodically, drives me insane.

The fistee will probably want to either lie on her back with her knees bent or lie propped on her elbows and knees. The fister will want to have both hands free and to be sitting or kneeling in a comfortable position. Take your time coaxing her vagina into a relaxed, receptive state and incorporate plenty of whatever clitoral, nipple or anal stimulation she finds most arousing. Insert one finger at a time until you're up to four. Your palm should be facing her stomach, and your knuckles should be pressing in the direction of her perineum, rather than grinding painfully against her pubic bone. Your partner may find it helpful to coordinate her breathing with your movements: inhaling as you withdraw your fingers and exhaling as you insert your fingers. If she bears down with her vaginal muscles as she exhales, she'll slide further and further onto your fingers. Take regular breaks to relubricate your entire hand and wrist. There are no Olympic medals for speed-fisting, and if you tease her to the point that she's begging for more, so much the better for both of you.

As you're working more and more of your fingers into her vagina, you'll probably find yourself instinctively adopting the hand position referred to as either the "duck" or the "swan." In this crucial fisting position, you tuck your thumb across your palm and narrow all four fingers together in a shape that resembles a beak (hence the bird names). The goal is to make your hand as narrow as possible in order to sneak it through the tight ring of muscle around the vaginal opening:

> I like being fisted, if they listen to my instructions to make the little duck thing before jamming their whole hand up my cunt.

You may find it helpful to incorporate a twisting motion as you gradually work more and more of your hand into her vagina. If she's sufficiently aroused and your hand is sufficiently lubricated, the moment will arrive when the widest point of your hand across your third knuckles slips inexorably into her vagina. When your hand has pushed past the muscles ringing the vaginal opening, it will naturally fold up into a fist, snugly surrounded by the strong, hot walls of her vagina.

Once inside, there are a variety of ways to move your hand. You can rock it slightly back and forth; circle it slowly; clench and unclench your fist; tap the inner walls of the vagina; or even thrust deep into her vagina. Many women have sensitive cervixes, so unless your partner specifically likes this kind of stimulation, you should refrain from pummeling her cervix.

Fisting—opening and closing my hand while it is inside—is great. Touching her cervix is a charge. Needless to say, I love it done to me, too.

Vaginally, I enjoy a whole hand or rapid, vigorous hand thrusts.

Don't forget the rest of your partner's body. The experience of fisting, like that of any other form of penetration, can be greatly enhanced when it's teamed up with simultaneous clitoral, anal, oral, nipple or full-body stimulation. If both your hands and mouth are occupied, your partner should feel free to stroke herself or you with her own hands.

My partner's best orgasms are when I have one finger up her ass, my whole other hand in her vagina, and my mouth on her clit.

I like to be gently stroked somewhere else (feet, ass, face) while being forcefully penetrated. I also like her to use her tongue to penetrate my mouth in the same hard rhythm as she is fucking me.

Your partner may or may not orgasm during fisting. Some women find the sensations of being fisted so transcendentally intense that orgasm seems irrelevant. Whether or not she comes, you'll eventually find yourself at the point where you need to remove your hand. If she has just orgasmed, her vagina may feel a lot smaller all of a sudden. Don't be alarmed. What went in must come out. Ask her to bear down with her vaginal muscles as you slide your hand slowly out, unfolding it as you go. If her vagina feels suctioned shut, you can break the seal by slipping another finger into her vaginal opening.

Fisting is a powerful experience for both parties involved. Both you and your partner may experience an altered state of consciousness. Allow yourselves plenty of time to come down from your high. Your partner will probably feel conscious of her vagina for several days thereafter. It's conceivable she could spot a little blood, but unless the bleeding is heavy, there's nothing to worry about.

Vaginal Intercourse

We're purposefully allotting neither more nor less space to vaginal intercourse than to any of the other sexual activities and playthings addressed in this book. The myth that intercourse is the be-all and end-all of sexual experience, and that most other activities are "foreplay" to the main event is one that has something of a stranglehold on our collective libido. In reality, intercourse need only be the "main event" when procreation is the goal (and in today's world of biomedical technology, even this is not always the case). An emphasis on the primacy of penis-vagina intercourse devalues not just the experience of gay and lesbian couples, but the experience of bisexual and heterosexual couples who have learned that there's more to sex than just sticking the proverbial plug in a socket. The negative results of this single-minded approach to sex are manifold: If the pleasures of "outercourse" were openly acknowledged, surely we'd see a decrease in the rate of teenage pregnancies, the spread of sexually transmitted diseases and the number of preorgasmic women.

I do think there is this standard (even in the lesbian/bi community) that penetration is the real thing—the ultimate thing, and that if you don't like being fucked you are uptight or boring. We have to get over that. Life is too short to spend trying to conform to other people's standards for pleasure. Claim your own desire!

With this disclaimer off our chests, we hasten to add that intercourse certainly deserves a place in the Sexual Activities Hall of Fame. Intercourse provides full-body contact, mutual stimulation and an intermingling of flesh that is highly arousing on many levels, both physiological and emotional. The discussion of vaginal intercourse that follows is equally applicable to both opposite-sex and same-sex couples and to penis/vagina intercourse or dildo/vagina intercourse.

EXPECTATIONS You and your partner should be clear as to your respective expectations and assumptions around intercourse. If you're in agreement that intercourse is just one facet of your sexual interaction, you'll probably have fewer concerns about whether or not it will lead to orgasm. If you do have orgasm as your goal, you'll need to bear in mind that anywhere from fifty to seventy-five percent of women do not achieve orgasm from penetration alone, as penetration does not provide enough of the clitoral stimulation that most women need to reach orgasm. You may decide to incorporate additional stimulation that would bring both you and your partner to orgasm during intercourse. In any case, please don't get stuck on the physiologically-unlikely goal of a no-hands orgasm for both partners, as this will only limit your enjoyment of intercourse.

Sometimes it's hard to get penetration and stimulation at the same time. Sometimes it's too awkward (physically or because of my partner's feelings) to do it myself.

I much prefer oral sex over fucking. I do love both, but the fucking part is mostly for my honey so he can come inside me. He's a hard come and does it best inside me.

Another popular intercourse expectation is that of simultaneous orgasm. Marriage manuals of the fifties and sixties touted this as the summit of sexual bliss, thereby establishing a standard that is extremely difficult for most couples to live up to. Arousal patterns vary from person to person and from occasion to occasion. If you're monitoring your partner's level of arousal, you're bound to be a bit distracted from your own. Simultaneous orgasm promotes an ideal of egalitarian reciprocity that doesn't have a whole lot to do with the average Joe or Jane's sexual responses. Of course, if you do experience simultaneous orgasm, that's grand. Don't be surprised if it happens more by sheer accident than by design.

LUBRICATION Lubricant is a key accompaniment to any type of penetration, and intercourse is no exception. Unless your partner has a great deal of natural lubrication, consider adding some from a bottle—this will make intercourse more comfortable for both of you:

We use condoms with extra Astroglide even though I naturally lubricate a lot myself. We apply it periodically as we go, to stay nice and slippery at all times. It makes it feel better and allows us to go on for a long time.

We do occasionally hear from men and women who complain that "too much" lubrication makes it hard for them to get enough friction to reach orgasm. If this is the case, you can try adjusting your angle of penetration so that the penetrator is rubbing against the edge of the vaginal opening, rather than sliding straight in. Or you can wear condoms–latex tends to suck up lubrication and to add friction to the proceedings.

DIFFERENT STROKES One final consideration to bear in mind is that different individuals have different tastes in terms of their preferred style, angle and depth of intercourse. You might like long, leisurely strokes or shorter, rhythmic strokes–or you may enjoy combining shallow and then deep strokes in a pattern. You might like to keep your hips close together, grinding against each other, or you might like to rock your hips away from each other. If you and your partner have different tastes, you can incorporate both your preferred methods into one intercourse session.

I've always enjoyed unhurried, exploratory, playful penile penetration.

Psychologically, I dig just about any hard and rapid fucking.

The angle of penetration can also affect the level of stimulation you both receive. A man may want to angle his penis against the edge of the vaginal opening to get the maximum stimulation on the sensitive glans and underside of the penis. Or, if he angles his penis high against the top of the vaginal opening, each stroke can tug on the woman's clitoral hood, thereby indirectly stimulating the clitoris. Women may enjoy pressure on one part of the vaginal wall more than another.

I like to have sex in several different positions. I need friction on my cock from different areas to easily reach orgasm.

G-spot stimulation occurred with a partner whose penis was curved to the left a little bit, so I guess he hit the spot!

Women have a wide range of preferences when it comes to the depth of thrusting they're comfortable with. Different positions accommodate deep

thrusting better than others, and some women find this quite pleasurable. Others, including women with sensitive cervixes or women who have had hysterectomies, may prefer a shallow thrusting, focusing on the outer third of the vagina. The vaginas of many male-to-female transsexuals are too shallow to accommodate deep thrusting.

I think a lot of my pleasure in intercourse or penetration comes from stimulation of the cervix, so length is important.

I enjoy penetration with a cock but really have to focus on staying open and relaxed. The only position that works for me is on my back with legs wide open and bent. I can't take too much thrusting.

Whenever you are on the receiving end of any kind of penetration, you should always feel you can control the depth of thrusting. You can manage this unobtrusively by wrapping your hand in a donut-shape around the base of your partner's penis or dildo. You'll easily be able to control the depth of each thrust, and, if your partner is a man, his penis will still feel pleasurably enveloped by the combination of your hand and vagina.

POSITIONS There has probably been more written about intercourse positions than any other topic in the history of sex manuals. Folks have been snapping up illustrated copies of the *Kama Sutra* for the past fifteen centuries, not for the Hindu philosophy of the text, but for the chance to admire illustrations of couples entangled in the "yawning position" or the "lotuslike position." The sixteenth-century Arabic manual, *The Perfumed Garden*, lists forty different "postures for coition." In the early nineties, a manual purporting to teach a "coital alignment technique" which would guarantee bigger, better and one hundred percent simultaneous orgasms for both parties, generated a publicity storm far greater than the book's actual techniques warranted (*The Perfect Fit* simply instructs men to position themselves during intercourse in the missionary position so that the pubic bone will stimulate a woman's clitoris). Obviously, position books have a powerful and timeless appeal .

What's behind this obsession with positions? Well, as any ballroom dancer can testify, it takes a little practice to get two bodies moving in time on the dance floor. It stands to reason that it would also take a little practice to get two bodies moving in a way that's mutually arousing, stimulating and comfortable off the dance floor. Just as no one instinctively knows how to waltz divinely, no one instinctively knows how to perform intercourse divinely. Yet most position books on the market should be taken with a grain of salt. Either they promote one sure-fire patented technique that is guaranteed to please each and every reader, or they present one hundred and one different sexual positions, all of which are minor variations on the same basic themes. Don't be intimidated by either extreme—position books are fun for their erotic visual content, even though the advice they offer is of dubious value. There are really only a handful of basic sexual positions, and you and your partners can have a great time adapting these positions to your unique body sizes, physical capabilities and erogenous preferences.

As you read the following, bear in mind that we address the active partner in all sexual situations in the second person; "you" may be a man or a woman.

Missionary: Legend has it that the missionary position derived its name from Pacific Islanders, who were surprised to observe missionaries having intercourse in a position they themselves never used. In the missionary position, the receptive partner lies on her back while you lie on top of her. This position is frequently disdained as being somehow old-fashioned or "oppressive" to women, as it limits the receptive partner's movement and, in and of itself, provides little direct clitoral stimulation. In fact, many women feel there are plenty of reasons to enjoy the missionary position.

I like to be on my back. I like to feel the weight and skin of another person on my body. So much more of my body gets stimulated that way. When I sit on another, only one small part of me gets stimulated.

Oh god—I'm still a feminist if I like the missionary position, aren't I? I like it because I can still reach my clit that way. I can't come when I'm on top.

I actually enjoy it the most in missionary position. It's easier for me to relax—otherwise, it feels really great, but I can't come.

There are several enjoyable variations on the missionary position. In a male/female couple, the woman can keep her legs down straight, thereby narrowing her vaginal opening and increasing pleasurable friction on the man's penis. This variation also makes it more likely that her partner's pubic bone will rub against her clitoris. Another alternative is for the woman to spread her legs and bend her knees—this allows for deeper penetration and also makes it easier for her to move her hips. For some women, freedom of movement is crucial to reaching orgasm during intercourse.

This is the way I have an orgasm: my partner on top, my legs on his shoulders or chest, while I grasp his shoulders for leverage with my legs, so I can help pump.

I do orgasm with penis penetration if I can move my body freely.

Woman-on-top: Although the name of this position implies opposite-sex intercourse, it's equally delightful whether there's another woman-on-bottom or a man-on-bottom. In this flip of the missionary position, you lie on your back with your partner straddling you; she can be facing your head or facing your feet. In one variation, she lies down with her back on your chest.

Man on back, woman's back on his front, semi-sitting, semi-lying down. This is a tough one to maneuver, but so worth the effort!

Woman-on-top is excellent for women who would like to control the depth of thrusting, such as those recovering from vaginismus or childbirth or those who have had hysterectomies. It's also a particularly comfortable position for pregnant women or women who are considerably smaller than their partners. Women who are larger than their partners and who enjoy deep penetration may find they want to sit directly on their partner, rather than kneeling.

Vaginal intercourse, rear entry

The woman-on-top position is versatile and allows easy stimulation of her nipples and clitoris. Many men find that they are more relaxed and experience less intense stimulation when they're on their backs, so they can delay ejaculation more easily in this position:

I like penetration especially when I'm on top and can angle it deeply into my body.

I have very large breasts and like to be on top with my partner licking and sucking them.

Me on top means I get to control the whole thing, including when he comes. I can do it slowly and move in twisty ways that just seem to get me in the right place. Plus, I get to look at him from a neat angle.

Rear Entry: Also referred to as "doggie-style," this position places your partner on her stomach or on her elbows and knees while you either stand or kneel behind her. It's very comfortable for women in the later stages of pregnancy, larger women and those who are smaller than their partners. This position has a lot of fringe benefits—it's great for G-spot stimulation, it allows easy stimulation of the nipples and clitoris, and it's conducive to vibrator play. The woman can lie on her stomach or on pillows with a vibrator pressed against her clitoris.

From behind is when I want really intense stimulation.

My fave is "doggie" style. I get the most G-spot stimulation, and I can better control how much penetration I get.

In rear entry, the natural curve of the vagina coincides with the curve of the erect penis or curved dildo, so deep thrusting is more comfortable in this position than most others. And there's no question that it's arousing to hang on to your partner's hips and move her to and fro—rear entry allows both of you a pleasurable freedom of pelvic movement.

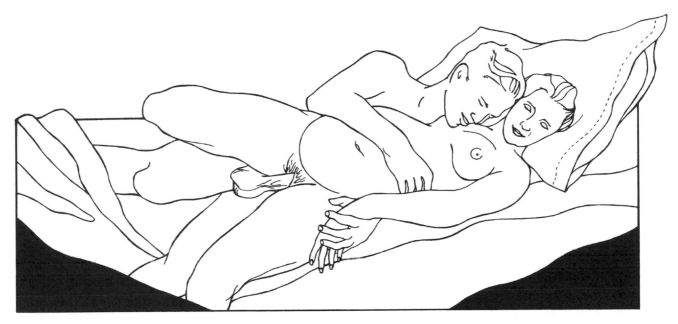

Vaginal intercourse, side by side

I like my lover to push herself as hard as she can when I'm behind her.

Some people find it depersonalizing not to be able to see a partner's face during intercourse, and associate rear entry with sex between animals:

Doggie-style is nice once in a while, but it seems a bit impersonal despite the stimulation opportunity.

Rear entry is also commonly associated with anal intercourse—even though it's only one of many possible positions for anal sex. Being the sexually diverse and creative animals humans are, many people find these two factors erotically inspiring.

I like being penetrated from behind. We often play-act as a gay male couple, so penetration from behind adds to that fantasy.

Side by side: In this position, you and your partner either lie facing each other—with thighs intertwined—or lie facing the same direction in a spoons position. A slight variation puts your partner on her back, draping her legs over your thighs. Side by side positions are good for long,

leisurely intercourse, as the stimulation they provide is somewhat less direct than that of other positions.

Side by side is a great warm-up—it builds the tension.

The spoons position allows the receptive partner to control the depth of thrusting, and since it ensures that neither partner will have to support the other's weight, it's another excellent position for women in the late stages of pregnancy. It's similarly convenient for two people with a wide discrepancy in size or height. Finally, side by side is a good position for older people or those with disabilities that limit stamina or mobility.

Once I did something fabulous when we were in the spoons position. I bent over so that I was perpendicular to his body. It was very easy to move and set rhythm freely, and penetration was at a very nice angle.

Sitting: Sitting positions create a relaxed and intimate mood. They allow for lots of full-body contact without intense genital stimulation. You can sit intertwined on a bed or you can sit on a chair, with your partner straddling you. Intercourse on a chair can be a particularly good position for couples with a wide discrepancy in size, pregnant women or any women who want to control the depth of penetration.

Definitely my favorite position is with my partner sitting "Indian style" with my legs around his waist and our arms wrapped around one another. This not only gives the richest penetration, but it also allows us to touch and have our hands free to roam one another's body. It is a good intimate, as opposed to sexual, position.

My current favorite is a variation of the woman-on-top position—screwing on a chair. The chair position is great, because it's restful, allows full stomach to stomach contact and allows the man the chance to caress the woman's neck, back, shoulder blades, ass and anus—hmm, delightful!

Standing: Couples who happen to be the same body-type may enjoy intercourse standing up. Standing up is not the most common position for intercourse, although you may enjoy variations of this position in which your partner is sitting on a counter, tabletop or airplane bathroom sink while you stand facing her. Standing positions lend themselves to the fantasy that both of you are so swept away by passion that you have to grab each other no matter where you are—which gives them an undeniable and widespread appeal.

Anal Penetration

There are just as many physiological reasons for men and women to enjoy anal penetration as there are for women to enjoy vaginal penetration. The anus is rich in nerve endings and participates with our genitals in the engorgement, muscular tension and contractions of sexual arousal and orgasm. Pressure and fullness in the rectum feels pleasurable to some men and women, just as vaginal fullness feels pleasurable to some women. Anal penetration can stimulate both the perineal area and G-spot in women and the bulb of the penis and prostate gland in men. Many of us find anal stimulation intensely pleasurable.

I enjoy both vaginal and anal penetration. I think my anus is more sensitive than my vagina, and I don't admit this to a lot of people.

You may already have discovered that anal stimulation greatly enhances and intensifies masturbation, oral sex or intercourse. After all, it's hard to miss that power-packed little bud of erogenous sensitivity located only inches from your genitals. Anal stimulation is an integral part of many folks' sex lives. Some individuals with disabilities that numb sensation in their genitals retain the capacity for pleasurable sensation in the anus. Women who have grown disinterested in vaginal penetration, perhaps after childbirth or with the onset of menopause, may prefer exploring anal penetration. Anal penetration offers men the experience of being physically entered, while countless men and women alike describe anal penetration as being a uniquely relaxing and meditative experience.

Despite these physical truths, those of us who enjoy anal play are understandably reluctant to stand up and be counted. From the time we're old enough to start toilet-training, we're taught that the anus is the dirtiest part of our bodies and that it needs to be brought under strict control. The same orifice that was a source of innocent pleasure during infancy becomes a source of shame and confusion in childhood. Many of us learn to hold a lot of tension in our anus, and the resulting health problems such as constipation or hemorrhoids convince us that the anus is, at best, a neutral area and, at worst, a painful one. It's no wonder that many adults are unable to conceive of the anus as an erogenous zone.

As for anal penetration, I've never tried it because it seems kind of awful. Doesn't appeal to me personally though people I know enjoy it.

Although our focus here is on encouraging you to get to know and love your anus, we should note that feelings of shame and transgression can be highly erotic, and that some people doubtlessly enjoy anal play in part because they feel they're messing around where they shouldn't. If the anal taboo is preventing you from taking pleasure in this sensitive and stimulating portion of your anatomy, we hope the information in these pages will help you overcome your negative associations. If the anal taboo is enhancing your pleasure, let us be the first to assure you that anal play is naughty, kinky and downright nasty.

Recent years have seen a slight lifting of the anal taboo: We in the sex-toy business can testify to a surge of interest in anal pleasure. On the one hand, the AIDS epidemic has spawned general confusion around the relative riskiness of anal play—popular perception has conflated anal sex and disease-transmission to such an extent that many people incorrectly believe that AIDS can be transmitted via anal intercourse even if neither partner is infected with the AIDS virus. On the other hand, the mere fact that anal intercourse is now routinely referred to in newspaper articles, public health brochures and schoolrooms across the nation has brought anal stimulation out of the closet. Once something is normalized as a topic for discussion, it's just a hop, skip and a jump to normalizing it as an activity. We field countless questions about anal play every day in our stores, while the classic guidebook *Anal Pleasure and Health* remains one of our best-selling books month after month.

Inhibitors

FEAR OF FECES Probably the most common factor that inhibits folks from experimenting with anal play is the fear of encountering feces. To address this appropriately, let's review a little anatomy. The anal canal is less than an inch long and leads into the rectum, which is anywhere from five to nine inches long. The rectum leads, in turn, to the colon, which is where feces accumulate until you're ready to defecate. The rectum is only a passageway, not a storage place, so it's unlikely you'll come across more than a few traces of feces in the course of your explorations. The fact that the rectum's sexual status suffers due to its participation in the digestive process is somewhat arbitrary. After all, the digestive process starts with your mouth, and nobody considers kissing a disgusting activity.

Still skittish? You might want to take a bath together before indulging in anal play, or better yet, you could pop on a latex glove or condom before making your first foray. Some people feel more confident if they rinse their rectum out with water, using a turkey-baster syringe or an enema. Unless you're preparing for some deep penetration or anal fisting, we wouldn't encourage the use of enemas. Enemas take time and finesse—you have to monitor the temperature of the water you're using, the water pressure and the height of the enema bag. A simple dip in the tub is sufficient preparation for most anal activities.

FEAR OF DISEASE The second primary inhibitor to anal experimentation is the fear of disease transmission. Anal sex is so linked in the popular imagination with gay male sex, and gay male sex has unfortunately become so linked with HIV transmission, that many people assume that anal sex in and of itself will cause disease. Neither of these associations is particularly logical. Plenty of gay men never engage in anal intercourse, and plenty of heterosexuals and lesbians do. Specific activities don't transmit disease; viruses transmit disease. Unprotected anal intercourse, like unprotected vaginal intercourse, is simply one way in which someone infected with an STD can conceivably transmit it to his partner.

The lining of the rectum is considerably more delicate and richer in blood vessels than the walls of the vagina, so it's easy to scratch or tear the tissue of the rectum, and easy for bodily fluids to pass from the rectum into your bloodstream. You should never insert anything into your anus that does not have a completely smooth surface, and you should never engage in penis/anal intercourse without putting a condom on the penis. To prevent possible bacterial infections, never switch your attentions from a woman's anus to her vagina without stopping to wash your hands, change your glove or change your condom.

Forget my behind; that's not a turn-on for me. All I can think of if someone messes with it is, "Quick! Scrub up with soap so you don't give me an infection!"

HOMOPHOBIA Anal sex is inextricably linked in many people's minds with gay male sex.

I have occasional anxiety about the homosexual act of anal play, but I like the forbidden nature.

This is just one more manifestation of the tyranny of the notion that intercourse is the main event of any sexual encounter. If sex by definition presumes sticking a penis into a vagina, then gays and lesbians are presumed to simulate this one "true" sex act by engaging in anal intercourse or by strapping on dildos to penetrate each other. In fact, sexual orientation is not defined by how you fuck, but who you fuck. There are gay men who never engage in anal intercourse, lesbians who've never seen a dildo, and heterosexual couples who love anal sex. The fact that the taboo against anal sex is partially motivated by homophobia is one more example of how homophobia restricts not only the freedom of gay people, but ultimately the freedom of all sexual people.

Anal Dos

DO RELAX The anus is ringed by two sphincter muscles, one right on top of the other. The external sphincter is the one you voluntarily control when you allow yourself to defecate. The internal sphincter is involuntary. This muscle will tighten up reflexively if you try to force your way into your anus, resulting in the excruciatingly sharp pain familiar to anyone who has rushed anal penetration. With practice and patience, it's possible to gain some control over this internal sphincter, but it will always serve as the guardian of the gateway, tensing up if you try to insert too much too soon.

Before you try to incorporate anal play into sex with a partner, set aside some time to do some anal exploration yourself. Lubricate both your finger and your anus, and position your finger at the anal opening. Concentrate on your breathing: Inhale and tighten your pelvic muscles, exhale and release your muscles. As you exhale, try bearing down slightly with your muscles, and sweep the tip of your finger into your anus. Leave your finger in place while you continue to inhale and exhale. You should be able to feel your two sphincter muscles contracting and releasing around your fingertip. If you're comfortable with the way your fingertip feels, you may want to insert your finger all the way into your rectum. Try moving your finger in and out or in a circular movement. You'll probably find it pleasant to angle your finger toward the front of your body: toward the perineal sponge and G-spot in women

and toward the bulb of the penis and prostate in men. Maintain a relaxed pace. If anything hurts or causes your muscles to tense up, stop moving or stop what you're doing altogether. The point is to enjoy yourself and to learn about what feels good.

DO USE LUBE The anus and rectum don't produce any lubrication of their own, and you absolutely must use some kind of lubricant any time you engage in anal penetration. Bear in mind this cautionary understatement from one of our customers:

Trying to put a dildo up my butt when I did not have lube was not a good idea.

Since water-based lubricants dry up more quickly than oils, some folks feel that oil-based lubricants are optimal for anal play. We would still suggest that you avoid the risk of using oils. Instead, shop for thicker varieties of water-based lubricant, such as Embrace or K-Y Jelly, and use them abundantly. Look for lubes that don't contain nonoxynol-9, as this is a potentially irritating to delicate rectal tissue. As a fundamental precaution, if you've been on the receiving end of an oil-based lubricant you should refrain from being on the receiving end of penis/anus intercourse for the next few days, as oils could linger in your rectum and destroy the next condom that comes your way.

Unfortunately, some lubricants and lotions containing anesthetic ingredients such as benzocaine are specifically marketed for anal sex. What's wrong with this picture? The last thing you want to do is to numb sensation in your anus, thereby deadening your awareness of what's going on in your body. The network of nerve endings in your anus and outer rectum is your best defense against hurting yourself. As with any kind of penetration, pain is a warning signal that you should stop what you're doing.

DO RESPECT YOUR ANATOMY The anus and rectum are made of smooth, highly expandable tissue—it's physiologically possible for your rectum to expand to accommodate an entire hand if you're anesthetized during surgery or if you're a practitioner of anal fisting. As with vaginal penetration, physiological capabilities have little to do with personal preferences. You may be perfectly happy with a pinkie's worth of anal attention, or you may enjoy anal intercourse with a large dildo. If you insert anything longer than nine inches, you'll come to the entrance to your colon. Devotees of deep anal fisting may wish to delve into the colon, but average aficionados of anal penetration are happy to restrict their paddling to the relative shallows of the rectum.

Knowledge of the shape of the rectum is especially relevant to comfortable anal penetration. The outer or lower rectum tilts toward the front of your body for about three inches, at which point it curves back to the spine for another few inches, and then tilts slightly forward again where it meets up with the sigmoid colon. You'll need to keep these curves in mind when you insert a finger, dildo or penis. You'll want to angle toward the front of your body in order to follow the initial tilt of the rectum while simultaneously angling gently upward to negotiate the first curve of the rectum. Practice by feeling your way along slowly while experimenting with body positioning—just as no two snowflakes are alike, no two rectums are alike, and you'll need to adjust to your own idiosyncrasies. If you're inserting anything more than four inches long, it should be flexible enough to adapt to the curves of your rectum.

Do Use Common Sense Anything that goes into your anus should be smooth, seamless and free of rough, scratchy edges. It's all too easy to damage the delicate tissue lining the rectum. This means you may need to file down the plastic seams on your anal beads.

You should also make sure that there's no way you can lose hold of whatever is going into your anus. That butt plug or battery vibrator you're wielding should have a flared base, so that even if you let go, it won't slip out of reach into your rectum. At a bare minimum, your toy should be over seven inches long so that you can keep your grip on it. If you do happen to let a toy slip into you, it's more than likely that if you wait patiently in a relaxed position, it will come back out the way it went in. Many of us, however, find it hard to be patient and relaxed with a rudderless sex toy on the loose in our bodies, and in certain instances, the toy can get pushed all the way up into the colon, at which point surgical intervention will be necessary to remove it. Save yourself the possible headaches: Choose and use your toys carefully.

Do Communicate If you're on the receiving end of anal penetration with a partner, you should feel as much in control as you do during solo play. It's up to you to help your partner negotiate your rectum safely and comfortably. Communicate about what feels good, and let your partner know immediately if you experience any pain. You should be able to stop what you're doing at any time. Anal play can be an extremely intimate encounter with a partner provided you trust each other sufficiently to relax and enjoy.

Fingers

Fingers provide probably the most common source of anal stimulation. The light, sensitive touch of a finger is the ideal way to titillate the anus and coax it into opening up. If you're going to play with your partner's anus, we suggest you put on a latex glove or a finger cot. Not only will this take care of any hygiene concerns you or your partner might have, but you'll be protecting your partner from your fingernails and any rough skin. Start by applying lube around the anal opening and circle your finger around the soft folds of anal tissue. Take the time to look at your partner's anus: You may be surprised at how sweet and innocent it looks—not like an "asshole" at all. Many people find that gentle stroking of their highly enervated anal opening is all the anal stimulation they desire.

I like the feel of a finger pressing lightly against my asshole.

I adore digital pressure to the outside of my anus.

If your partner becomes sufficiently relaxed, she or he may bear down and slide right onto your finger. Your fingertip should be reaching toward the front of the body, rather than crooking up toward the tailbone. The sphincter muscles may tense up automatically as soon as you enter, so hold your finger still at first until the anus relaxes around it. Then feel free to insert your finger more deeply, exploring the outer rectum. You can circle your finger, tap and stroke the walls of the rectum, or move your finger gently in and out. If your partner is experiencing anal penetration for the first time, she or he may find the sensation a little unsettling. The primary association we all have with pressure in our rectum is that we're about to defecate, so your partner may feel briefly uncomfortable while adjusting to the sensation.

We hope it goes without saying that anal penetration is a great adjunct to other types of stimulation. In fact, many couples regularly incorporate anal fingering into their oral sex or intercourse routine.

During sex, an occasional fingering by my girlfriend while I'm inside her is great.

I enjoy my partner putting a finger in my anus during oral sex. But it makes me come a lot faster. I also like her tongue on and in my anus.

My favorite position is when I'm on my back in a pleasure swing, with my knees to my chest, while my cock is sucked and stroked and a finger is penetrating my butt.

Anal Fisting

Like vaginal fisting, anal fisting is something of an art form, and is spoken of in almost spiritual terms by its practitioners. At first blush, the notion of anal fisting strikes many of us as impossible at best and dangerous at worst.

Fist? Don't people need diapers after that?

The truth is that the rectum is highly expandable, and every human being's rectum is capable of accommodating a hand without sustaining damage. The proportion of human beings who are able to voluntarily relax their anus to this extent is, however, relatively small. People who engage in anal fisting frequently take hours to build up to any one session, and experience it as almost a meditative union of mind and body, involving total relaxation and receptivity. Fisting is an esoteric sexual discipline that has been practiced around the world throughout history.

All the basic rules of anal play—relaxation, lubrication and communication—apply ten-fold where fisting is concerned. Never go into a fisting session if either you or your partner is drunk or stoned.

Drugs can numb your awareness of pain, and pain during anal penetration is always an indication that what you're doing is not right. Given the delicate nature of the rectum, it's especially important to make sure your nails are filed short and smooth and that you're covering them with a latex glove.

Since water-based lubricants dry up more quickly than oils, some people feel that oil-based lubricants are the only way to go when it comes to fisting, arguing that latex gloves are thicker than condoms and are unlikely to break down from contact with oil during the limited time period they're worn. We would still suggest that you avoid the risk of using oils.

Anal fisting is frequently and misleadingly listed as an activity that's high-risk for sexually transmitted diseases. Although fisting could conceivably cause tears in the rectum, which would be vulnerable to subsequent encounters with infected bodily fluids, fisting is not inherently more risky than any other type of anal penetration. However, the fister should always wear a latex glove to minimize the chance of transmitting infection.

The techniques described in the section on vaginal fisting are applicable to anal fisting. We don't feel, however, that anyone can read one or two pages on the subject of anal fisting in a general interest book and consider him or herself sufficiently educated to take a crack at this quite sophisticated sexual practice. If you're interested in learning more about fisting, we recommend you track down an excellent book devoted to the subject, *Trust: The Hand Book.*

Anal Intercourse

Anal intercourse is an activity that has many fans, and it's been practiced in all civilizations throughout history. If you and your partner would like to experiment with anal intercourse, please discuss your intentions ahead of time. As with any anal play, intercourse requires considerable relaxation and good communication, and it's best not to embark on it on the spur of the moment. One bad experience with rushed, forced anal penetration is frequently all it takes to make someone swear off anal sex for life. That dense concentration of anal nerve endings that communicates exquisite pleasure when approached respectfully communicates agonizing pain when handled roughly.

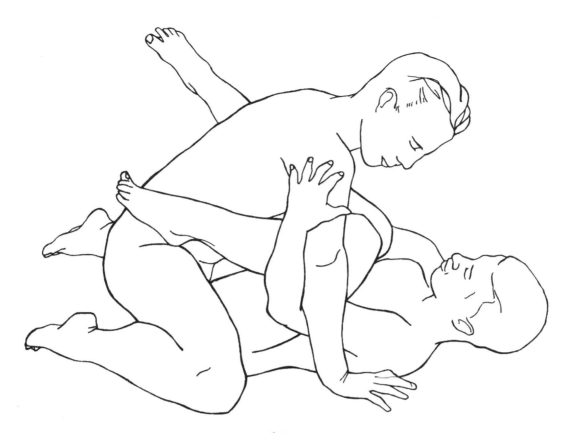

Anal intercourse

I've only once had anal penetration that was pleasant, because he knew to go slow and use lubrication.

The following discussion of anal intercourse applies to both opposite-sex and same-sex couples and to penis/anus intercourse or dildo/anus intercourse.

EXPECTATIONS Get clear with your partner about your respective expectations. Are you assuming that anal intercourse will be just like vaginal intercourse in terms of preparation, pace and sensation? Bear in mind that the anus and rectum require a more deliberate and gradual approach than the vagina does. You may not be able to insert your entire penis or dildo, or to thrust as vigorously as you do during vaginal or oral sex. You and your partner should have discussed in advance whether or not it's okay for you to come while inside the rectum. As you approach orgasm, your movements may become a little less controlled, and this could cause your partner to tense

up and experience some discomfort. As a fundamental safer sex precaution, you should always wear a condom during anal intercourse regardless of whether or not you ejaculate. You may find that your anxieties around inflicting pain or the more lengthy process of getting your penis inserted causes your erection to subside. Try not to be too goal-oriented in your approach, and allow yourselves to have fun exploring the range of sensations—let your level of arousal ebb and flow. After all, nobody has got a stop watch trained on you.

If you're being penetrated, you may have anxieties that you're taking "too long" to relax and feel that you should grit your teeth and bear any painful sensations out of some sense that "the show must go on." Please respect your own responses, and don't buy into the popular misconception that anal sex "has" to hurt. It will be a more pleasurable experience for both of you if you're completely relaxed and receptive. If the physical sensations become too much for you or you feel frightened and out of control, by all means, stop what you're doing.

The pleasure derived from being penetrated results from the internal massaging pressure and fullness in the rectum. Direct prostate stimulation leads many men to orgasm solely from being anally penetrated. Some women, though fewer than men, can also orgasm solely from anal intercourse. If orgasm is your goal, you should certainly incorporate other types of genital stimulation into what you're doing. A vibrator on your clitoris, a dildo in your vagina, a hand around your penis, a nipple clamp tugging your nipple or a cock ring snapped around your testicles can all contribute to your experience of anal intercourse. Some people feel that anal intercourse produces unique sensations of serenity and intimacy, and it may be that these sensations will be powerful enough to make orgasm seem irrelevant.

Anal intercourse is infrequent, but an exclusive "high."

POSITIONS Despite the common assumption that anal intercourse almost by definition takes place in a rear-entry position, all the positions used in vaginal intercourse can be adapted to anal intercourse. The most important consideration for any position you adopt is that the receptive partner should control how and when penetration takes place. For convenience's sake and to avoid a morass of pronouns, let's assume that Tarzan and Jane are about to try anal intercourse for the first time. Jane has fashioned a beautiful dildo harness out of jungle vines, and Tarzan is eager to enact his fantasy of feeling Jane moving inside him.

Before Jane attempts penetration, she starts by teasing Tarzan's anus with her finger. She applies plenty of lubricant with her fingers, taking the time to really work the lubricant past the anal opening and into the rectum. (Some people find it helpful to co-opt a vaginal cream applicator in order to insert lube well into the rectum.) Once Tarzan's anus is happy and relaxed and able to comfortably accommodate two of Jane's fingers, Jane positions the tip of her banana dildo at Tarzan's anal opening and holds it there. Tarzan inhales and exhales a few times, while contracting and relaxing his sphincter muscles. When he feels ready, he bears down onto Jane's banana. Jane moves forward into him ever so slightly, but she

holds the banana still just inside his rectum while his muscles adjust to the sensation. After Tarzan has gotten used to the sensation of fullness, he asks Jane to move her hips slowly back and forth.

Tarzan and Jane quickly become expert in anal intercourse, and try all the following positions. In missionary position, Tarzan lies on his back with his knees pulled to his chest and his feet over Jane's shoulders. This allows for deep penetration, prostate stimulation and face-to-face contact, although Tarzan doesn't have much freedom of movement and sometimes his legs get cramped.

In rear entry, Tarzan is on his elbows and knees, while Jane penetrates him from behind. Jane likes the fact that this position allows her to do a lot of pelvic thrusting, while Tarzan likes the deep penetration it affords, not to mention that Jane can easily reach around and play with his penis. Sometimes they try a variation where both are standing up with Tarzan bent slightly at the waist and bracing himself against a tree. When Tarzan wants total control of the rate of penetration, Jane lies on her back while he straddles her and sits down on the dildo. This is a convenient position in which to stimulate each other. When neither of them wants to support the weight of the other, they lie side by side in a spoons position. This does not allow for deep penetration or much thrusting movement, but it is a comfortable intimate position, which allows plenty of opportunity for full-body stimulation.

You may want to try all the same positions as Tarzan and Jane, or you may make up your own variations. Just stick to the golden rule of anal sex, and make sure that the receptive partner has ultimate control over the movement and pace of penetration. Some people get an added erotic thrill by identifying anal intercourse as a power play, in which the receptive partner is the submissive bottom under the control of his or her dominant penetrator. This dynamic can enhance your experience, especially if you are aroused by the taboo of anal sex as a forbidden activity. There are just as many people for whom power play would be distasteful and who prefer to experience anal intercourse as an equal melting together of two bodies.

When being fucked I like to straddle my partner who is lying on his back. I like to have control of how the penis enters me until I've loosened up enough to actually be fucked by him. When fucking I like to be sitting up with my partner sitting in my lap so that we can kiss and play with each other's nipples—so that it seems more equal than dominant/submissive.

Intercourse Inhibitors and Enhancers

Inhibitors

Sometimes intercourse is more easily said than done. A few of the more common inhibitors have already been discussed above: fear of penetration, vaginismus, lack of sufficient lubrication and excessive lubrication. We'd like to add a few words about two more experiences that are specific to men and can interfere with pleasurable intercourse.

PREMATURE EJACULATION   Whether you are ejaculating "prematurely" or not is in the eye of the beholder. There are no absolutes when it comes to how long intercourse "should" take place before a man ejaculates. Whether the time involved is a minute or an hour, ejaculation is only premature if either partner wishes it had been delayed. It's worth noting that very few gay men report problems with premature ejaculation—presumably since they're not worrying about whether or not a female partner will reach orgasm, they don't feel pressure around how long they do or don't take to ejaculate. As men age, the rate at which they reach orgasm slows down naturally.

In the past, remedies for premature ejaculation tended to focus on trying to counteract sexual arousal or to deaden sensation in the penis. You're probably familiar with the stereotype of a man reciting baseball statistics to himself during intercourse so he can "last longer," and the adult industry does a booming business in numbing gels sold as "erection prolongers," which contain anesthetic ingredients.

Fortunately, in recent years therapists and their patients have learned that the best way to gain control over one's physical responses is to increase rather than decrease awareness of sensation. Common and highly effective treatments for premature ejaculation involve learning to identify the moment of "ejaculatory inevitability" right before

orgasm. If you feel that you're reaching orgasm sooner than you'd like, practice the following stop-start exercises. Start by masturbating. Pay attention to your level of arousal, and when you feel you're about to reach orgasm, stop moving, stop touching yourself for a moment and let the arousal ebb slightly before starting up again. Repeat this a few times and see how long you can stimulate yourself each time before you have to back off again. After fifteen minutes or so, consciously allow yourself to come. The fact that you've built up to orgasm slowly and deliberately could well result in a particularly enjoyable orgasm.

The next step is to incorporate this stop-start technique into partner sex. Gradually intensify the stimulation you're receiving in each session, so that you gain confidence that you can control your responses under increasingly arousing circumstances. It's usually recommended that a man learning to control ejaculation progress from masturbating with no lubricant, to masturbating with lubricant, to intercourse with his partner on top of him while he lies still, to intercourse with him moving. Some men utilize a variation of the stop-start method known as the "squeeze technique." With this technique, you forestall an imminent orgasm by grasping the area right below your

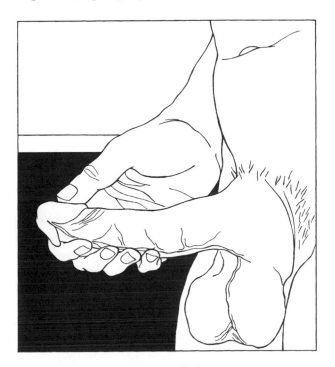

Squeeze technique

glans between your thumb and forefingers, and squeezing. After a few seconds of squeezing, you can resume stimulation and build yourself up to the point of ejaculatory inevitability again.

You may also find it helpful to use your PC muscle to delay ejaculation. Since orgasm is accompanied by contractions of the PC muscle, consciously relaxing this muscle at the point of high arousal can help you back off from the edge of orgasm. Similarly, positions such as woman-on-top are useful, as they reduce muscular tension throughout your body and make it easier for you to focus on and control your pelvic muscles. On the other hand, some men find that contracting, almost clenching, their PC muscle when they feel on the verge of orgasm helps them bring their arousal down a notch. Through consciously contracting and relaxing your PC muscle, you can learn to take an active role in modulating your level of arousal.

Bear in mind that you're not going to gain control over your body by denying yourself sensation. Instead, let yourself take conscious pleasure in the different levels of arousal you're capable of experiencing. As you learn to postpone the immediate gratification of orgasm, you may well discover a subtle range of sensation that is infinitely more gratifying.

ERECTILE DYSFUNCTION More commonly referred to by the loaded term, *impotence,* the inability to sustain an erection is something that all men experience at one point or another in their lives, whether as a result of a few too many drinks, physical fatigue or lack of desire. Recurring erectile dysfunction is another matter, and is generally the result of ongoing physical rather than temporary situational problems.

It's interesting to note that until about ten years ago, the medical wisdom was that eighty to ninety percent of all erectile dysfunction was caused by psychological factors and only ten to twenty percent was believed to be the result of physical problems. Today, the exact opposite is believed to be true. Erection is a complex physical process, and problems may arise at each stage of this process. For an erection to take place, your brain must send a signal pumping blood into the penis, the tissues in the penis must fill with enough blood to create

an erection, and the erectile tissues must expand against their surrounding membrane with enough force to squeeze shut the veins that would normally carry blood back out of the penis. Nerve damage caused by pelvic surgery, spinal cord injuries, multiple sclerosis or diabetes can interfere with the signal the brain sends to the penis. Hardened arteries or injuries to the pelvic area can interfere with blood flow into the penis. Diabetes, smoking, pelvic injury and aging can all reduce the elasticity of the erectile tissues, resulting in blood leaking out of the erection.

If you have had recurrent episodes in which you couldn't sustain an erection, the first thing to do is determine whether this failure has physical or psychological causes. All men who are physically capable of having erections have several erections throughout the course of a night's sleep. A doctor can set you up with a device like a mechanized cock ring, which will measure the quantity and firmness of the erections you have throughout the night. If you are having erections while you sleep, presumably your difficulties with erection during waking hours are psychological, not physiological in origin. Maybe you are forcing yourself into sexual situations you don't want to be in. Maybe your sex life has become oppressively goal-oriented, rather than focused on pleasure. Consider taking a sabbatical from partner sex, or restrict your partner interactions to nondemand touching, such as massage. You may want to contact a sex therapist to discuss your feelings and some of the possible origins for your current inability to sustain an erection.

If you do find that there are physiological causes for your erectile dysfunction, please don't be disheartened. You and your doctor can explore a number of treatments, including a vacuum pump that you can use to pump up erections as desired, injections that produce temporary erections or surgical implants. Before you leap into any radically invasive treatment program, take the time to evaluate how crucial erections are to your sex life. Many men find that as they get older and are less able to have erections on demand, they expand their sexual activities to include more nongenital touch, oral sex, playing with vibrators, penetrating their partners with a dildo or penetrating their partners with a soft penis. It may be that your partner is less attached to intercourse than you might think and would be happy to build a sex life based on any one of the numerous pleasurable alternatives.

Enhancers

ADDITIONAL STIMULATION People's preferences with regard to how much and what kind of additional stimulation they crave during intercourse can range from "less is more" to "more is more."

I don't like a lot of extra stimulation during fucking, preferring to concentrate on the act.

I don't think two people have enough hands to stimulate everything that wants to get stimulated on me!

There is nothing better than vaginal, anal and clitoral stimulation all at once, especially if I have my nipple clips on at the same time!

We ourselves, as you may have guessed, are of the "more is more" school, and we encourage you to experiment with a wide range of sensations during intercourse. Take advantage of the fact that intercourse is a full-body experience. While joined at the hips, your hands and mouths can roam freely over each other's chests, backs, shoulders, butts and thighs. You may want to focus attention on traditional erogenous zones, or you may find the unexpected arousing.

I love having the hair on my head pulled, especially at the back of my neck.

I really enjoy being scratched on my legs, not too hard, but hard enough. I enjoy having my nipples bitten and my chest rubbed (I sound like a pine cabinet!).

I like it when a man slowly introduces his tongue in my mouth and fucks my mouth with his tongue the exact same way his cock is fucking my cunt. At that point, my mouth comes alive and my imagination soars.

During penetration, I love having my breasts touched at all times. The whole breast, not just the nipple.

As mentioned above, the majority of women need clitoral stimulation in order to reach orgasm during intercourse. Who provides the stimulation may depend on what position you're in. In the missionary or woman-on-top positions, it can be easier for a woman to stimulate herself.

I usually only climax with clitoral stimulation, so this for me is a must. I prefer to do it while I enjoy my partner stimulating my nipples. Oh yes, put a tongue in my ear and your teeth across the back of my neck.

Rear entry or spoons are convenient positions if you want to reach around and stimulate your partner's clitoris. Some women find that, once they are sufficiently aroused, the indirect clitoral stimulation from intercourse is enough to bring them to orgasm, and that additional direct clitoral stimulation might numb them out.

Sometimes clitoral stimulation distracts me when I'm getting ready to come while fucking.

I like clitoral stimulation beforehand, but if I get too much I lose sensitivity.

Both men and women can appreciate having their nipples stimulated during intercourse. Face-to-face positions allow you to suck, lick and bite each other's nipples, while nearly all positions allow for nipple pinching and tweaking. Many people find that the more aroused they are, the more vigorous attention their nipples crave.

Nipple stimulation is practically mandatory to a "hot" experience. I can practically come with a combination of tit biting/licking and lip kissing. The hotter I get, the harder I like my nipples tweaked/pinched. I get annoyed if my partner is gentle with my nipples.

I love breast stimulation even to the point of it hurting—actually that really gets me hot.

Nipple stimulation gets me "over the top" and into orgasm faster than anything.

I have neurological disabilities. It took me a long time to understand that it's okay to have my nipple pinched while I masturbate—it speeds up my ejaculation time.

I have a nipple piercing, which feels good if it is gently played with.

Anal stimulation is another popular intercourse enhancer for men and women alike. Preferred techniques range from the simple pressure of a finger or thumb stroking the anal opening, to some form of penetration: a finger, several fingers, a dildo or a plug. Nearly every intercourse position lends itself handily to one or both partners reaching around to play with the other's anus. Men may enjoy feeling a finger stroking the prostate gland during intercourse—to do so, reach about three inches into the rectum, and stroke toward the front of his body. Some women find double penetration extremely arousing. It provides stimulation of the sensitive perineal area between the vagina and anus, while the sensation of pressure on both sides of the vaginal wall can be quite exciting for both parties involved. Of course, for every woman who finds double penetration double the fun, there's a woman who finds it unpleasantly overwhelming.

My favorite thing is to have a butt plug in while I'm fucking either a penis, finger or dildo. That's a great feeling—like you are totally filled.

I enjoy anal stimulation/penetration, but combined with vaginal penetration, it's sometimes distracting.

Many men also appreciate having their testicles played with during intercourse. Try reaching between his legs and forming your fingers into a ring around his scrotum and the base of his penis. Either hold on, applying a gentle pressure, or tug gently on the scrotum. You could also try palming each testicle separately, but bear in mind that a fluttering, light touch may feel more ticklish than sexy.

My favorite stimulation during intercourse is a firm yet gentle grasping of the entire scrotal sac.

It conveys a sense of control that overcomes my wife's sexual reticence.

I like to have a woman stroke and squeeze my testicles during sex.

SPATIAL ARRANGEMENTS From the humble pillow to the elaborate pleasure swing, devices that adjust your physical positioning are time-honored intercourse enhancers. If you're penetrating a woman who's lying on her back, try raising her hips by placing pillows beneath them. This elevated posture allows for deeper penetration—also, the angle of penetration will follow the natural curve of the vagina, allowing your pubic bone to rub against her clitoris. Similarly, if you're penetrating a man who's lying on his stomach, he may enjoy having pillows piled beneath his pelvis. Some men (and women) prefer to masturbate by rubbing against a pillow or bolster and can easily employ this useful technique during rear-entry intercourse.

One position toy on the market is a long web strap attached to buckling cuffs that fit around each ankle. You lie on your back, run the strap around the back of your neck and fasten each cuff around your ankles, thereby comfortably suspending your legs in the air in a highly receptive posture. The idea is that the strap will support you in sustaining a position that might be tiring to hold on your own. Since the pressure this strap puts on your neck may dismay your chiropractor, you might be better off exploring the pleasures of Sportsheets, a soft Velcro bed cover, which comes with four anchor pads and four adjustable restraints. The anchor pads secure to the sheet with Velcro—attach the restraints to the pads, and attach your partner to the restraints and you can position him or her any way your imagination and his or her flexibility allow.

You can also enhance your positioning by having one person sitting or lying down, while the other person stands. For instance, your partner can lie on his or her back at the side of the bed, while you stand on the floor or kneel against the side of the bed. This allows your partner the leverage to raise and lower his or her legs and hips for different angles of penetration, and provides a delightful weightless feeling. Alternatives include intercourse with the receptive partner perched on a table or counter. Different heights will obviously work better for different-sized people.

For the ultimate weightless sensation, try a swing or sling. Hanging chairs have been in existence since ancient times, testament to the timeless appeal of being suspended in mid-air. Your partner can sit in the swing, being rocked to-and-fro onto your penis or dildo, or your partner can straddle you while you lie in the swing. Many people find that being cradled in a swing creates a relaxed, receptive state that greatly enhances and facilitates deep penetration, G-spot stimulation or fisting. Swings are enjoyed by pregnant women and large people, who may particularly appreciate a temporary release from gravity. They're also a boon to folks who suffer from debilitating back pains or other disabilities that limit stamina and mobility.

Swings can range in price from fifty dollars for a simple hammock to between one hundred and two hundred fifty for a genuine sex swing complete with adjustable straps and stirrups for the legs. Installing a swing is a far simpler undertaking than you might think. All you need are two or three eyebolts and some lengths of chain, both of which are easily purchased at any hardware store. Make sure to screw the eyebolts into ceiling beams, rather than into plaster, and use the lengths of chain to adjust the height of the swing to your specifications. *Voilà*. Not only will you be the envy of all your friends, but you'll never have trouble getting a housesitter when you want to go on vacation!

VIBRATORS The same toys that provide delightful stimulation during solo sex are ready and waiting to serve you and your loved ones during partner sex. One of the most common reasons a male/female or female/female couple gives for buying a vibrator is that they'd like to increase clitoral stimulation during intercourse. Penetrating a partner provides direct stimulation to the most sensitive part of a man's penis—his glans—and therefore the vast majority of men reach orgasm from intercourse alone. The majority of women, however, require additional attention to the clitoris in order to reach orgasm during intercourse. This is where a vibrator can be of invaluable assistance.

Any and every style of vibrator can be incorporated into intercourse. It's easy to tuck a battery vibrator or vibrating egg between two bodies, and it's even possible for a woman to take a no-hands approach and wear a vibrator between her legs in a leather pouch or harness. You may be worried that introducing a Hitachi Magic Wand or a Panasonic Massager into your intercourse routine will be the equivalent of slipping between the sheets with a Mack truck, but it ain't so. Even the larger plug-in vibrators rest unobtrusively against a woman's clitoris when you're in woman-on-top, rear-entry or side-by-side positions. Some people also find it comfortable to slip a wand vibrator between their pelvises while in missionary position. Coil vibrators are a less convenient shape to position between two bodies, but you may find that a long G-Spotter attachment on a coil vibrator provides the perfect way to reach the clitoris while holding the vibrator off to the side of your bodies.

As even the most attentive lover can become distracted by his or her own pleasure during intercourse, your best bet would be for the receptive partner to hold the vibrator and control its intensity, pressure and positioning. You may want to experiment with placing a vibrating cock ring at the base of your penis or dildo, although as this moves on and off your partner's clitoris in time with the thrusting of your penis or dildo, the cock ring won't provide reliable, consistent clitoral stimulation. It will provide consistent stimulation to the penis, which some men like and some men find overwhelming.

Men whose partners are using a vibrator during intercourse are often pleasantly surprised at how good the indirect vibrations transmitted through their partner's body feel on their own genitals. A man being penetrated may enjoy holding a vibrator against his penis in all the ways described above.

FRENCH TICKLERS French Ticklers are devices that look like a cross between a condom and a Creepy Crawler. They fit like a cap over the head of a penis or dildo, and they're covered with rubber nubs and fronds. The idea behind French Ticklers is that the sensation of the little tickling fronds going in and out of a woman's vaginal opening will somehow be unutterably pleasing to her. Presumably, French Ticklers sprang from the same great minds who brought us textured condoms. While we certainly believe there are some women who might derive pleasure from the sensation of rubber nubs or ribbed condoms whispering in and out of their vaginas, the whole notion has about as much in common with the average woman's experience as does the story of the princess and the pea.

French Ticklers and a few other stimulus-styled condoms didn't work with women and annoyed me.

About ribbed condoms: Thanks for making me feel like I have no nerve endings. I couldn't tell the difference. Can anyone?

One variation on the French Tickler has some pleasure potential. This is a rubber ring with a knob protruding off one side. The ring is designed to fit around the base of a penis or dildo, with the knob positioned upward, so that it will rub against the woman's clitoris during intercourse. Not every woman will be able to get the knob positioned comfortably or to get consistent, sufficiently intense stimulation from it, but at least this device reflects a rudimentary knowledge of female anatomy. We sell dozens of these doohickeys—for lack of a technical name, called "clit rugs"—in our stores. We suspect their primary function is as a communication tool for initiating the subject of clitoral stimulation during intercourse.

My favorite sex toy is something we call "the rubber thing." It came in the mail with a box of condoms. I refuse to call it a "French Tickler," since it looks like it came from a factory in New Jersey. Some may call it a "cock ring." It has an added appendage for strategic female stimulation during the act of union. But whatever you call 'em, they're GREAT!

COCK RINGS Cock rings are rings designed to fit around the base of the penis and the scrotum, restricting blood flow out of the penis. The resulting pressure can be very pleasurable and can heighten sensation in the penis and testicles. Since cock rings act to constrict the veins that would allow blood to drain out of an erection, some men find that wearing cock rings prolongs their erec-

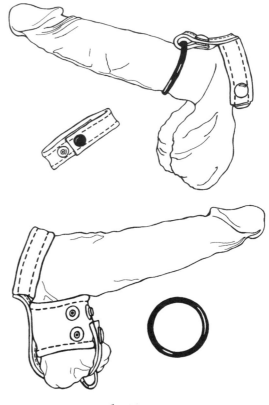

Cock rings

tions or even makes their erection firmer, a side effect that can enhance intercourse for both parties involved.

My most enjoyable sex toy was a cock ring. It was interesting and added about two hours until my orgasm, and when I came—Wow, Bam, Pow, Shazam...

I like when he uses a cock ring and fucks me with his enlarged and super-hard cock.

I enjoy the feel and look a cock ring provides. When I get aroused without the cock ring, my balls pull way up into my body and almost disappear. With the ring around my scrotum, they stay out. It looks great without being painful or uncomfortable.

Of course, this sensation of pressure that some men find arousing may be downright anti-erotic to others.

Our most disappointing sex toy was a cock ring. My partner said it hurt too much for him to enjoy anything else.

If you wear a cock ring that is too tight or if you wear it for too long, you'll cut off your circulation and you may experience bruising. In most cases, the damage from burst blood vessels is minor and only temporary, but why risk it? Stick to wearing easily removable cock rings and don't wear them for more than half an hour at a time. Try not to fall asleep with your cock ring on. Some men do enjoy wearing cock rings for hours at a time, but you should only do this after you've gained enough experience to have a realistic sense of your own limits.

Cock rings come in three varieties: metal, latex or leather. The only way to don the solid metal or latex variety is to put them on before you're erect. You'll need to drop one testicle at a time through the ring and then tuck your flaccid penis down through the ring. Metal cock rings should really only be used by men who have considerable experience with these toys. After all, once you've got the darn thing on, and it's constricting the flow of blood out of your erection, orgasm will be the only pleasant way to make your erection subside. If your metal cock ring begins to feel painfully tight, and you want to remove it, you have two options: Apply ice to your penis, which should shrink that erection down to size, or go to the emergency room and have the ring clipped off. Latex cock rings are slightly less problematic, as you can cut these off as necessary in the privacy of your own home without resorting to power tools.

When all's said and done, you're better off with the leather strap variety. These fasten with either snaps or Velcro, and the moment you begin to experience any discomfort, you can unfasten them, and release the pressure. Furthermore, leather cock-and-ball toys are available in a delightful array of styles: Some have straps that separate each testicle; some have straps that stretch the testicles downwards; some are fitted with D-rings, so you can attach a leash to them; and some are decoratively studded. Leather cock-and-ball toys provide not only sexual but aesthetic stimulation to the wearer and his partner.

KEGELS Don't forget that one of the easiest, most effective ways to enhance any type of penetration is to keep your pelvic muscles well toned. Kegel exercises can provide a delightful way to "warm up" before intercourse, as they increase blood flow to the genitals and increase awareness of genital sensation. A toned muscle is a flexible muscle, and you're likely to experience a great deal more pleasure with strong pelvic muscles than without. Your partner can also enjoy feeling you rhythmically contract and relax your pelvic muscles during intercourse.

Safer Sex

Please don't ever engage in either vaginal or anal intercourse without following some basic safer sex guidelines. Penis/vagina and penis/anus intercourse are activities that transmit viruses and bacteria with alarming efficiency. The friction of intercourse can easily create minute breaks in the tissue of the vagina, rectum or penis, through which bodily fluids can pass. Men should always wear a condom during intercourse to avoid the mingling of bodily fluids. The Reality female condom is another option that can be used as a barrier both for vaginal and anal intercourse.

Intercourse without Penetration

One of the reasons people frequently give for enjoying intercourse is that it allows them simultaneous genital stimulation and full-body contact. We didn't want to leave the topic of intercourse without pointing out that it's possible to reap these simultaneous benefits independent of penetration. Penetration by a penis is fraught with so many consequences, from pregnancy to disease transmission, that it's a shame the variety of full-body "intercourse" techniques aren't more widely discussed and encouraged. Dry humping is dismissed as an archaic adolescent activity simply because it doesn't involve sticking one body part into another. Yet few things feel better than rubbing two bodies against each other, and as anyone who's ever humped a lover's thigh until she or he saw stars knows, there's nothing "dry" about dry humping.

I love to rub against both men and women. I can easily have an orgasm by persistently rubbing against anything hard, like legs.

Dry humping can be a big turn-on, especially when my boyfriend has an erection, and I can feel it through his clothes.

Certain terms for dry humping have come to be associated exclusively with lesbian sex: *frottage* (from the French *frotter,* to rub) and *tribadism* (from the Greek *tribein,* to rub). Both describe the activity of rubbing your clitoris against any part of your partner's body that gets you off, such as her pubic bone, thigh, hip, elbow or knee. One of the great things about dry humping is its ease and versatility. You can be naked or clothed; rolling around the floor in the privacy of your own home or climbing onto each other in the back seat of a parked car; locked in a full embrace or poised on one another's knees.

I really enjoy tribadism with women—I lie on my back, wrap my legs around them and rock—thrilling.

My girlfriend jokingly tells me it's not her I love but her leg. When we're naked, I love to close my eyes and straddle one of her delicious thighs, rubbing my cunt slowly and firmly up and down.

Given the full expanse of your partner's body as your playground, you may be surprised to discover how creative you both can be.

I also love to have a woman hump my ass with her clit. You know, this actually is my favorite!

Once I was about to take my girlfriend's boots off, and I got inspired to rub my cunt on the toe of her boot. She just lay back in a chair watching me, while I gave her a "shoeshine" she'll never forget.

Another variation on dry humping especially for men is *interfemoral* or *intercrural intercourse.* These are the terms for rubbing your penis between your partner's thighs and getting off from the friction this creates. Some classical scholars speculate that this was actually the primary type of intercourse indulged in between Athenian male citizens and the young boys they initiated into adulthood. So much for the popular notion that all those classical Greeks were obsessed with anal intercourse. You may enjoy rubbing your penis against your partner's perineum, between the cheeks of his or her butt or in his or her armpit. Tit-fucking—rubbing your penis in between your partner's breasts—is yet another variation on this theme.

There's a lot of pleasure awaiting you if you let your imagination lead you beyond the confines of traditional sex.

Once, after some time apart, my boyfriend and I made love simply with his hand stuffed inside me and me making love to his cock with my hand wet with my juices, lying as if we were having intercourse, and it was wonderful—like taking apart the elements of traditional fucking and intensifying them.

CHAPTER 11

All About Dildos

A dildo is any object designed (or recruited) for vaginal or anal insertion. Dildos don't vibrate, although many battery vibrators are dildo-shaped. They don't even move unless you put them into motion. Dildos have been around in one form or another, in one culture after another, since the beginning of civilization. According to one source, *The Prehistory of Sex*, dildos *predate* civilization—three-dimensional "phallic batons," including a gorgeous sculpture that clearly resembles a double dildo, have been found in Upper Paleolithic art created over thirty thousand years ago. Dildos are represented in Greek vase paintings of the fifth and fourth centuries B.C. and were worn by actors in classical Greek stage comedies. Throughout the Hellenistic Age, the coastal city of Miletus in Asia Minor was well known as the manufacturing and export center for dildos made of leather or wood. In a Greek dialogue from the third century B.C., one woman complains to another that all their acquaintances are borrowing her beautiful new scarlet leather dildo before she's had the chance to try it herself. The *Kama Sutra* refers to dildos made from wood, tubular stalks or reeds tied to the waist, while a nineteenth-century Chinese painting depicts a woman acrobatically entertaining herself with a dildo strapped to her shoe.

Dildos may be sex toys with a long and honorable history, but in this day and age they just can't get no respect. Kids use the word as a pejorative; sex-toy shoppers hesitate over how "unnatural" it seems to play with a disembodied phallus; and many bristle at the implication that they would crave a "penis-substitute." The bottom line is, dildos make people nervous. Yet we're convinced that it's well worth overcoming your dildo-induced anxiety.

Why Would I Use a Dildo?

The truth is it's natural for the vagina to balloon during sexual excitement, leading many women to crave the pressure and fullness of penetration. It's natural for those of us who appreciate anal stimulation to enjoy feeling the anus contracting around a dildo. Isn't it a bit arbitrary to insist that anything that goes into the vagina or anus should be attached to a human body? After all, we work out on Stairmasters and whip up romantic dinners *à deux* in our Cuisinarts with no concern that we're indulging in "unnatural" pleasures. Instead, consider the theory that the word *dildo* derives from the Italian word *diletto,* or *delight*—dildos are unquestionably among the most delightful sex toys around.

Sometimes a Cigar Is Just a Cigar

The notion that a dildo is a substitute for nature's fine creation, the penis, implies that dildos are second-rate stand-ins for "the real thing." This second-best status has given dildos a bad rap. Women who have fought to overturn the notion that intercourse defines a sexual experience sometimes throw out the baby of pleasurable penetration with the bath water of preconception. For years, it was assumed assumed that lesbians played exclusively with dildos in a simulation of heterosexual intercourse—after all, what else is there for two women to do in bed? In a classic example of cutting off your nose to spite your face, many lesbians responded to the stereotype by condemning dildos as tools of the patriarchy. After all, if a dildo is supposed to be a replacement for a penis, the desire to wear a dildo could be seen as a form of penis envy. Similarly, men who are led to believe that dildos are "fake penises" may react by taking an adversarial stance toward the very toy that could bring them so much pleasure in bed.

Please allow us to set the record straight: A dildo is not a penis-substitute any more than riding a bike is a substitute for taking a stroll. A dildo is an object that allows you to penetrate yourself or your partner in a marvelous variety of ways. Dildos are a logical, dare we say, natural response to the fact that while many of us enjoy having our vaginas or anuses filled, no two of us have exactly the same preferences in terms of the length, width and shape of the object filling us. Why should your experiences with penetration be defined by the dimensions of your current partners' penises or fingers? Few of us limit our dining experiences to eating only whatever is in the refrigerator at home. Think of dildos as the take-out food of the sexual realm; they offer novelty, spice up your routine and teach you about the range of your appetites.

Variety

Not only are no two vaginas alike, but no one vagina is alike all of the time. At different times in her life, at different times during the menstrual cycle and in different intercourse positions, a woman's vagina will accommodate different-sized objects. A wardrobe of different sizes, shapes and colors of dildos is just as crucial to the well-equipped penetration maven as a wardrobe of clothes for all seasons.

In some positions, the contractions of my cunt are too strong for my partner, so we'll use the dildo.

Dildos are good when you can't get enough.

Safety

The primary distinction between sex with a penis and sex with a dildo is that sex with a penis requires a certain amount of negotiation with your partner, whereas sex with a dildo puts you squarely in the driver's seat. You and you alone are in charge of your experience with a dildo, which can take some getting used to. Many of us unconsciously rely on our partners to set the pace of a sexual encounter. Even those of us who regularly masturbate with vibrators may be inclined to abandon ourselves to the vibrations rather than to direct the flow of sensations. Dildos are the ultimate self-assertion tool—it's up to you to manipulate them for your own pleasure. This means that they are also great self-awareness tools, and are particularly helpful for women and men who want to experiment with penetration without the performance anxiety of having a partner present.

Women who are nervous about penetration, or those suffering from vaginismus, can gain confidence through playing with dildos. Post-menopausal women may want to use dildos to keep their vaginas toned for intercourse. Male-to-female transsexuals are required to exercise with dildos (referred to by the medical establishment as "dilators") to keep their surgically created vaginas from contracting shut. Men and women who want to experiment with anal penetration often find solo play with dildos a great way to learn their own preferences and limits. Furthermore, dildos are the ultimate safe-sex fuck-buddy. As long as you keep your dildo clean and condom-clad, it will never infect you or your loved ones with any virus or bacteria.

Fantasy

Best of all, dildos can provide the key to unlock many an inspiring fantasy. Whether you're playing alone or with a partner, dildos offer an easy, safe, fun way to enact scenes from your erotic imagination.

I especially enjoy using the Family Jewels when I'm with a partner—partly for the menage à trois fantasy—partly because it's a turn-on for my partner.

My favorite method of masturbating is riding a dildo with a vibrator. I guess it reminds me of riding a horse!

I like using a dildo while getting fucked or sucking my partner and imagine being with two men.

Dildo Dos

Do Relax

The key to comfortable penetration of any kind is to relax. Your vagina and anus are surrounded by pelvic muscles, and if these muscles are tense or contracted, you won't find penetration a pleasant experience. A lot of us carry tension in our genitals without even being aware of it. Before you settle in to play with a dildo, bring some attention to bear on your genitals. Do Kegel exercises in order to get the blood flowing throughout your pelvis. Put the tip of the dildo at the entrance to your vagina, inhale and contract your vaginal muscles, then exhale and bear down with your vaginal muscles. As you bear down, slip the dildo inside your vagina. If you feel your muscles tensing, deliberately contract and relax them around the dildo. You may find you enjoy squeezing and releasing a dildo, as this enhances awareness of sensation in your vagina. Try combining muscular contractions with moving the dildo: For instance, tighten your pelvic muscles as you slowly slip the dildo out of the vagina, then relax your muscles and let the dildo sink back inside the vagina. Whatever you choose to do, keep breathing and don't force any more of the dildo into your vagina than you can comfortably accommodate. The same considerations apply to anal play with a dildo. Remember, you're the one in control of the experience.

Do Use Lube

Dildos are dry. They don't self-lubricate the way genitals do. Furthermore, dildos frequently have a slightly gummy, porous texture that absorbs moisture. Please always use lubricant with dildos. We don't care how much lubrication you produce on your own—two slippery surfaces slide together much more comfortably than one slippery and one dry surface. Apply lubricant to the dildo and to your vagina or anus. Nobody likes dildo burn, and there's no reason to experience it. The dildo that struck you as impossibly large when you took it for a dry run could well seem the perfect fit once you lube it up.

Do Keep Your Dildos Clean

Dildos come in all types of material. Some dildos are completely smooth and nonporous; others have tacky surfaces and are quite porous. You could transmit infection if bacteria and viruses linger in the pockmarks of your porous dildo. At the very least, wash your dildo with mild soap after each use. Rinse it thoroughly, and let it dry completely before putting it away. Viruses and bacteria won't live on a dry surface.

You can save yourself time and trouble by using condoms with your dildos. Even if you use your dildo exclusively in your own vagina, you can benefit from using condoms; they'll prevent you from reinfecting yourself with a yeast infection and can add years to the life of a cheap rubber dildo. Change the condom every time you swap a dildo with a partner or every time you move the dildo from your anus to vagina. After all, no dildo will ever complain of being forced to wear "a raincoat in the shower."

Do Use Common Sense

Babies will put just about anything into their mouths, and adults have been known to put just about anything into their vaginas and anuses.

I've been penetrated by a pickle, a long-neck beer bottle and a big stick ice cream.

Although we applaud this kind of enterprise and ingenuity, we implore you to use common sense and not to put anything fragile, anything sharp or anything with rough, jagged edges into your body. If you're using a plastic hairbrush handle, make sure that the plastic seams are filed down. Don't use anything wooden that could splinter or anything glass that could shatter, and don't insert an open bottle neck-first—the resulting suction could make it very difficult and dangerous to remove. Certain dildos produced by the adult industry contain wire rods, and you should avoid these. While the wire allows the dildo to be bent or cranked into all kinds of interesting configurations, the metal can tear through the soft rubber of the dildo all too easily. In a worst case scenario, the wire could poke through the dildo and perforate your vaginal or anal walls. There are many materials that make perfectly safe and pleasurable dildos, so there's no excuse for playing with fire.

Styles and Sources

Whereas vibrators can be found camouflaged as "massagers" in department or discount stores, the natural habitat of the dildo is and always will be the sex shop. When Good Vibrations first opened in 1977, the only type of dildo commercially available was the great-big-Caucasian-penis lookalike. The good news is that, since the mid-eighties, more and more cottage industries have sprung up to meet the challenge of producing good quality, imaginatively designed dildos. Now there are more styles and sizes of dildos available than you can shake a stick at, and even the mainstream industry is making an effort to produce dildos in a greater variety of skin tones, as well as in playful colors and materials that don't attempt to imitate nature. You can find generic rubber dildos in any adult bookstore in the country, but you'll only track down upscale silicone, latex, lucite or wood dildos at sex boutiques. See the resource listings for addresses of retail and mail-order sources for dildos.

As discussed in the vibrator chapter, many battery vibrators are dildo-shaped and can be used for penetration both before and after their motors give up the ghost. However, battery vibrators are either made of hard plastic or of a softer material encasing a hard plastic battery case. Unless your preference is for firm penetration, a battery vibrator won't necessarily prove as pleasant as a soft,

resilient dildo. Our focus in this chapter is on dildos, nonvibrating toys designed purely and simply for penetration.

Adult-Industry Dildos

Mainstream commercial dildos, marketed as "novelties," are made of either vinyl or synthetic rubbers molded into flexible, more or less representational penis shapes. While the vinyl variety are lightweight (most are hollow), and nonporous, the synthetic rubber variety are heavy, porous and difficult to keep clean. Grime works its way into the air bubbles under the surface and is impossible to scrub out. Furthermore, scrubbing will only produce unappetizing little rubber pills all over the surface of your dildo. If you own a rubber dildo, please make sure to use condoms with it at all times. On the bright side, rubber dildos are quite flexible, and they will soften up with time, handling and heat to become even more flexible.

The newest material in the adult industry is something we call "jelly jewel rubber"—it's nonporous and easier to keep clean than most rubber. For simplicity's sake, we use the generic term "rubber" to describe all these soft materials. They're actually formulated from PVC (Poly Vinyl Chloride), a plastic that's used in everything from fetish fashion to rainwear to floor tiles.

Vinyl and rubber dildos are primarily produced in either the unique peachy-orange tint that the adult industry has designated Caucasian skin color (think "flesh"-colored Band-Aid) or in a flat black color. While this black color doesn't remotely resemble any human being's skin color, it does go nicely with all your evening wear. In the past couple of years, some novelty manufacturers have produced dildos in somewhat more realistic brown skin tones, and jelly rubber now comes in a wide range of brilliant crayon colors.

These dildos run anywhere from one-and-a-half to two-and-a-half inches in diameter and six to twelve inches in length. Prices ranges from ten dollars for the budget models up to seventy dollars for the larger realistics. Some dildos are set on a handle that allows for delightful maneuverability; some flare at the base, allowing you to wear them in a dildo harness; some come complete with scrotum and testicles; and some feature rubber

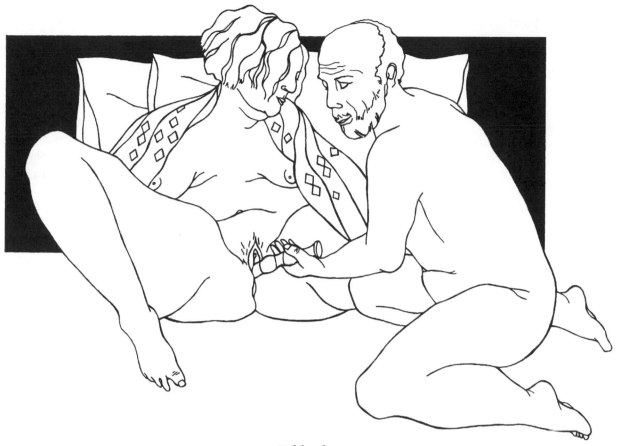

Dildo play

nubs at the base, ostensibly as clitoral stimulators for women. Double dildos are those with a head at each end, designed for two people to use at once. We'll discuss double dildos at greater length later in this chapter. What follows is a description of some of the noteworthy trends in mainstream dildo production.

FAMILY JEWELS The original manufacturers of the soft rubber Family Jewels were a married couple living in Kansas City, Missouri. When Family Jewels sprang onto the scene in the mid-eighties, they were instant attention-getters due to their extremely realistic detailing and coloring. Not only did Family Jewels sport delicately painted blue veins and a lifelike scrotum, but they actually came in three different skin tones—Caucasian, "mulatto" and black—and the skin tones were realistically shaded from the glans to the shaft. Adult novelty manufacturers were quick to pick up on a good idea, and competition from companies such as Doc Johnson put this mom-and-pop operation out of business for a spell until their son revived the family business.

REALISTICS Realistic dildos are soft rubber models that, according to their packaging, are "molded directly from an actual erect penis. Hand-colored and detailed to capture every vein, bulge and crease of a real erect cock." In its most extreme form, this marketing ploy has resulted in dildos modeled after the genitals of famous gay and straight porn stars such as Jeff Stryker, Kris Lord and Sean Michaels. Most realistics are available in Caucasian skin tones, some in black skin tones, and all are sized from big to bigger—few are less than two inches in diameter or eight inches in length. The only "miniature" realistic dildo we've ever seen is a perky five inches long and, in a swipe at corporate America, it's named The Executive!

The larger realistics are so long and heavy they frequently sag under their own weight, giving the impression that Jeff, Kris and their pals don't have their hearts in their work. What keeps these drooping dildos from falling off our display shelves are their suction cup bases. The removable suction cup adheres to any nonporous surface, such as glass or bathroom tile, for easy mounting. While realistics have a unique aesthetic niche, they're not cheap, they're hard to keep clean and they're too bulky to be very comfortable when worn in most harnesses. Many realistic dildos also come in a vibrating version, with an attached battery pack. Uncircumcised realistics come complete with sculpted foreskins—alas, we've yet to find a model with a retractable foreskin.

PROSTHETIC PENIS ATTACHMENTS We call them PPAs. These are hollow vinyl shafts, usually attached to an elastic strap. The idea behind PPAs is that some men may have trouble sustaining erections, may want to continue penetrating their partner after they themselves have reached orgasm, or may want to penetrate their partner with a longer, thicker "penis" than the one nature gave them. A man can slip a PPA over his flaccid penis, snap the elastic strap around his waist and continue to have intercourse with his partner. Sometimes female customers express interest in

buying a PPA as a budget alternative to buying a complete dildo and harness set. Without some kind of stuffing, however, the PPA is prone to being squeezed out of shape. Furthermore, an elastic strap is a highly inefficient means of fastening any kind of dildo to your body—it's hard to thrust in and out of your partner with conviction when the dildo is wobbling and snapping against your torso with every move. Anyone who wants to wear a PPA would be better served by wearing it in a quality dildo harness.

In general, PPAs strike us as inefficient sex toys. They appear to be extremely uncomfortable for both the wearer and the wearee—at the very least, you'd want to slather the inside and the outside of the vinyl sheath with lubricant. We sell a penis-shaped ice mold made of thin vinyl, and we've heard that this works well as a PPA when worn in a harness, providing marginally more sensation for the wearer than a standard PPA.

JELLIES The adult-industry dildo of the nineties is the jelly dildo. A complete line of dildos, double dildos and plugs is made of a specially formulated rubber, which is soft, pliable and full of air bubbles beneath the dildo's surface, giving it a festive carbonated appearance. They are available in pink, orange and—just like the soft drinks of the nineties—in "crystal" clear jelly. The flexible nature of jelly dildos makes them popular for packing. (*Packing* is the term used when genderbenders, pre-operative female-to-male transsexuals and girls-who-wanna-have-fun wear dildos underneath their clothes to simulate that realistic bulge at the crotch.)

I love your Jelly Boy dildo! (There's a "plug" for you—no pun intended.) Good size, texture, pliability-to-hardness ratio, and I love that pink day-glo color!

The latest development in dildo technology is a new, improved jelly rubber that is sleek, elastic and available in luminous jewel tones, such as emerald, ruby and sapphire. At Good Vibrations, we refer to this gorgeous material as

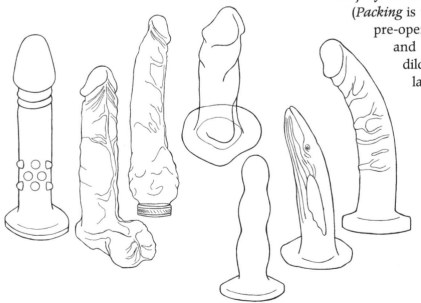

Various styles of dildos

"jelly jewel," though elsewhere you'll see it referred to simply as "jelly rubber." Jelly jewels have a translucent glow almost like stained glass, though the material does fade or even discolor with age. It does, however, retain its supple feel come what (or who) may. The beauty of jelly jewel rubber is that it's spawned a mini-revolution in the adult industry, releasing manufacturers from their focus on quasi-"realistic" styles and skin tones. Now sex toys can look truly playful.

A related development is the flexible plastic spine that's inserted inside one line of jelly jewel dildos. This spine is segmented into plastic "vertebrae," so the dildo can be bent into a variety of different angles. Best of all, the spine can't perforate the rubber in the way that uncovered metal wires can, so you can enjoy these dildos in complete safety.

Silicone Dildos

The dildo revolution got its start in the early eighties when a holistic health practitioner in Brooklyn began experimenting with molding silicone into prosthetic devices that would be more pleasurable and comfortable to use than what was then available in the disabled community. As word about these unique products spread to the owners of women's bookstores and sex boutiques, demand increased, and an industry was born. Currently, there are fewer than ten silicone-manufacturing businesses around the world.

Silicone—the same substance used in surgical implants—is an expensive and delicate raw material, which must be kept sterile and dust-free. Manufacturers continually tinker with their formulas to make their silicone products both resilient and strong, and they must monitor the degree of moisture in the air for successful casting. Silicone manufacturing is a labor-intensive process, done by hand with handmade molds. Consequently, the demand for silicone dildos far outweighs the supply. So far, the prohibitive cost of silicone as a raw material and the difficulty of mechanizing production has kept adult-novelty manufacturers out of the field. Instead, silicone manufacturing is the exclusive province of cottage industries, whose owners have put imagination and empathy into their work, are responsive to their consumers and take personal pleasure in the products they create.

So what's so great about silicone dildos? Texture, for one thing. Silicone is delightfully firm yet flexible, neither too floppy nor too hard. Yes, if Goldilocks and Baby Bear were to select one dildo to take into their sweet tiny bed, it would doubtless be made of silicone. Furthermore, silicone has a smooth, nonporous, velvety surface that is enticing and easy to clean. It retains heat and warms up to body temperature quite fast. Hygiene fiends are always pleased to hear that you can safely boil silicone products for up to five minutes, or the efficiency-minded can pop silicone dildos into the top rack of their dishwashers. Silicone is available in a rainbow of colors, including marbled swirls, gold and silver glitter and glow-in-the-dark.

Best of all, silicone manufacturers have created molds in a wide variety of sizes and shapes. These dildos come finger-slim to fist-wide in a range of nonrepresentational styles, including dolphins, diving women and even a snake coiled around a tree limb. Due to the high costs and low volume of production, silicone dildos aren't cheap, weighing in anywhere from twenty-five to seventy-five dollars, depending on the size of the model. A couple of silicone models are available with hollowed-out shafts, so you can insert vibrating eggs inside them for an extra treat.

At its best, silicone is highly resilient and can be yanked, tugged and mauled with no ill effects. Over the years, however, all our manufacturers have experimented with their formulas and some batches have proved sturdier than others. If the surface of a silicone dildo is broken in any way, the silicone will tear through with distressing ease. Do what you can to avoid breaking the surface tension—don't attack your dildo with tooth and nail. Alas, there is no way to securely glue your silicone dildo back together again once it breaks.

Latex Dildos

Latex dildos are made of the natural rubber from rubber trees, and they're produced only in Europe. As a result, they're hard to find in this country. They're available only in black (just like your tires) and generally consist of a latex sheath enrobing a foam-filled core. One real show-stopper you may encounter in a sex boutique is an inflatable latex dildo, which can be pumped up from about one-and-a-half to three inches in diameter. We've also seen a delightful latex whip which consists of a dildo-shaped handle attached to numerous long latex strips. Now if you can crack this whip while the handle is inside you, we'll know you've been doing your Kegels.

Latex is nonporous, so these dildos are easy to keep clean. But if you spill oil of any kind on the dildo, you'll wind up with a tacky, gummy mess, as oil destroys latex. Rubber tappers are in the vanguard of the movement to preserve the rain forest, and we look forward to the day when condoms and latex dildos are recognized as the ecologically sound investments they are. Yes, every day can be Earth Day when you're playing with your sex toys.

Leather Dildos

Leather dildos have a timeless appeal, based more on aesthetics than practicality. Hand-stitched and available only in leather specialty shops, leather dildos should always be used with condoms. Stitched seams are hard to keep clean, and the dyes and chemicals used in treating the leather could prove irritating to your genital tissue. Leather dildos are generally available in basic black.

Dildos as Art Objects

Over the years we've been pleased to run across dildos elegant enough to display on any art-lover's coffee table or altar. One of these is a Lucite dildo, distributed by a sex education organization as a "condom demonstration model." Certainly this rose-tinted acrylic sculpture provides an easy way for educators to display condoms, but it also makes a great toy for anyone with glass-slipper fantasies. The Crystal Wand is another acrylic dildo, S-shaped for ease in reaching the G-spot or prostate. A lucite model from the aptly-named "Inner Space" company has a magnifying effect—women can use this in conjunction with a flashlight and mirror to take a look at the cervix and the inside walls of the vagina.

The Kegelcisor is a chrome-plated brass rod that resembles a barbell. Marketed as a vaginal-exercise device, the Kegelcisor comes with instructions for doing Kegels and a hefty price tag of up to one hundred dollars. Nobody needs a resistive device in her vagina in order to do Kegels cor-

rectly—however, many women find this cool, heavy, space-age toy makes an appealing dildo.

My first vaginal barbell was taken away from me by an airport security guard, who claimed I couldn't get on the plane with this potential weapon in my purse. Of course, they lost the barbell before returning it to me, so I wrote a letter to the airline officials asking just how many times one of their airplanes had been hijacked by an elderly woman brandishing a sex toy. Eventually, they reimbursed me for my "item."

Occasionally, we're approached by a woodworker who has had the imagination to turn beautiful dildos on his or her lathe. Everyone knows how sensuous fine-grain woods can be, and when they are shaped, sanded and varnished into flowing forms, they are downright irresistible.

You'll notice that these artistic dildos tend to be made of unyielding materials. They are all smooth and safe for insertion, but a hard dildo isn't going to be to everybody's taste. Although one woman may find that a firm dildo is particularly effective in providing the precise pressure that stimulates her G-spot, another may find it cold and unfriendly. Whichever side of the fence you fall on, make sure to use plenty of lubricant when you experiment.

Ben Wa Balls

While they aren't exactly dildos, we're including ben wa balls in this category because they are insertable toys. Many women and men have heard exaggerated claims about the pleasure potential of these marble-sized balls. Even if ben wa balls really were decent sex toys, they'd have a hard time living up to their hype. According to legend, the women of ancient Japan used to insert two hollow ivory balls filled with mercury into their vaginas, then sit back and enjoy the sensation as the balls rolled around inside them. This legend is based on some lapses in logic: Mercury is a highly toxic substance, and the vagina is not a gaping cave that anything is likely to "roll around" in.

Probably, ben wa balls were small ivory spheres inserted during intercourse to enhance sensation. The modern-day incarnation comes in two forms. Ben wa balls are two gold-plated ball bearings about three-quarters of an inch in diameter, and duotone balls are two metal ball bearings encased in larger, hollow plastic spheres about one-and-a-half inches in diameter joined by a nylon cord. Some women enjoy ben wa balls for their fantasy value or use them to tune into subtle sensations in the vagina. You probably won't feel any more sexual sensation from ben wa balls than you would from a tampon, though we have heard from women bus drivers and motorcycle riders who say they enjoy wearing ben wa balls on the road, as their vehicle's vibration sets the balls in motion. Some women find that ben wa balls provide stimulation during intercourse, even though they don't move around much. Please bear in mind that you should not use ben wa balls anally, as they could easily slip into your colon and out of your reach. We'll discuss anal beads in the chapter on anal toys.

Over all, duotone balls have more potential, as the heavy ball bearings roll around inside their plastic casing when you rock your hips or tug on the string, thereby creating a sensation of movement. You might want to position duotone balls half-in/half-out of your vaginal opening for maximum effect. There are numerous variations on the theme of duotone balls: Some vibrate, some are encased in rubber, some are encased in silicone and some strings feature up to four balls.

I think duotone balls are especially fun to wear in public for secret surprise stimulation. They were a great pick-me-up when I was on crutches (swinging hips).

Some women adopt a "bigger is better" approach and insert Chinese healing balls instead of ben wa balls. Slightly larger than a golf ball, healing balls are made of weighted metal that produces a lovely tone, like a distant wind chime. These two balls are designed to be rotated in your palm, thereby stimulating acupressure points and improving the circulation of vital energy through your body. Perhaps you'll find acupressure points inside your vagina that you never knew you had.

Vegetables

We once received a testy note from a customer who was tired of our unremitting praise of silicone dildos—she wrote to let us know that in her opinion "a microwaved zucchini" was infinitely superior to any dildo on the market. You too may be among those who are happiest with a cornucopia of nature's dildos. If you do play with produce, make sure to avoid potentially irritating pesticides—either peel your vegetable or slip a condom on it. If you don't own a microwave, you might want to blanch your chosen vegetable in some boiling water in order to render it warm and flexible.

I thought using a carrot for penetration might be nice. It was cold!

In a classic example of art meeting postmodern life, there are now silicone dildos shaped like corn and zucchini, for those folks who want the relationship with their dildos to last past dinnertime.

The Sybian

The Sybian reminds us of one of those mechanical bucking broncos you see in bars. The dildo (interchangeable so you can buck with the dildo of your choice) is mounted on a saddle-shaped block. You adjust the rotation and speed of the dildo by separate controls. The dildo does not thrust; if that's your preference you're on your own to bob up and down on the saddle. The Sybian excels at stimulating a woman's G-spot and will add a delightful new twist to masturbation. It retails for almost fourteen hundred dollars. There's a demonstration video for twenty dollars, which the manufacturer will credit to the purchase of the Sybian.

Buying a Dildo

You may find yourself a little overwhelmed by the sheer number of options available to the dildo-buyer, but you can quickly narrow the field by considering the following variables:

Aesthetics

Would you like a dildo that resembles a penis or one that doesn't? The choice is yours. We've rarely come across a customer who doesn't have a distinct aesthetic preference, and there's no predicting tastes in the matter. The blushing baby-dyke just back from the Michigan Womyn's Music

Festival may well demand a realistic Jeff Stryker dildo, while the biker dude who just rode in on his Harley may be purchasing a Dolphin dildo for his old lady.

Color may influence your selection process: Folks who are disappointed by the limited palette of realistic dildos are frequently relieved to find silicone dildos in purple or jelly rubber dildos in green. Others may want a realistic dildo that most closely approximates their own skin color. Some customers who have had their "colors done" even whip out their color chips when torn between a cream- or lavender-colored butt plug. The fact that the dildo or plug is destined to go where the sun don't shine is apparently irrelevant to those who take personal style very seriously.

Intentions

Different sizes and styles of dildos suit different circumstances. Many people find that they enjoy a thicker dildo when they're playing alone and can control the pace and timing of penetration. If your partner is manipulating the dildo, you'll probably want it to be slimmer than one you'd masturbate with. Similarly, if you plan to insert your dildo to the hilt, you'd be happiest with one that's not much more than four inches long. But if you want to thrust the dildo in and out of yourself, if your partner is manipulating the dildo, or if your partner is wearing the dildo in a harness, you'd be better off with one that's at least six inches long. Several of the adult novelty dildos on the market have the shaft set on a handle like a nightstick for easy control. Or you can get creative with a double dildo.

I like to use a long double dildo, putting one end in my cunt and stroking the other end, pretending it's my cock.

Size

While it's true that the average person can accommodate many different sizes of dildos, it's also true that most of us have a decided preference for one size or another.

I like small penises, or better yet, dildos. With very small penises, I orgasm easily. The dildo shouldn't be more than five-and-a-half inches long and one-and-a-quarter inches in diameter, and penises should be even smaller.

I love the feeling of being filled up, so big dildos, lots of fingers and a fist make me real happy. When they say that size is not important—well, it is for me.

We stock a wide range of sizes in our stores, and first-time dildo buyers are frequently intimidated by the abundance of alternatives. Male customers seek reassurance that some of the models are "awfully big, aren't they?" while women wonder which model is "average." Frequently, shoppers ask store staff, "Which size should I get?" as though all we need to do is check a customer's glove or shoe size to determine the dildo dimensions of their dreams. Alas, although Good Vibes staffers are an intuitive bunch, there's no way for us to channel the right dildo size for you. Here are some things to consider in making your selection:

Obviously, the diameter of the dildo you're selecting is more important than its length, as you can control how deeply you insert the dildo, but there's no way to adjust for an uncomfortable width. Are you currently enjoying penetration from someone's fingers or penis, a candle, a hairbrush handle, a cucumber? You may want to select a dildo that approximates the measurements of an object you already know and love, or you may want to seize this golden opportunity to size up or down. Perhaps you've always fantasized about trying out a two-inch-thick dildo, or perhaps you'd like a dildo slimmer than your partner's penis.

If you're a woman who has recently undergone genital or abdominal surgery, if you've never experienced penetration, or if it has been a long time since you did, you should take the time to measure your vagina before purchasing a dildo. Don't be afraid to think small. Medical dilators sold to post-operative male-to-female transsexuals start at about one-third of an inch in diameter and go up from there, while dilators sold to women with vaginismus start at just under an inch in diameter.

Head for the nearest produce stand and select some carrots, zucchinis and cucumbers. Wash them well, dress them in condoms, and try them on for size. When you've found a vegetable that suits your taste, cut it in half and measure its diameter. Remember, diameter is the distance across, not around a circle. The same considerations apply if you're selecting a dildo for anal penetration. Take the time to research your preferences before you make your purchase—you'll be glad you did.

My most disappointing sex-toy experience was the purchase of a too-large dildo when I first dared to buy one. I was all excited—got it home, practically tore off the wrapper and hopped into bed with it only to find that its width was an irritant, even with lube. I felt embarrassed that size didn't equal pleasure for me and kept trying to use it for a while. Eventually I braved the trip to the sex-toy store again and got other sizes!

Most of our dildos run between one and two inches in diameter, with the best-sellers in the one-and-a-quarter to one-and-five-eighths inch diameter range. While people who enjoy vaginal or anal fisting may want dildos greater than two inches in diameter, the average Joe or Jane is generally content with this range.

Shape

Dildos vary greatly, not only in length and girth, but in their shape as well. Some are textured with "veins," some are rippled, some have a head larger than their shaft, and some of the more creative silicone styles undulate in unexpected ways—imagine slipping first the arms, then the head, then the breasts of a diving-woman dildo into your vagina. This is another instance where previous experience with penetration can help you make your selection. Do you particularly enjoy the sensation when your vaginal opening expands and then contracts around something? You may find yourself intrigued by a rippled dildo. If you enjoy vaginal fisting, you may be drawn to a dildo with a large head and slimmer shaft. Or you may be someone who has never understood what all the fuss about "textures" and "ribbing" is about, and you'll be perfectly happy with a simple, smooth model.

Playing with Dildos

You can use a variety of methods to incorporate dildos into your sex life. We recommend that you experiment by yourself first, so you can get a sense of what sizes, styles and strokes you enjoy before springing a dildo on your partner. You may find you want to insert the dildo and simply rest with it inside yourself; you may want to tantalize yourself with gradual insertion; or you may want to pump away vigorously.

I like to put my dildo up my butt and just lie there motionless.

Initially I like to hold the "head" of the dildo just at the opening of my vagina, usually with some lubricant. My orgasm may occur at this point, or one inch inside, or all the way in.

In any case, have respect for your anatomy. Insert the dildo gently, and position it to correspond with the angle of your vaginal or anal canal. If you're playing with a curved dildo, angle the curved tip toward the front wall of your vagina, rather than down toward your perineum. The firm pressure of a dildo can be highly delightful to women who enjoy G-spot stimulation. Be particularly cautious when inserting a dildo anally, and don't jab it into the walls of your rectum.

The first time you and a partner play with dildos together, take turns manipulating the dildo by hand and show each other what angles, strokes and speeds feel good. If you're penetrating your partner with a dildo, be especially attentive to his or her body language or any expressions of discomfort. When you have a finger, fist or penis inside somebody, the direct skin contact makes it easy to follow the shape of the vagina or anus and to respond immediately to any resistance or tension. You can't expect the same immediacy when wielding a dildo, and you need to pay close attention to your partner's reactions. With time and practice, the dildo may come to feel like an extension of your own body.

I love using dildos on a female partner by hand, not a strap-on, to really adjust to her pleasure.

I've used dildos with male and female partners, because they enjoy them, but it's sometimes awkward (handling that is) because dildos aren't as "natural" as fingers.

If you crave a no-hands experience, dildos may seem kind of frustrating. They're certainly not going to move unless you take them firmly in hand, and if you let go of them they're apt to shoot right out of your vagina when your PC muscle contracts. Don't despair. There are a surprising number of options when it comes to Dildo Management.

Doc Johnson, one of the major adult-novelty manufacturers, has come out with a dildo you can hop on and ride. It's a inflatable vinyl ball about eight inches in diameter with a dildo mounted on the top. You sit on the dildo and either squat, kneel or lie down with the quasi-beach ball squeezed between your thighs. Not only does the dildo stay firmly in place, but when you bounce around on the inflatable ball it generates a delightful motion through the dildo. Stormy Leather produces a web strap with a snap-in latex ring—slip your dildo through the ring, buckle the strap around your mattress, the seat of a chair or your motorcycle, and the dildo is ready for you to mount.

Teaming Up Dildos and Vibrators

If you like the way a vibrator feels, and you like the way a dildo feels, you've probably already figured out that playing with both at once is an extremely pleasant experience. We mentioned some of the ways you can combine vibrators and dildos in our vibrator chapter, but we'll review them briefly here.

Many battery vibrators, as you'll recall, are phallic in shape. The fundamental error in the design of these vibrators reflects their manufacturers' disregard of anatomy and sexual response. The nerve endings that can respond to vibration are located in the clitoris, the vaginal opening and the anal opening. There are very few nerve endings inside the vaginal canal or the rectum. Therefore, if you insert a battery vibrator that has vibration concentrated in the head, you're not really going to feel the vibrations anywhere they might do you good. Many of the cylindrical battery vibrators have the strongest vibration concentrated at the base, but this means you'd either need to insert the vibrator completely to feel the vibrations at your vaginal or anal opening or you'd need to tilt the vibrator strategically against your clitoris. We suspect that many women who say they've been disappointed by vibrators have tried shoving phallic battery vibrators in and out of their vaginas to little effect.

Really, the best way to enjoy penetration and vibration is to use two toys at once. Yes, specialized technology provides the best results every time. Select a dildo whose size and shape appeal to you, and hold your vibrator against the base of the dildo—the vibrations will ripple throughout your entire genital area. Many coil-operated vibrators are packaged with a funnel-shaped attachment, which when placed against the round base of a dildo, creates a suction that transforms the dildo into a powerfully vibrating toy. Battery vibrators can also be pleasantly combined with dildos: Some folks tuck a vibrating egg against the clitoris while playing with a dildo, and some attach a vibrating cock ring right onto the dildo.

My favorite method of masturbating is using a lubed-up dildo that one hand is pushing in and out, while the other hand is either rubbing my clitoris or using a vibrator on my clitoris. If using a vibrator, I'll also hold the vibrator against the dildo and up against my anus. YEOW!

Soft rubber dildos tend to absorb vibration, but silicone is a divinely effective transmitter of vibration. In fact, a couple of silicone dildos on the market are especially designed to be teamed up with vibrators—their hollowed-out shaft fits a Pink Pearl vibrator, and when the pearl is switched on, the dildo vibrates dramatically from tip to base. Given the limited lifespan of most battery vibrators, it makes much more sense to purchase a silicone dildo from which you can remove the vibrator than one with a vibrator sealed inside.

You may be thinking, "It all sounds so complicated!" Let us assure you that it's actually easier to enact sex-toy combinations than it is to describe them. The great thing about sex toys is, not only the sensations they provide, but the sense of unlimited possibilities they inspire. We've learned a lot over the years from our creative customers, some of whom have graduated from buying sex toys to designing and manufacturing them for others. All it takes is a sense of humor and a sense of adventure to whip up some unique sex-toy recipes of your own.

Double Dildos

Double dildos consist of a shaft anywhere from twelve to eighteen inches in length with a "head" at each end. In theory, you mount one end of the dildo, either vaginally or anally, your partner mounts the other end, and you both ride the same dildo like a seesaw to mutual orgasm. The reality of a double dildo experience does not always live up to the ideal. As always, if you expect the dildo to take on a life of its own you'll be disappointed. One or the other of you will need to hold the middle of the double dildo and get a push-me/pull-you motion going.

Double dildos are available in rubber, jelly rubber and silicone—one jelly model even has a flexible plastic spine, so you and your partner can

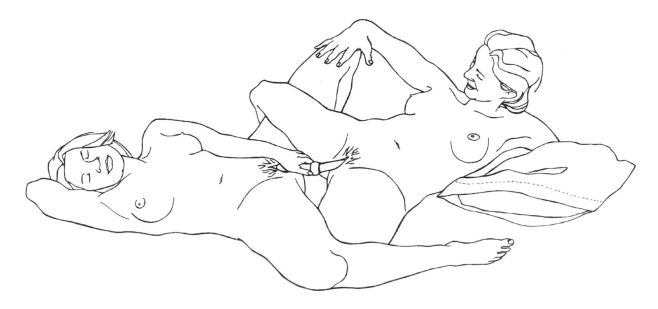

Playing with a double dildo

bend the dildo into the optimal configuration for both of you. The vast majority of double dildos are one size throughout, which can be problematic for couples with different size preferences. Certain jelly rubber models are gradated in size, or look for the Dills for Does line of silicone doubles; these have a different diameter at each end. Dills for Does has also come out with the brilliantly simple "Coupler," a neoprene pad perforated with three holes—you can slip any two dildos with bases through the holes and fasten them together into a double dildo.

Although they have an undeniable fantasy value, you may find double dildos just aren't all they're cracked up to be.

Double dildos haven't worked as well as I've always hoped. They're fun sometimes, but generally take too much effort and coordination for me to be able to really let go. This has been true with men and women for me.

Double dildos are great for the voyeur in me.

Unless you and your partner are roughly the same body size, it may be hard to coordinate riding the same toy. By far the most reliable position is one in which both of you lie on your sides facing opposite directions with your legs scissored together. If you're trying to use a double dildo for anal/anal insertion or vaginal/anal insertion, you may need to crouch doggie-style facing away from each other. People are frequently disappointed that a toy that promises simultaneity and intimacy actually puts them at arm's length from a partner.

Double dongs are disappointing. Can't get one to work right—always flops out or pulls you too far from your partner.

The same folks who find sixty-nine (simultaneous oral sex) to be more distracting than pleasurable will doubtlessly be similarly unimpressed with double dildos. If you'd like to experiment with double dildos, don't invest in an expensive silicone model the first time around. Your best bet would be to keep your expectations low and to approach the experience as a novel type of acrobatic foreplay. If you're disappointed with the results of your experimentation, you can always keep that double dildo around as an extra-long single dildo. If you're thrilled with the results, more power to you!

Dildo Harnesses

We're pleased to have arrived at one of our favorite topics: how to "wear" a dildo in a harness. Dildo harnesses fit around your hips and hold a dildo in place against your pubic bone so you can penetrate your partner. At Good Vibrations we sell dildo and harness combos to couples of all sexual orientations and field plenty of requests from folks who are looking for X-rated videos featuring dildo and harness scenes. If our customer base is at all representative, dildos are being routinely strapped on all across this great land of ours. Women are wearing them with women; women are wearing them with men; men are wearing them with women; and men are wearing them with men. Yet harnesses are one taboo topic that will probably never make it onto TV talk shows. Harness shoppers are the customers most likely to whisper their desires to the salesperson, and a successful harness sale often calls for all the tact, diplomacy and good humor the salesperson can muster.

What is it that makes dildo harnesses such highly-charged playthings? Strapping on a dildo is the ultimate genderbender. A woman who pops on a phallus can expect to feel everything from ridiculous to sublimely powerful. After all, when a woman looks down and sees the archetypal symbol of male privilege bobbing between her thighs, the experience can subvert all preconceptions of who she is and what her role is during sex. Similarly, a man who straps on a dildo is accepting the radical idea that his penis isn't necessarily center stage in every sexual scene, while a man who is anally penetrated by a dildo-wearing partner must embrace his own receptive, submissive side. Dildo-wearing presupposes a willingness to submit to a range of emotions, to explore a range of fantasies and to role-play.

My male lover enjoys getting fucked by me wearing a harness and dildo. As a woman, this experience has been extremely empowering for me. It changes the way you view sex—suddenly the "shoe is on the other foot," so to speak.

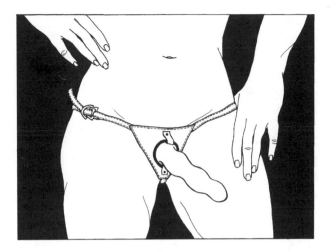

Single-strap harness

While strap-ons are toys commonly associated with lesbians, probably half our harness sales are to heterosexual couples planning to explore anal intercourse with the woman as the active partner. Heterosexual and gay men also strap on dildos—in order to penetrate their partners if they can't sustain an erection, to enjoy a method of penetration that is completely risk free, to penetrate their partners while having their penises stroked, or to double-penetrate a female partner both vaginally and anally. What all couples—gay, lesbian or straight—enjoy about dildo harnesses is the variety, adventure and drama they add to a sexual encounter.

Most of all, I love to fuck my partner with a strap-on. I love to make him suck my realistic cock and then slowly and lovingly fuck him and talk dirty to him till he screams with pleasure and comes explosively.

STYLES AND SOURCES OF HARNESSES Harnesses are available through adult bookstores, mail-order catalogs, sex boutiques and leather specialty stores. By and large, adult bookstores stock cheaper, less functional models, and you'll be better off seeking your harness in a specialty store or through a mail-order catalog. Leather stores that cater to a lesbian clientele are also good resources for quality harnesses.

Dildo harnesses are made of hip and leg straps that radiate out from a central ring or a flap of material with an opening cut in it. You slip the dildo through the ring or the opening in the flap—

the base of the dildo rests against your body and is secured when you tighten the hip and leg straps of the harness. Any dildo you wear in a harness must have a flared base or it will fall out of the harness.

When you're wearing a dildo in a harness, the dildo rests against your pubic bone, higher up on your body than a penis is or would be. This positioning gives the wearer more control over the movement of the dildo. A harness with some sort of central flap of material generally supports a dildo better than one that consists solely of a ring attached to straps.

The majority of harnesses found in adult bookstores are cheaply made with vinyl, latex or stiff leather bodies and elastic waist straps. Unfortunately, elastic is not an ideal material to use in securing a relatively heavy object to your body. It sags, stretches out of shape and snaps back and forth, making it difficult to control the dildo. One adult-novelty harness designed for women is an all-one-piece latex brief and dildo. Since these only come in one or two sizes, they tend to fit poorly with the dildo positioned a bit too low for optimal control.

The best, most functional harnesses have leather or nylon web hip straps that fasten securely either with D-rings, buckles or Velcro. These harnesses come in two basic styles: those that have one center strap running between the legs and those with two leg straps, one running around each thigh. Devotees of the single-strap style like the simplicity of the fit and find the G-string effect of the center strap either unobtrusive or pleasurable. Devotees of the two-strap style may find

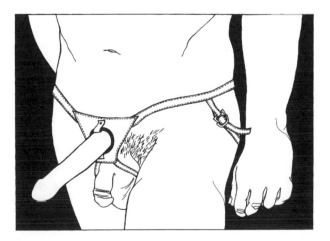

Two-strap harness

G-strings irritating and prefer strapping the harness around the thighs, thereby leaving their own genitals unimpeded. Men can only comfortably wear the single-strap style if they're using the ring of the harness as a cock ring—i.e., with the ring worn around the base of their penis and scrotum—rather than wearing a dildo in the harness. Men who wish to wear a dildo in a harness must use a two-strap model and position the dildo above their own genitals.

Stormy Leather's Jewel harness provides a particularly comfortable way to wear those realistic dildos that come complete with scrotum and testicles. In the past, folks who wanted to wear realistic dildos in a harness had to contend with stuffing a bulky mass of rubber under the flap of their harness, where it would chafe against their skin. The Jewel harness has a free-hanging ring positioned in front of a flap of material, and two leg straps that snap into the ring. When you slip a dildo with balls through the ring, the base of the dildo rests securely and comfortably against the flap of material rather than against your skin. Stormy's Terra Firma harness also positions the dildo in front of the harness flap. Best of all, the leg and waist straps of this two-strap harness fit directly around the center ring, holding the dildo firmly against the wearer's body.

One cloth harness we've carried is a long sash of cotton fabric that must be knotted around the dildo, wrapped around your thighs and tied around your waist. While this sash is certainly versatile, easily washable and innocuous in appearance, mastering its use can be intimidating to anyone who's not an Eagle Scout.

When selecting a dildo harness, you'll want to consider price, size and style. If you're experimenting with harnesses for the first time, you might want one of the less-expensive fabric and nylon web models. If you're convinced that you have many happy harness years ahead of you, you'll probably want to invest in a comfortable, long-lasting leather harness.

Consider the size of the dildo you plan to be using—you should select a harness with an opening or ring that fits snugly, but not too tightly around your dildo. Ideally the ring in your harness should be made of flexible latex, rather than unyielding metal. While some people prefer the aesthetics of metal, it can be rough on more delicate silicone dildos. Most leather harnesses have a ring around the harness opening as reinforcement—soft leather stretches, and nobody appreciates having the harness opening stretch to the point that the dildo falls right through. Style is strictly a matter of personal preference.

Don't forget to keep your harness as clean as you would any other item of intimate apparel. Hand wash your harness with mild soap and water, and let it dry thoroughly before putting it away. You should be careful not to dry your leather harness in front of direct heat, unless you fancy a cracked, saddle-worn look and feel.

HARNESS COMPONENTS AND VARIATIONS Harness-sporting customers frequently want to know how they can stimulate themselves while they are penetrating their partners. A surprising number of options are available. Those harness-wearers who crave vaginal penetration can purchase a double harness, which features a second hole positioned over the wearer's vagina covered by a strap that snaps a dildo in place. (Double harnesses are designed for use with two separate dildos, not with a double dildo.)

Leather cuffs are an accessory that allows you to turn your single harness into a double harness providing either vaginal or anal stimulation. The cuff has a hole in the center, and the ends of the cuff snap or Velcro shut. Cuffs can be used by both women and men. Simply slip a dildo or plug through the hole in the cuff, insert the dildo or plug in your body and snap the cuff in place around the center strap of the harness. Cuffs work best with single-strap harnesses, but some folks are also willing to adjust the leg straps of a two-strap harness in order to wear a cuff between their legs. Since a cuff will hold the entire length of the dildo or plug inside you, you should make sure to select a comfortably short model.

Small battery vibrators offer the best way for harness-wearers to get clitoral stimulation. Vibrating silicone dildos transmit vibrations beautifully to both the harness-wearer and her partner. Some women obtain clitoral stimulation by tucking a vibrating cock ring around the base of the dildo between flesh and harness. Others substitute a vibrating-egg vibrator. A variation on the cuff described above is a small leather pouch designed to hold a vibrating egg or pearl—the Vibro Cuff snaps in place around the center strap of a harness. The vibrator's battery pack can be easily tucked into the waist strap of the harness.

One of the most ingenious examples of how sex-toy technology spawns attendant technologies is the Slip Not. The Slip Not is a donut-shaped foam pad with a tiny hole in its center, and is designed to address the problem of what to do when the dildo you want to wear has a very small base and falls through the hole in your harness. Simply slide the Slip Not all the way down to the base of your dildo so that it rests between the dildo base and the harness opening, and it will act like a safety belt for tiny dildos.

Finally, we should note that not all dildo harnesses are designed to fit around the hips. The Lip Service (variants sold under several different names) is a harness that straps over the head, positioning a dildo over the wearer's mouth, giving a new twist to going down on your partner. In other versions of this toy, the dildo straps over the wearer's chin. The Thigh Harness (variants sold under several different names) fastens a dildo onto the wearer's thigh, offering a whole new dimension to bouncing your loved one on your knee. The Thigh Harness opens up a range of new positions for enjoying penetration, and two partners can each strap on a Thigh Harness to penetrate each other, an alternative to double dildos that allows full-body contact.

TIPS AND TRICKS Wearing a dildo in a harness demands a fair amount of coordination, imagination and attentiveness. When you strap on a dildo for the first time, you may unconsciously expect it to be transmuted into a sentient part of your body, and you may be disappointed at how much energy is required to control it.

Using a strap-on dildo with a lesbian lover was disappointing—because I couldn't feel what was happening with her.

Don't despair—with a little practice and a lot of feedback from your partner you'll quickly gain command of the situation. Ideally, the dildo you wear in a harness will have a slight curve to it, so that it will match the natural curve of your part-

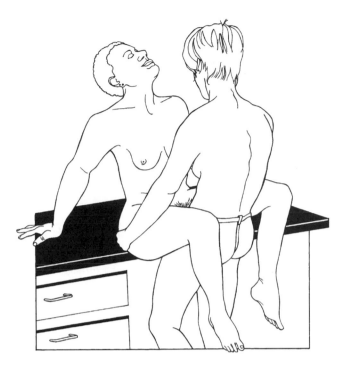

Intercourse with a dildo harness

ner's vagina or anus. It's easier to control a firm dildo than a soft, floppy one. Needless to say, you should take care to apply lubricant both to the dildo and to your partner's vagina or anus. Most people find that it's best to wear a fairly long dildo in a harness, given that the harness will take up about half an inch of the dildo's length. Furthermore, if you want to get into a stroking rhythm, it's best to use a dildo long enough that it won't ever pull entirely out of your partner.

With my partner using a long dildo, I can lie on my front, be fucked from behind and masturbate all at once. The best thing about her wearing a dildo is that her hands are free and she's able to be more on top of me. Plus, she can reach my nipples and/or clit from behind.

Reinserting a dildo can interrupt the flow of things, as dildos don't have the self-lubricating properties of penises. Remember, you won't be conscious of the dildo you're wearing in the same way you would be conscious of a part of your own body—you'll feel pretty silly if you find yourself pumping energetically away in mid-air, leaving your partner high and dry.

Of course, some couples prefer the close body contact of inserting a dildo to the hilt and rocking their pelvises together without thrusting in and out—short dildos are perfect for this method of penetration.

All the positions that apply to penis/vagina or penis/anus intercourse are relevant to intercourse with a dildo. A man wearing a dildo in a harness should position the dildo above his genitals—he may find that strapping on a dildo opens up some intriguing options.

I like vaginal and anal penetration. I would love it if he could wear a strap-on below (or above, I guess) his penis without hurting his balls. Possible?

It's possible for a man in the missionary position to simultaneously penetrate his female partner in the vagina with his strapped-on dildo and in the anus with his penis, or for a man in the rear-entry position to penetrate his partner in the anus with a dildo and in the vagina with his penis. One toy is specifically designed with this kind of fun in mind. We call it the Acrobat, and the manufacturer calls it the "Ultimate Triple Stimulator." It's a cock ring with a dildo molded onto one end and a vibrating egg attachment molded onto the other. A man can slip his penis through the cock ring and wear the dildo for double penetration on a female partner. The vibrating egg attachment provides either clitoral stimulation or testicular stimulation, depending on how it's positioned on your penis. A woman can wear the same toy in a dildo harness along with a second dildo for double penetration on a female partner.

Dildos and Genderbending

Packing

Despite our conviction that dildos are not "penis-substitutes," we'd be remiss to ignore their fantasy potential. Over the years, we've sold a lot of dildos to women who plan to "pack" them, that is to wear the dildos underneath their jeans to simulate the bulge of a penis. Some of these women are pre-operative female-to-male transsexuals who want to complete their male appearance. (In many cases,

female-to-male transsexuals live as men without ever going through with the expensive, complicated and less-than-satisfactory penile-construction surgery.) Sometimes they're women doing a little genderbending for the sake of entertainment and sexual role-playing. Most often, they're practical and adventurous gals who want to be ready for action when they head out for a night on the town.

The first thing to know about packing is that the dildo that makes a great sex toy in a harness is not necessarily a great choice to stuff into your boxer shorts. Just as a man finds it uncomfortable to walk around with a full erection, a woman finds it uncomfortable to walk around with a stiff dildo straining beneath the buttons of her 501s. Transsexuals and those seeking the most realistic appearance gravitate toward soft rubber or foam rubber dildos that are too floppy to actually penetrate anyone with—Vixen Creations makes a convincing packing dildo out of silicone.

If you want the bulge of the dildo beneath your pants to look authentic, you should probably wear a smallish dildo in a Jewel harness, so that it can be tucked neatly in your crotch. If you're packing with the intention of using your dildo with a partner, you'll want a somewhat firmer dildo, but ideally one that is flexible enough to bend without breaking: Rubber dildos tend to be better than silicone dildos. If your dildo is fairly long and firm, you might want to wear it snapped onto the leg strap of your harness with a harness cuff. This way, you avoid having the base of the dildo jammed awkwardly into your pubic bone. It's easy enough to move the dildo into place when the time comes to use it.

Sucking

Dildos also make great toys for any woman who's ever had her erotic imagination sparked by fellatio, with its blend of seduction, submission, vulnerability and dominance.

My favorite method of masturbation is simply lying on my back with my legs spread far apart rubbing my clit while I fantasize that someone, anyone, is sucking my "dick."

Role-playing with a dildo can be a safe yet arousing way to enact fantasies of fellatio, whether you're watching your girlfriend suck your "cock" or you're pretending to be your husband's gay lover. You and your partner can select the dildo that best resembles the penis of your imagination. And you can truthfully swear that you'll never come in his or her mouth.

Dildo Laws

No chapter about dildos would be complete without a mention of the ridiculous legislative restrictions that exist in certain states with regard to buying and owning dildos. Dildos are explicitly targeted in states with laws criminalizing "obscene devices." For instance, in Texas an obscene device is defined as "a device including a dildo or artificial vagina, designed or marketed as useful primarily for the stimulation of human genital organs." We've heard that in both Texas and Arizona, it's against the law to own more than six dildos, as possession of more than six is supposed to indicate intent to sell—never mind that some of us simply *own* a different dildo for every day of the week.

Due to these laws, adult bookstores in certain states find themselves in the ludicrous position of labeling dildos as "novelties" and "condom demonstration models," as though public health educators were the sole dildo-buying citizens. Adult bookstores that don't toe the line run the risk of being busted and having everything from vibrators to penis-shaped soap-on-a-rope confiscated as contraband. How sad that the same toy once celebrated in art and literature throughout the classical world receives such ignominious treatment today.

All About Anal Toys

Anal toys are designed to insert in and/or vibrate the anus and rectum. Like dildos, which have been in existence since time immemorial, anal toys have a long and distinguished history. One European doctor of the Victorian era instructed his male clients to insert wooden eggs rectally—his theory was that the pressure against the prostate gland would help route semen back to the bladder, preventing wasteful ejaculation of precious sperm. We have to assume that those gentlemen who went about their daily duties with a wooden egg up their rectum were enjoying themselves as much as our customer who remarked:

Butt plugs under clothing can put a different twist on your day.

The anus is an erogenous zone for men and women alike, and as children nearly all of us engage in some sort of anal exploration.

From a very early age (six or eight), I enjoyed inserting objects into my anus but did not actually masturbate until I was twelve or so.

As we grow into adolescence and adulthood, we encounter numerous societal taboos around anal play, ranging from the extreme—indulging in anal pleasure is dirty and perverted—to the subtle—indulging in anal pleasure is immature and potentially risky. Yet the truth is that anal play need be no more dirty or risky than kissing. If you follow a few commonsense precautions, playing with anal toys is completely safe as well as fun. At Good Vibrations, we sell ever-increasing numbers of butt plugs and anal vibrators to individuals and couples all across the country. And a finger-slim vinyl butt plug is the number-one best-selling product of the nation's largest adult novelty manufacturer, proof that the simple pleasures of anal play will always triumph against ignorance and prejudice.

Once More with Feeling

To recap what you've read in previous chapters: Please do take the time to relax your sphincter muscles before inserting anything into your anus, as relaxation is a prerequisite to enjoyable anal play. Do use plenty of lubricant. Make sure that any toy you insert anally is completely smooth and nonabrasive, has a flared base so that it won't slip out of reach into your rectum, and (if longer than four inches) is flexible enough to align with the curves in your rectum. Finally, don't transfer your toy from anus to vagina without either washing the toy or covering it with a new condom. The simplest, most convenient approach is to wear a condom on your anal toy every time you play.

Styles and Sources

As with dildos, you're not likely to run across anal toys at your local department store. You'll find anal toys in adult bookstores, mail-order catalogs or sex boutiques. See our resource listings for specific details.

Butt plugs

Butt plugs are dildos designed especially for anal use. They are flared at the base so they won't wiggle out of reach, and they frequently are pyramid- or diamond-shaped, tapering to a narrow neck. This diamond shape allows you to "wear" a plug inside your rectum. Once you sneak the widest point of the plug past your sphincter muscles, your anal sphincter will clasp around the narrow neck, holding the body of the plug snugly inside you.

Variations on the diamond plug generally fall into the ripple category. Some are shaped like Christmas trees, with three increasingly larger ripples ranging from the tip to the base of the plug: As you get progressively more aroused and receptive, you can make your way from one ripple to the next. Some have corkscrewlike ridges down the length of the shaft; others have an undulating shape resembling beads strung close together. The rationale for these rippled shapes is that many people enjoy the sensation of the anus repeatedly contracting and releasing around each bump and

ridge. Other people find this much anal activity more distracting than pleasurable, and prefer to slip a plug in place and then leave it there.

Butt plugs range in size from pinky-slim to fist-wide, but they are usually shorter than dildos. A standard butt plug is designed for you to insert to the hilt and leave in place rather than stroking in and out, as you might with a vaginal dildo. When inserting any plug, angle it up toward the front of your body. You may find it helpful to twist the plug slightly to get the widest part through your anal opening. When removing any plug, slowly jiggle it out of your rectum—a gentle twisting motion is also helpful here to ease the body of the plug past your sphincter.

You may enjoy wearing butt plugs during masturbation, oral sex or vaginal penetration. The pressure and sense of fullness plugs provide can be highly pleasurable, particularly in combination with other types of stimulation.

Sometimes while masturbating I use a small plug for prostate stimulation.

My wife enjoys inserting a plug while we are proceeding toward orgasm.

Some people like to wear butt plugs under their clothing throughout the day. We've certainly sold our share of plugs to customers who immediately take their new purchase off to the bathroom to pop it in place. Keep this possibility in mind next time an intimidating highway patrolman pulls you over—perhaps he's sitting on something that throbs even harder than his motorcycle. Why would someone want to wear a plug out and about? For the thrill of a sexual secret, as an act of obedience to a dominant partner, or in order to relax the sphincter muscles in preparation for anal intercourse.

I enjoy inserting dildos into my boyfriend's anus. I also insert butt plugs to relax him in preparation for a dildo.

Some women take advantage of the fact that plugs are available in slimmer sizes than most of the dildos found in adult bookstores.

I use butt plugs in the vagina—dildos are too big.

ADULT-INDUSTRY BUTT PLUGS The plugs produced by the adult industry average anywhere from one to two inches in diameter. They come in the following materials and styles:

Vinyl: The most commonly available plug is the peach, black or red vinyl variety. Slim vinyl models don't have enough flare to remain in place once inserted, so you or your partner should either hold this type of plug in place or treat it like a finger moving in and out of your rectum. The wider models are available either in the classic diamond shape or in a ripple shape. Vinyl plugs are reasonably resilient but not as flexible as plugs made from other materials. They are nonporous and easy to keep clean. A new extra-slim, shapely "Petite" plug in hot pink vinyl is proving that bigger isn't always better—it's one of the best-selling plugs around.

Jelly: Translucent, bubbly jelly rubber is available in pink, orange and crystal-clear colors. On the plus side, jelly plugs are attractive, soft and flexible. On the negative side, jelly rubber is porous—ideally, you should always wear a condom on these plugs.

Jelly Jewel: Your butt plug can positively glow if you buy one made of sleek, nonporous jelly jewel rubber.

Probes: Some plugs are set on a handle, which provides a convenient way to approach what one adult mail-order catalog coyly refers to as "the backdoor of Eros' temple." These nightstick-styled plugs have either a rippling shaft, a diamond-shaped shaft or a slim shaft ending in a fat round tip. Those made of either peach or black rubber should be worn with a condom, but the vinyl models are nonporous. Some probes vibrate, and one style contains tumbling pearls in its midsection—once inserted, the pearls create a massaging sensation just inside the anus. Probes make great vaginal dildos as well.

Inflatable: There are a couple of inflatable vinyl plugs on the market. These are attached by a hose to a rubber hand pump. After you've inserted the plug, you can pump away, inflating it to twice its original size. Unfortunately, these toys are better conceived than they are manufactured—the inflatable plug has a tendency to inflate unevenly, with all the pressure expanding one side of the plug. The resulting lopsided pressure can be uncomfortable at best and dangerous at worst.

Big, Bigger, Biggest: While the most popular plugs are under two inches in diameter, there's definitely a market for larger models. Most of these are made of soft rubber or vinyl and range up to four inches in diameter. Some are diamond-shaped, and others—in a nod to the practice of anal fisting—are shaped like a clenched hand and forearm. Needless to say, these large plugs should only be used by someone with considerable experience, who has trained him or herself to comfortably accommodate an object as large as a hand in the rectum.

SILICONE PLUGS Silicone plugs range anywhere from three-quarters to two inches in diameter. They come in a variety of colors, in diamond shapes or slim rippled shapes. One model, from Vixen Creations, comes in the shape of a rectal thermometer, so you can play doctor with ease and comfort! Silicone plugs have the same advantages as silicone dildos, namely a delightful resilient texture and a smooth, nonporous surface that is easy to clean.

METAL PLUGS Some leather stores or fetish boutiques stock metal plugs and eggs. Metal plugs are cool and heavy, providing a unique sensation. They are exceptionally weighty and hard, however, so you have to be careful how you move when they're inside you to avoid banging them against your spine or tailbone. These metal toys are completely solid except for a narrow hole running down their center—within the S/M community, folks sometimes attach electrodes to these plugs to transmit electricity. Unless you're very experienced with anal play, you shouldn't insert any toy that doesn't have a base or isn't on a string, so we don't recommend your playing with egg-shaped toys.

ANAL BEADS Anal beads are a very popular insertable toy, consisting of a series of plastic or rubber beads strung on a nylon cord. You can also find anal beads made of silicone or of jelly rubber. The beads range anywhere from marble-sized to softball-sized. Although we sell lots of the former size, we don't have too much demand for the latter. Anal beads are popular with folks who like to feel the anus opening and closing around each new bead. You may be surprised how visually

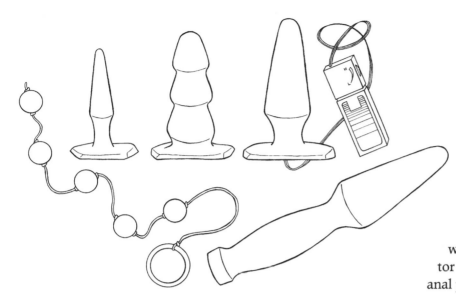

Various styles of anal toys

entertaining it is to feed the beads into your partner's anus and pop them back out again. Some people like to pull the beads swiftly out of the rectum while they're coming as a way of intensifying the orgasmic contractions. Other people find this sensation too intense at the moment of orgasm and prefer to remove the beads before or after orgasm.

I've been anally penetrated with fingers, dildo, vibrating plug and beads, all with enjoyment, but not at the moment of orgasm! A finger in my butt when I orgasm is okay, but the others draw my focus too much and I don't seem to be able to have as exquisite a sensation. But they all get me very excited!

As adult novelties are cheaply made, it's a good idea to do a little safety overhauling on your anal beads before playing with them. Plastic beads frequently have nasty, sharp seams, which might scratch your rectal tissue. But this is nothing that a once-over with a nail file won't solve. Softer rubber beads can be porous, so if you want to use them more than once, put a condom over them. You can knot the open end of the condom around the last bead. Some beads are strung on a cotton cord, rather than a nylon cord. It's going to be difficult to keep those cotton fibers clean—another good reason to put a condom over the whole strand.

Vibrators

Vibration provides a fabulous way to enhance anal stimulation and penetration. After all, vibration can titillate the myriad nerve endings of your anus just as it does those of your clitoris or penis. A vibrating butt plug can relax your anal sphincter, distracting you from any involuntary tension or resistance you might otherwise feel. Or you can use a vibrator externally in conjunction with anal penetration.

My favorite method of masturbating is sitting on a silicone dildo, with a vibrator over my cock. I'm filled and exploding all at the same time! It leaves me with a pleasant, dirty, spent glow. The anal sensations the next day or two cause erotic daydreaming.

VIBRATING BUTT PLUGS Many of the plugs described above are available with battery packs, so that you can insert your plug and set it buzzing. The most popular style we sell is a slim (one inch diameter), slightly rippled cylindrical model, but plenty of people opt for larger, diamond-shaped models. These have mild vibrations, generated by AA batteries, which are further muffled by the vinyl or rubber bodies of the plugs. Several jelly jewel vibrators contain a flexible plastic spine inside a long, slim tail—you can bend the spine inside the toy's "tail" to the angle that best suits your own tail.

A variation on this theme is a vibrating plug featuring a thin probe extending from a short cylindrical base. The slim shaft vibrates, and in some cases, makes a simultaneous rotating motion.

T-Vibes are hard plastic or jelly rubber plugs with an angled body extending off a flange that resembles a pacifier. These plugs have a great shape, which follows the natural curve of your rectum, and they vibrate energetically. As with plastic anal beads, you do have to go over these plastic vibrators with a nail file to smooth down any rough edges.

BATTERY VIBRATORS AND SLEEVES Many of the realistic rubber dildos on the market are also sold in vibrating versions, with battery packs attached. Some of these are styled especially for anal use, with a narrow neck and a flared base. More often, however, people use simple, cylindrical battery vibrators for anal play. Some men find that G-spot vibrators, which are curved at their tip, make good prostate stimulators (one more way in which the prostate and G-spot are analogous!).

Feel free to use battery vibrators for anal play, provided your vibrator is at least seven inches long and you can always keep hold of it—don't use a toy that doesn't have a flared base if you think you might lose your grip on it in the heat of the moment. If the vibrator itself seems too large to insert, you can adapt it for anal use with any one of a number of flexible vinyl sleeves. These sleeves fit over the top of a cylindrical battery vibrator and feature the nubs, fronds and fringes so beloved by adult-novelty manufacturers. The most practical model around is a simple finger-width style. By the time the vibrations get down to the tip of the sleeve, they're considerably diluted, but this anal sleeve is still a convenient way to experiment with anal vibration.

ELECTRIC VIBRATORS For a powerful and penetrating massage, electric vibrators can't be beat. If you're holding an electric vibrator against your clitoris or penis, the vibrations will probably be diffused throughout your genital region and indirectly stimulate your anus. For a more direct approach, try using a double-headed massager with one head positioned against your genitals and the other against your anus.

The insertable attachments sold for use with wand vibrators work well for anal insertion. The curved G-Spotter attachment is the best shape for anal use. Some men find this attachment just the ticket for tickling the prostate, while others find it a bit too short to hit the spot. The only coil vibrator attachment that should be used anally is the Twig, as even if this should slip off the vibrator shaft, it won't slip into your rectum.

Of course, these vibrator attachments come in a fairly limited range of sizes and shapes. Your best bet for combining anal penetration and vibration is to select a butt plug that pleases you and simply hold your vibrator against the base of the plug. As with the vagina, the nerve endings that are responsive to vibration cluster at the opening and outer third of the rectum, so using a vibrator externally should give you all the stimulation you desire. The funnel-shaped attachment packaged with most coil vibrators is ideal to press against the round base of dildos or plugs—it creates a suction that transforms the two toys into one.

Harnesses

If you do want to wear a butt plug inside yourself, either during masturbation or partner sex, you can use a cuff fastened around the center strap of a dildo harness. There's also a Plug Harness on the market—this has two adjustable leg straps so you can position a plug inside yourself but still have your genitals accessible for other activities. Or, you could take a more prosaic, low-tech approach to wearing a plug.

I like wearing my leather cock ring wrapped around the base of my cock and balls, with my butt plug adhesive-taped in my bottom. I wear them while shopping, doing errands and housework.

Customers buying a dildo harness for anal intercourse frequently make the mistake of approaching the counter with a harness and a diamond-shaped butt plug. Why is this a mistake? Well, standard butt plugs are designed to be left in place, not thrust in and out of your anus. You'd find it pretty uncomfortable to have the widest part of a plug yanked through your anal opening with each stroke of your partner's hips.

Instead, select a dildo, rather than a plug, that seems the right diameter to the receptive partner. Use the number of fingers the receiver can comfortably accommodate as your gauge. You'll probably find it helpful to select a dildo that curves up from the base, rather than one that is set perpendicular to the base, as this will align more naturally with the curve of the rectum. And remember that a dildo worn in a harness should be a little longer than a dildo used by hand, so that it will never slip entirely out of your partner's body. Extra length also comes in handy when negotiating body size discrepancies between you.

Buying an Anal Toy

You're far more likely to have a good time with the anal toy you buy if you're basing your purchase on personal preference. Do you like the sensation of having a finger or two inserted in your anus? Then you might want to purchase a plug. Do you like moving a finger in and out of your rectum, or do you prefer holding it still? If you enjoy movement, you might want to buy anal beads, a slim rippled plug or a dildo. If you prefer no movement, you might be happiest with a diamond-shaped plug. If you already own and enjoy a vibrator, try pressing it against your anal opening—if this feels particularly tantalizing, you may want to purchase a vibrating butt plug.

As with buying a dildo, the most important aspect of selecting a butt plug is deciding what size to get. Do your homework, and base your selection on fact rather than fantasy. We still have fond memories of the two female flight attendants who spent their time in front of the anal toy shelf boasting to each other, "My boyfriend's so macho, he only wants the biggest one!" Those of us who are less macho probably have more in common with the customer who wrote:

> *I bought a two-inch butt plug vibrator and savored the idea of using it only to find that it was too big!! And the vibration of the tiny bit that went in was so titillating.*

If you have as much fun playing with your anal toys as we do selling them, we know you'll be having a good time. We enjoy peddling products that fly in the face of our society's ridiculously obsessive anal taboo. There's the satisfaction of spreading the good word that anal play is both safe and pleasurable. And there's the sheer entertainment value of the enterprise—after all, imagine telling everyone at your high-school reunion, "I sell butt plugs for a living." Even habitually deadpan adult-novelty packagers can't help but take a tongue-in-cheek approach to marketing butt plugs—our favorite plug packaging promises, "Once you get used to this model, you'll begin to walk slower and enjoy the scenery. Every step you take will be an exciting adventure!" We couldn't have said it better ourselves.

PLUG SHOPPING CHECKLIST

✔ *Aesthetics.* If you'd prefer a plug that looks as good as it feels, select a jelly jewel or silicone model.

✔ *Expense.* If you're experimenting to determine your preferences, you may gravitate towards an inexpensive jelly rubber or vinyl model. If you know what you like and you're making a longterm investment, treat yourself to a silicone model.

✔ *Material.* We recommend using condoms regardless of the style of plug you select, but be aware that rubber and jelly rubber models are porous and will be harder to keep clean than plastic, vinyl or silicone.

✔ *Size.* Confirm the diameter that's right for you before you buy—using finger-width measurements is probably the easiest way to gauge your preference.

✔ *Shape.* If you enjoy the sensation of your anus expanding and contracting, you might want to buy anal beads or a rippled plug. If you prefer penetration without movement, you might want to buy a diamond-shaped model that you can "wear" in place. If you or your partner want to stroke in and out of your rectum with the plug, select a slim, curved dildo, rather than a diamond-shaped plug.

✔ *Vibration.* If you enjoy vibrations, check out any vibrating plugs or attachments that intrigue you. Select a vibrating toy that has a shape you like—even if you decide the vibrations don't float your boat, you'll still have an anal toy you can enjoy.

✔ *Safety.* Your anal toy should have a flared base. Make sure that the surface of your toy is completely smooth and nonabrasive, and be prepared to file down plastic seams on some new toys before you play with them.

CHAPTER 13

Fantasies

I like to fantasize when I'm walking around, in public places preferably. That way I can use my mind and imagination to get myself so worked up that I almost come without touching myself. And when I finally get myself alone, it's guaranteed phenomenal masturbation.

You've no doubt heard that the brain is our largest sex organ, but it may never have occurred to you that it's also an incredibly versatile sex toy. Without the brain responding to stimuli and sending messages to the rest of the body, we'd have about as much sexual feeling as pieces of furniture. But it's the brain's capacity to house a vast reservoir of erotic imagery–known as fantasies–that makes it a powerful sex toy, since fantasies can be endlessly tapped for sexual pleasure.

Fantasies, simply put, are mental pictures that trigger sexual arousal. Their content, importance and purpose vary greatly from person to person. Some folks summon them when they want to be sexual, others find they have little control over how and when their fantasies emerge, while still others don't fantasize at all.

Fantasizing, like masturbating, is an act of self-love as well as an assertion of sexual confidence and independence. You are responsible for turning yourself on; you don't have to wait for someone else to do it.

A fantasy can be anything from flashing on an act or an image:

Making love on a sailboat in the middle of the ocean under the hot sun with a breeze blowing.

To a well-scripted sexual encounter:

I'm a teacher, and a cute female student sits in the front row. She's wearing a very short skirt. When she sits down, I notice she's not wearing any underwear. She looks up at me, winks and grins. At the end of class she comes up to me and asks for an appointment so we can discuss her grade on the midterm. We set a time, she comes to my office, walks in, closes the door, turns around with her shirt open and explains the problem she's having and asks if I could help her.... As a dedicated professional, I have to help!

Whether it's explicit or vague, short or long, kinky or common, if it gets you hot, it's a fantasy. As a way to illustrate the variety of fantasies, both in terms of content and the way they are expressed, we have transcribed some of our customers' fantasies in this section. Perhaps you will discover new fantasies of your own as a result!

Popular Themes

Despite the fact that no two people's fantasy lives are the same, some popular themes emerge.

Sex with Someone Other Than Your Partner

It's common to fantasize about sex with someone other than your partner. Sometimes the other person is an acquaintance:

I'd love fifteen minutes with my community studies professor. I'd get her on her desk in her office, or against the wall. Unbutton the top two buttons of her shirt, suck her earlobe and run my tongue down her neck, across her right clavicle, over her shoulder and then untuck her shirt, pull it off, off with the bra, bite gently the outside of her tit, touch the back of her knee, run my spread fingers hard up the inside of her thigh, squeeze her cunt, and then she'd beg me to come home with her.

Sometimes the other people are total strangers:

I am at a prison where a group of men are assembled in a circle on the floor, hands cuffed behind their backs. I select a man, and the guard unlocks his cuffs—the man stays seated and undoes his pants so I can evaluate his erect penis. As I select several men, one at a time, each is allowed to touch/masturbate his cock. I have rejected one or two—their cocks weren't pretty enough—and they are now handcuffed again with their cocks exposed. I now allow my chosen ones (still seated) to stroke my thighs (I'm wearing a garter belt and stockings, no panties) and, eventually, to eat me. As I get more aroused, the chosen men become more active. They are up now, pulling my clothes off, stroking me, stimulating my breasts; there are hands, tongues,

cocks everywhere. I bend over the back of a straight-backed chair and while one penetrates me from the back I suck on one or more of the others. They jerk off and come on me while playing with my breasts and talking dirty to me. I come about a dozen times.

Voyeurism and Exhibitionism

I have fantasies of having sex in front of other people. Not friends but a crowd of strangers. They are not interacting or making any intrusive noises but are just watching and getting aroused. I imagine them masturbating very quietly without calling any attention to themselves.

I'm naked, lying on my back. Several yards away, a circle of men are behind glass, naked, watching me. They're restrained so they can't touch themselves. But I watch them become aroused as I masturbate, dance erotically, or walk around the circle teasing them, even reaching through "doors" in the glass to touch them. Each one wants me to choose him for sex.

Forced Encounters

I'm alone on a beach—caught up in watching the sunset. Suddenly there's a man behind me. He says he won't hurt me if I cooperate. He slits several access holes in my jeans so no one passing can tell what's going on. He proceeds to stimulate me with his hands in front while gently and persistently entering me anally from behind. I pretend that I hate it but become so aroused I climax several times before he even thinks about coming. Though this is a rape fantasy, he's really very considerate and gentle, and I feel no threat.

My current fantasy is being given up by my stepmother to be an indentured servant to a wealthy family and being seduced into wet nursing for their kids, then being broken into a bondage and fucking toy for the parents, their other servants, the guard dog, etc.

I fantasize about my ex-lover, who is pretty butch and much stronger than me, holding me down by my arms and ordering my ex-boyfriend to "force" oral sex on me.

Sex with Someone of Another Sexual Preference

I'm in a hotel's health club locker room, shaving. Two gorgeous men come out of the sauna naked except for towels wrapped around their waists. They're talking about meeting "the girls" in the lobby to do something touristy. One disappears to the lockers to dress. The other unwraps his towel and stands naked at the sink next to me. I watch him in the mirror as he begins to play with his huge dick. He's grinning at me, but still shouting banalities to his buddy. He makes himself hard, bends forward and licks the head of his own cock.

My favorite fantasy involves me and my girl- friend at a nude beach on the Mediterranean. We're sunbathing and we can't keep our eyes off each other's brown bodies. I stare at her while pinching my tit, she spreads her legs. We get so hot we decide to swim out to an island to get some privacy. On the island we encounter a man who has sex on his mind, too. Being obliging and greedy girls, we go for it. We take turns being fucked by him; he does one of us while the other watches and masturbates.

Sex with the Stars

I fantasize about mild S/M with five women and one of them must be Cher.

Although (or perhaps because) I am a lesbian, I have really hot fantasies about dominating famous men I find attractive. I've always been caught up in rock 'n' roll idolatry and one of my favorite scenarios is to dress up in a slutty little groupie outfit—you know, spandex and heels— only packing a vibrating dildo underneath. I gain access backstage and meet my idol. I approach him from behind as he's pouring champagne and press up against his ass, knowing he can feel my bulge. He turns and looks at me somewhat bewildered but before he can speak I push him down on the floor and place a stiletto to his chest and maneuver it expertly to pop the buttons on his shirt. I take off my shirt, revealing a cut-out leather bra, then slip off my skirt and expose my nice cock to him. "I named this dildo after you because it brings me such pleasure. Now

I'm going to use it on you so you can experience the ecstasy of being fucked by your own prick." His jaw drops, and I seize the moment to insert my cock into his mouth. I keep up a steady banter. "You narcissistic cock-sucker, if you can sing 'I still haven't found what I'm looking for' after I'm done with you, then there's no hope for you." Then I fuck him in the ass with my dildo, stopping periodically to sip champagne.

I used to get off on Madonna's tits (assorted shots from "Justify my Love" and "Cherish" videos), but now that I'm disappointed with her politics and totally unarousing book, that's gone out the window! Oh! Here's a good fantasy involving my favorite two characters from Love and Rockets *comics. Hopey (the more dykey of the two) is between my legs using her mouth, fingers and tongue on me, while Maggie holds my arms down above my head. Maggie talks to me about what Hopey's doing with a soothing, sexy voice and occasionally Hopey gives Maggie some orders. One of the most important details in my fantasies is what everyone's wearing. Bustiers, schoolgirl-type skirts, Doc Martens DRIVE ME WILD.*

I love to fantasize that Xena, Warrior Princess, and her sidekick Gabrielle save me from some sadistic warlords, but afterwards we're all so turned on that the three of us go out and fuck each other. Of course because she's so good at martial arts, Xena can get into all these outrageous positions! But my favorite part of the fantasy is when Xena lets me remove her armor and feel her up while she's still wearing her sexy leather outfit.

A very common fantasy is for a centerfold to surprise me while I'm masturbating. She is dressed and fully made up in centerfold clothing—lots of skin showing, but not necessarily showing anything sexual. I prefer voluptuous women with full hair and full lips like Loni Anderson. She steps through a door, coolly appraises what I am doing. I am stunned by her presence and freeze. She steps towards me, kneels down at the edge of the bed, bends over and takes my cock in her mouth. I can see her full breasts hanging and her long legs.

Group Sex

My wife and I are making it with another straight couple, with no holds barred between any possible combination. Lots of oral action between all four participants. A cock in my mouth and a woman sitting on my cock. A woman sitting on my face while a guy blows me. A woman sitting on my face while I fuck one of the women. Watching the other couple getting each other off while we get each other off while they get off by watching us get off...

Being used by two or more bi or lesbian women as their male sex toy and slut. I would love to be the object of an all-female gang bang.

Myself and two other women—I'm in the least dominant position observing the fierce, passionate loving that is taking place beside or above me. A woman kneeling over me with her cunt near my mouth is being entered from behind by her lover who is also my lover. I can be "ordered" around by both women—there's lots of freedom for me to do or see anything I want with either woman.

A man enters me anally while another man performs cunnilingus, and yet another man sucks on my nipples. I watch another woman being fucked and licked till she comes.

S/M, Bondage and Discipline

A close female friend of my wife is invited over for ostensibly social reasons. At some point in the evening, my wife orders me to undress, while they remain clothed. I am to perform menial chores, and later they restrain me. At their pleasure, I either have to pose or perform. They touch and stimulate me to orgasm.

I would like to own my own men who speak only when spoken to, live to serve and pleasure me and wear nothing. They will bathe me, brush my hair and always keep their asses handy.

A woman controls me and binds me on a couple of chairs or a bed. Then she spreads my mouth open with a ring-gag. She penetrates my anus with a strap-on dildo (and uses plenty of lubricant). After that she invites some people, both male and female, who use me for their sexual purposes. They have fun, and so do I.

Mild S/M fantasy where I am required to beg my partner to keep fucking me. If I stop begging then my partner stops and I lose my excitement.

Being submissive to my partner's dominant role. He tickles my tits while I stroke my clit. In my ear he tells me fantasies akin to 9 1/2 Weeks scenarios—the more graphic, rude and repulsive, the harder I come.

My favorite fantasy involves me being dominated by a man, being made to take off all of my clothing, then have sex with another woman while he watches.

Taboo Sex (Animals, Kids, Etc.)

This month I've been reviving childhood stories (made up) about two boys, who I now realize in retrospect were very hot for one another. I imagine I'm one of them and play out in my mind how these two teenagers end up in bed together and how they stroke and suck each other.

I fantasize about seducing young girls, especially virgins from eleven to fifteen years old. I love the idea of helping them discover their sexuality for the first time, giving them their first orgasm and their first experience of a cock. I also imagine introducing them to kinky sex—tying them up or handcuffing them, making them lick my asshole or watch dirty movies.

I saw a graphic illustration once of a black lab licking the cunt of its mistress. I imagine that big, bumpy tongue on my labia and clit and I have to squeeze my legs together and shiver!

Occasionally I fantasize about "corrupting"— more like initiating—a young man who is inexperienced but very interested in exploring sexuality with an older woman. I like imagining I'm a dominatrix who's schooling him in the fine art of submission.

I like the idea of two gay brothers doing it, and being exhibitionists in front of other family members.

Enjoying Your Fantasies

I fantasize about my lover (usually) when I masturbate–he kind of creeps in my fantasy like smoke. My hand is rubbing my clit real fast and frantic while I'm thinking how much I totally want him. Before I know it I'm panting and coming and oh, oh...

Most people use fantasies to increase their sexual arousal, whether they're enjoying (or antici-pating) sex with themselves or a partner. Over sev-enty percent of male and female respondents to a Kinsey survey reported fantasizing during sex with a partner. Anyone, however, can enjoy a sexual fantasy without expecting to engage in sex. Con-sider it a recreational activity, like walking in the park or talking on the phone–it's something we do to improve our mood, or relieve boredom or stress.

Sexual fantasies calm me down and stop me from obsessing and worrying.

We asked our customers to share their favorite times and places to fantasize and these answers topped many lists: during masturbation, during partner sex, during class, before falling asleep, after waking up, when taking a shower, in the car, on the bus, on an airplane, on the subway, while riding a bike, on the phone, at the office, at home, at the library, instead of doing homework, during meetings and lectures, walking down the street, on the beach, in the financial district.

These responses deserve special mention:

My fantasies most often occur during masturba-tion, but every so often they come out of the blue; for example–sitting on a bus, a man's crotch directly in front of my face. I begin to fantasize about taking out his penis and performing fellatio.

I like to fantasize before going to sleep because it increases the chances of better dreams.

Any time or place where I have more than two minutes without anything to do or read.

My favorite time to fantasize is when it is most inconvenient to do so. For instance, when I am with a customer at work, while I am driving, while I am on hold on the phone.

Some people have one reliable fantasy that they call upon when the mood hits. Others maintain a ready supply of favorites while still others make up new fantasies as they go. When asked about her favorite fantasy, one woman replied:

I don't have a favorite. It varies from fucking whoever my favorite fellow student is, strangers, dogs, bunches of people, multiple genders, groupies, old people, young people, boys, drag queens, famous people, someone I passed at the grocery store, in public, private, inside, outside, me as male, me as a different female, transsexual, etc.

Fantasies are a powerful aphrodisiac because they offer people a chance to enjoy sexual activi-ties they might not normally–or necessarily ever want to–experience. Just as many of us engage in nonsexual fantasizing (daydreaming), like enter-taining thoughts of winning a gold medal, living in an exotic foreign land or being rich and famous, so too can we enjoy the thrill of some chance sexual encounter brought to us courtesy of our imagina-tions. For most of us, the knowledge that we won't engage in these activities in our real lives only adds to the erotic charge of our fantasies.

We also use fantasies to explore different parts of our personalities. Take the example of the seri-ous, to-be-feared commanding officer who enjoys fantasies of submission and humiliation, or the supermom den-mother who fantasizes about being a professional stripper at the local nightclub. You can try on a new gender and other sexual preferences, experiment with their erotic appeal and learn something new about yourself.

My fantasies are often about being straight, which I'm not! One is of being a secretary, and my boss says he'll pay me extra if I fuck him, so we fuck on top of an executive desk in a high-rise with lots of windows.

Fantasies can also function as a rehearsal for a scenario you would actually like to act out. Perhaps you met someone recently—you could mentally role-play a variety of scenarios about how to intimately approach that person. Maybe you're considering trying out some new toy or technique with your partner, and you want to envision a variety of ways to approach the subject and meet with success. These fantasies can sometimes be as much—or more—of a turn-on than the real thing.

Many couples have found that sharing fantasies is a good way to find out what a partner likes. Of course, if keeping your fantasies private is necessary for them to be effective, you may want to think twice about this!

Acting Out Fantasies

Your fantasies don't have to remain entirely in your head. Transform some of them into reality via a few of the games described below. They can revitalize routine sex and settings. All this requires is a sense of adventure and a willingness to experiment.

Role-Playing

You can play with personalities, themes or relationships by placing yourself in imaginary situations and letting a new sexual dynamic emerge. If you've fantasized about a life of movie stardom, it's not too difficult to don some sunglasses, a haughty attitude, and cast yourself as the toast of Hollywood. Your partner can be whomever you desire—an adoring fan, the lead in your newest movie or the casting director.

These folks like to play with a specific theme that excites both of them:

Our favorite fantasies are more or less variations on a theme, a semi-S/M scenario.

My partner portrays a large, heavy gay male in some dominant, fairly dangerous position—we've played with the Star Wars *empire, Nazi Germany, the record industry, a Satanic cult, the Victorian era, and we're currently using characters from a* Godfather-*type Mafia. I'm a woman, but I usually portray a femme-ish gay male in a bottom-type position—a slave, or loved*

submissive boy. We do a lot of verbal domination and occasional verbal humiliation.

This couple leaves the fantasy, and the type of sex, up to chance:

All our game requires is some dice and a willing attitude. First we swap fantasies, describing what we'd like done to us or what we want to do. Then we roll the dice and the high number wins. The loser must perform the desired act, doing everything in her or his power to make the fantasy real. Sometimes it's as simple as giving head. Other times the fantasy can take days and involve a significant amount of work. We do have one rule though: The loser is allowed to say no.

Choreographing the sexual encounter can be almost as much fun as engaging in it; the anticipation can be a heady aphrodisiac. Shop for props and costumes or try drafting a script for yourself. If you're intrigued by role-playing and just need a few more ideas, read a book of fantasies, some erotic fiction or watch an erotic movie. You might find characters, settings or activities you'd like to imitate. There are also game books as well as card and board games that offer some imaginative suggestions.

Common Roles

- school girl/boy and head mistress/master
- rich widow and delivery person
- commanding officer and enlisted soldier
- truck driver and hitchhiker
- secretary and boss
- star and groupie
- priest/nun and parishioner

Talking Dirty

Ever considered bringing someone to a higher state of arousal through your impressive, obscene verbal skills? Unaccustomed as most of us are to hearing and using sexually explicit language, using it with your partner can lend an intense charge to a sexual encounter. And it lends itself well to different locales—you can unexpectedly set someone's pulse racing in a public place or during the middle of the workday (one individual likes to leave nasty messages on his girlfriend's voice mail). Countless respondents to our survey mentioned explicit language as something that turns them on during sex.

I get off on talking dirty and reading erotic literature while we fondle and fuck. I do like crossing the line of propriety.

Using words like cunt, cock, fuck, pussy *and others is exciting to me and my partner.*

Most folks are intrigued by the idea of explicit sex talk but don't know how to begin. Start with writing your own list of dirty words. If you need a little help developing a sexual vocabulary, track down something like *The Dictionary of Sexual Slang*. Read a variety of erotic material, from the explicit to the euphemistic. Watch an X-rated movie, paying special attention to the dialogue you find arousing. Take a look at which words hold a special sexual charge for you. Similarly, read and watch erotica with a partner to discover which words are a turn-on for him or her. You may find that you each respond better to one type of language over another. For example, "I crave the feel of your sweet lips on my ripe, juicy peach" might stir your lust more than "Suck on my pussy until I explode" or vice versa. You may find you respond particularly well to certain words or phrases, or just to certain styles.

Dirty talk right up close to my ear is the ultimate. Especially P words, like "pound your pecker" or "pump my pussy you pud." The air-expunging P-sound is like a Smart Missile running right smack into an erogenous zone, a G-spot inside my brain somewhere.

I enjoy talking dirty as long as it doesn't get explicit—I like it to be very suggestive and mysterious.

If you're suffering from a bit of performance anxiety or are fearful you won't be taken seriously, practice. Talk to yourself in the mirror or while puttering around the house—just make sure no one's home! Practice using your hot words while you're masturbating. If you usually moan, try substituting words as you get excited or voicing the fantasy you're having. Phone sex can be a good place to start; if you're calling a service you may be emboldened by the anonymity. We'll talk more about this in the next section.

If you're struggling with your script or subject matter, relax. You don't have to memorize the text of a pornographic bestseller, you've got plenty of material inside your brain. Describe a past sexual encounter or, if you're with your partner, try relaying the sexual activity you're engaging in at the moment. Give your partner a verbal list of the many ways you like to be made love to or elaborate on what you'd like to do to her or him. Fantasies and erotic dreams lend themselves well to storytelling; you can have your partner ask you specific questions to draw out the details. Or make a game out of it by taking turns making up parts of the story.

Keep in mind that your language doesn't have to be explicit to be erotic. Role-playing can present you with new options for communicating sexually to a partner. You may find that just hearing your partner speak to you in the commanding voice of a drill sergeant is enough to set your pulse racing.

There's no wrong way to talk dirty! If your partner doesn't enjoy the activity as much as you do, perhaps you don't share the same turn-on around certain stories, words or themes. You may talk yourself into a frenzy of desire when the subject is dominance, whereas your partner's preference might be for sex with a science-fiction twist. Take turns indulging each other, and you should both be happy. If you like sex talk but it leaves your partner cold, you might ask yourself how important it is to you. Your partner may not want to participate in the dialogue, in which case you could simply get off from your own storytelling.

Phone Sex

Although phone-sex lines have been around for years, since the onset of AIDS, phone sex—paid and unpaid—has increased in popularity because it's a completely safe and discreet way to get off. Anyone can understand the appeal of phone sex; just think about the last time you spoke to someone whose voice you found surprisingly sexy. Imagine yourself in a receptive, aroused state while that caller switches from extolling the virtues of a new long distance service to describing the contours of her or his fine physique!

This popular activity often involves masturbating while engaging in sexually explicit conversations over the phone. Most people think of nine-hundred numbers or paid phone calls to anonymous operators when you mention the term phone sex, but certainly any two (or more) people can engage in their own version of phone sex.

My lover lives in another town so phone sex is fun. We'll masturbate and describe to each other what we're touching, how it feels—it's a great way to let the other person know what turns you on.

My first experience of lesbian sex was on the phone with my best girlfriend when we were fifteen. We were too chicken to actually do anything to each other for a while so we told each other what we wanted to do over the phone.

You know what else is fun? Getting a phone call when you're in the middle of masturbating—or even just stimulating yourself while you're on the phone. It's exciting and risky. Kind of embarrassing, but fun.

With the growing popularity of cellular phones, you can get pretty creative about where and when you place that provocative call. Think about calling him at the office the next time you're nude sunbathing. Or dial her car phone when you know she'll be stuck in rush-hour traffic and let her know what's really on your mind. Nasty messages on answering machines and voice mail can be another fun game—just make sure you dial the right number!

The phone-sex industry offers several different options for the libidinous caller who's willing to pay for the call:
♦ You can dial a sexually explicit recorded message.
♦ You can speak live to one operator who will share nasty thoughts and fantasies tailored to your specifications.
♦ You can hook up with a party line—one or several other callers who get each other off as a group. For a hilarious and hot transcription of the phone conversation between a man and a woman

---

Tips for Enjoying Phone Sex

♦ *Get in the mood.* Before you make the call spend a little time relaxing with a glass of wine or some favorite music and fantasize about what you want to talk about. You may want to wear some sexy clothing, or nothing at all.

♦ *Get comfortable.* Set yourself up in your favorite chair or stretch out on the bed. Find a position that will allow you to hold the phone and play with yourself at the same time. Speaker phones free up both hands, while cellular phones allow for maximum mobility around the house (or garden or pool or office)!

♦ *Be prepared.* Have some lube nearby and some tissues or a sex towel. If you plan on using sex toys, put them within easy reach and make sure they're all plugged in.

♦ *Take charge.* To get your money's worth out of commercial phone sex, be prepared to initiate the sex talk, otherwise you may waste time while the operator tries to figure out what you want. Remember, the longer you're on the line the more money the company makes, so they're in no hurry to get you off (pardon the pun). It might help to set a timer if you're the type who loses track of time and would not be prepared for a five-hundred-dollar orgasm.

---

who hook up via this last option, pick up a copy of Nicholson Baker's novel *Vox.*

Engaging in phone sex can be a great way to learn how to talk dirty—they say the best way to learn a foreign language is to immerse yourself in it. It also enables you to explore some of the fantasies or qualities you find particularly arousing. Southern accents may leave you cold while British accents turn out to be just the thing to raise your temperature. Many folks find the anonymity of the exchange allows them to be more daring when it comes to vocalizing their desires.

Phone sex is the ultimate in intimacy. Having to be verbal, explicit and direct is a potent erotic combination because I'm a shy person.

Phone sex is wonderful for connecting my penis and my prostate to my mind. I feel safe talking dirty when I'm not face to face with someone. It's an intensified form of shared imaginations; the negotiations are very different, and they keep shifting with words instead of actions.

Commercial phone-sex companies cater to every conceivable sexual preference and proclivity. You can sample everything from "the voyeuristic journey of female bodybuilder fantasies" to "cross-dressers waiting to meet you." The FCC does regulate what words and subjects can be discussed over the phone lines, so don't expect to explore fantasies of bestiality, incest or sex with clergy members with professional phone-sex operators. Phone-sex advertisements can be found in many sex magazines, tabloids, gay newspapers and directories. Make sure to read the rate information in the ad, as charges can vary drastically between companies.

Pagers

Once an annoying little beeper used primarily by on-call doctors, the pager is now a sophisticated, affordable device that offers the erotic possibilities of a vibrator, a computer and a phone. Everyone from expectant parents to security guards enjoys the instant communication offered by the pager, but not everyone has discovered that pagers can be used for erotic expression and arousal. Invest in a pager with a digital readout and the caller can leave short, steamy messages for the recipient. Combine this with a vibrating model, and your sweetheart will receive your sexy sentiment along with a titillating buzz!

I wanted to eat in the restaurant at Nordstrom's but there was a wait, so they gave me a pager to carry around while I shopped. I put the pager in my breast pocket and when it buzzed I shrieked! I certainly gave the sales clerks a good laugh; they must see that little sex toy work its magic all the time.

Exhibitionism and Voyeurism

Most people associate exhibitionism with the flasher who gets off by showing his genitals to a shocked stranger, and this activity is illegal. Many of us, however, possess exhibitionist tendencies that we can act on safely with consenting partners. Some people like the thrill of having sex in semi-public places because the chance of getting caught increases their arousal. Some enjoy performing acts of exhibitionism for their lovers' eyes only, because it turns one or both of them on.

We love to have sex in a public place with the risk of being discovered at any minute.

I love to be sexual in dangerous places.

I like being watched when I masturbate, which works out well since my husband says he gets turned on by watching me.

I get off on a little exhibitionist teasing. I have nice breasts and will frequently wear something scant and revealing.

I enjoy spending long hours in public with a woman who is exhibitionistic within the bounds of fashion and style (short skirts, heels, deep necklines, sheer fabrics). If she is affectionate and sexual, all the better.

If there's an exhibitionist in you but you're not sure how to let her or him out, go to a strip club, rent an instructional strip video, check out stripping scenes in erotic videos, and then practice some of the moves you see. Observe people around you and notice what turns you on so you can appropriate any of the things you see for your own exhibitionist behavior. You may find that certain clothes, an attitude, even a hair style catch your attention. Experiment with wearing tight, sheer or revealing clothing. Masturbating somewhere besides your bed can make you feel more exposed or daring. Ask your partner if you can masturbate in front of him or her or start walking around the house naked. For encouraging guidance on unleashing your sexy inner self, read Carol Queen's engaging book, *Exhibitionism for the Shy*.

Voyeurism is the flip side of exhibitionism—voyeurs are folks who enjoy watching others have sex. Voyeurism can be fun when you indulge in it with willing partners. Watching your partner strip or masturbate, peeking through the keyhole as she or he bathes, making X-rated home videos together—these are ways to express your voyeuristic side. Alone, you can enjoy voyeurism by going to strip shows, looking at pornographic materials and overhearing the neighbors having sex!

I enjoy lingerie (wearing it, being admired in it, taking it off, or doing it with it on). I also enjoy looking at pictures of my lover and me having sex.

Once I watched my best friend make love and it was totally beautiful!

Love voyeurism! When I was in NYC, I could watch hetero sex across the courtyard and homosexual activity across and one floor up. Made me very hot.

Cross-Dressing

If you find yourself partial to the costumes involved in role-playing or you're simply fond of your girl or boyfriend's clothing, dress up! Many of us get an erotic charge out of putting on and wearing the opposite sex's clothing; it's a harmless way to indulge our fantasies. Even though it's often associated with drag queens, cross-dressing is more common among straight men. And there are plenty of women who have "passed" as men over the ages, as well as modern-day "drag kings" with fully-developed male personas. We'd like to expand the definition of cross-dressing to include anyone who gets a sexual charge from dressing up in clothing not typically associated with his or her particular sexual identity. For example:

I'm a butch girl who occasionally loves to dress up in sexy lingerie.

Sex Toys

We were tickled to see how many people include sex toys in their descriptions of favorite fantasies. In some instances, they are one of many props that enhance a scene:

I fantasize about being in a ménage à trois with two other bisexuals and a room full of toys, ties and swings.

I want to have a group of five or six women kissing, sucking, fucking and touching me all over after I have done the same for each of them. I want to be last so I am as hot as I can get. We use dildos, feathers, crops, restraints, blindfolds, wax and oils.

In other fantasies, they play the starring role:

I have this one super fantasy that involves me and my girlfriends simultaneously getting off every night with vibrators in our dormitory at a Catholic girls' school.

I fantasize about fucking a guy with a strap-on while I jack him off.

We like to remind people who shop at Good Vibrations of the enormous fantasy potential of their purchases. A woman strapping on a dildo and harness suddenly finds herself with a "penis" and can have some fun with the new perspective it provides her. This woman may be a perfect candidate:

Although I am a femme lesbian, I always seem to fantasize that I have a dick.

Cock rings are another example of sex toys with fantasy appeal. Adorning that penis with a lovely collar not only perks it up, but it can tease out some of those stud fantasies.

I enjoy the look and feel a cock ring gives. It's ornamental in a way that makes me feel a bit daring and more confident.

Group Sex

FRIENDS AND INTIMATES Sex with more than one person at a time is a popular, hot fantasy. In a recent survey of *Men's Confidential* readers, eighty-four percent of the predominantly heterosexual male respondents said they fantasize about masturbating in front of or with other men. Although more people have an interest in group sex with friends than act this out, several customers shared actual experiences of multiple mouths and hands exploring their bodies.

The hottest foursome I had involved butch/femme play, dildos, blow jobs, lingerie and latex. We made a lot of noise and broke my friend's bed.

I like masturbating with other guys—it's quick and just about sex—which is not usually the case when I'm with women.

I like to experiment with threesomes. Usually it has been two women and one man, although I would like three women.

I would like group sex if it were with good friends.

When it comes to sex, the more the merrier! I've managed several times with two women and a man, and am still looking to try two women.

If this sounds like fun, why not throw a party? You could be the first person on your block to do so, and it sure beats sitting around waiting for someone else to do it! Plan it like you would any party—send out invitations (ask for an RSVP) and prepare delicious finger food. You may want to let your guests know in advance what your party rules will be (i.e., safer sex, consensual activity, polite behavior, etc.). Arrange your house or apartment so there are comfortable areas to play in and furnish them with sheets, pillows and cushions. Cue up an X-rated video or put on some sexy music to help get things started. Make plenty of party favors available to your guests: condoms, gloves and dams, lubricant, vibrators, dildos, massage oil, whipped cream, soft mitts, paddles and anything else you think will inspire your playmates. You're all set to earn your reputation as the hottest host or hostess in town!

JACK-AND-JILL-OFF PARTIES AND SEX CLUBS
Group-sex parties have become increasingly popular in the age of AIDS. Some (but definitely not all) are governed by strictly enforced rules regarding consensual behavior and no-risk activities. These parties usually feature courteous guests, safer sex accouterments and toys, and provide a secure, playful environment for those who want to voyeurize, exhibit, role-play, fantasize, masturbate and experiment.

I love to watch sex between people at sex parties, especially two men having sex together.

Folks interested in exploring group sex, but who are frustrated by the logistics of organizing their own parties, could investigate this alternative. You can usually only find these parties in certain major cities, and attendance is often by invitation only, so getting hooked up with one requires some work.

Larger versions of these parties are sometimes held in clubs and are a bit easier to find. Look for announcements in local sex newspapers or magazines. Although sex clubs are subject to regulations (usually from the local health department) that seek to prevent the spread of AIDS, not all clubs follow them, so you won't always find safer sex practiced. Try to find out in advance if the club adheres to safer sex guidelines and avoid the ones that don't.

Parties and clubs cater to a gay, lesbian, straight, mixed or S/M clientele; inquire in advance if you don't know the group's particular slant.

Games

If you've ever played strip poker, spin the bottle or adapted an ordinary board game for sexual purposes, you've discovered the erotic potential of game-playing. Adult board games, card games and word games abound and run the gamut from those intended to improve erotic expression to those that script out sexual scenarios. One of Good Vibrations' most popular impulse buys is a pair of Dirty Dice. One die lists a variety of actions—lick, suck, kiss, etc.—and the other lists body parts—lips, below the waist, etc. You both win with every shake of the dice.

Games often introduce an element of chance into sex play; the unpredictable outcome of the encounter can be particularly exciting. It's also liberating to simply agree to play by someone else's rules. With many games, not only are you relieved of any responsibility for planning the next move, you're being told what to do. This can be a nice break for those who tend to choreograph sexual encounters, as well as a welcome change for people whose imaginations may need a little jump start. Games also give you permission and guidance when it comes to exploring fantasies you might otherwise be too embarrassed or shy to bring up with a partner. Finally, if you've been intrigued by many of the suggestions for acting out your fantasies but aren't sure where to start, games can be a great way to try on a new persona, practice talking dirty and engage in a little exhibitionism, among other things.

Concerns about Fantasies

Many of us have an unwritten code about what is appropriate material for fantasy. When our imaginations cross the line, we might feel guilt or fear that something's wrong with us. Remember the beauty of fantasy is that it's all in your head! No one need be invited in that you don't want, so the only judge and jury is you. If your fantasies are bringing you pleasure and not causing anyone else pain, why not leave the thought police out of it?

Nonetheless, the only person who can give you permission to enjoy your fantasies is you. If you are worried about them, you might want to examine the reasons behind your concern. There are a few common anxieties people experience when it comes to fantasies.

Guilt That Fantasies Aren't about Your Partner

Generally, I don't like to have fantasies that are too involved and that he's not in, because it makes me feel too distant and not as connected with him.

As noted earlier, many people's fantasies don't involve their current partners. There are no rules that say they should. We feel a sense of obligation to feature real-life lovers in our dreams. But just because you spend all day working for an autobody shop doesn't mean your daydreams have to all take place in cars. Perhaps you feel okay fantasizing about someone else while masturbating, but not during sex with your partner. You'll certainly agree that fantasizing about someone else doesn't mean your partner is dispensable or any less desirable, so why not just enjoy the fantasy as you would sex toys or erotic books and videos—as fun and easy ways to heighten your arousal. Trying to restrict your fantasy life only inhibits

your experience of sex. If you'd like your lover to figure into your fantasies, try substituting her or him in a leading role (or as a bystander) and see if you can sustain the charge.

If your partner is giving you grief about fantasizing about someone else, chances are he or she isn't being honest about his or her own fantasies or perhaps doesn't fantasize at all. Try explaining that your fantasies aren't an indication that you want someone else, they simply increase your sexual excitement, and in the end you both benefit. Reassure your partner of your affection and ask if he or she has any fantasies to share. If none of this works, you might be better off keeping your fantasies to yourself!

Anxiety Over Fantasies That Stray to Taboo or Forbidden Behaviors

Oh dear. My sexual fantasies are totally politically incorrect and in the past have caused me to suffer guilt. I often fantasize about being completely under the control of a majestic woman. I also fantasize about multiple sex partners and prostitution.

This is probably the most common, troublesome impediment to enjoyment of our fantasies. Many of our customers punctuated their descriptions of unusual fantasies with the disclaimer "This is only a fantasy," meaning, "I would never do this in real life." For most people, this reassurance is what enables them to push the boundaries of the erotic imagination.

Nonetheless, some people fear that if they are fantasizing about some taboo-breaking activity, they must harbor a secret desire to actually do it. There is absolutely no indication that having a fantasy automatically leads to acting on that fantasy. In fact you may fantasize about a specific scenario or activity precisely because it's outside the realm of your experience. When Jack Morin surveyed men and women about their peak erotic experiences and their most arousing fantasies for his book *The Erotic Mind,* he found that power play was a key component in exciting fantasies twice as often as it was in real life encounters. Certain themes that might be anxiety-provoking or inhibiting to enact in real life can be powerfully arousing in the security of our fantasies.

Taboo subject matter is infused with erotic significance almost by definition. The forbidden, the mysterious and the dangerous have a seductive appeal. As behaviors become less taboo, we are less likely to rely on them for fantasy material. Not long ago a woman showing a little leg from underneath heaps of petticoats would send a guy into erotic overload.

Fantasizing Too Much or Too Little

Some folks feel that they fantasize too much. Just as with masturbation, there are no standards against which to compare yourself. If your fantasies interfere with your ability to do anything else, then you'd be wise to seek professional help. If they're *not* hurting anyone, and you just feel a guilty pleasure for having an active imagination, enjoy yourself—we salute your filthy mind!

If you feel that you don't fantasize and would like to, you can stimulate your imagination in several ways. Focus on an erotic memory, read some literature, look at a magazine or watch an X-rated movie. Or pay attention to the thoughts and images that pass through your mind when you're masturbating or having sex. You may be assuming that you don't fantasize simply because you don't have a full-fledged erotic movie running in your head, complete with plot and dialogue. Yet any image, memory or fleeting thought that you use to heighten arousal counts as a fantasy.

If you feel that fantasies aren't necessary to your sexual enjoyment, that's fine. Just as there are no rules against fantasizing, neither are there any saying it's compulsory.

Anxiety over Fantasies You Don't Want to Have

You may feel that the fantasy you use to get off is one you'd rather do without. Perhaps you're a survivor of sexual trauma and your fantasy relates to the abuse. Maybe there's an evil ex-lover dominating your erotic thoughts, and you wish he or she would find someone else's dreams to haunt. Our sexual scripts are affected by the major emotional and psychological events in our lives, and it stands to reason not all of these will be positive.

If you're unable to accept your fantasies, or if they exacerbate a sense of low self-esteem or self-hatred, you can take steps to change your pattern. Attempt to separate your fantasy from your sexual activity. When you're masturbating, concentrate on your physical feelings, and explore a full range of sensuous touch, rather than focusing solely on genital stimulation. If you find your attention wandering to undesirable thoughts or images, consciously guide it toward other less destructive, yet arousing thoughts and images. Gaining control over problematic fantasies doesn't mean you have to give up having a rich fantasy life. Read a variety of erotic literature or rent some X-rated videos to discover new images to supplant the old ones. In order to reprogram your fantasies, you'll need to explore what it is that gives the current, troubling fantasies their erotic charge. Jack Morin's provocative book, *The Erotic Mind,* is a groundbreaking exploration of the complex nature of sexual arousal and has an excellent section devoted to transforming "troublesome turn-ons." We can't recommend this book highly enough to anyone who wants to learn more about the nature and power of the erotic imagination.

What Now?

Perhaps you've been reading this chapter wondering, "How do people come up with this stuff?" Some folks are highly creative and capable of scripting incredible fantasies using only their imaginations. Others draw on dreams or memories of past sexual experiences. You can elaborate on the activity or change the characters, but the plot has already been written. Most of us do all of the above, as well as employ a variety of visual and written materials to fill our fantasy universe and heighten our arousal—a discussion of these erotic materials follows in the next chapter. Remember, the best thing about fantasies is the freedom they give us to be and act any way we want. A creative fantasy life contributes to a fulfilling, arousing sex life.

CHAPTER 14

Books, Magazines and Videos

I first encountered the wondrous world of graphic erotica as a boy of ten who filled his bike tires at a neighborhood gas station. The owner and some of his customers constantly played "pick up" games of poker, using one of those decks with amazingly candid black-and-white photographs of sex on the backs of all the cards. That was forty years ago and I still recall, vividly, and with no small excitement, a few of those breathtakingly arousing scenes.

This man eloquently demonstrates the power of visual or written imagery to elicit a sexual response. Not only can we enjoy heightened sexual arousal in the process of reading or viewing sexual materials, but we can store the memory to draw upon at a later time. You don't have to lay in a lifetime supply of nasty playing cards though; for many people, good fantasy material is only as far away as the nearest book, magazine or video. Whether your preference is for romance novels, lesbian erotica, *Penthouse* letters, underground comix, underwear ads or adult movies, you don't have to look far to satisfy your tastes.

If you already use books or videos to spark your libido, this section may suggest additional materials you might enjoy. If you've never indulged in this pastime, you may end up with some ideas about how to start. If you've ever been surprised to find yourself aroused by something you had no idea was erotic, you may want to try some of the more explicit materials we recommend in this chapter. If you aren't interested in erotic books and videos, that's fine. Porn isn't everyone's cup of tea, and we don't expect it to be. But if you're uncomfortable with the idea of reading or viewing sexually explicit materials, and aren't sure why, you may want to read on.

To get in the mood, think back to your own first sweet encounter with sexual imagery. Many a youth's surprise sexual awakening resulted from exposure to images depicting anything from hints of a sexual undercurrent to explicit behavior.

I first orgasmed while masturbating to Batman! *It was an episode where Batgirl was "captured" by some evil villain—she was in a cage—Batman and Robin were slow in saving her—this was a big turn-on to me at seven.*

I saw a Playboy *photo with a woman with flour on her pussy; she was supposed to be a cookie going into the oven. I was eleven, and I wanted to try this because it turned me on so. I got baby powder and put it all over my pussy. I got so excited by this, I started to explore myself. I played with my cunt until I came. I had no idea what was happening, but it was fun!*

It seems like everyone has a memory of stumbling on a cache of porn under a family member's bed—it almost makes one believe in a porn Santa who delivers little bundles to the naughty and nice. Remember the bra ads in the Sears catalog or those passages from dog-eared Victorian novels? Now you're in the proper frame of mind to read about today's options in the world of porn. At the end of this book you'll find a bibliography of erotic books and videos, so you can finally retire that beat-up old copy of the *Sports Illustrated* swimsuit edition and try something new.

Before launching into a description of the various types of explicit material available, we'd like to confess that we find efforts to discriminate between "erotica" and "porn" pointless at best and tedious at worst. The only criteria Good Vibrations has for selecting the erotic books and X-rated videos we carry is that consenting adults produced them with the goal of inspiring sexual arousal. If what you read or view gets you off, you may call it what you will.

While we use the terms *erotica, porn* and *smut* interchangeably, we frequently refer to written works as "erotica" and to films or videos as "porn." This is purely a convenience, and we certainly don't mean to imply any moral or aesthetic judgment in doing so. Consumers, reviewers and media people who discuss sexually explicit materials often seem compelled to make distinctions between "good" erotica, which is defined as displaying literary or artistic merit, and "bad" smut, which is defined as hopeless trash. Needless to say, these distinctions are purely subjective—one person's sublime erotic literature is bound to be another's tawdry smut.

The bottom line in assessing the value of "erotica" or "porn" must be: Does it arouse you? People who critique a piece of erotic writing or an X-rated video without divulging whether or not it turned

them on are missing the point. Of course, it's challenging to speak openly about our sexual desires and appetites—it's much safer to criticize a story's clumsy plot device or a video's poor lighting than to confess to the fact that it got us wet. It takes courage to recognize and cop to what makes you hot, but once you do you end up with a clear, honest picture of yourself, along with the ability to name—and claim—your desire. And, your recommended reading/viewing list will be a much sought-after resource among your friends!

Knowing what turns you on will help if you're searching for "hot" books or videos. Customers often ask us to recommend titles. We ply them with any number of questions in our attempts to discover what they're more likely to enjoy. Try filling out our Erotica Shopping Checklist before you venture into a store.

Keep in mind that one person's arousing read is another's certified snooze. If you're not sure what kinds of sexual activities you'll like to read about or see portrayed, think about what sorts of fantasies work for you, or try to recall the last movie or book you read that elicited some kind of erotic response. By all means explore a variety of materials—your libido may be two steps ahead of your conscious mind. Erotic anthologies and compilation videos are great ways to sample a variety of styles, themes and activities without going bankrupt investing in a library of sexually explicit materials.

Books

Whether you want to read alone to get yourself "in the mood," recite erotic passages to your lover or re-enact scenes from what you're reading, the printed word has tremendous potential to inspire our sex lives. It can transform everyday sex into a euphoric communion or fuel your fantasies with people, places and positions you might never have dreamed up yourself.

Where to Shop for Books

If only purchasing your erotica were as easy as buying a *Soap Opera Digest* in the check-out line at the supermarket. And why shouldn't it be? After all, you could argue that soap operas have almost as much sex in them! Unfortunately, when it comes to finding erotic books people usually run into a few problems. Here are your options:

Chain bookstores. Most folks patronize chain bookstores because they're convenient. Sadly, you'd think their buyers had never heard the adage "sex sells," since they carry so few erotic titles. They tend to carry books published by mainstream houses, which results in a limited selection since most of the more diverse material is published by smaller presses. Even if your chain carries erotica, where do you go to find it? We've never seen erotic fiction nicely displayed in a section all its own (this might offend the sensibilities of those purchasing the latest fitness books from the counter display). If it's mixed in with the rest of the fiction, you either have to browse through thousands of titles or know the name or author of a specific book. Maybe the erotica is shelved with the nonfiction sex books, but where are those? If you're truly lucky, your store will have a sexuality section and you may find erotica there. Unfortunately, many stores shelve sex books in their general "health" section and you usually won't find fiction there.

Independent bookstores. These shops can come through for you. If the owner is fairly progressive (and book readers tend to be), you might find a good selection, or he or she might stock your recommendations. They are also more likely to carry books by smaller publishers.

Gay and lesbian bookstores. If you're lucky enough to live near one of these, they should carry a pretty good selection of gay and lesbian erotica. If they don't, get them to! These stores will also carry titles published by smaller presses.

Adult bookstores. You might find a selection of smut books and sex magazines, but don't expect advice or information from the sales staff.

> ## EROTICA SHOPPING CHECKLIST
>
> ✔ *Activities.* What types turn you on? Will descriptions of taboo activities light your fire or douse it?
>
> ✔ *Orientation.* Are you interested in a specific orientation (straight, lesbian, gay, bisexual, transgendered) or is a mix desired?
>
> ✔ *Voice.* Are you interested in a specific point-of-view, for instance a woman's perspective, a gay male perspective or a partnered perspective?
>
> ✔ *Genres.* What kinds of themes entertain you in other media, for example: science fiction, film noir, historical fiction, adventures in far-off lands? Erotic materials are available in a wide range of genres.
>
> ✔ *Language.* Do you prefer explicit sexual references or colorful euphemisms?
>
> ✔ *Comparison shopping.* Is there a similar title you can suggest to the clerk for comparison's sake?
>
> ✔ *Format.* With books, would you prefer short stories over novels? With videos, perhaps you'd like a compilation rather than a full-length feature.
>
> ✔ *Quality.* Are literary merit and high production values priorities?

Sex boutiques. If you live in an urban area, this is your best bet. You should find a pretty diverse selection, an informed staff and a welcoming environment.

Mail-order catalogs. Mail-order sex-book catalogs are not nearly as common as toy or video catalogs—our Sexuality Library remains one of the few in existence. (It's very difficult to turn a profit with a mail-order book catalog.) However, some adult catalogs, gay and lesbian catalogs, and mainstream book clubs have erotica sections.

Fiction

There is a wealth of erotic fiction available today in nearly every genre—science fiction, horror, epic romance, among others. Some folks prefer the subtle or romantic, while others want access to the explicit language of sex; it is the latter that we'll focus on here. The bulk of erotic fiction appears in short-story anthologies (many authors) or collections (one author). Erotic novels, fairly scarce up until the nineties, are gaining in popularity. Some novels claim to be "sexy," but be wary, since this is a common advertising ploy, and in reality the sexual content is often microscopic or nonexistent.

WOMEN'S EROTICA This category covers contemporary erotic fiction penned by women and includes straight, lesbian and bisexual authors. Up until the late eighties only a handful of authors and editors—Lonnie Barbach, the Kensington Ladies, Anaïs Nin, Pat Califia, Tee Corinne and Susie Bright—filled this niche. Their books were published primarily by small, independent, often feminist publishers and were underground hits with readers who appreciated the emergence of erotica emphasizing women's sexual gratification.

I've read tons of erotica but I can still count on this one story in Barbach's Pleasures—*which I first read ten years ago—to turn me on when everything else fails.*

Macho Sluts *by Pat Califia definitely enlivened my fantasy life.*

My first taste of women's erotica were the stories in Herotica—*how delicious! I relished the breadth of sexual experiences described and that the women's desires—whether kinky or conventional—were central to the plot.*

Large publishing companies jumped on the bandwagon, and today dozens of new titles appear annually. You can now find stories, published by both mainstream and independent publishers, that reflect a variety of themes, characters and sexual tastes. Tales written by and about large women, stories of lesbians losing their virginity and erotic musings by women of color are just a few examples of how real-life diversity is finally being reflected in the growing body of sexual literature.

Not surprisingly, you will definitely find greater representation of female sexual experience (that's ladies' orgasms too, please) in women's erotica than you will in some other genres. You'll also get a more flexible definition of "erotic." Some material billed as erotica is less explicit than a "Dear Abby" column, so browse before buying.

Lesbian erotica, published primarily by small presses, is also an expanding category. Look for well-known, prolific authors like Tee Corinne, Robbi Sommers and Pat Califia or sample the cream of the crop from a new series, *Best Lesbian Erotica.* If you think only women write lesbian erotica, read the anthology *Switch Hitters: Lesbians Write Gay Male Erotica and Gay Men Write Lesbian Erotica,* proof that good smut transcends gender. Women and men of all sexual preferences enjoy lesbian erotica and its focus on female sexual pleasure.

My lover and I spend hours reading to each other, taking turns with lesbian erotic stories.

For my own pleasure, I buy lesbian erotica even though I'm straight. I really like the writing and romance that I find within the pages.

GAY PORN As you might expect, male sexuality is front and center in gay porn, authored primarily by men—John Preston and Samuel Steward among the more prolific—but also by a few women such as Anne Rice and Pat Califia. Perhaps because it rarely confuses its priorities—one-handed reading is as important as the quality of the writing—gay porn never fails to deliver what it promises: no-holds-barred graphic depictions of sex. Consequently, there has always been a large market for gay male porn (both written and visual), whose fans include a growing number of lesbians and straight women. You don't have to look farther than the nearest gay bookstore to find volumes of gay sex writing featuring surfers, body builders, truck drivers, leather daddies and urban professionals, but if you want to sample a variety, check out series such as *Best Gay Erotica* or *Flesh and the Word.* S/M themes are far more prevalent in gay porn than in women's erotica.

I like hardcore sex, and gay porn dishes it out reliably.

I like the abundance of sex in gay porn—lesbian sex stories are too focused on emotional conflict for me.

SMUT At Good Vibrations we've affectionately named this genre "dimestore smut"—inexpensive (under six dollars), devourable, mass-market collections of explicit writing often by anonymous or pseudonymous authors, with roots in classics like *Autobiography of a Flea* and *Fanny Hill.*

Smut doesn't pretend to be anything other than writing about sex—its goal is to get you off. These books specialize in colorful language, meticulously detailed sex scenes and taboo activities. Smut books generally favor content over form (i.e., no Pulitzer-prize aspirations), or as one of our coworkers so aptly described them, "They offer little of lasting literary merit but plenty of enjoyable rambunctious lechery." This genre is becoming so large, however, that some authors are making a name for themselves. Look for those who've written several books, this is often a good indication of their popularity.

Smut books are my choice for a sure-fire turn-on. They skip the flowery euphemistic language that bogs down some women's erotica and describe nasty, naughty sex on page after page.

No, it's not great literature—but I don't care. The erotic exploits of the naughty Victorian lads and ladies are jolly good spicy fun.

Smut can also be full of stereotypes, so if you're looking for politically correct sex, skip these books. The genre includes an abundance of "Victorian pornography," though many of these supposed period pieces are "unearthed" (written) annually. These books are printed by the truckload; they can be as formulaic in style as their tamer sister, the Harlequin romance, but more diverse in theme—you won't find gay priests, sadistic heterosexual twins or lesbian jet-setters in a Harlequin!

I read hundreds of Harlequins when I was a teen but got so frustrated that the sex scenes were always left up to the imagination. I love reading those cheap-o pornographic paperbacks; they never leave me hanging!

The diversity apparent in more mainstream erotica is also being reflected in smut. There are spin-off imprints with gay and lesbian themes such as Bad Boy and Rosebud. The British publishing company Black Lace produces nothing but women-authored smut, and Carroll & Graf publishes various "period" lines focusing on adventures from the Victorian era to the Roaring Twenties to the Jazz Age. These books have also found their way onto the shelves of a few airport bookstores, which often give them equal display space alongside the current bestsellers. No wonder so many people fantasize about sex on planes!

AMERICAN MASTERS Henry Miller, Anaïs Nin and Marco Vassi wrote quite a bit of sexually explicit literature in their day and have achieved cult status among many erotica lovers. All three were masters of their craft, using their polished, explicit prose to explore the limits of human sexual behavior—you'll find countless taboos explored in these writings. Miller and Nin can be found in most bookstores; Vassi's work goes in and out of print and will probably be harder to find.

I recently picked up an Anaïs Nin erotica book and started to read some while I was alone. It got me rather hot and bothered and I KNEW that I must read this with my husband in bed. It proved to be very scintillating fodder.

MULTICULTURAL EROTICA The nineties produced a welcome trend: erotic titles that represent a variety of cultural perspectives. Although erotica is still primarily Eurocentric, you can now find separate erotic anthologies from Asian, Latino and African American communities, as well as a variety of ethnic voices represented in large compilations like *The Mammoth Book of Erotica*. Men and women of all orientations are usually represented.

EUROPEAN If you like your erotica on the dark side, you'll enjoy the wave of European titles that have hit the U.S. lately. Distinguished by quality writing, a willingness to explore taboo subjects, and lush, uninhibited prose, these titles offer a nice alternative to some of the more sanitized collections cranked out by large publishers. Look for the Velvet series published by Creation Books.

EROTIC SERIES Otherwise known as "find a need and fill it—over and over and over." Spurred by the success of a single erotic title or theme, publishers capitalize on its popularity by releasing subsequent volumes annually. As of this writing, the classic women-authored erotica series *Herotica* is up to six volumes, the cutting-edge *Best American Erotica* is in its fourth year, and *Best Gay Erotica* and *Best Lesbian Erotica* have released two volumes.

SCIENCE FICTION, SUPERNATURAL, GOTHIC
Tales of aliens or the supernatural have always tickled our imaginations, it's no surprise they make good fodder for sexual fantasy. Anthologies featuring well-known authors as well as little known writers abound on a variety of subjects—alien sex, lesbian vampires, gay intergalactic hunks, and futuristic stories about prostitution, to name a few. For a large selection of futuristic erotica, check out the books by Circlet Press.

SADOMASOCHISM The sheer number of titles in print with S/M themes reveals what a powerful hold S/M has on our fantasy life. Nearly all of the genres we've discussed so far include books that deal with various forms of power play. So whether you're looking for women-authored stories of bondage and discipline, gay leathersex encounters, tales of schoolmistresses disciplining impertinent lads and lasses, or otherworldly crimes against nature, you shouldn't have to search very hard to find them.

LITERARY AND HISTORICAL ANTHOLOGIES
There's always an anthology in print of steamy passages culled from classic and contemporary works of literature. Since you might not otherwise have known your favorite author had a few erotic stories stashed away in the closet, these comprehensive anthologies can be very enlightening and exciting. They should delight any student of literature frustrated that the nasty stuff never made it onto the required reading list. Unfortunately, sometimes the editors stretch the limits of what they consider erotic, but if you cast yourself back to the time, place and conditions under which the pieces were written, you may just get yourself in the mood!

AUDIO EROTICA Those of you who want to spice up your morning commute or your next road trip can now enjoy audio versions of erotic fiction from classics of the Victorian era, such as *The Pearl,* to the more contemporary *Herotica* series. Passion Press is one company specializing in this genre.

Thank god for rest stops. When I put in one of those naughty tapes I often need to pull over and satisfy myself!

MISCELLANEOUS FICTION What's left? We can't fit everything into a nice neat category, and the sex writing we didn't cover usually focuses on extremely specific themes. As the erotica market continues to prosper you'll be seeing even more thematic books—we'd welcome works devoted to sex and food, sex and music, sex outdoors, and sex on various forms of public transportation, to name just a few!

Erotic Nonfiction

FANTASIES Nancy Friday broke ground in the seventies when she published a collection of hundreds of women's sexual fantasies. This important work acknowledged the fantasy lives of women, but more to the point, these fantasies were impossible to read without getting turned on.

The threesome I had with two other women was initiated by reading a Nancy Friday fantasy that got us all so hot we could not contain ourselves any longer!

Friday published subsequent collections of both women's and men's fantasies, and these volumes remain some of the best fantasy fuel around. Although other collections of fantasies have materialized, Friday's volumes were the most commercially successful and are still in print. Her books can be found in the sex section of almost any bookstore.

BIOGRAPHIES You know the saying, "Truth is stranger than fiction"? Substitute the word *hotter* for *stranger,* and you'll catch our drift. Individual sex histories found in collections like *Good Sex: Real Stories from Real People, Sex: Real People Talk About What They Really Do,* or "kiss-and-tell" biographies and memoirs can make for some steamy reading.

SEX MANUALS, SURVEYS, ETC. If you've gotten the least little bit turned on while reading this book, then you know first hand what this category is all about. Often reading about the sexual practices of others can be as arousing as any fiction!

As a young girl I would sneak into my parents' bedroom and read anything I could get my hands on—Fanny Hill, The Joy of Sex, Everything You Always Wanted to Know About Sex..., cheap porn books of my dad's. I would read and rock, sometimes for hours. I didn't have my first successful orgasm 'til eighteen, when I read The Hite Report.

We read sex manuals to each other and then carry out the suggestions.

PERSONAL ADS Personal ads are one cheap way to get off whether you like your porn short and sweet or short and hardcore! You don't have to look farther than your nearest alternative newspaper or check out the alt.personals news group on the Internet.

Midnight ritualistic phallic worship. Masculine, aggressive masseur seeking similar for heavy mutual dirty talk, jerk off, showing off, chanting, phallic appreciation, late night my place. Visual/verbal buddy-to-buddy fantasy, not physical.

The schoolmaster provides home tutoring, training and discipline for the behavior problems of wayward, gum-chewing girls (eighteen) who cannot seem to complete their assignments. Slim, austere appearance; firm, loving hands deliver correction. A ready smile rewards earnest efforts at improvement.

We like to read the personals and then fantasize about me contacting one of the advertised women to play with.

Erotic Art Books

Although erotic art books run the gamut of sexual expression—from collections of fine-art nudes to *Playboy* centerfolds—only you can say what you do or don't find erotic (or what you consider "art," for that matter). But there's no denying the power of a visual image to elicit a strong erotic response, so we encourage you to view a variety of images and learn what pleases you most. Erotic art books tend to fall into the following basic categories, though some combine elements from each. Many are also accompanied by erotic or instructional text. With the exception of really famous artists, there's a limit to the number of erotic art books you'll find in chain bookstores. You probably have a better chance of locating erotic art books in alternative or lesbian and gay bookstores, sex boutiques, some mail-order catalogs and art collectors' catalogs or shops.

PILLOW BOOKS The origins of the pillow book date back to second-century B.C. China. These were manuals for married couples, complete with instructions on foreplay, intercourse, techniques, positions and advice, all lavishly illustrated so one could learn and practice at the same time. The originals no longer exist, but the form has reinvented itself over time and across cultures—the most famous pillow book being the Indian *Kama Sutra of Vatsayana*. This book is almost always in print, but don't confuse the classic edition (beautifully illustrated with Indian paintings) with more sanitized modern versions. Publishers like to rewrite the text and add lots of softcore photos of happy Caucasian couples demonstrating the positions.

There's actually been somewhat of a pillow book renaissance lately, resulting in an abundance of tiny, pocket-sized editions—the perfect size for slipping under a pillow. You can find some with gay and lesbian themes, as well as those that show multiple-partner sex.

I love those Eastern sex manuals because they show such a healthy respect for sex of all kinds—you can find two women, sometimes men, lots of voyeurism and threesomes.

EROTIC PHOTOGRAPHY Perhaps you prefer the work of certain famous contemporary photographers like Robert Mapplethorpe, Herb Ritts or Jan Saudek, or you're attracted to the star quality of a collection of Betty Page photographs. You might be a fan of collections that focus on a specific activity or lifestyle like S/M, cross-dressing, fetish wear or sex work:

The S/M photographs in Sexual Magic *by Michael Rosen validated and inspired me. He captures the eroticism, the creativity and the passion of his subjects.*

Erotic by Nature is a superb book, intelligent and exquisitely put together. I'm savoring every morsel, particularly the stunning photography.

The female nude can be found in everything from collections of lesbian sex photographs, art-history tomes and airbrushed *Penthouse* publications. Male nudes are the subject of many gay photography collections. The pictures in some of the historical collections of erotic photography are worth a thousand words—grainy images of spankings, nymphettes and illicit encounters offer a welcome peek into our prudish past. Fetish photography is also very popular. Taschen publishes a number of beautiful historical and fetish photography books.

FINE ART Collections of erotic fine art are popping up all over the place these days—there's even a fantastic playing-card deck adorned with fifty-two different fine-art nudes (which we would dearly love to send to the gentleman whose quote opens this chapter). Some books focus on a specific time period, others on the works of different artists, others on a specific theme such as the nude or previously banned work.

Once in a while we run across a crafty collection of erotic folk art that usually features work spanning several centuries and cultures. Whether you're curious about those Victorian canes or the sexual significance of the Navaho Kachina doll, you won't find the answers in an ordinary collection of erotic art.

Magazines

Magazines are appealing for several reasons: You've got visual erotica at an affordable price, sex information, fiction, the infamous "Letters to the Editor" section and a new issue to devour every few months. There are a multitude of sex magazines serving almost every imaginable sexual interest. Whether your tastes run toward bondage and fetish gear, lesbian culture, erotica for eggheads or more traditional skin magazines, you usually don't have to look beyond large newsstands or adult, gay and lesbian bookstores.

Gay men's magazines are hot. Those boys are easy on the eye and supply the leading men in my erotic daydreams.

I've enjoyed nude-men magazines since I was ten. I like imagining I'm with the models as I jerk off to them.

I use magazines of a not terribly hardcore sort to arouse myself, Playboy *and* Penthouse. *I am mostly interested in pictures of women (*Vogue *is often a good choice) who are sophisticated-looking and partially dressed.*

You may have noticed a boom in the 'zine market in the last decade. 'Zines are usually low-budget publications (black and white, printed on newsprint or photocopied on inexpensive bond) with a specific theme, sometimes sexual in nature. If you can get your hands on them, you'll find cutting-edge sex writing. Look for these in alternative bookstores.

I get off on stories in 'zines. I enjoy new fantasies, new writing, new images. Depending on how horny I feel I will read for ages, until my cock aches to be wanked.

I love the sex 'zines because they fly in the face of conventional sex magazines and cater to a greater variety of sexual tastes.

Unfortunately magazines and 'zines are more often labors of love than money-making endeavors. Their creators either burn out or run out of money so there can be a pretty rapid turnover in this field.

Comix

Graphic Novels

Many classic X-rated stories like *Story of O* and *Emmanuelle* have been illustrated in the popular genre known as graphic novels. You might find these in adult bookstores and definitely in adult comic stores.

I remember getting really hot once looking at an illustrated story involving a stern, domineering woman and her Great Dane. It reminded me of a really kinky version of Cruella de Vil in 101 *Dalmatians.*

Underground

Artists and cartoonists often use the traditional comic book format to explore very untraditional sexual themes in the genre known as comix. Look for these in adult comic bookstores.

Videos

Thanks to the era of cable television and video cassette recorders, many people have discovered the pleasures of watching X-rated films in the privacy of their own homes. The presence of substantial adult sections in video stores indicates that more than a few people are indulging in this recreation. An estimated thirty percent of all video rentals are X-rated tapes, and the adult video industry is a multi-billion dollar business.

Who's Watching

When I was in high school I came home early from a date one night and walked in on my parents watching an X-rated flick in our living room. They were sitting together about two feet from the TV and looked up at me, mortified at being caught.

If it's hard to imagine our parents having sex, it's probably even harder to imagine them enjoying porn! But not all porn is consumed by men in small booths in the red-light district. Our parents, siblings, children, friends, coworkers and anyone else you can't imagine all watch porn. We started carrying X-rated videos at Good Vibrations in 1989 after literally hundreds of women and men asked us to. As porn critic Susie Bright reminds us:

Contrary to the stereotype that porn viewers are inarticulate raincoaters who have miserable sex lives, people who watch erotic movies have sex lives and they aren't incapable of getting a date. They like movies and they like sex. Their sexual tastes run from real romantic to the kinkier-the-better.

People watch erotic videos for the same reasons they read or view other sexually oriented material—to get aroused, to get new ideas or collect fantasy material, to learn about sexual techniques or behaviors, to get more comfortable with sex. Many couples watch X-rated movies together as a means of igniting sexual desire or sharing with a partner the types of activities they find enjoyable. Later in the chapter we'll share customers' revelations about how they prefer to use porn. For now, let's talk a bit more about the industry.

What to Expect

A VERY BRIEF HISTORY   Porn experienced its Golden Age around the same time the contemporary sex manual hit its peak. The counterculture of the late seventies and early eighties spawned a slew of directors whose films reflected the sexual liberation of the times. Films by the Mitchell Brothers, Radley Metzger, Richard Mahler, Henri Pachard, Robert McCallum and Anthony Spinelli (among others) were characterized by an unprecedented cinematic quality while delivering hot sex, realistic relationships and believable story lines. Peep shows, however, continued to be the primary marketplace for porn, creating a demand for fast and cheap production. The talented directors were simultaneously being ignored by Hollywood, and the combination resulted in a loss of incentive to continue making quality pornography.

The recent invention of the video camera made filmmaking more accessible to a growing number of entrepreneurs with vision. It also resulted in a huge audience of home viewers, and adult producers began churning out volumes of assembly-line porn at rock-bottom prices. Most of the porn that's been released since the mid-eighties is mediocre, formulaic and sloppily produced.

The nineties have brought some positive changes to porn. Now that it's clear men aren't the sole consumers of porn—forty percent of video rentals are to the much-hyped "women's and couple's market"—producers are releasing instructional couples videos, such as Nina Hartley's popular series, along with comedies and dramas highlighting authentic female pleasure. Certain contemporary directors are breaking away from the pack. Andrew Blake's films are praised for their high production values and beautiful casts—these are the ultimate porno eye candy. Paul Thomas' films have earned a lot of fans for delivering strong plots, eliciting compelling performances and portraying female orgasms.

Our national "hard body" obsession is now extending to porn, with both positive and negative results. Performers of the seventies looked more like real people, and many contemporary viewers are frustrated by the fact that most of today's porn starlets are walking Barbie-doll advertisements for plastic surgery. Those seeking a greater diversity of body types have to rely on women-produced, independent and amateur videos in their quest for silicone-free breasts. On the bright side, viewers who have resented the fact that for years female performers were held to certain standards of beauty, while the appearance of male performers was secondary compared to their ability to get it up, appreciate the fact that heterosexual porn now features a bevy of beautiful men—from Sean Michaels to Rocco Siffredi.

While we resent the plastic-surgery norm, there's no question that the glamorous starlets of the nineties are doing a lot to bring porn into the mainstream, becoming the latest darlings of our celebrity-hungry culture. When the girls of Vivid Video are featured on a billboard dominating Sunset Boulevard, and sexy, articulate starlets pop up everywhere from the *Tonight Show* to the E! Entertainment network, surely there's a sea change in societal attitudes at work.

COMMERCIAL PORN   Even though commercial porn has been around for decades, it rarely rises above a certain level of mediocrity thanks to the combined efforts of censors and unimaginative filmmakers. Emphasis is placed on cranking out hundreds of fast-buck films each year, resulting in hoards of barely distinguishable films. Poor sound quality, lighting and faulty tapes are some of the production problems you may encounter. One-dimensional plots, bad acting and formulaic sexual encounters are among the most common complaints. This doesn't mean there aren't exceptions or that even the bad ones won't turn you on. We're just reminding you because forewarned is forearmed! If you don't expect Academy Award-winning material you won't set yourself up for disappointment. Your ability to suspend your normal

standards will vastly increase your enjoyment.

Commercial X-rated videos follow fairly rigid industry conventions with regard to the activities depicted. You can expect predominantly heterosexual sex focusing on male sexual pleasure, a "girl-girl" scene, lots of fellatio, external come shots, anal and vaginal penetration. Sex toys are an ever-increasing presence in porn. Adult toy manufacturers now arrange brand-name tie-ins by featuring certain porn starlets on the packaging for their products and positioning these products in the starlets' videos.

Unfortunately, there's almost no condom use outside of gay porn (where it's the norm). Producers claim that condom use is "performer's choice," but few performers want to identify as someone who demands to use condoms—they rely on regular STD testing and the fact that up-to-date health certificates are required on most sets. A common argument within the industry is that the audience wants to see a fantasy, not a safe-sex scene, but strategic lighting and camera angles can disguise the fact that a condom is even in use. Furthermore, what better way to teach viewers how to eroticize safer sex than to depict a really hot condom encounter? In fact, some independent producers, such as Candida Royalle, do just that.

The appeal of any given porn movie depends on you and your tastes. You might find that just seeing sexually explicit acts performed in your living room is an instant turn-on. Or you may require your porn to meet certain standards in order for you to feel any erotic charge. As these customers illustrate, erotic enjoyment can hinge on a particular star, certain production elements, a particular theme or plot device:

Marilyn Chambers is so charismatic, with real star quality. I think most women find it easy to identify with her.

Most porn actors can't act, so I like Andrew Blake's movies because there's practically no dialogue. They're pretty, with good music, and they're woman-centered.

In The Felines*, the gradual buildup of erotic tension between the young woman and her hosts is refreshing for a porn film. Several passionate* *anal sex scenes between the husband and mistress provide all the immediate gratification you could wish for.*

Even if they're sometimes hokey, I like porn movies with suspenseful plots. They're dark and shadowy, which I find irresistible when combined with sex. Hey, I thought Twin Peaks *was twisted TV porn.*

A particular director or producer's special touch can make all the difference to some viewers:

I prefer the newer videos, which are superior visually and feature good-looking couples. Most films directed by Paul Thomas are, in my opinion, vastly superior to the others. Skin tones are warm, the camera shots are smooth and lingering and, most importantly, the people in the film are given long and continuous stimulation (i.e., the women actually orgasm).

I am interested in videos that reflect honesty, humor and emotional reality and are also professional and artistically sensitive. The best example so far is Andrew Blake's work.

One of the best things about Every Woman Has a Fantasy, *which was co-written and produced by a woman, is the very believable story line. Along with the well-written script and good acting, this made for a refreshingly good and exciting erotic film.*

People's criticisms of pornographic videos run the gamut. Many people bemoan the fact that women's sexual gratification is rarely the main event in porn and is sometimes absent altogether. What's more, depictions of female sex can be stereotypical and downright misleading, as this customer points out with the reference to the orgasm-from-thrusting:

The whole video was fucking and come shots. The woman was supposedly just getting off from the thrusting, but it would've been so nice to see her masturbate and to watch the expression on her face as she came.

In addition to equal time for female orgasms, our video customers often ask for sex and story lines that mirror real life.

I really don't get turned on watching some abnormally large guy pound some woman into the floor while she fakes it. Romance and good settings and camera work are a must. I usually get lesbian videos because they are sometimes more romantic, and there are no gruesome guys around.

I can't believe how ugly some of the men are. Give me a break! Like I believe this gorgeous girl is going to suck him off as he sells mops door to door.

LESBIAN AND FEMINIST PRODUCTIONS As we noted earlier, a lot of this criticism comes from disappointment when porn isn't as cinematic, well-acted or poetically scripted as our favorite Hollywood movies. Attempts to subvert industry conventions have come primarily from independent filmmakers or production companies that specialize in lesbian-made or women-oriented films. These alternative producers give long-overdue screen time to the female experience of sex, and also frequently go out on a limb when it comes to presenting sexual activities that the industry shies away from. For example, female ejaculation, sex between interracial couples and erotic depictions of safer sex activities can be found in these films. Some independent films are also more experimental in format. As the demand for alternative videos increases, expect the quality and availability to steadily improve. For now, your best bet on finding these tapes will not be the local video store, even adult ones! Seek out a sex boutique, a gay or lesbian bookstore, or check the ads in alternative sex magazines.

I watch new lesbian-made videos as soon as they are released. The best part is seeing real lesbians having real sex. The worst part is waiting a year for another one to come out.

I like those Femme videos because the women and men aren't Barbie and Ken types. They're more like your yuppie next-door neighbors.

They have intelligent conversations and buildup to the sex, which is gracefully filmed—it's not one glaring genital close-up after another.

Clips was much more creative than most erotic movies. The short vignettes mean you don't need to watch the whole thing at once. The masturbation scene is done really well, with an exotic mask and special effects.

GAY MALE PORN Gay male porn has been a booming industry for years, resulting in more diversity in style and content than straight movies, and earning this genre a wide range of fans, including plenty of women. Gay porn features exceptionally attractive men, and condom use is the norm in these productions. Look for these in the adult section of your video store, gay book and video stores, and mail-order catalogs.

My boyfriend and I watch male-to-male porn together. We try to emulate what they're doing on the screen.

I'm a lesbian who watches boy porn with my girlie for no more than ten minutes before we get nasty.

AMATEUR TAPES The amateur videos you find in adult bookstores are actually what's known as "pro-am," or professionally amateur videos. Basically, successful filmmakers shoot real people engaging in real sex—these aren't polished actors or actresses, and there are no scripts. Amateur videos tend to be low on production values and talent, but long on enthusiasm and sincerity. They depict a wider range of physical types than commercial porn does, and multiple-volume series such as *Masturbation Memoirs, Video Virgins* and *San Francisco Lesbians* depict women who are authentically turned on in loving detail. If you prefer your porn slick and glossy, however, you may not appreciate the real-life awkwardness that's on display in these videos. Amateur tapes appeal to the viewer who might be tempted to film the couple next door having sex if it weren't against the law!

Never have I seen anything as beautiful, moving and erotic as these on-screen orgasms. Masturbation Memoirs fulfilled a visual erotic and educational dream, touched me profoundly and raised my consciousness.

SEX-EDUCATION TAPES There are a number of sex-education tapes available, from talking-head sex therapy to porno-educational endeavors like porn star Nina Hartley's guides to various sexual techniques. The videos in the latter category set out to turn you on, and although those in the former category may not intend to, you can find yourself suddenly aroused by the explicit sex talk or participants' demonstrations. Several sex-education series have been a hit with our customers—each tape is dedicated to a specific issue relevant to the series theme. All of these sex-education tapes are a great way to get no-nonsense, explicit sex education. There's no common source for these tapes, so we've listed a few of the popular ones in the videography at the end of the book.

Watching the women in the masturbation circle in Betty Dodson's SelfLoving *video made me feel like I was part of a women's jill-off club—I came with the best of them!*

Concerns

I don't want to watch certain activities. If you're worried about viewing scenes you may find disturbing or shocking, review the following suggestions on how to choose a video, so you can get as much information as possible before you rent or purchase a tape. Read the box copy or, if you have the good fortune to be in a store with savvy clerks, ask for more information. If you notice that specific activities or situations make you uncomfortable, read some books that address the topic to gain some outside perspective.

View the video by yourself to freely and honestly explore your range of reactions to the erotic material. You won't be inhibited by someone else's presence, so you can focus all your attention on what is or isn't turning you on. You may discover that an activity you were convinced was repulsive holds a particularly explosive charge. Sometimes you just have to feel it to believe it!

In my college anti-porn feminist days I stumbled on a cache of Penthouse *magazines someone had collected for a term paper. I got so wet looking at those women I knew something was amiss with our rhetoric.*

Should women be involved with porn? Some people register surprise when they hear that a feminist sex-toy store is peddling pornography. Women's participation in porn, whether as consumers, producers, actresses or critics has spawned years of debate in the women's movement. While volumes have been written on all sides of the issue—and we urge you to read them—we'll take just a minute to illuminate our perspective.

Conditions in the porn industry, as in any industry, vary widely. Women are not any more exploited in porn than they are in any other industry, and in some ways less so—they're better paid for one. Furthermore, women have been taking more and more control as producers and performers since the early eighties.

We are opposed to limiting or restricting access to sexually explicit materials. Although images of women in X-rated films can be as stereotyped and demeaning as in mainstream films, we doubt that eliminating porn would result in economic and social equality of the sexes. We believe porn reflects the social, sexual mores of our society, rather than creates these mores. Restricting the production and consumption of porn only perpetuates the lowest-common denominator of mainstream X-rated videos. The only way to combat the existence of low quality is not to censor it, but to produce more and better porn. As we've seen from our customers' comments, they want porn, they enjoy porn, they just want better-made porn! Entrepreneurs are you listening? It's time to get your hands dirty!

And remember, if you're bored, uncomfortable or just plain in a hurry, you can always use that popular button on the remote control—fast forward!

I can't believe my lover likes that stuff! You may be in a relationship where your partner doesn't exactly share your penchant for porn.

She got really pissed when I watched X-rated videos of other women. I tried to explain that I think of her when I watch them (and I really do), but she refused to believe it. So I was damned if I did, and my balls would explode if I didn't.

Attempt to find out what he or she is objecting to. If, like this man, you find your partner feels hurt that you need outside stimulation to get aroused, perhaps you can read the chapter on fantasy together. Find out what fantasies or images, if any, turn on your partner. Draw a parallel between the images we invent ourselves and those we pick up from books and videos. Stress that you're not watching porn as a way of unfavorably comparing your partner to the actors and actresses on screen, you're doing it to enhance the arousal you can share with your partner. Expecting one person to be the sole source of your arousal unnecessarily confines your sexuality and is simply unrealistic.

Perhaps the source of your partner's objections is embarrassment or discomfort with specific activities or behaviors A discussion might help you identify the disturbing components of the porn she or he has seen (or possibly only heard about). Your partner may have never actually seen an X-rated tape, in which case you can try to find out what you'd both like and watch one together. Or, he or she may be more comfortable initially watching it alone. To a certain extent, porn is an acquired taste, and it can take a few viewings to let go of your internalized judgments and just enjoy your visceral responses. If, after all's said and done, your partner simply doesn't enjoy porn, you can politely ask that he or she not rain on your parade, and continue to indulge privately.

Videos always get my girlfriend soaking wet, and she's not a porno fan.

I can't believe I like that stuff! You may have your concerns that porn, while pleasurable for the individual, is somehow harmful to society. Despite the common myth that porn "degrades" women or inspires violent behavior, numerous academic and government studies have been completely unable to demonstrate any causal link between consuming sexually explicit materials and performing antisocial acts. For an excellent overview of this subject, we recommend Nadine

Strossen's *Defending Pornography: Free Speech, Sex and the Fight for Women's Rights.*

Remember, fantasy is not real life. Images of forbidden, taboo or degrading activities can excite us even though, or especially because, we have no desire to act them out. Ironically, it is often the acts or behaviors we find most disconcerting that are the most titillating; that they are forbidden infuses them with erotic appeal.

Shopping for Videos

WHERE TO GET VIDEOS All adult bookstores and almost all video stores have a video section from which you can rent X-rated tapes. We realize this isn't going to work for all of you—the idea of venturing into the adult section of your local store might be intimidating. We can testify that the clerk probably has as much interest in your taste in porn as he or she does in your taste in cereal, but undoubtedly there are some of you who fear your penchant for dildo-packing cowgirl tapes might make it into Liz Smith's next column. If you're too shy to make your selection from your neighborhood store, you could a) travel to another town to rent tapes; b) subscribe to the *Playboy* channel; or c) purchase tapes from mail-order catalogs that promise discretion and confidentiality. You can't usually purchase adult tapes from mainstream video stores, but you can from adult bookstores.

HOW TO CHOOSE VIDEOS If you are game for venturing into the adult section of your local video store, you may be instantly overwhelmed by the rows of seemingly identical boxes. If you're a sex video novice, trying to choose one can be a complete crap shoot. Here are some tips:

♦ Think about what might appeal to you in a porn movie. Are you looking for certain kinds of sexual activities, certain couplings, certain famous porn stars, particular directors or an interesting plot? If you're clear about your personal criteria, you'll at least have something to look for.

♦ Read the box. While the information on the box is not always helpful or accurate, it may mention or allude to something you're interested in.

♦ Read reviews. Just like mainstream movies, adult movies are reviewed, and reviews can provide some hints about the sexual content, the plot or the actors involved. Look for these in magazines

like *Adult Video News* and *Screw,* although keep in mind that these are trade magazines designed to sell videos, so don't expect critical analyses. For more thoughtful reviews, sex 'zines and on-line magazines can be a great resource, as can almanacs like *Only the Best* or the *X-rated Videotape Guides.*

♦ Look for award winners. Publications such as *Adult Video News* sponsor annual awards ceremonies, and awards are usually noted on box copy. This can work, but bear in mind the disagreements you've had with the Academy Award judges in the past.

♦ Ask friends for recommendations. Obviously not everyone is comfortable quizzing friends about their tastes in porn, but personal recommendations can be invaluable in separating the wheat from the chaff. Surfing computer bulletin-board services, Usenet News groups and websites is an excellent way to learn about other people's porn preferences while maintaining your anonymity.

♦ Ask the store clerk. This isn't always easy either, but if you can muster up the courage, you may tap into a valuable resource.

♦ Look for a rating system. Some retailers and reviewers use rating systems to help viewers narrow down titles of interest to them.

At Good Vibrations we've compiled a selection of adult videos we believe to be a cut above the rest. These are distinguished by at least one of a variety of criteria: good acting, superior filmmaking, unusual sexual activities, sexually explosive scenes, believable or compelling plots, woman-oriented or educational content. We've listed the most popular of the titles in the videography, so if you're interested in becoming one of the millions of erotic video fans, you'll have a good place to start.

Enjoying Porn

Now that you have access to this plethora of sexually oriented materials you may wonder what to do with it all. We'll let our customers offer some suggestions.

Enhance Masturbation

When I was younger I used to read erotica while masturbating. I always liked to have my orgasm coincide with the characters' so I'd reread the same exciting paragraph over and over....

I prefer to lie on my stomach while I'm looking at sexually explicit material and rub my penis against a cushion. I actually buy soft cotton socks so that I can ejaculate into them if I get aroused beyond the point of no return.

I read mostly Penthouse *letters to the editor, and Victorian pornographic novels, such as* The Pearl *and* My Secret Life. *Also lesbian fantasies. I read them while using my plug-in vibrator. I rarely finish reading more than a page or two before climaxing and enjoy teasing myself by taking away the vibrator to make the good feelings last. I have two magazines from ten years ago that I still use.*

I read books to myself silently and then masturbate when I become wet. It's fun to see how long I can keep from touching myself.

Turn On Both Partners

If I'm with a partner, sometimes halfway through the film I'll be so horny we'll have to turn it off and have sex.

We often read stories silently at the same time and then focus the arousal on each other when we are done reading. I sometimes read to him aloud. We look at magazines a lot together, but while he is more turned on by Playboy, *I am turned on by the more hardcore photographs of actual penetration. Because of this we aren't aroused by the same pictures.*

Watching porn with a partner is a good way to start a sexual encounter—then let nature take over. With myself, I read a lot of porno books/magazines and then build up the fantasy with my imagination.

My ex-lover and I would watch gay men's porn every time. It was great. I would watch, and she would fuck me; her back was often to the TV.

Discover New Ways to Enjoy Sex

We use books, movies and videos, both erotic and nonerotic, as sources of ideas for characters and locations for our fantasy universe, then we make up our own plots and characters.

Watching videos with a partner is educational; it's a way of opening a discussion about what we like. Sometimes we'll stop a tape and play a scenario again as we do the same. I find that I like to do more than I like to see. For example, I enjoy anal penetration but am turned off by viewing it.

Alone, reading or watching videos can substitute for fantasy—it gets me hot, and I'll try to time my come to coincide with a hot come in the writing or the video. I don't like photos—I never find them sexy—but fucking scenes either described or shown in videos can be good, especially if the woman seems to convincingly get off.

I read books and magazines at bedtime and then use any new images or ideas to fuel my fantasies later on.

I use porn videos for education and anticipation of pleasure while beating off alone. I also use them nonsexually with a partner to actually see examples of things each of us likes so we can discuss them.

Learn about Our Own and Others' Pleasures and Desires

I read erotica and fantasize myself with the characters I desire. I prefer lesbian erotica to hetero. I consider myself straight, but I always fantasize, read and daydream about making love to women.

I love reading/looking at erotica by myself and then masturbating. I enjoy doing this to recharge right before my partner comes home or the baby goes to sleep. I also enjoy doing it with a partner. It keeps communication going sexually, and I sometimes learn new things my partner fantasizes about and vice-versa.

Do It Yourself!

Are you a pornographer? If you've taken your own X-rated videos, penned some erotic verse or snapped some nasty photos of your sweetheart, you qualify! You can write, direct and star in your own erotic fantasies, and your partner will probably appreciate the imaginative and personal touch. If you're looking for a place to start, try writing down one of your fantasies. Many of our questionnaire respondents reported getting rather excited as they were describing their earliest memories of masturbating, their favorite sexual encounter or their experience of orgasm. Give it a try!

I'd like to act out a scene from a book or video and then record it for posterity's sake!

I love drawing my own erotica and have been doing it all my life; for the most part attempting to sensitively and beautifully depict hetero, homo and bisexual acts of oral sex in classic pencil-on-paper style.

I write highly personalized stories for my lover and then read to her.

When my old boyfriend moved away we used to write erotic letters to each other.

CHAPTER 15

High-Tech Sex

Where would we be without our machines? If you're excited about the sexual possibilities of an appliance like a vibrator, you'll no doubt be intrigued to know what something as technologically sophisticated as a computer can offer your sex life. That big square box sitting atop your desk may not be your idea of an attractive date, but warm her up and get to know her better and you'll be surprised at the amount of pleasure she's capable of providing. Looking for an erotic pen pal? Want to meet other folks interested in exhibitionism? Care to try your hand at an X-rated computer game? Want a discreet way to buy that new condom you've heard about? With the right equipment and an adventurous spirit you can do all of these things and a whole lot more. Call it what you will—cyber sex, virtual sex or high-tech sex—getting off with your computer requires not only the equipment, but imagination, and most definitely a passion for experimentation!

How to Get On-Line

Thanks to widespread use of personal computers, technological advances and the sexual inclinations and curiosities of your fellow users, an enormous on-line sex community has evolved seemingly overnight—and it's just a flick of the power switch away. We've provided a brief review of a few of the ways you can enjoy adult entertainment courtesy of your computer. For a more exhaustive discussion in greater technical detail, refer to one of the books on the subject in our bibliography.

Equipment

To access on-line activities and resources requires:

A modem. This device connects your computer to other computers through your telephone line. Speed is an important consideration—the faster your modem, the less time you'll spend waiting to receive images and information over the wires—so we recommend investing in the fastest modem currently available. If you're considering purchasing an ISDN modem, keep in mind that despite being very fast, they do require the installation of special digital phone lines and aren't supported by all on-line services. Most folks wait to buy an ISDN modem until after becoming more familiar with on-line technologies. Cable television companies are also jumping into the fray and may soon offer an attractive alternative to telephone-line-based connections—in the not-so-distant future, we could all be accessing the Internet through our televisions.

Software. The type of software you need depends on whether you want to access computer "bulletin boards," the Internet, or large commercial on-line services. We'll elaborate on these three options in the following section.

A computer. You can get started with electronic mail, on-line chatting and message posting with the simplest of computers. You'll need a color monitor to view images, and if you want to get involved with some of the latest Internet activities such as live video or audio chat, you'll need a fairly state-of-the-art machine.

Bulletin Board Services (BBS)

BBSs are private affairs. Each BBS functions as an island, with its own telephone number, its own collection of services, its own policies, and its own focus dictated by the person who runs its central computer. When you sign up with a BBS, you're authorized to call up this central computer via your modem and exchange messages with the other members (a.k.a. users) of the BBS. BBSs appeal to users looking for a particular community, and function as on-line social clubs as much as anything. You can find boards devoted to fetish worship, swinging, and gay and lesbian networking. They are also popular among people who want to download or post pictures. Since non-local users must pay long-distance rates, BBS universes are primarily populated by the local community. And while the "home town" feel of BBSs is nice, more BBS owners are looking for ways to link their services to the Internet in order to reach folks around the world.

In addition to possible long-distance charges, some BBSs charge monthly fees for the services they provide, but there are plenty of free services out there. To find some in your area, look in the phone book, computer magazines, or ask your nearest computer-literate pal. To access a BBS, you'll need a basic communications software package—this type of software is usually included when you buy a modem.

When you first log on to a BBS, you'll be asked to pick a username or handle. This is the name you'll be known by when you post electronic messages or when another user sends you electronic mail. Be creative, but practical, when choosing your name since "buxom" will attract quite a different response than "icequeen."

The Internet

The Internet represents the largest collection of public and private computer networks in the world, and all these networks are in constant communication. To explore the vast resources of the Internet, you usually gain access through a local Internet Service Provider (ISP). You sign up with a single ISP, which charges either monthly or hourly fees—you then access any part of the Internet you desire by calling up the ISP's central computer system. The beauty of this set-up is that you pay no more to surf a Web page maintained by someone in Zimbabwe than you do to read a news group posting from someone right in your own backyard. Your Internet account serves as your personal "on-ramp" to the much-ballyhooed information superhighway, allowing you access to the World Wide Web, Usenet News groups and a host of other services. Thanks largely to the emerging popularity and consumer appeal of the World Wide Web (described later in this chapter), the Internet will probably make BBSs obsolete.

Quality of customer service and reliability varies widely among ISPs. Some are user friendly, providing easy-to-install software packages. Others are expert friendly, and prioritize maintaining a fast infrastructure in order to minimize noticeable delays. You may be able to find information on ISPs in your local phonebook (under the headings "Computer On-Line Services" or "Internet"), in computer magazines or from friends. Many local and long-distance telephone companies now provide ISP services as well. Try speaking to the technical support personnel of any prospective ISP to help determine if their services and software can accommodate your level of expertise and computer hardware.

As with a BBS, you'll have to pick an on-line name when you first sign up with your ISP. You will be able to assume different names and identities when trying out some of the services, but this first "login" name will be a permanent part of your e-mail address.

Commercial On-Line Services

For many years, large, national commercial on-line services like Prodigy, CompuServe and America Online dominated the world of on-line services, distancing themselves from the "chaotic" Internet by creating an orderly, menu-driven world where chat rooms, stock tips and weather updates could all be accessed with a simple click of the mouse. Each of these commercial on-line services used exclusive proprietary software and created much of their own content—on-line interaction between users of different systems was limited to exchanging e-mail at best. Now the Internet has captured the global imagination, emphasizing freedom, diversity and universality of access over isolationism and monolithic corporate control. Most commercial on-line services have responded by committing more resources to providing Internet access for their users. Their convenience and offers of free introductory periods make these fine places to start out on-line. Unless you are in a remote area, most of these services can be accessed from a local telephone number. Because they offer more features and proprietary content, commercial services tend to charge a higher monthly fee than ISPs.

Some commercial on-line services, however, take an active role in protecting users from "objectionable" material within their domain. In addition, some users complain that these commercial on-line services aren't prioritizing Internet technology and are slow to adopt cutting-edge features—this complaint is especially valid when it comes to sexual content on-line. If you get the feeling you're missing something with these services, you may well be right. It can't hurt to check out another service or to look into signing up with a "pure" ISP. Some people find advantages in both worlds and maintain two accounts or more.

What To Do On-Line

Now that you've completed your refresher course and have outfitted your cyber den with the proper equipment, we'll explore some of the ways to get naughty on-line.

Hot Talk

If you believe the pen is mightier than the sword, wait till you see what erotic conquests are just a tap of the keyboard away. Do erotic love letters turn you on? Do you enjoy reciting your sexual escapades for friends or lovers? Do you fantasize about having an alter ego of a different gender or sexual orientation? If you answered yes to any of these, you're a good candidate for the many text-based sex activities available on-line. As with phone sex, the appeal of hot talk has to do with the interactive fantasy component. You can be as nasty as you want to be with other users—sharing erotic stories, describing sexual encounters, initiating virtual sex acts—either publicly (which has the voyeur and group-sex appeal) or privately. Because no one ever sees you, you can try out different names, personalities, genders or sexual preferences.

There is an anonymous quality that allows one to be a bit of a voyeur without any involvement, and that is kind of fun.

Perhaps because you may never see the other users, a particular type of intimacy and conversation develops. Shy people often feel freer to assert and/or reveal themselves in this faceless format; the overall effect is a very strong sense of community.

The Net allows an unguarded level of conversation that I would never, or only rarely, be able to engage in with women I meet every day. I find that informative, fun and stimulating intellectually as well as sexually.

With electronic sex you don't have to worry about catching a disease or being rejected. I can experiment with all kinds of sex because there are no consequences.

Hot talk currently takes five main forms:

Private e-mail. This simple, direct method of communication is mail intended for a single recipient to read at leisure. Your e-mail is typically "signed" with your on-line alias or login name, but you should be aware that sometimes other users can find out more about you by looking up your user profile (called "fingering"!). You can use e-mail to exchange sweet seductions with a trans-Atlantic pen pal you've never met or to spice up your lover's boring day at the office.

Some BBSs and Internet service providers offer "anonymous re-mailer" services, which either replace your name with a random name, replace it with an alias you choose, or replace it with a special key that allows a response to be delivered correctly but gives no clue as to your identity. This way no one need ever know that underneath the Superman persona lurks a Clark Kent (or a Lois Lane for that matter).

Public discussion groups. Also known as forums, message bases or conferences, these exist for more public discussions on topics of shared interest. Groups are identified by very specific topic headings, to keep all participants "on the subject." You can exchange ideas on sexual politics, technique and pornography with hundreds of other users. Sample topics range from "how to give/receive a good rim job" to "where to see authentic female orgasms in porn." Chances are that if more than one or two people have expressed an interest in the same topic at some point, a conference or discussion group has popped up on that subject. Some discussion groups are "moderated," meaning you cannot post to the group directly but must mail your submissions to the moderator, who may edit your posting or refuse it for straying too far from the subject or for other reasons. On BBSs and commercial on-line services there will be a menu option for forums or discussion groups. BBS forums are generally limited to local users, so it may be possible for the dedicated to keep up with all of the discussions on any given board.

Usenet News. On the Internet, most discussion groups are organized into a huge hierarchy known as Usenet News. People around the world submit nearly a million posts per day to over ten thousand news groups. Usenet News is organized by subject. Top levels in the hierarchy include "comp" for computers and "sci" for science, as well as "alt" for discussions of an "alternative" nature. This is where you'll find "alt.sex," the news group for more general discussions about sex. Sex being the popular subject that it is, however, hundreds of more specialized groups have been added like alt.sex.bestiality, alt.sex.sounds, alt.sex.strip-clubs,

alt.sex.movies—get the idea? There is a group somewhere in the alt.sex hierarchy for nearly any sexual specialty you can think of! Remember, the longer the group name the more specific the topic, so whether you'd rather chat about *Star Trek* or sheep, you can log right in to alt.sex.fetish.startrek or alt.sex.sheep.baaa.baaaa.baaa.moo!

As with e-mail, "anonymous posting" functions have been introduced. News is generally held for only a few days or weeks before it is deleted, but most groups have dedicated fans who carefully maintain "archives" of that group and these are available for the asking. Although Usenet News can be accessed through point-and-click graphical interfaces, it's been a key feature of the Internet for so long that many people still use text-based commands such as "rn" and "tin" to read and post news.

Mailing Lists. Mailing lists are somewhat like discussion groups, but based on e-mail. Members subscribe to a mailing list on a specific topic, then submit e-mail destined for all members to a special group e-mail address. Discovering mailing lists can be difficult and instructions for joining vary: Generally you must be clued in by someone in the know or chance upon a reference in Usenet News or on the Web.

Live Chat. On most systems, you can engage in "live" chats with other users, i.e., written conversations taking place in real time. The best chats are like cocktail parties in a huge mansion. You enter by the lobby where you check out the other guests, find out where the action is and then move from room to room and mingle. Each line you type is displayed along with your handle to everyone in that room. Some rooms are private and you need an invitation to get in. A chat room can be hidden and known only by the user who created it and those invited inside, a handy feature when a sexy brain across the country gets you excited and you decide its time to make way for the nearest electronic bedroom. Most chat programs have a way to send private messages to a user, which show up in a separate part of the screen. Chat rooms or something similar should be on the main menu of your BBS or commercial on-line service. On the Internet, "Internet Relay Chat" or "IRC" is a popular chat system, and chat extensions or "plug-ins" are being integrated into the World Wide Web.

Downloading Pictures

Make room under your bed (or at least on your hard drive) for the newest form of visual erotica–electronic pictures. Considering the popularity of skin magazines, erotic art collections and porn videos, it should come as no surprise that viewing and downloading pornographic photos is one of the most common on-line activities for the libidinous user. With varying degrees of difficulty, you can access photos from your BBS or commercial on-line service, some Usenet News groups or the Web. Most files are stored in "graphics interchange format"–the name of the file will have the suffix ".gif"–and can be seen using GIF viewer software on most computers. This viewer software may be included with your communications package–if not, it can usually be downloaded for free along with the photos.

BBSs. Most sex-related BBSs boast a large cache of photos that tend to reflect the particular theme of each board, so don't look for nude-in-nature photos on a bondage board. The files should be grouped by topic, with short descriptions of each file. When you've decided on a file, pick a download protocol that's shared by your BBS and the communications package you are using. Start your download, and when you are finished you'll have a copy of the file on your computer. Uncompress it if necessary, and fire up your "viewer" to take a look. If this doesn't work, try using a different protocol during download, but be aware that some files have critical flaws that make them incompatible with some or all viewers. If you need help with this process, consult other members or the BBS owner.

Internet. On the Internet, many of the Usenet News groups are devoted to pictures and movies, particularly in the alt.sex category. They are known as "binary" groups and are organized in the same way the text files are, with topics as specific as alt.binaries.dead.porn.stars or alt.pictures.erotica.furry. These pictures are encoded as text; instructions for decoding them can be found in the "Frequently Asked Questions" (FAQ) files that are posted periodically to the group. Often it takes several posts to complete a single picture, and these can be tedious to piece together and decode.

Another way of obtaining picture files over the Internet is via "File Transfer Protocol" or FTP. Internet machines known as Anonymous FTP Servers dedicate huge amounts of disk space to public files, which often wind up being filled to overflowing with nasty pictures. Chief among the traditional tools for retrieving these files is the text-based command "ftp," which begins a login and download process reminiscent of the process for retrieving files from a BBS. Tools like "archie" can help to automatically search thousands of FTP sites for files of interest. Many commercial on-line services will also provide file retrieval tools or an FTP menu option. File transfers happen automatically on the World Wide Web.

Sound complicated? Perhaps so. Some of these tools and activities have been around since the early eighties, yet people who knew how to use them were few and far between. Luckily the newest way of viewing images as well as participating in nearly every other on-line activity we've been discussing is far more user friendly–the World Wide Web has turned the Internet into a pop superstar almost overnight.

The World Wide Web

If you're not sure how to start your foray into on-line sex, we enthusiastically recommend the World Wide Web. As two women who previously had

Favorite Websites

The websites that made our list are either visually entertaining, provide useful information or serve as jumping-off points to other sex-related sites. Bear in mind that hundreds of new websites are created daily, and old ones are being updated continuously. The URL addresses listed here may change; if you can't find a site through the URL below, try searching its name.

Annie Sprinkle's Home Page
http://www.infi.net/~heck/sprinkleshow.html
Annie offers anatomy lessons, including her "public cervix announcement," tips such as "how to have an energy orgasm," and workshop and performance dates.

Ars Erotica Magna
http://www.dd.chalmers.se/~niky/aem.html
An absolutely fantastic collection of Western erotic art from prehistoric times to the present.

Ask Isadora Home Page
http://www.askisadora.com
Our favorite sex advice columnist answers all your sex questions and provides folks with similar interests a place to meet and chat on-line.

Bianca's Smut Shack
http://www.bianca.com
This immensely popular site invites you to tour Bianca's shack, chat with others about a variety of sexual subjects, read reviews and glean sex information.

Elf Sternberg
http://www.halcyon.com/elf/altsex/shortdex.html
For those too impatient to wander through the alt.sex newsgroups, the alt.sex FAQ (Frequently Asked Questions) is kept by this gentleman.

Feminists for Free Expression
http://www.well.com/user/freedom
Educational pamphlets and an impressive speakers' bureau outlining positions on free speech and the arts, the internet, sexual harrassment and pornography.

Good Vibrations
http://www.goodvibes.com
Visit our antique vibrator museum, discover this month's best-selling toys, books and videos, read the latest *Good Vibes Gazette,* learn about the history of our worker-owned cooperative, and ask us your sex questions.

Libido
http://www.indra.com/libido
Our favorite literary sex magazine offers images and excerpts from each issue.

The Masturbation Home Page
http://www.zonarosa.com/~mick/auto.html
Stories, photos, newsletter, FAQ and information about play-parties.

Naughty Linx
http://www.naughty.com
A directory of sex-related sites.

The Safer Sex Pages
http://www.safersex.org
Up-to-the-minute information about safer sex, including a cut-and-fold display of lesbian safer sex guidelines, counselor information, links to condom suppliers and a video visit to a condom factory.

Society for Human Sexuality
http://weber.u.washington.edu/~sfpse
Maintained by students at the University of Washington, this site offers the largest source of sex information on-line. They've compiled an extensive library of sexual materials on every conceivable sexual topic, along with links to other sites. This is *the* source for good, up-to-date sex information.

The Transgender Resource Guide
http://www.cdspub.com
Maintained by Creative Design Services, this site contains a wealth of information, resources and links.

some interest in sex on the Internet, but neither the time nor the patience to master complicated commands, we now confess to emerging bleary-eyed from lengthy spells of Web surfing. And lest you think we are alone in our carnal pursuits, let us inform you that Web users now number twenty-three million, and are expected to exceed one hundred fifty million by the turn of the century. Even if only ten percent of users are sex surfing, that's still a pretty big party! Apparently Web surfing is such a popular pastime at the workplace that corporate head honchos are starting to pull the plug on their employees' on-line access.

WHY IS THE WWW SO POPULAR? As its name implies, the Web attempts to organize and provide access to the amazing tangle of information available on the Internet by weaving together sites with related content. Thanks to graphics interface programs (known as "browsers"), which allow users to simultaneously display and access text-based, visual and audio information, "websites" present information in an attractive, accessible format. The Web also makes it easier to navigate the immensity of the Internet through a system of "hypertext links"—users simply click on a highlighted word or phrase on one screen, and they're immediately transferred ("linked") to a new screen. In one second you're reading about a sex club in San Francisco and in the next second you're shopping at a toy store in Denmark.

Aside from offering an incredibly easy way to view images on-line, the Web's popularity continues to flourish because:
♦ There are no restrictions on who can create Web pages and they aren't too difficult to produce.
♦ It's relatively inexpensive to create a Web page, meaning everyone from Joe hobbyist next door to large commercial interests are getting in on the action.
♦ It's an extremely affordable way to communicate with people worldwide.
♦ It's a tremendous source of information on almost every conceivable subject.

THE LAY OF THE LAND The easiest and probably most affordable way to access the Web is through an Internet Service Provider. You'll also need browser software like Netscape Navigator or Microsoft's Internet Explorer, which allows you to view color graphics and video clips as well as to hear sounds. Generally when you sign up with an ISP, they supply you with the necessary software. Commercial on-line services such as America Online and Compuserve offer their own browser software. Your browser will provide a simple point and click menu system that will help you find and organize the "pages" on the WWW. You can also buy a device, marketed as WebTV, that hooks up to your television so you can surf the Net through your TV instead of your computer.

If the Web is one large directory, the individual addresses or listings are the "sites." Within each site there can be an infinite number of pages. Since you can hop around within or between sites rather than travel in a linear fashion, it's easy to lose your focus. That's why all sites have a "home page." This is the first page you'll see when you link to a new site, and it often serves as a table of contents for the rest of the site. It becomes valuable as a home base since it's very easy to get lost in the site. Most pages offer an easy link back to their home page.

The URL (Uniform Resource Locator) is simply the address for a website. When you're looking a site up by its URL address, make sure to type in the address exactly as written.

How do you find websites? If you know the URL address, you simply type it in and off you go. Most folks, however, discover websites simply by clicking on the hypertext "links" that appear in one site that allow you to jump into another site or page. For example, you may be reading some sex therapist's advice column extolling the merits of vibrator use, and the word *vibrator* might be linked to the Good Vibrations' website. If you click on it, you'll find yourself on our home page! Many sites contain a section of "hot links" or "cool links" that will send you to their favorite sites.

A search engine offers another useful way to find websites. Consider it the directory assistance of the on-line world: It helps you locate specific subject matter as well as specific sites. Type in a word or series of words and a search engine will find all the sites containing these words in their name or site description and bring them up in a list. There are numerous search engines; many are accompanied by directories that try to categorize subjects to help in your search. Once you start using search engines, you'll quickly discover the importance of precise vocabulary. Searching on the word *sex* for example will yield thousands of entries and can be incredibly overwhelming (unless you're simply curious about the sheer volume of sex-related sites). Narrowing down your search if you have a specific interest—for example, typing in "queer resources" or "safer sex"—will save time.

SEX ON THE WEB If you're surfing the Web with sex on your brain, you're in good company. Thousands of other users are burning the midnight oil or killing time at their desk jobs in a quest for Net sex. What follows is a brief discussion of some of the things you might do or see on the Web, but we encourage you to dial up and see for yourself.

Sex information. It's safe to say you won't find such easy access to so much sex information anywhere else. If you've ever tried to find a sex-related book at a public library you probably discovered that it was lost, stolen or mysteriously missing. Even if you were lucky enough to locate one, you may have been too embarrassed to check it out. Although you may not find the text of these same sex books on-line (some day you will, we believe), you'll certainly find a company to sell it to you. You're also bound to locate the same subject matter covered by somebody else somewhere on the Web. For example, you'll find sex magazines, advice columns, archival collections of research materials, resource listings and chapters from sex books devoted to every single conceivable sexual topic.

There are several advantages to this hodge-podge of sex information. One of our favorites is the tremendous variety of perspectives you will be exposed to during your roamings on the Web. You may have started with a visit to Parents Place looking for tips on nutrition, dropped in on their chat group on gay parenting, read about a great sex education book for kids, which then linked you to the sex shop selling the book. There you're intrigued by a link to the Feminists for Free Expression and soon you're reading about women defending pornography. We can only hope that this exposure broadens individual understanding and tolerance of alternative sexual viewpoints.

Another advantage is the kind of information you'll come across on the Web. Bookstores and libraries naturally only carry work by published authors, and to be a published author (at least when it comes to sex writing) usually requires some professional credential or specialized knowledge. Since anyone can make a Web page, you can find out what the people next door, who love talking about sex, are really doing! Jane Doe enthusiastically writes about her personal requirements for satisfying oral sex, while John Doe shares what he looks for in his favorite pornography. Some of these virtual-sex pioneers develop quite a following, their opinions sometimes trusted more than a professional's.

Be warned, however, that it's very easy to get sidetracked by all the intriguing sounding links you'll encounter on your travels, and eventually lose sight of your original mission. Most browsers have a "bookmark" option that will record an address for you to return to later. Or if you find yourself deep into a chain of links and you want to go back to an earlier site, most browsers will show a history of your travels and allow you to return to any point along the way.

Networking. Maybe you just had a baby and want to find other moms who will share their experiences about postpartum sex. Perhaps you're contemplating a sex change and want to get recommendations for good doctors. Or it could be you're moving to a new city and want to know what businesses in the area are queer friendly. You can find websites dedicated to special interests, which usually offer a host of valuable resources, provide a place to ask questions, and sometimes allow you to chat with other users. Anyone who's ever tried to get information, resources or advice like this on their own knows the search can be frustrating and difficult. The Web offers discretion, up-to-date referrals and a welcoming embrace from other folk with interests like yours.

Visuals. Regardless of whether your tastes are for *Playgirl* or *Fat Girl*, countless sites offer you the opportunity to download erotic pictures, view video clips or access live-action video. Invest in a fast modem, or the wait won't be worth your while (unless watching your nudes appear v-e-r-y slowly increases your arousal). On-line sex magazines

As Time Goes By

Every new technological development in art or communication is seized almost immediately for use in expressing sexual ideas or creating sexual materials. From Stone Age carvings, to the printing press, to the development of films, to the video revolution, to the design of CD-ROMs and most recently, the explosion of interest in on-line communication, sex has been the subject matter of each new medium.

It's widely taught in literature classes that the first novels were composed in eighteenth-century England. It's less widely noted that *Fanny Hill*, one of the first novels published (in 1749), was a piece of classic porn that's been setting readers' pulses racing ever since. Among the earliest film reels available are clips of the gay ladies and gentlemen of the twenties having amorous escapades. It's a chicken-and-egg conundrum whether VCRs became must-have appliances due to their convenience for viewing X-rated videos in the privacy of one's home, or whether adult video became a multi-billion dollar business due to the advent of video technology. And now computer engineers are busily programming more truly interactive adult CD-ROMs, while ever-increasing numbers of consumers surf the Internet, swapping tips, sharing tales and accessing information about sex.

Some might argue that the inevitable use of each new technology for erotic expression is proof that we're a nation of techno-nerds who feel more comfortable with impersonal gadgets than with face-to-face communion. We prefer to see the link between sex and technology as proof that most creative impulses are intimately linked to sexuality—humans instinctively seize upon each new medium as a way to explore our boundaries, to add excitement to the human experience, and to reach out and touch someone.

Visit the Good Vibrations website and you'll find pages of product descriptions and reviews, sex information, event listings, sex trivia, frequently asked questions, news and history, but our single most visited page is the Antique Vibrator Museum. Our on-line "museum" features photographs of dozens of vibrators dating back to the turn of the century. How fitting that the vibrator, a cutting-edge medical technology appropriated for pleasure in its day, seduces surfers of the Web, a cutting-edge communications technology appropriated for pleasure in our day!

(see resource listings) can be a great source of more tasteful and diverse erotic imagery, and different sites will cater to specific sexual interests. But just as in the real world, the majority of material mirrors what you'll find on the newsstand. Some sites will give you a taste of what you'll get if you pay a subscription fee, which then entitles you to greater access. So despite the popular myth that everything on the Net is free, those nude photos of your favorite celebrities come at a price! You should also know that unless you have a pretty fast modem, video clips can take forever to download.

Another burgeoning Web sex activity is "live nude chat." This combines a bit of phone sex, computer sex and stripping in one pay-per-view feature. With most companies, you meet a playmate who'll take her clothes off and masturbate for you in real time. Some have an audio option, though text seems to be the preferred method of dialoguing with one's date.

Discreet Shopping. It didn't take long for commercial interests to discover the incredible sales potential offered by the Web, and the implications for sex-related businesses are even greater. Here you've got a discreet, easy and convenient way for folks to order from the privacy of their own homes. Retailers can provide far more detailed information about products on a website than they can in a paper catalog. This, combined with the relatively low costs involved with developing a Web page, resulted in hundreds of commercial sex enterprises flocking to the Web. Whether you're looking for fetish wear, sex toys, educational sex videos or latex products, you'll find on-line shops dedicated to these and many others. As with the visual material we discussed above, the kinds of shops you'll discover resemble those you'll find in the real world. Countless "adult" bookstores exist, but so do a plethora of more unique shops. Folks who may not be able to afford the start-up costs of a retail store in their town's commercial district can still do a brisk business out of their home with a Web page attracting customers from all over the world.

On-line consumers enjoy a couple more perqs than their real-world counterparts. Since most users are accustomed to unlimited amounts of free information, most commercial businesses that hope to succeed will offer information, services or resources in addition to their product line. For example, visitors to Good Vibrations website (www.goodvibes.com), will find replicas of our antique vibrator museum, sex trivia, information about our cooperative business structure, chapters from this book, answers to customers' most frequently asked sex questions, and much more. This abundance of information results in much more savvy consumers and allows potential shoppers to become more familiar with a company before they decide to patronize it. It's worth noting that word travels fast on the Internet, so a company that treats customers poorly or engages in bad business practices can lose its reputation overnight.

Since there are literally thousands of sex-related sites out there, your quest will take you on a unique path reflecting your own interests. To help you get started, we've included a list of some of our favorite websites in this chapter. Although these sites represent just a slice of what's out there, they provide a good jumping-off point for a variety of interests.

Censorship and Privacy

Censorship

The information superhighway, with its free-flowing exchange of sex information and erotica through public, private and commercial on-line services, has naturally become a fertile breeding ground for legislative interference. The electronic world puts a new spin on the age-old problem of coming up with a legal definition for "obscenity." In prosecuting obscenity charges in traditional media, the courts abide by local community standards. But how do you define community if your audience spans the globe? Whose community

standards determine what is obscene? In the spring of 1996, as part of the Telecommunications Act, Congress passed the Communications Decency Act (CDA), which seeks to police all forms of electronic communication—from television to radio to the Internet—and to censor all "indecent" materials. To illustrate the vague and difficult interpretation of "indecent," the Electronic Freedom Foundation (EFF) drafted a list of websites that might be defined as indecent under the terms of the CDA—these included everything from The Sistine Chapel to the Breastfeeding Home Page to the Evangelical Network. Free-speech advocates challenged the CDA as unconstitutional as soon as it was passed, and so far, legislative attempts to restrict content on the Internet have been blocked.

Liability issues are a related concern. Some BBS owners and Internet service providers have been held directly responsible for sexually explicit files and e-mail found on their systems, despite lack of evidence that the system owner had knowledge of the contents. Unfortunately, this has resulted in some self-policing—some owners may not allow certain types of images or discussions on their BBSs. More often, providers have been forced to collect and turn over users' e-mail and other files—usually images deemed obscene or hardcore (i.e., erect penises) and images of children—to cooperate with law enforcement. Luckily, for every person who would like to stamp out the slightest hint of sex on-line, there are ten who consider it their personal responsibility to provide a safe and free environment for the exchange of sexual ideas and materials. Numerous individuals and organizations have rallied to defend First Amendment rights on-line.

What you can do:
♦ Parents concerned with children's access to sexual materials on the Net can use one of the filtering programs (like Surfwatch or Net Nanny) currently available. Many adult websites will provide links to this software. System administrators can help limit children's access by requiring a photo ID or a credit card in order to use adult services.
♦ Individual users can behave responsibly. Engage in sex "netiquette." These guidelines were established by other users to help ensure a polite, consensual experience that does not jeopardize your

service provider's livelihood or fellow users' enjoyment. Contact your BBS owner or ISP if someone is posting illegal material.

♦ Defend your right to have access to sexually explicit materials. E-mail your Congressional representatives regarding legislation that infringes on free speech, then rally your friends to do the same. Check in with organizations like the Electronic Freedom Foundation or Feminists for Free Expression for news and updates regarding freedom of electronic expression. EFF can also provide assistance and advice to service providers and users.

Privacy

Security of commerce over the Internet is receiving a good deal of media attention, as is the occasional story of an Internet "stalking." Ironically, what makes these stories newsworthy as compared to their real-world counterparts is largely their rarity. Consumers fearful of credit card fraud by hackers probably don't realize that they expose themselves to far more fraud in their daily lives whenever they use their credit cards. Many on-line companies offer some kind of protection when ordering, and encryption technologies will very soon bring true security to the average consumer for the first time in history. If you have reservations about a company's credibility, try verifying their legitimacy by another means (call them up, ask for references and the number of years they've been in business, check with the Better Business Bureau, etc.).

As for stalking, you should know that, yes it is possible for virtually anyone to read your e-mail, impersonate you, find out any personal information you may have given when you signed up, grab your password, or log all of your on-line activities. This, however, is rare. Bear in mind that it's also possible for someone to tap your phone lines and bug your house, but this has probably never happened to you. It's good to be aware of the risks, but this shouldn't prevent you from exploring or having a good time. People's fear of crime on the Internet has more to do with their ignorance of this new technology than with any statistically greater threat from on-line activities. The Internet is probably one of the friendliest, most accessible communities you could ever hope to enter, so our advice to you is to log on, exercise common sense and enjoy.

CD-ROMs

What are they?

They've got all the makings of a good sex toy— they're shiny, round and smooth—but most folks unfamiliar with CD-ROMs wouldn't expect them to show up in a list of erotic accessories. Little do they know what pleasure awaits those who scratch the surface of adult CD-ROMs! Short for "compact disc-read only memory," these disks look just like the CDs you put into your stereo, only you insert them into your computer. You can buy an external CD-ROM drive to hook up to your computer, but most computers sold today come packaged with an internal drive. CD-ROMs have a huge storage capacity—one CD-ROM holds about five hundred times more data than a floppy disk, so it can accommodate more complicated programming. For the user this translates into some fancy features and tricks—you can access encyclopedic amounts of information, view color photographs and full-length movies, play complicated games, and display and manipulate cool color graphics.

Put simply, most adult CD-ROMs are kind of a hybrid porn flick and computer game. In many of these, pornographic film clips reward players who solve a puzzle, traipse down some hallways, open certain doors, answer some questions, click on hidden hot spots, or simply choose the right buttons. Unlike videos that run sequentially, CD-ROMs allow you to hop around and explore different parts of the story or the action. Whereas you can watch a video from start to finish in a couple of hours, you can kill a day unearthing all the different parts of an interactive CD-ROM and rearranging the order in which you view your film clips. Since most of the film clips are from mainstream adult video, you see a standard range of activities: heterosexual intercourse, lesbian sex, triads, come shots. You'll also find plenty of adult CD-ROMs that are just large catalogs of erotic photographs without any movement or interactivity.

Interactive Games Versus Linear Movies

The word *interactive* gets abused frequently in the adult CD-ROM industry. Most of the adult CD-ROMs currently available, many of which masquerade as interactive games, are really just porn films transferred onto disk—these also get referred to as "digital films." Beyond giving users a fast forward or pause option and the ability to view scenes in a different order, the viewer has no way of manipulating the action. Truly interactive CD-ROMs require some kind of participation from the user, which ultimately determines the outcome of the game. For example in The Dream Machine you interact with seductive female escorts who help you create your own fantasy. You peek behind a bunch of doors and watch porn clips, then answer questions that determine what your next clip will be. In this way, your fantasy is tailored to suit your individual sexual preferences.

Another interactive game, Space Sirens, teaches users a wonderful lesson in foreplay. You're a sex slave trapped in an alien pod with space sirens and you can't leave until you sexually satisfy them. You manipulate dildo and hand controls to "stimulate" each siren—you can caress her hair, "touch" her tits, take her underwear off and even fuck her. The catch is you can't come before she does (you both have orgasmatrons monitoring your excitement level) or she sends you packing with a few choice words. Since your humble authors were never able to satisfy our sirens, we don't even know what treats they might have bestowed upon us if we had!

As you can see, this technology has exciting implications for adult entertainment. We think the ultimate interactive CD-ROM would give you millions of different options—you could cast, direct, produce and star in your own adult film!

The Bad News

There are drawbacks to CD-ROM technology, mostly because it's still in its infancy. The video segments play in an area only about one-quarter the size of your computer screen. The photo-resolution breaks up if it's any bigger, so the film is often cleverly framed in some kind of graphic background. Similarly, the computer playback is slower and more stilted than that offered by your VCR. Why watch a CD-ROM instead of a video you ask? Videos don't allow you to interact with the action. And think of how many folks can now secretly watch porn on their lunch breaks at work! There's a reason so many of these games come with a "kill" button that will instantly replace your screen with a mock spreadsheet.

There's some speculation that CD-ROMs may go the way of the eight-track tape. They may ultimately be surpassed by some new and improved technology or image, and movie-viewing may happen entirely over the Internet. This may be, but until then, we recommend checking one out.

Let Me At 'Em!

We've listed a few of our favorite CD-ROMs in the discography. We chose them for their good production quality, which in the CD-ROM world means minimal out-of-synch talking (a common problem), smooth video play, decent graphics and color. We listed primarily interactive games since these seem far more popular than linear movies. Most popular, contemporary porn films, however, now exist on CD-ROM.

Many CD-ROMs are hybrid or cross platform, meaning they'll run on either a Mac or a PC, but make sure to check the box before purchasing, just in case. The box will also list the system requirements necessary for running the CD-ROM.

As for price, interactive CD-ROMs currently retail between forty and sixty dollars, and digital films between twenty and forty dollars. For easy access to hundreds of titles and reviews of adult CD-ROMs, check the World Wide Web. Otherwise your best outlets are mail-order catalogs, some adult bookstores and computer magazines.

Virtual Reality (VR)

These two words will escort us well into the twenty-first century. If you don't have a grip on what "virtual reality" is, you're not alone—it's actually a fairly primitive technology at this point, and expectations and enthusiasm for this medium outpace its "reality." Virtual reality is the by-product of computers and 3-D technology. The idea behind this technology is to envelop the user, by manipulating sight, sound and touch, in an artificial environment that closely approximates reality. What this means in layperson's sex lingo is that someday you'll be able to feel like you're having sex without really having it. Think of the last time you had a vivid, sexually explicit dream—when you woke up, you could've sworn you'd had sex, right? That's what this is supposed to be like.

Virtual-reality entertainment utilizes a cornucopia of gear: a helmet that serves as the video projector creating your 3-D visual reality and sound system, and data gloves that enable you to manipulate objects in the simulated environment. Currently, personal-computer users can also hook up 3-D stereoscopic glasses to their computers and phones and play virtual-reality games with other users. Serious players can sit in a Cyberchair, which tilts and slides with the player's movements and can be programmed with hot or cold sensation as the player moves through different environments. While there are no genital data gloves as yet, we expect those won't be far behind, as virtual reality's implications for adult entertainment are clearly appealing.

Virtual 3-D Audio

Although VR is far from refined and light-years away from being as affordable as stereo equipment, you can get a taste of the technology for the price of a compact disk. Virtual audio is a new way of digitally recording in full fidelity three-dimensional sound. When you listen to the recording through headphones (it won't work without them), you experience the activity as if it were happening all around you. *Cyborgasm* and *Private Erotica*, available on CD or cassette, offer sexual vignettes enhanced by virtual audio (unfortunately, although immensely popular, their availability has been sporadic). You hear the feverish whispers and moans of someone you'd swear was lying beside you. Watch out for the clicking stilettos or the cracking whip as they approach you from behind! The only equipment you need for this toy is a cassette or CD player and a set of headphones.

My favorite piece on Cyborgasm *was the lion tamer. I felt totally trapped in a cage at the circus, craving my master's attention and affection, helpless, raw, hungry and exposed.*

The Communications Revolution

The World Wide Web and virtual reality are all examples of the advancements made in the name of the communications revolution. Promises of interactive television, hundreds of cable channels and video phones tickle the imagination, and their sexual ramifications boggle the mind. Imagine how much phone sex will change when you have the option of seeing the caller on your computer screen. What couch potatoes we'll become when it is possible to choose any erotic video ever made by scrolling through a list of selections on our TV. Or perhaps it will inspire a sexual fitness craze that will replace our obsession with workout tapes.

Some folks fear that these advancements only make us more dependent on machines—who'll bother to have sex with a real person if virtual sex feels the same? It's worth bearing in mind that even the most realistic simulation is still only a simulation, and could never replace the real thing. Similarly, computer sex doesn't satisfy the need for physical stimulation or companionship, and vibrators don't diminish the desire for a big slurpy kiss on the mouth. The primary appeal of the new generation of high-tech toys is their potential to exercise our most powerful low-tech toy—the erotic imagination. These tools enable us to expand our fantasy realm and to learn more about pleasure.

This little taste of technology is just the beginning—who knows what new technological treats are waiting around the bend to seduce us? Whatever they are, we're tuned in, plugged in, logged on, pumped up and ready to chart new erotic terrain well into the twenty-first century!

S/M and Power Play

My favorite thing is when my lover takes total control, dominates me, doesn't ask what I need or want because she knows already; she just goes right ahead and takes me, talking to me the whole time.

I like to take the cord to my bathrobe and bind my partner's hands to the bedpost. I get excited by the feeling of power—the ability to tease and bring him to orgasm without his intervention.

Do either of these sentiments ring a bell for you? We think it's a safe bet that you find both the thought of being overpowered by a partner and the thought of overpowering a partner quite arousing. Sexual power play has always had a near universal appeal, but many of you who readily incorporate aspects of dominance and submission into your sex lives might be surprised to learn that these could be described as S/M activities.

The terms *S/M* or *S&M* evolved from abbreviations of the word *sadomasochism,* which the dictionary defines as the "perversion" of deriving sexual pleasure from either the infliction or the experience of pain. Popular misconceptions about S/M can be traced to this dictionary definition and are aggravated by the fact that *sadomasochism* is frequently used to describe the nonsexual dynamic between people involved in coercive or abusive behaviors: A bullying boss or battering husband is referred to as a "sadist," while anyone physically or emotionally self-destructive is referred to as a "masochist." Hollywood moviemakers have done their bit to exacerbate stereotypes about S/M. When not casting screenplays full of psychopathic transsexual or transvestite villains, they like to spice up their thrillers with plots involving murderous practitioners of "S&M." Talk about having your cake and eating it, too—the public is invited to revel in titillating images of spike-heeled dominatrixes or leather-clad masters, but by the final reel of the movie, all the evil sadists and pathetic masochists have been incarcerated or killed, and kinder, gentler virtue is triumphant.

In fact, S/M has nothing to do with coercion, either sexual or nonsexual. The common denominator in all S/M play is not a violent exchange of pain but a consensual exchange of power. The distinction that S/M is about eroticized power play, not about physical or emotional abuse, is crucial to understanding and demystifying the subject. Some people in the S/M community feel that *sadomasochism* is therefore an inaccurate and inappropriate word to describe their experience, preferring terms such as *dominance and submission, sensuality and mutuality, sexual magic, radical sex* or *power and trust.*

As the definition of S/M has broadened to include any eroticism that revolves around role-playing, power exchange and heightening sensation, there's been a notable upsurge of interest in the topic. With growing awareness of the risks of sexually transmitted diseases, many people are intrigued by the prospect of sexual play that is highly arousing yet doesn't presume genital sex. S/M clubs and organizations across the country offer lectures, workshops and play-parties enabling participants to explore power play in a safe, structured context. The negotiation and communication required before two or more people embark on an S/M session can improve your chances of achieving sexual satisfaction, whether you're relative strangers meeting up for a one-night adventure or you're a long-term couple looking to break out of the rut of predictable sex.

When you factor in the popularization of fetish items such as leather, lingerie, collars and corsets as seen on MTV and in fashion magazines, you have the phenomenon our friend Susie Bright dubs "S/M lite"—S/M imagery that has permeated mainstream culture. Many adult-industry manufacturers added S/M lite toys and lingerie to their product lines in direct response to customer demand. Good Vibrations customers snap up each new S/M primer added to our book and video catalog, and the success of our "Bound to Please" department of restraints, paddles and nipple clamps leads us to suspect that S/M play is sweeping the nation.

Of course, there's nothing new under the sun, and power play has been a compelling aspect of human sexuality from the get-go. One archeologist has even theorized that one of the Venus figurines, statuettes of naked women that date back to Ice Age Europe, depicts a woman whose wrists are bound together by bands of fur (see the entertaining chapter "S&M on the Steppe" in Timothy Taylor's *The Prehistory of Sex*). If erotic bondage

was good enough for our ancestors twenty-five thousand years ago, why shouldn't it be good enough for us today?

The following chapter briefly introduces you to an erotic style enjoyed and explicated by a wide range of articulate spokespeople. If what you read here sparks your curiosity, we encourage you to contact one of the numerous social and educational organizations available to people interested in exploring S/M—national organizations may be able to refer you to a group or chapter in your own town, and we've noted some of these in our resource listings. You can also find an abundance of excellent books and videos about S/M—some of our favorites are noted in the bibliography and videography. The Internet is an excellent resource for information about all alternative sex styles.

Let's Define Our Terms

About Power Exchange

In S/M play, one partner assumes the dominant or "top" role, while the other assumes the submissive or "bottom" role in a pre-arranged encounter that is commonly referred to as a "scene." This role-playing can take subtle to elaborate forms, and scenes may last for a few minutes or a few days. At the subtle end of the spectrum, you might play a dominant role by directing your partner to wear a particular item of clothing or to assume a particular position in bed. You might play a submissive role by agreeing that you won't allow yourself to reach orgasm until your partner gives you permission to come. At the more elaborate end of the spectrum, you can make an erotic contract with your partner in which one of you serves as obedient sex-slave to the other. A day later, you might each switch roles. The bottom line is, you can't dominate your partner unless he or she allows you to take control, and you can't submit to your partner unless he or she accepts control. The interdependency and fluidity of the power exchange implicit in S/M is expressed by the slash between the letters *S* and *M*—the two poles of the S/M experience are connected. One can't exist in isolation from the other.

Why, you may be asking yourself, would anyone want to take a dominant or submissive role during sex? To which we respond, come now, have you taken a look at your own sex life lately? Sex between two people rarely proceeds along a strictly egalitarian path of mutual arousal to a simultaneous orgasm—more likely, each partner takes turns controlling the sensations the other is feeling. An ever-shifting power dynamic is fundamental to any human interaction. The range of feelings that arise during sex are hardly restricted to hearts-and-flowers sentimentality—protectiveness, vulnerability, abandonment, selfishness, curiosity, spite, pride and love are all emotions that may ebb and flow in an intimate encounter.

> *Sometimes I'm almost frightened by how determined I am to make my partner come purely for my own selfish pleasure, just to hear her scream and watch her lose control.*

You might recoil at the thought that humiliating a partner could be arousing, but who hasn't enjoyed teasing a lover in the manner described below:

> *I like to rim my most recent male partner or lick his butt, because he moans a lot when I do. He hates to be involuntarily demonstrative, yet he finds it pleasurable, so he's in this quandary. He usually makes me stop because he's embarrassed about moaning.*

It occurs to us that the gentleman described in this quote might benefit from a stern mistress or master who'd tie him down, lick him to distraction and refuse to release him until his moans of pleasure were fully audible. After all, he's withholding pleasure, not only from his partner, but from himself—perhaps if someone else takes over the task of "punishing" him for his demonstrative ways, he'll no longer feel compelled to punish himself by censoring his responses. Abdicating control and putting your partner in the driver's seat is a highly effective way to make an end run around your own sexual shame and self-denial.

The Fantasy Connection

A closer look at your own sexual fantasies may give you some further clues as to the appeal of power play. Many people enjoy fantasies that

break down into one of two categories. One popular fantasy theme is that of being completely subjugated by kidnappers, rapists, aliens, etc.:

> *I fantasize being forcefully "taken" with one or more men watching and waiting their turns, while my partner directs the action.*

The complementary and equally popular fantasy theme is that of being in complete erotic control of a stable full of love slaves, some real-life authority figure, a celebrity, etc.:

> *In my fantasy I'm dominating a man and a woman who are completely at my disposal for any activity I plan for them, i.e., bondage, spanking, anal penetration with dildos...*

Power play is central to our erotic imaginations, and practitioners of S/M often argue that consciously addressing this fact has brought a heightened self-awareness, honesty and integrity to their sexual life that so-called "vanilla" (non-S/M) sex cannot provide.

Who's on Bottom?

What, specifically, is the appeal of taking a submissive role? In many ways it mirrors the appeal of subjugation fantasies. The implication that you are so desirable and alluring that an overpowering dominant will stop at nothing to possess you is the crux of time-honored fantasies ranging from ravishment by bodice-ripping pirates to prison-yard gang bangs. The fantasy that you inspire overwhelming desire frees you to be swept away by your own sexual desires—at the same time, you're allowed to abdicate responsibility for anything you might say or do. This surrender can be a particular relief to those who either feel guilty or ambivalent about sex.

> *I've just recently begun experimenting with dominance/submission—seems to free me up to "lose control" more easily.*

It can also be liberating to those who crave lots of sensation in order to reach orgasm. Whereas you may feel embarrassed by your own high tolerance for stimulation or for being a "hard come" in vanilla sex situations, as a greedy, "insatiable" submissive you can be an object of pride and respect.

I like being bound and teased–I'm excitingly embarrassed by how kinky I can get when provoked or manipulated to respond sexually. It lets me be free to enjoy sex deeply.

Submissive scenarios can also be a pleasant relief to individuals who have plenty of responsibility in their daily professional lives and yearn for the opportunity to relinquish control in their personal lives. The popular misconception that S/M is somehow sexist or demeaning to women has its roots in the presumption that the dominant in any S/M scene will necessarily be that individual who has the greatest economic and social power. Yet, there's no direct correlation between an individual's actual socioeconomic status and her or his preference in sexual role-playing–many wealthy, powerful executives of both genders quite fancy a spanking in their off hours. Furthermore, this "S/M is demeaning" model implies that the submissive is viewed as the partner of lesser value, which isn't the case. After all, it takes two to tango–we'd hate to see anxiety over political-correctness inhibiting any of our reader's pleasure in taking a spin around the dance floor.

I like being tied up and teased or even left for a while. I like to play the helpless wench (maybe if I were helpless in real life, I'd be a dominatrix). I like to be forced to think about it until I'm in a frenzy of desire and begging for it.

The classic contradiction of being a submissive is that while you are ostensibly subservient to your dominant, you remain the center of attention, which implies that you are very valuable. This promotes a pampered, childlike security that counterbalances the vulnerability involved in expressing your craving for subordination. In childhood, we all experience a painful sense of powerlessness. Willingly abdicating control as an adult can give you a paradoxical sense of power– after embracing weakness and dependency, you can come out of the experience reassured of your strength and autonomy.

Who's on Top?

What, specifically, is the appeal of taking a dominant role? The appeal is that you're on top!–your partner has entrusted you to run the show. You control what happens and who gets off when. You also have the responsibility for your partner's safety and enjoyment. Ideally, you shouldn't do unto your submissive anything that hasn't at one time or another been done to you. You may want to focus on your partner's pleasure:

S/M is something I'm doing with my current partner. I find tying her up and having her "at my mercy" while I'm playing with her nipples, pussy, etc. is very erotic and also quite fun.

I tied her up and went down on her for an hour or so–she was so swollen and sensitive. Then I used her vibrator directly on her clit and gave her at least ten orgasms. That was fun.

You may want to focus on your own pleasure:

My partner goes down on me while I whip her with a crop. Her pain is commensurate to my pleasure.

I strap a dildo onto my partner and order him to lie back while I ride him. He's not allowed to move, to touch me or to touch himself. It makes him crazy to have my breasts right over his face, and my ass bouncing right over his cock without his being able to touch me.

Just as being a submissive frees you to yield control and embrace vulnerability, being a dominant frees you to take control and embrace authority. The dominant can explore feelings frowned upon in our society–selfishness, cruelty, superiority and lust for power–and act these out in the context of pleasing a partner. Your partner's trust can be highly intoxicating, and the experience of tapping into your own "dark side" can be quite liberating. The flip side of this freedom is the responsibility for maintaining complete focus on your partner, ensuring that his or her physical or emotional limits are not transgressed, and being the one who is taking care of the situation. It can take courage, especially for the novice dominant, to muster up the self-confidence and panache necessary to carry off a scene. Willingness to assume this responsibility and to expend the energy involved in sustaining a scene is a gift from the dominant to the submissive.

I really like S/M role-playing games. I'm a top. I find pleasure in creating a scene for my lover. It's a custom-made gift created with the deepest of love.

What about Pain?

While it's true that S/M is not fundamentally about pain, it's equally true that some S/M activities—such as whipping or applying nipple clamps—may sound pretty darn uncomfortable. It's more accurate to describe these activities as producing sensation than producing pain. Think about it. If you were from another planet and you walked into an aerobics class, you might be astonished to learn that the students had paid to undergo this torture. We live on the beautiful California coastline, and every weekend the coastal highway is filled with bicyclists pedaling their way to the top of each hill with grim expressions that hardly seem to denote recreational bliss. Yet, if quizzed by an alien, both the aerobics students and the bicyclists would likely say that they were proud to have worked their way up to this level of exertion, and that actually their physical activities serve to pump intoxicating levels of endorphins through their bloodstreams. Even when physical exertion is painful, there's a big subjective difference between pain that you're controlling and training yourself to surmount and pain that you didn't expect or request.

Similarly, if you were to walk in on a scene of a man being flogged, you might assume that he was in great pain, but he would probably describe himself as being in an altered state of heightened sensation. Sexual arousal affects how we perceive pain. You've doubtlessly had the experience of enjoying certain types of stimulation during sex—hair-pulling, nipple-biting, scratching—which you wouldn't enjoy in the slightest once your arousal had subsided. It's a bit arbitrary to coo proudly over the scratches and bites you've received during passionate lovemaking and then pass judgment on the crop marks somebody else received during his or her passionate lovemaking.

It's also worth noting that individuals with neurological disabilities that dull their perception of physical stimulation sometimes experience pleasure exclusively from the intense sensation provided by certain S/M activities. And some able-bodied individuals who pursue intense sensation do so as an almost meditative discipline, a way of triumphing over and transcending the flesh.

What about Fetishes?

Certain objects, materials or body parts can trigger sexual desire in individuals who fetishize them. Clothing fetishes are probably the most common, and many people harbor fetishes for uniforms or lingerie, or for materials such as leather or latex. A fetish can be mild—the object or material helps enhance a sexual scene—or extreme—the object or material is essential to sexual arousal. We are mentioning the topic here, as folks with fetishes sometimes become part of their local S/M communities in order to have a chance to dress-up in and be close to the material or clothing they love. The point is, don't assume that because somebody loves leather, she or he necessarily enjoys S/M play. Likewise, someone who enjoys S/M doesn't necessarily love leather. Dressing up in fetish clothing, be it lacy lingerie or studded leather, is one of the most universal ways of being sexually adventurous, but while costuming may be part of an S/M scene, it doesn't serve as a signpost.

I joined the Outcasts, the lesbian S/M group, so I could meet women who'd appreciate my wardrobe. Now I'm thinking of starting a group called the Outfits, especially for girls who like to dress up.

What's the Appeal of S/M?

It's Exciting

Few things are as dampening to sexual excitement as predictability. Eroticism thrives on drama, particularly the drama of surmounting obstacles, whether these obstacles are long distances, family ties or religious proscriptions. In his groundbreaking book *The Erotic Mind*, psychotherapist Jack

Morin suggests that the equation for unforgettable sex is "attraction + obstacles = excitement." He lists four "cornerstones" or common contributors to sexual arousal: longing and anticipation, violating prohibitions, searching for power and overcoming ambivalence.

Half the thrill of sexually engaging with a new partner is the thrill of the unknown: the myriad possibilities of seduction, the opportunity to present whatever side of yourself you choose, the mystery of your new partner's responses. Hot sex requires an "other" to react against, and sustaining your identities as separate individuals is crucial to sustaining a sexual spark. Many long-term couples know that the key to keeping their sex lives fresh is to take neither each other nor each other's availability for granted. The common experience of having passionate sex after a big fight is just one example of how asserting differences or raising a temporary obstacle can stoke the sexual fires.

S/M play incorporates these erotic "cornerstones," and can reintroduce the thrill of the unknown into even the most familiar of relationships. Preparing for an S/M scene involves building anticipation, exploring taboos and prohibitions, negotiating power and defining limits of physical and emotional resistance. S/M combines the drama and unpredictability of seduction with the security of pre-arranged boundaries. The heightened mutual awareness you must bring to an S/M encounter is what makes S/M play so much more memorable for its practitioners than vanilla sex.

It's Dramatic

S/M involves accessing your imaginative, playful side. In preparing for S/M play, you are essentially preparing for erotic theater—you choose to incorporate whatever dramatic tension, aspects of your fantasies, props or costumes you find most arousing. Role-playing, as anyone who ever played cops and robbers as a kid can testify, is both fun and liberating. You are freed to express parts of yourself you don't express in daily life, and you can play-act frightening or dangerous situations while remaining completely safe. The use of the word *scene* to describe an S/M encounter is in keeping with this theatrical metaphor.

It's Safe

S/M play is safer sex, in the same way that playing with sex toys is safer sex. Both these sexual variations de-emphasize genital intercourse or the exchange of bodily fluids and emphasize a full-body approach to sex. The S/M community has been active in advocating safer sex through its organizations and classes and in upholding safer sex guidelines at parties, events and workshops. The one creed linking the vast variety of S/M activities is that all S/M play must be "safe, sane and consensual." According to this maxim, no one should embark on an S/M scene without clear communication as to each party's physical and emotional limits or without a certain level of mutual trust. Excessive drug or alcohol consumption, which could impair a dominant's judgment and blunt a submissive's awareness of having exceeded physical limits, is also discouraged.

It's Inclusive

The S/M community is somewhat unique in including and incorporating individuals of different ages, backgrounds and sexualities. While there are and always will be specific organizations for gays, lesbians or heterosexuals involved in S/M, the community as a whole tends to be inclusive on the basis of a shared interest in power play. It's also worth noting that the S/M community puts a high premium on experienced practitioners, and that this is one sexual subculture in which age and maturity can be seen as a turn-on, rather than a turn-off. How refreshing.

What Next?

Defining Your Desires

If you're intrigued by the thought of experimenting with sexual power play, you may be wondering, where do I go from here? First, examine your own desires and expectations. Your sexual fantasies can reveal a lot about what aspects of power exchange you find most exciting and what types of role-playing appeal to you. Of course, it's possible that your most exciting fantasies are those you have no intention of acting out. Some people's fantasies are in counterbalance to their actual sexual behavior:

Even though I define myself as a top, my fantasies are as a bottom. I have straight fantasies, which freaks me out. I only think this way while fantasizing. Once sex is over, if I think of men, I'll be nauseated!

Many people enjoy two types of fantasies: the "I'd never do this in a million years, but I sure get hot thinking about it" fantasy and the "I'd leap at the chance to make this one come true" fantasy.

I want to be topped by five or six butch leather dykes. I want an enema. I want to be whipped and pierced. Those are the ones I want to actually happen. The fantasy that makes me come the fastest these days is of getting fucked by men in hotel rooms for money. But I don't necessarily want that to actually happen.

Think about what key elements inspire your hottest fantasies: Is it certain positions, certain words, the idea of being spoken to in a certain tone of voice, certain items of clothing, certain locations, certain smells? Identifying these elements could help you identify the components of a satisfying scene.

Get specific about what activities you do and don't want to explore. An excellent exercise is to make three lists: one list of all the erotic activities you've tried and know you like; one list of all the erotic activities you're sure you don't want to try; and one list of all the erotic activities you're curious about possibly trying. This will give you a frame of reference for how to proceed. You'll probably find it interesting to do this exercise once a year to see what activities move from one list to another over time—so much more functional and so much less discouraging than dusting off that list of New Year's resolutions!

Finding a Playmate

Suitably armed with all this self-knowledge, it's time to broach the topic with a partner. We know, this is the scary part. You could bring the matter up in a general way, by asking what he or she thinks of erotica such as *Story of O* or by describing that sexy panel of dominatrixes you saw on a daytime TV talk show. You can comment that you've had S/M fantasies and are curious whether he or she does. Don't be disheartened if your partner's first response is a nervous joke about "whips and chains." There's a lot of misinformation generally available about S/M, and it's likely that the same person who expresses discomfort with the idea of whips has a fantasy bank full of army sergeants, schoolmistresses and prison matrons. It may just take time to tease out the details as to what types of role-playing might appeal.

Sometimes it's easier to discuss your fantasies with someone you've just met than with a long-term partner or spouse. Unfortunately, the more attached to someone you are, the more afraid you can become of revealing information that you fear your partner might find off-putting or silly. In either case, it helps to be as specific, nonthreatening and nonjudgmental in your language as possible, for instance, "Sometimes I pretend that you own me, you've kept me locked in my apartment all day, and now you're coming over to have your way with me," as opposed to "Why don't you ever take charge in bed!" Or, "Yesterday, I imagined tying your hands to the bedposts and taking an hour to go down on you," as opposed to "You never let me take as long as I want!" Whatever response you get, remember that naming your own sexual desires is a brave act and you deserve a respectful response. Of course, you should try not to respond to any of your partner's suggestions or counterproposals with defensiveness or hostility.

Despite the most tactful communication on your part, you may find your proposal rejected. You have the option of seeking other like-minded potential partners at S/M classes, social events or through personal ads. If you are in a monogamous relationship, you'll probably want to discuss your partner's reservations on more than one occasion, to see if you can reach some common understanding. Ideally, you'd be able to compromise on activities that would satisfy your curiosity without making your partner feel badgered or bullied into trying something against his or her will. It's possible that your partner has simply leapt to the conclusion that your interest in trying something new implies dissatisfaction with your current sex life; she or he may just need some reassurance. Some people think that sex should always be spontaneous and may protest that planning a sexual scenario seems cumbersome and artificial. You can remind your partner that in your courting days, both of you probably put lots of time into planning your every encounter, but romance never suffered for it.

Negotiating a Scene

If you've both acknowledged interest in exploring power play, it's time for some fun research. Here's where those lists you wrote—detailing activities you've tried, activities you haven't tried but are curious about, and activities you have no interest in trying—come in handy. You and your partner could each draw up a set of lists and swap them as a basis for discussion. If either of you draws a blank at possible activities, you may find books and videos helpful and inspirational.

I watch porn videos nonsexually with a partner to actually see examples of things each of us likes. Then we discuss what we'd like to do.

Perhaps the first thing to agree on is who'll take the dominant and who'll take the submissive role. This decision can be based on anything from personal preference, to who has more experience, to flipping a coin. You should then clarify what activities you're each interested in trying and which you absolutely do not wish to try, for instance, "I'd like to be tied up and spanked, but I don't want to be blindfolded at any point." You should each know the other's level of experience with those activities on the "done this" list, as well as with any sexual activities you wish to incorporate into the scene. If you'd like to beat your partner with a crop, he or she may be understandably curious to know just how many times you've wielded a crop before. If you'd like to be tied up and anally penetrated with a dildo, your partner should know whether or not your previous experience of anal penetration has involved anything larger than a pinkie finger. The fact that you have the opportunity to enact some of your fantasies does not mean that every activity you undertake will flow as pleasurably and effortlessly as it does in your fantasies. Don't throw common sense out the window with your inhibitions.

TIMING If you're at a play-party or negotiating with someone you've just met, your negotiation may serve as the foreplay to your scene. You might step right into your respective roles and work out the details with the dominant adopting a top persona to interview the submissive. Or you may prefer to stay out of role during your discussion and to set a future date to play. There's certainly nothing wrong with giving yourselves time to let some anticipation build.

Couples who've been enjoying power play for some time probably won't need an elaborate negotiation before each scene. Advance notice could simply take the form of telling your partner over breakfast that you've got something planned for her when she comes home that night, or leaving explicit invitations on his voice mail. You may have developed your own personal ways of signaling your intentions—putting on a particular collar or wearing a particular pair of boots.

You'll need to know how much time you've got together, as the pacing of your scene will vary depending on whether you have an hour before you have to get home and pay the baby-sitter, all night before you have to get to work or an entire carefree weekend ahead of you.

LOCATION As with any kind of date, the classic "my place or yours" is a relevant consideration, and your decision may be dictated by any number of things: who has more privacy at home; who has more toys; who has eyebolts screwed into the wall; who has a four-poster bed; who has to get up early for work, etc. If you and you partner live together, you may wish to escape your daily routine and situate your scene in a hotel room or at a play-party.

Will it be a public scene? If all or part of your scene takes place at a restaurant, bar or public space, you need to be discreet to avoid harassment or intrusion. You may, however, each have different ideas as to what constitutes "discreet." Set your guidelines ahead of time—how are you willing to be addressed and treated in public? Maybe you're willing to wear a collar, but not to be led on a leash. Maybe you're willing to be addressed as "Mistress," but not to have your partner sit at your feet in the taxi. It can be extremely arousing to be out on the town with your scene—don't let a misunderstanding ruin the mood.

Nothing excites me as much as secret public sex. I enjoy being ordered to wear butt plugs, vibrators, ben wa balls or bondage under my clothes and then to be covertly disciplined in public.

If you're planning to get together at a play-party or with more than one person, you should negotiate how you're both going to interact with other people. Is there one particular person or several people who are welcome to join you? To what extent are you willing to have others participate in your scene: physically, genitally, voyeuristically? You can avoid a lot of unnecessary jealousy or bad feeling if you think things through ahead of time.

PERSONAS You may be perfectly content simply to define your roles as dominant and submissive, without any further elaboration. Or you may want to establish some parameters. Is the top to be referred to as "Mistress," "Master" or "Sir"? Is the bottom allowed to make eye contact with the top? Should the bottom speak only when spoken to? You may want to assume very specific roles, which will determine what kinds of things you wear, say or do. This is where you can let your creative juices flow. Now's the time to unlock your fantasy treasure chest and release a character or two. Perhaps you've always longed to play Roman senator and slave boy; Catherine the Great and stable hand; priest and nun; schoolmarm and student; doctor and patient; inquisitor and p.o.w.; parent and child...the list is endless.

I like to act out being some hot daddy's sex slave. I am kept naked and servile.

My partner pretends to be a bad little girl, and I'm the teacher giving her a bare bottom spanking.

I like to pretend to be corrupting or initiating a much younger man who is inexperienced, but very interested in exploring sex with an older woman.

Whether or not you adopt specific characters, you'll probably find it both helpful and fun to dress up for your scene. You may well have a greater sense of conviction as a dominant when

you're clad in leather or chains or boots or spike heels. Your feelings of vulnerability and helplessness as a submissive could well be enhanced by revealing or restrictive clothes. Clothing can add a sensual impact, not to mention sound effects, that greatly enhance a scene—the sounds of stilettos clicking, leather creaking, zippers being forced open and fabric tearing can be highly arousing. You don't need Princess Di's income to afford this kind of disposable wardrobe either—trips to the Goodwill can keep you costumed in style, and you may find that shopping becomes its own form of foreplay.

HEALTH AND SAFETY GUIDELINES A top should make sure to get basic medical information from the bottom, so as not to endanger her or his health during the scene. Someone wearing contact lenses should not be tightly blindfolded. Someone with asthma or a cold shouldn't be gagged. You should both communicate about back pains, joint troubles, heart conditions, epilepsy, diabetes, high blood pressure or any other conditions that could affect tolerance of pain, range-of-motion and flexibility.

It's also crucial to discuss safer sex guidelines and what genital sex, if any, you are willing to have. An S/M scene doesn't necessarily include sex.

I really love S/M as a turn-on prelude to sex, but also S/M can be a complete sex act in itself. With a good spanking, I can feel as good as if I had sex.

You should be very clear in advance whether or not your scene might include masturbation, oral sex, penetration of any kind or sex toys, and what safer sex precautions you choose to follow in each case. While this negotiation is particularly important when you're playing with a new partner, even long-term partners might find that they have different limits or desires around genital play during an S/M scene than during vanilla sex.

SAFE WORDS Both partners need a way to clearly communicate if they are feeling overwhelmed and want to slow down or stop the action altogether. Safe words afford a quick and easy way to alert your partner to the fact that you need a break. Usually, couples agree on words or signals that will be completely unambiguous. *No, don't* or *stop* are inefficient safe words, as you may well find yourself deep into role-playing and crying out these words without the slightest desire for anyone to stop doing anything. *Yellow* or *red* are frequently used to mean "slow down" or "stop." Some couples agree to use the top's first name as a signal to ease up, or you can simply say, "safe word." The bottom line is, select a word that's easy to remember. It's also helpful to have a safe signal, such as snapping your fingers, in the event that one of you is gagged.

Expectations

S/M involves exploring fantasy and playing with illusion. As with any case of bringing a fantasy to life, you're far less likely to experience a disappointing discrepancy between dream and reality if you try to clarify your expectations and motivations ahead of time. Power play is a blend of mental, emotional and physical stimulants, and simply going through the physical motions will probably not be particularly arousing in and of itself. Ask yourself what feeling you want to get out of your experience. Do you want to feel powerful, awe-inspiring, vulnerable, frightened, taken care of? Once you have a sense of the emotion you're seeking, you can figure out how best to go after it.

The same physical activity will be appealing to different people for different reasons. It helps to figure out not just what you like, but why you like it. You might want to be tied up because you like the sensation of immobility or because you like being exposed or the illusion of being someone's property. Is it important that you are being punished for an invented infraction, humiliated by a cruel dominant, trained by a loving master? The distinctions are crucial to the success of your scene. Neither you nor your partner can expect to intuit what intangible components will provide satisfaction and enhance sensation. Talk about it—S/M play provides a unique opportunity to get specific about naming your desires.

Finally, be realistic. Bear in mind that you can't do everything you've ever dreamed of in one session. If you leave each other wanting more, you're far more likely to play together again than if either one of you feels overwhelmed by what happened between you.

Toys and Techniques

Before we embark on our discussion of toys, we'd like to point out that just as clothes don't make the man, toys don't make the scene. Although there's a tendency to equate S/M with the use of equipment, many people incorporate power play into their sex lives without a single prop. That you're intimidated by whips and can't tie a knot to save your life doesn't mean you can't be a thrilling dominant. Anyone's flair with toys can be enhanced if she or he has played without them first. The power of the human voice and an authoritative manner are greater than any ropes and chains.

Imagine ordering your partner to keep her legs spread wide open while you tease her clit, or directing your partner to keep his hands clasped over his head while you go down on him—if the punishment for disobeying is that you'll instantly stop what you're doing, chances are good that you will be obeyed to the letter. A friend of ours has a motto, "It's not the toys, it's the technique." Keep this in mind as you read on.

Bondage

Restraining your partner or being restrained is a highly popular activity—many of our questionnaire respondents listed bondage among their favorite sex games.

> *I like being restrained either physically or by verbal request, oops, I mean command.*

> *I love going down on my lovers, especially when they are tied up.*

> *I do like tying people up and being tied up. I mostly like the feeling of not being able to move and having to give up control.*

> *I enjoy being tied up with silk ties and slowly stimulated.*

Bondage can be appealing for many reasons. You may be inspired by the idea of rendering your partner helpless, so that you can tease or torment her or him at your leisure. Or you may like

Bondage

the idea of erotically displaying your partner spread-eagled on the bed and exposed to your merciless scrutiny, posed gracefully with arms overhead, strapped to a chair or just plain hog-tied. You may want to dress your pet in a collar and leash and do some obedience training. Cock-and-ball toys provide a specific type of bondage that serves to simultaneously restrict and display a man's genitals.

> *I've had fun being handcuffed, tied up, etc. One of the most fun sex-plays I've had was when I allowed a partner to tie up my cock and balls and pull me by this "leash."*

SAFETY TIPS   Whatever your pleasure, bear in mind some basic safety guidelines. One common-sense rule of thumb: Don't do anything that will constrict joints or cut off circulation. If you're tying rope, cords or a scarf, don't use any knots that tighten with resistance—slip knots are bad, bowlines are good. If you're knot-illiterate, it's time to dig up that old Boy Scout manual or to look for a similar reference guide. A lot of people tie each other up with thin scarves or stockings, not realizing that the soft, slippery material is hard to untie and can tighten, resulting in pinched nerves or

even permanent nerve damage. Whatever material you use, make sure you've left enough room to fit a finger between the bond and your partner's wrist or ankle. You'll also feel more secure if you keep a pair of scissors, preferably bandage scissors (these have a blunt edge on the blade that would rest against the body), within arm's reach.

No one should be kept completely restricted for longer than half an hour, and you should be careful not to let your partner's arms or legs fall asleep. You're both responsible for monitoring bound body parts regularly for cooling or numbness, signs that blood has stopped flowing into the extremities. Be particularly attentive to someone in standing bondage or who's holding his or her arms overhead—your partner's elbows should be slightly bent to reduce stress on the joints. Never suspend anyone by his or her wrists, ankles or neck. Never tie anything around someone's neck or otherwise restrict breathing—if you're using a gag of some kind, check regularly to make sure it's loose enough that your partner can breathe and make noise. And, finally, don't ever leave someone who's bound or gagged alone in the room—this is no time to go answer a phone call. Sure, you may want to pretend to "desert" your bottom for several minutes at a time, but you should keep an eye on him or her from wherever you are hiding.

PROPS AND PROCEDURES   It can be intimidating to hop into the driver's seat and tie somebody up if you've never done so before. Take your time and enjoy the sensuous feel of whatever bondage material you're using. You can entertain and distract your partner with a running commentary on exactly what you're going to do next. This may be the perfect occasion to whip out a blindfold or to wrap a scarf over her or his eyes—you won't feel scrutinized, and your partner will feel vulnerable and filled with anticipation.

Supplies: Bondage materials run the gamut in texture and price range. Rope, clothesline and scarves are all cheap and readily available. Just keep your safety precautions in mind when using these materials. A trip to a hardware store is something of a field day for a bondage fan—you'll find snap hooks, double clips, chain and eyebolts at bargain prices. You can screw eyebolts or hooks into your bed frame, walls, baseboards, door frame or ceiling–hang that macramé plant-holder from the ceiling hooks when your mom comes to visit, and no one will be any the wiser. Mountaineering or backpacking stores are also great resources and carry panic snaps, clips that release easily even if weight is pulling on them–these should be used for any standing bondage.

Restraints: Some people really like the idea of co-opting household supplies for their sex scenes, but many others prefer to buy something designed especially for what they have in mind, and therefore there's a thriving restraint industry in this country. Restraints, bonds and cuffs (we'll use these terms interchangeably) are available through sex boutiques, leather specialty stores and a growing number of mail-order catalogs. While it may seem like a bit of an investment to buy restraints, consider the advantages: They are wide, padded, comfortable, and much safer than thin cords. Furthermore, cuffs are highly decorative. Some of the leather and suede restraints we sell could practically double as evening-wear accessories, while many of the fabric restraints are so sporty, they look like something you'd order from a backpacking catalog.

Less expensive restraints are made of nylon webbing or fabric–they wrap around the wrist or ankle and fasten with either a buckle or Velcro. You can find varieties that have a long lead, which you then tie wherever you please, or that are set with D-rings. The advantage of the D-ring variety is that you don't necessarily need to tie any knots, provided you purchase a little hardware. You can fasten the restraints together with a double clip, slip a leash clip over the D-rings, or use chain to fasten the restraints to an eyebolt in your wall. Of course you can also just tie a rope or scarf to the D-rings and fasten the other end wherever it suits you.

In the past few years, a remarkable number of fabric bonds have come onto the market. You can buy bonds in every color of the rainbow, including some dazzling neon shades that would coordinate beautifully with Barbie's Malibu dream house. The quality and sturdiness of these bonds can vary quite a bit, and the ties of some of the cheaper fabric varieties rip off the body of the restraint with a simple tug or two. If you do have the chance to shop for restraints in person, rather than by mail, check how well the fastening is reinforced, and make sure the leads are sewn down securely.

On the luxury end of the scale are leather bonds. Most leather bonds are padded, and some are fleece-lined, for a plushy, snug fit. The buckling variety fasten with wide buckles–some buckles are designed so that you can slip a padlock through and lock the restraint shut. These buckling models are all fitted with D-rings. If tying restraints onto your partner strikes you as a bit intimidating, you'll appreciate how easy it is to be suave and commanding with buckling bonds. Leather restraints are most commonly available through leather specialty stores. If you're shopping in person, check that all rivets and snaps are secure and that the restraint fits comfortably, but not so loosely that it could slip off.

Handcuffs: Handcuffs have a certain classic appeal, but they should be used with caution. Make sure the cuffs you purchase have a safety catch which locks them into position, so that they won't tighten further after being fastened–make sure the safety catch works with a pin, not a lever. Don't even think about buying handcuffs unless you're willing to pay top dollar. Be careful in positioning persons wearing handcuffs so they're not ever lying with their body weight on top of all that sharp metal. And, as with any locking toy, keep the key handy! If you like the idea of playing with locks, your best bet would be to key all your padlocks and cuffs to one standard key.

Accessories: There are a number of options for mixing and matching bondage components. One handy product is the Bond Voyage, a web strap, fitted with sturdy plastic D-rings, that buckles around any size mattress, enabling you to tie your partner right down to the bed. The Bond Voyage is great both for travelers and for those folks who don't want to install hardware in their walls or ceilings.

Bondage belts are another attractive accessory. These are wide leather or fabric belts fitted with D-rings. You fasten the wearer's wrist restraints to the D-rings on the belt, creating a fetchingly submissive look. Bondage belts also provide a great way to hang on to your partner and tug him or her back and forth during intercourse.

For a spread-eagle effect that doesn't require a lot of effort, you might want to try a spreader bar—an adjustable metal bar with cuffs on either end. You can fasten the cuffs around your partner's wrists or ankles and adjust the bar to spread the wearer's arms or legs as far apart as you'd like. Just the thing for those Scarlet Letter, Puritan-in-Stocks fantasies.

Flagellation

Slapping, spanking, whipping and paddling all fall into the category of flagellation. From a casual smack on the butt during intercourse to an all-out flogging, flagellation runs the gamut of sensation. As an activity that inhabits the fine line between pain and pleasure, flagellation inspires a good deal of judgment and disapproval in those who've never experienced its charms.

If you're on the receiving end, you may enjoy enacting a fantasy role-play: naughty child receiving a spanking; unruly student getting rapped across the knuckles; P.O.W. being tortured; mutinous sailor undergoing a flogging. You may want the flagellation to be largely play-acted, with more bark than bite. Or, you may want to test your own limits of physical endurance, whether to prove your devotion to a dominant, to earn a certain reward, to feel completely present in your body or purely to attain that endorphin buzz. Either way, you're bound to experience a certain amount of fear, a rush of adrenaline that only serves to heighten and intensify sexual arousal.

Sometimes all I want is more sensation. I get greedy to have my cunt filled, my face slapped, my nipples bitten—all at the same time in order to get that "fucked into oblivion" feeling.

If you're on the administering end, you'll want to keep up your end of the fantasy role-play. Tailor your actions and comments to the story behind your scene: Are you punishing your partner for wrongdoing, disciplining your partner for his or her own good, abusing or indulging, or testing limits? You get to enjoy the excitement of performing a forbidden activity, the rush of displaying physical strength and the challenge of coaxing your partner into accepting ever-increasing levels of sensation.

When I take a crop to my partner's ass, I feel as though I'm feeding him. It's a strangely tender act.

SAFETY TIPS   In general, aiming for fleshy areas is safe, while hitting bone, joints or over any internal organs is not safe. This means you should avoid the head, the neck, the spine, the area between the rib cage and pelvis, the backs of the knees and elbows and the shins. This leaves you with the well-padded butt, thighs, upper arms and shoulders. Hitting breasts in moderation is okay, unless your partner is pregnant, nursing, prone to cysts or has silicone implants—these can burst if struck directly.

If you're slapping someone on the cheeks (the only part of the face you should be hitting), support the head with your other hand so as not to jerk the neck or jaw. Be careful not to box the ears—a blow over the ears can cause dizziness at best or a burst eardrum at worst.

When using an instrument such as a whip, crop, paddle or cane, you should be aware that the tip of the instrument carries the greatest force. When wielding a whip, aim it so that the tips of the tails land first, to avoid the "wrap" effect, in which the tips wrap around and hit the side of your partner's body with considerable speed and impact. Until you've developed your aim and perfected your technique, it's a good idea to put pillows on either side of your partner to absorb the wrap.

PROPS AND PROCEDURES   The key to safe and pleasurable flagellation is a gradual buildup. The strength of your blows should escalate in time with your partner's mounting arousal. Don't rush it. The more turned on someone is, the higher the pain threshold. You should start with very light blows and only increase their intensity as your partner indicates she or he wants more. Contrast the slapping, spanking or beating with other types of stimulation. Kisses on a freshly slapped cheek or feathery touches on a newly spanked butt can feel exquisitely sensitive and tormentingly good. If you're using a specific instrument, such as a crop or whip, you can alternate your blows with teasing the instrument around your partner's body—for instance, gently poking the tip of the crop against her clitoris or softly brushing the strands of the whip across his thighs.

You'll need to find out whether or not your partner objects to any marks, as this will affect how light or heavy your touch should be. The narrower the instrument you use, the more likely it is to leave marks.

An excellent rule of thumb is not to try any technique on a partner that you haven't experienced yourself. Test that crop on your own inner arm, thigh or shoulder before you swing it toward anybody else's back. We hope it goes without saying that you should not hit a human being with any implement before practicing your aim and finesse on an inanimate object, such as a pillow. Bear in mind that the shorter an instrument, the easier it will be to control, and the longer, the more difficult.

Supplies: Plenty of household objects lend themselves to flagellation scenes, from the classic belt (watch out for the buckle) to hairbrushes to rulers. Different shapes generate different kinds of sensation. Broad, flat objects produce a sting that's spread over a wider area, while thin, round objects produce a stinging burn and can cut the skin, if you wield them with a heavy hand. A broad, flat object, like your hand, a belt or a paddle will have a more concentrated impact. The tips of a whip will have a forceful sting—again, the greatest force of any instrument is at its tip.

Obviously, the lighter and softer the material, the harder you can hit with it without causing pain. Given a doeskin whip, you can pretty much wail away with impunity, but you'd better lighten up quick if you switch to latigo leather or neoprene rubber. By and large, the more tails a whip has, the more diffuse its impact—a single-tailed whip, like a bullwhip, can do the most damage, and is no toy for an amateur.

Implements designed especially for flagellation fall into several categories. Slappers are slim paddles made of two flaps of leather, sewn together at one side. The cracking sound of one flap hitting the other creates a dramatic effect, while the actual sensation produced varies from mild to heavy depending on how stiff and thick the leather of the paddle is. Straps and paddles are easy to control and produce a wide range of sensations, depending on the materials used. Thin straps or those encasing flexible steel produce more of a sting, similar to getting smacked with a ruler. Riding crops are usually made of flexible fiberglass rods encased in leather with a leather flap at one end. These are about two feet long, easy to maneuver and quite versatile. Whips are made of nylon, suede, leather or rubber in a variety of lengths—different materials will create different sensations. Canes are usually made from thin, supple wood, although one company produces canes and rods out of synthetic plastics. Given their thin, flexible design, canes can deliver a highly cutting sting.

Whatever you choose to use will depend both on the sensation you're looking for and the scene you're creating—a cane will be just the thing for those English schoolboy fantasies, while whips are ideal for a flogging scenario.

Suppliers: Some of the most creative and artistic entrepreneurs in the sex field are designing and crafting S/M tools. Many of these folks had no intention of becoming entrepreneurs until they became involved in S/M, saw a need for better quality toys, and decided to fill it. Adam and Gillian's Sensual Whips and Toys is a company in Long Island run by a couple who started out making their own nylon whips for personal use, but they received so many inquiries from friends in their local S/M community that they went into business. Now they have a mail-order catalog of whips and paddles, all guaranteed to be "feel-tested" in their workshop.

Although there are mail-order catalogs that specialize in S/M products, you will find the greatest variety and selection at a leather specialty store. We've seen whips and floggers in red, purple, silver and gold leather, of such beautiful craftsmanship that it can be exciting just to run your hands over them. Equestrian stores can be similarly inspiring.

I went into this riding store once and got incredibly turned on by all the sexy equipment. I was sneaking a peek at the display stand of riding crops, when the nice elderly woman who ran the store came over and said, "I see you're admiring our whips!" I got so flustered, I nearly knocked over the stand.

Hygiene: A reminder that you should follow safer sex precautions with your S/M gear, just as you would with any toy. If your instrument has come into contact with bodily fluids, such as blood or ejaculate, you should clean it thoroughly before using it again. In a perfect world, we'd all have separate toys for each of our partners, but most of us can't afford not to share. Clean your instrument with soap and water, then apply a disinfectant, such as rubbing alcohol or Betadine. Diluted hydrogen peroxide or bleach make good detergents, but they can be hard on leather. Clean each tail of a whip individually. Rinse thoroughly and dry. With leather products, it's a good idea to use a conditioner after your cleaning routine to keep the leather supple.

Senses and Skin

SENSORY DEPRIVATION Sensory deprivation is a popular way of enhancing an S/M scene. When one sense is restricted, all the others become heightened and more sensitive. The classic example of sensory deprivation is using a blindfold—with vision removed, suddenly every sound, smell and touch is intensified. Once blindfolded, you feel completely at the mercy of your partner, wondering what's about to happen next. For the novice dominant, blindfolds are an invaluable tool for creating suspense.

Blindfolds can be homemade out of scarves, bandannas, ties and so forth or specially purchased. The sleep masks sold in drugstores work fine, or you can spring for a sexy black leather and fleece blindfold from a leather specialty store. Of course, this particular form of sensory deprivation won't be appealing to people who derive much of their sexual arousal from visual stimuli.

I'm paraplegic and have no sensation from the chest down. I get my pleasure largely from what I see, smell and taste. I don't like to have sex with the lights out, because I won't get aroused unless I can see my partner.

You can restrict your partner's hearing by using ear plugs, or simply control what she or he hears by using headphones. Some people enjoy exploring near-total sensory deprivation through mummification, a process whereby the bottom is completely encased in a material such as plastic wrap (with holes left for breathing). On a less elab-

orate level, you can control the sounds, smells and tastes your partner is allowed to experience during a scene as one more way of emphasizing your overall control of the situation.

PLAYING WITH TEMPERATURE We bet you remember that scene in *9 1/2 Weeks* where Mickey Rourke slid ice cubes down Kim Basinger's silken shoulder. After all, it spawned a slew of derivative ad campaigns for everything from perfume to liquor. And with good reason. Ice has an immediate erotic appeal, whether it's applied to cool an overheated body, dripped teasingly onto nipples, slipped startlingly into a vagina or contrasted with heat. Imagine trailing ice along a warm, freshly-spanked butt—the contrast of extremes can feel torturously good.

If ice is the time-honored cold toy, candles are the classic hot toy. Dripping melted wax on your partner's skin is perfectly safe, provided you use plain, paraffin candles. Scented, colored or beeswax candles melt at a higher temperature, and could burn or blister your partner's skin. Before you drip wax onto your partner, test a drop on the inside of your own arm. You might want to start by holding the candle high, so that the wax will be cooler before it hits the surface of your partner's skin, and gradually move the candle closer. Try dripping hot wax and cold ice in rapid succession for maximum sensation.

I love sensual massage with oils and hot candle wax followed by kisses all over. The wax is exciting because it is shocking, warm, sensual. I sometimes like to have it scraped off with a dull knife.

Clamps

Clamps create sensations ranging from a slow, dull ache to a mean bite. What's their appeal? The same as that of having your skin pinched, bitten or otherwise tightly grabbed onto. As always, the pleasure this type of intense stimulation can produce is in direct relation to how sexually aroused you are at the time. Although people can—and do—put clamps almost anywhere on the body, we're going to focus on the most common erotic sites: nipples and genitals.

SAFETY TIPS Apply the clamp slowly and gently, gradually releasing the tension. When you first put a clamp on, you'll probably experience a sharp bite for about thirty seconds. This will gradually subside, as blood flow to the clamped area is cut off. Unless you flick, tap or pull on the clamps, you'll be feeling a dull ache and pressure, rather than a sharp pain. If you jostle the clamps in any way, the sharp sensations will return—this may be exactly what you want, and certainly there are plenty of people who enjoy these surges of sensation. Inevitably, when you remove the clamp, the blood flow back into the numbed tissue will produce a brief, intense pain. You can reduce this pain by releasing the clamp slowly and delicately. The longer the clamp has been on, the more it will hurt to remove. A good rule is not to leave clamps on for more than about thirty minutes at a time.

STYLES AND SOURCES Clamps are the ultimate in inexpensive toys. From clothespins to office supplies, there are countless everyday objects that can be co-opted for this kind of play. Test any clamp on the crease between your thumb and forefinger first to get a sense of what it will feel like on other tender areas of your body. You can adjust the tension of clothespins by wrapping rubber bands around one end or another. The more skin being held in the clamp and the wider the object you're using, the milder the sensation will be—for instance, a loose wire office clip will feel like a massage tool as compared to the nasty pinch of a miniature clothespin.

NIPPLE CLAMPS Plenty of products designed first and foremost as nipple clamps are available in sex stores and from mail-order catalogs. These are generally made of metal, have padded vinyl tips and are frequently attached to each other with a length of chain. When Good Vibrations first started carrying nipple clamps, they literally flew out the door, and we had to wonder why we'd taken so long to add them to our product mix. After all, we've heard countless people over the years express their enjoyment and appreciation of intense nipple play.

Due to my having very responsive nipples, I like rough nipple play and also like to pinch and lick

my own nipples, either during or outside of having sex with a partner.

Nipple stimulation is very, very exciting and also very relaxing. I feel it tingling in my cervix. And if it were being done to me for long enough, I think I could get to an orgasm from this alone.

I love nipple pinching, pressing and sucking. Love breast stimulation even to the point of it hurting—that actually really gets me hot.

Alligator clips have broad, flat pincers and tighten with a screw. These fit better on men than women, as they don't expand enough to stay on larger nipples. Alligator clips are named for their serrated metal pincers, but you should never apply one to your skin unless the pincers are well-padded with vinyl. Tweezer clips have two long, slim pincers that slide shut—they are highly expandable and versatile. Japanese clover clamps look something like a metal figure eight with small rubber pads for pincers. Clover clamps are designed so that when you tug on them, the pincers tighten, intensifying sensation. Skirt-hanger clips have wide padded pincers and distribute an achey sensation over a wider surface area.

If you enjoy nipple stimulation, why not experiment with nipple clamps? Wait until you're so aroused that pinching and tugging on your nipples with your fingers feels tantalizing, rather than unpleasant. Position the clamp behind the tip of your nipple, rather than right on the tip, where it will not only feel quite uncomfortable, but might fall off. If you're playing with miniature clothespins or other tiny clamps with a ferocious bite, you might want to position these around the aureola, rather than directly on your nipple. Once your clamps are in place, you make the call as to whether to leave them alone or to mess around with them further.

Nipple clamps—what a turn-on! When they're flicked, my switches go off!

Women with cystic breasts and women with silicone breast implants should be cautious about using clamps, and all women should be aware that their sensitivity levels may fluctuate with their menstrual cycle, so that a pair of clamps that feels delightful one week could well feel unbearable the next. Similarly, pregnant or nursing women may feel disinclined to play with clamps.

GENITAL CLAMPS All the nipple clamps described above can easily double as labia, clitoris, foreskin, penis or scrotum clamps. You'll probably encounter more people who enjoy having clamps placed on their outer labia or scrotal sac than the more sensitive, nerve-rich clitoris or glans of the penis, but anything's possible.

A nipple clamp on my clit can be exciting.

Piercing

Although piercing is not an S/M activity per se, there's some overlap between the S/M community and the body modification community. *Body modification* is the term used to describe the act of creating permanent adornments such as tattoos or piercings. These types of adornment are found in tribal cultures all over the world and have existed since the beginning of recorded history, which is why the term *modern primitive* is often used to describe someone who is exploring body modification today.

Throughout history, piercings have been done for ornamentation, as a rite of passage, to convey status and to augment erotic sensations. The Apadravya, a vertical piercing through the glans of the penis, is mentioned in the *Kama Sutra* as a means of providing additional stimulation during intercourse. Today people's motivations for getting piercings can range from the playful to the spiritual. Some people get piercings as a way of claiming ownership of their own bodies; some as a rite of passage; some as a way of heightening consciousness of their bodies; some as an endurance test; some for sexual stimulation; and some for purely decorative purposes. The traditional sites for piercings are nipples, genitals, ears, face and bellybutton.

Nipple piercings are common among both men and women, and nipple rings may be used to enhance sensation in the same way that nipple clamps are. You may find that nipple piercings enhance your awareness of and the sensitivity of your nipples.

Since getting my nipple piercing, I like the fact that I can get really turned on by having something other than my dick played with. Having a woman tug on the ring with her teeth and tongue feels indescribably good.

Women can opt to get one or more labia piercings, to pierce the clitoral hood or to pierce through the base of the clitoris. Clitoral hood piercings are frequently ring-style piercings with a ball bearing positioned to rest strategically against the clitoris.

Men have a variety of penis piercings to choose from. A Prince Albert is a ring-style piercing that extends along the underside of the glans from the urethral opening to where the glans meets the shaft of the penis. A frenum piercing is usually a barbell-style piercing along the underside of the shaft of the penis. Some men get a frenum ring-style piercing, so that the ring can be swung up to encircle the head of the erect penis, creating a modified cock-ring effect. All but the largest and most obtrusive penis piercings can be left in during intercourse for extra stimulation. Many people comment that their piercings have enhanced their awareness of their genitals in a way that augments sexual feelings.

If you're interested in finding out more about piercings, check out the resource listings. Permanent piercings should only be performed by professionals working with sterile tools and sterile jewelry. This is not a do-it-yourself kind of activity.

Emotional Issues

Before leaving this topic, we'd like to reiterate that power play offers a unique blend of physical, mental and emotional components, and the result is that S/M games can be frightening. For one thing, you're experimenting with activities that many people you know would casually label "sick" and "perverted." For another, you're exposing some of your deepest fantasies to a partner and, in the process, you're expressing feelings that aren't as "nice" or "loving" as you've been led to believe sexual feelings should be. S/M can bring up strong emotions, painful memories, shame, surges of anger and guilt. It's important to honor the fact that you're getting in touch with feelings that may not be pretty, but which are nonetheless real. You and your partner should trust each other enough that you can discuss what emotions are coming up for you, both during the scene, if necessary, and after.

It's always a good idea to spend some coming-down time with your partner after a scene. Whether you're feeling purely positive or somewhat ambivalent about what just happened, you owe each other positive reinforcement for the energy you each put out, the risks you each took and the experience you shared. Discuss what thrilled you, frightened you and turned you on. How do you feel about yourself? What might you do differently next time? Keep your focus on feelings and the overall impact of a scene. There's no need to do a play-by-play or to critique technical details.

If you or your partner is a survivor of assault or abuse, a lot of powerful feelings can come up in the context of a scene. You'll both need to be extra respectful of and communicative around emotional danger zones. Some survivors have found S/M to be helpful in the healing process, but the ways in which this is true will vary greatly from person to person. In any case, remember that S/M isn't therapy, and be cautious about overstepping your boundaries.

Ultimately, S/M wouldn't have the potential to be frightening if it didn't also have the potential to be an exhilarating, empowering way to play. We placed this chapter near the end of our book, because the subject of power play brings together much of what has gone before. S/M blends communication, touch, fantasy and sex into an eroticism that can be as exciting, creative and highly pleasurable as you want to make it.

CHAPTER 17

Where Sex Toys Come From

Now that you've read through several chapters full of descriptions of sexual products, you may well be asking yourself, "Who comes up with this stuff, anyway?" And how could you be expected to know? It's highly unlikely that *Fortune* magazine will ever do a cover story on the dildo industry. There are no Dun and Bradstreet stats on porn peddling. Sex toys are practically a billion-dollar business in this country, with sales expanding rapidly, but the industry is so marginalized that it's invisible to anyone not working in it. We'd like to pull back the curtain and tell you what we know about the people who design and manufacture sex toys.

Sex-toy manufacturers break down into three categories: those who don't admit they're making sex toys; those who make novelty toys; and entrepreneurs who launch cottage industries in the interest of combining business and pleasure.

When Is a Sex Toy Not a Sex Toy?

The earliest vibrators were marketed as cure-alls for any number of bodily ailments and advertised as contributing to the "health, vigor and beauty" of men and women. This disingenuous marketing strategy continues today.

These vibrators are sold in drugstores, department stores and discount stores, yet they are marketed exclusively as massage tools. The product illustrations show models running the massagers up and down their aching necks and shapely calves, and packaging inserts refer to "facial attachments" and "foot attachments," as though there were no possibility of using these appliances anywhere between your navel and your knees. Even phallic-shaped battery vibrators advertised in the back pages of magazines or in discount mail-order catalogs generally feature product illustrations of a female model pressing the tip of the vibrator against her forehead or cheek to massage her migraine—putting a new spin on the old standard, "Not tonight dear, I've got a headache."

The Prelude 3 is the only quality electric vibrator ever marketed for sexual purposes, and it was promoted with mail-order ads in men's magazines throughout the seventies. By 1978, realizing that it would be impossible to break into a mainstream retail market with this truth-in-advertising approach, the Prelude marketers dropped all sexual references from their packaging and promotion, and the Prelude took its place next to all the other "housewares" and "personal-care products" in drugstores across America.

Most of the brand-name appliance companies manufacturing and distributing electric vibrators make absolutely no reference to the sexual possibilities of their products, although to the initiated, tips from the instruction booklets such as "Always ready to help you in providing refreshing relief at the end of a busy day" or "Removes everyday dullness" are certainly evocative. The only exception to this See No Evil, Hear No Evil marketing strategy is a discouraging one—a Midwestern company includes the caution, "This unit is not intended for use on the genital areas of the body" in its instruction booklet. We've had to field many an anxious call from customers alarmed by this warning.

The advantage to this camouflaged approach is that distribution of electric massagers isn't restricted to sex stores and, unlike cheaply made novelty vibrators, massagers are subject to the same kind of consumer scrutiny and standards as any other type of appliance. The disadvantage is that customers can't get honest information and advice about using their products and may fear that they're the only perverts in Sears' history to consider slipping that handy back massager south of the tailbone.

Despite the manufacturer's head-in-the-sand stance, we've found that those of our sales reps who hail from large appliance companies get quite a kick out of Good Vibrations' approach to selling their products. After all, the staff of these companies is well aware of the versatility of electric massagers. In a local newspaper article about our store, the national sales manager for Hitachi was quoted as saying, "We approach the massagers as personal-care items.... The people we hire know what it's for without our having to say it."

Most adult bookstores or mail-order sex catalogs don't stock brand-name electric vibrators because their wholesale cost is considerably higher than that of novelty toys manufactured in the Far East. Customers are too intimidated to demand high standards from their products, which leads to the current schizophrenia in the sex-toy market. You can buy good quality products in a limited range of styles, none of which, ostensibly, is for sexual use. Or you can buy inferior quality products in a wide range of styles, marketed explicitly for sexual uses.

Mainstream appliance companies dare not risk the wrath of the Religious Right or the threat of potential legal liabilities by acknowledging that their products make great sex toys, and consequently they miss out on the possibility of creating even more pleasing and functional toys. We and our customers long for the day when Hitachi, Panasonic, Pollenex, Sunbeam and Wahl can safely acknowledge the versatility of their products and feel free to develop sexual attachments for their massagers or to devise powerful, reliable battery models.

Legal Restrictions

It's not entirely fair for us to heap scorn on appliance companies for their failure to disclose the pleasure potential of electric massagers or to chastise adult-novelty manufacturers for their less-than-forthright packaging without acknowledging the legal constraints affecting how sex toys can be marketed. As noted in the chapter on censorship, several states criminalize the sale of products "designed or marketed as useful primarily for the stimulation of human genitals," defining these as "obscene devices." In California, a manufacturer or retailer who provides explicit information as to how to use and enjoy sex toys is vulnerable to prosecution under the state's "pandering" laws. Furthermore, any implicit or explicit claims as to a sex toy's efficacy could subject the toy to FDA regulation as a medical device.

What are the results of all these restrictions? Manufacturers of electric massagers market their products with copy that is coy at best and alarmist at worst. Adult-toy manufacturers position themselves as being in the "novelty" business, and their packaging emphasizes the "fantasy" value, rather than the function, of their products. In certain states, consumers can't even find retail outlets for sex toys. And in many adult bookstores, owners explicitly forbid clerks from offering advice to customers for fear of legal liabilities.

And yet, many of the recent developments in the adult industry make us optimistic about the potential for positive change. The adult-toy industry is growing by leaps and bounds, fueled by escalating consumer demand—presumably the "cocooning" trend among baby boomers is boosting all kinds of "home entertainment" sales. In 1996, several adult-toy manufacturers organized the first annual Adult Novelty Manufacturer's Expo, where manufacturers could network with distributors and retailers about product quality and design. Although adult consumers are still predominantly male, the trend of the nineties is an effort to cater to "the women's and couples' market." A growing number of adult manufacturers are gearing products toward heterosexual couples, while a growing number of adult bookstore owners are steering clear of the legally (and physically) sticky realm of on-site video viewing booths in favor of creating "upscale" shopping environments that will have greater appeal to women.

You may have heard of the two Fairvilla Megastores in Florida—these adult superstores, each over ten thousand square feet in size, adopt an approach to merchandising and layout that is similar in some ways to that of Good Vibrations. The stores are open, airy and well-lit; customer-service staffers are readily available; and products are organized in categories, with less threatening items such as cards and T-shirts up front and the more "hardcore" items such as dildos and videos in the back.

Like any other American industry, the adult industry is one in which money talks. Businesses such as Good Vibrations are having a small, but growing, impact on adult manufacturers, not because manufacturers have a deep-seated yearning to support our educational mission, but because we speak for a "sophisticated" clientele that is increasingly the consumer base for adult products. If stores such as the Fairvilla remain successful, other adult retailers will begin following this model. It would be much easier for an upscale adult establishment to challenge zoning restrictions and other obscenity laws than it would be for a "dirty bookstore" to do so. It requires considerable financial resources to take on the legal system. Just as the owners of the Adam and Eve mail-order catalog successfully challenged federal

indictments for interstate trafficking in obscene materials, a major adult retailer with deep pockets and his or her eyes on the prize of mainstreaming sex-toy shops might be able to overturn antiquated state statutes. Meanwhile, you can do your bit to revolutionize the adult industry by seeking out those stores and mail-order companies whose approach to presenting sexual materials best fits your personal politics.

The Adult-Novelty Business

Manufacturing Toys

First, let's dispel a popular myth. The people who manufacture sexual novelties are neither cigar-puffing Mafiosi dedicated to the destruction of our nation's moral fiber, nor sexually insatiable swingers dedicated to spreading the gospel of hedonism. In fact, the women and men who work in the adult industry are, by and large, a conservative bunch, chock-full of family values, and dedicated to making a living. While a handful of manufacturers are educated consumers of sex toys, we've always been astonished at how few of our novelty packagers or their sales reps have even tried their own products or have any interest in doing so. They are equally bemused at our sincere enthusiasm for sex toys and our concern for product quality, function and appearance. In the adult-bookstore business, products sell based on packaging alone, and our reps can't quite understand why we're so fixated on what's actually inside their boxes.

Novelty toys hail from all over the globe. Some of our most popular battery vibrators are manufactured in Japan. Japanese vibrators feature rotating figurines with faces and vibrating attachments shaped like animals—part of General MacArthur's post-war legacy to Japan was laws forbidding the manufacture of sex toys resembling genitals. These toys are extremely expensive by novelty standards—wholesaling anywhere between twenty-five and sixty-five dollars each—so Japanese exports account for only a small percentage of the sex toys sold by adult retailers in the States. They do tend to be better quality than other battery vibrators.

Certain novelty products are made in the United States, primarily rubber dildos and plugs,

Joni's Butterfly

As proof of the "make-a-quick-buck" manufacturing philosophy of the adult industry, consider the tale of "Joni's Butterfly." Joani Blank, the founder of Good Vibrations, knew that a no-hands, wearable clitoral vibrator would be a very popular and sensible design, and she mentioned this to one of our novelty distributors. He took her rough sketch of the idea off to Hong Kong, and came back with a finished toy. Joani had several improvements to suggest: The vibrator was too bulky to wear during intercourse and the elastic leg straps were too flimsy to hold it firmly in place, but the molds had already been made and production was underway. To Joani's dismay, her name (albeit misspelled) was permanently attached to just the type of shoddy battery toy she's spent her professional life decrying. Since very few novelty manufacturers get patenting or trade protection on their products, countless Butterflies flooded the market, and Joani received no royalties for any of these.

The moral of the story is, if you have an idea for a sex toy that you'd like to see realized exactly as you envision it or if you'd like financial compensation for the idea, your best bet would be to produce and patent the toy yourself. If, however, you'd just like to get your idea on the marketplace in some form, and you aren't attached to being paid for it, you should definitely consider forwarding a description of your better mousetrap (in writing) to one of the adult manufacturers in Southern California. Now that manufacturers are required to attach a disclosure label to any packaging that features sexually explicit imagery, you can easily find the address of companies such as Doc Johnson, California Exotic Novelties and Topco on their product boxes.

only because they can be made as cheaply or more cheaply here than they would be elsewhere. Most vibrating novelties are made in China, Taiwan, Korea and Hong Kong, where battery packs are produced much more cheaply than they would be in this country. The vast majority of novelty toys are made in Hong Kong, as it's a huge international manufacturing and export center with few restrictions on trade in sexual materials. In contrast, Taiwan has strict laws against exporting products of a sexual nature, and it's a capital offense to manufacture phallic-shaped vibrators in the People's Republic of China. Factories in Taiwan and the People's Republic of China produce the internal mechanisms of many battery vibrators, but will not produce graphic novelties. When Hong Kong reverts to governance by China, the political transition will definitely have an impact on the novelty industry. Korea, Thailand and Malaysia may well become the next centers of sex-toy commerce, and some U.S. manufacturers are improving their vibrator technology now in hopes of bringing production of battery novelties stateside.

Most of these Hong Kong factories produce novelties purely as a sideline. For instance, a doll factory might also manufacture blow-up dolls. A factory producing hair dryers and small massagers might also produce battery vibrators. Most novelty toys are manufactured with no more concern, attentiveness to detail or loving craftsmanship than the toy you fish out of a Cracker Jack box, and the kindest way to describe their quality would be to say that they tend to have a built-in obsolescence. Adult-novelty customers are frequently too embarrassed by their purchases to demand the same quality control from sex toys that they would from household appliances or other consumer goods. The nineties, however, have brought an upswing in the quality of novelty toys. In order to stay competitive in a marketplace that's filling up with more and more producers and distributors, manufacturers are taking steps to improve quality control. All things are relative, however, and you'd be wise to keep your expectations low.

Marketing of Toys

Once adult novelties make the long boat trip from Hong Kong to the States, they are packaged and marketed by American distributors. Product packaging is geared toward facilitating slatwall display—toys are sealed in cellophane, then carded or boxed with hang-tabs. At typical adult bookstores, customers don't get to handle, or even see, what they're purchasing until they get their toys home.

Sometimes samples of the products are displayed behind a glass counter—more commonly, the closest the customer gets to viewing the product is checking out the illustration on the box. The recent trend toward plastering boxes with photos of porn stars and starlets—marketing the "fantasy," rather than the product—makes it that much harder to get a clue as to what you're buying.

In stores such as ours, where we display samples of all products on the shelves for customers to handle and compare before making their selections, the standard sealed, carded and hang-tabbed packaging is cumbersome and annoying. Yet when we protest to our suppliers that we don't want to buy battery vibrators in shrink-wrapped cases covered in photos of comely porn starlets, they roll their eyes at our lack of business savvy: Don't we realize that packaging is what sells?

You can't really blame our suppliers—after all, celebrity tie-ins are big sellers. X-rated celebrities have dominated novelty packaging in recent years: You can purchase a star's favorite toy, a love kit of products featured in the star's recent video, or for the ultimate in celebrity worship, an artificial vagina or dildo sculpted directly from the star's body. It would take a major revolution in the adult retailing field—for instance, the success of many more stores across the nation that merchandise products the way we do—to produce changes in novelty packaging. On the plus side, more and more manufacturers are including detailed depictions of the product and its specific features on the box (right alongside the sexy celebrity).

Design of Toys

The one thing that frustrates us even more than poor quality or cheesy packaging is the frequently idiotic design of adult toys. Manufacturers do little or nothing to combat our society's mystification around sex, marketing products with dubious claims and minimal regard for the facts of human sexual response. In some case, manufacturers just aren't particularly well educated about human sexuality themselves. In others, they're exploiting people's sexual insecurities for the sake of selling products. After all, it's quite common for people who find a sex toy disappointing to assume that something must be "wrong" with their own responses, rather than with the design of the toy itself.

HOW CONSUMERS ARE MANIPULATED For one thing, the adult industry adopts a distinctly retro and inaccurate view of female sexual response. In the world according to novelty manufacturers, women crave penetration from a penis above all else, and bigger is always better. Novelty dildos are only available in big to jumbo-sized penis styling, and nearly all battery vibrators are insertable and phallic in shape. In adult novelty-land, women require only the mildest form of clitoral stimulation to be slingshot to the heights of orgasmic bliss. The classic example of this "less is more" approach to clitoral stimulation is what we like to refer to as "the nub syndrome." The nub syndrome refers to the way in which adult-novelty manufacturers tip their hats to the existence of the clitoris by decorating the base of many dildos with little rubber bumps; adorning French Ticklers with rubber fronds; and covering all clitoral vibrators (such as Joni's Butterfly) with vinyl spines. Sure, some women may actually enjoy the extremely subtle massaging sensation provided by these nubs, just as some women enjoy ribbed condoms or ben wa balls. We, however, have encountered far more women who find the nubs pointless at best and annoying at worst.

Alas, X-rated movies do nothing to set the record straight on female pleasure. We can't count the number of videos we've seen in which a masturbating porn starlet arouses herself by sucking greedily on her plastic battery vibrator and then plunging the vibrator vigorously into her vagina for one shuddering "orgasm" after another. Women in standard X-rated movies are presented as being obsessed with tracking down any phallic

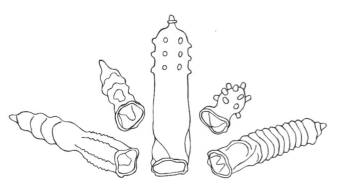

The nub syndrome

object within a five-mile radius and pumping it in and out of themselves with a fervor verging on the ridiculous. Bear in mind that a man playing with a vibrating sleeve would never be depicted lovingly tonguing the mouth of the vinyl sleeve before slipping his penis inside. And it's unlikely you'd see a man in an X-rated movie reach orgasm without some sort of stimulation of the glans of his penis. Viewers seeking authentic depictions of female sexual pleasure have to restrict themselves, by and large, to watching videos produced by women or for women.

While women who buy adult novelties and view adult videos may wind up feeling inadequate in terms of their sexual responses, men are likely to feel inadequate in terms of their sexual prowess. Novelty manufacturers take advantage of male insecurities about penis size and "potency" to sell a plethora of "penis extenders" and "erection prolongers." Penis extenders are hollow vinyl prosthetic devices that fit over the head of the penis. Other such prosthetic devices fit over the entire penis, whether it's erect or not, and are held in place with elastic straps. Erection prolongers are usually numbing creams. Both types of products perpetuate the questionable notion that it's better for a man to avoid feeling sensation than for him to "perform" as anything less than one hundred percent stud.

Never mind that not all women crave long, thick penises. Never mind that a man who wishes to penetrate his partner when he's not erect could easily and pleasurably do so by wielding a dildo. Never mind that numbing your penis and distancing yourself from the sensations you're feeling is probably the single worst way to gain control over your sexual responses and the timing of your orgasm. People in the adult industry live in the same sex-negative society as the rest of us, and if manufacturers discontinued all merchandise that plays on people's sexual insecurities, they'd have to abandon factories full of molds and throw out warehouses full of products.

ABOUT BLOW-UP DOLLS Blow-up dolls—inflatable vinyl mannequins sporting tunnel-shaped mouths, vaginas and anuses—are designed primarily as penis-receptacles. There are male blow-up dolls, complete with inflatable, vibrating penises;

there are transvestite blow-up dolls, complete with inflatable breasts and penises; and one of the most popular gag novelties of the past five years has been an inflatable sheep, but female blow-up dolls continue to dominate the field. You can purchase a stunning variety of blow-up dolls—dolls with vibrating mouths, vaginas or anuses; dolls with squirting breasts; dolls with lubricating orifices; dolls with "apple-pie pussy" flavoring—all made of extra-durable vinyl that will hold up to three hundred pounds.

We have to confess to a certain amount of discomfort around the topic of blow-up dolls. We've never carried them in our store, and we've yet to meet anyone who's ever tried one. The samples we've seen are quite unappealing: expensive, cheaply made, crudely detailed, smelling strongly of plastic, with vinyl seams you could cut yourself on. We can truthfully say that we don't carry dolls because they are poorly made and don't provide much physical stimulation to the user, but it's further true that we don't carry them because they make us uncomfortable. After all, when you preach the philosophy that sex toys don't simulate human touch, but rather provide alternatives to and enhancement of human touch, it's unsettling to encounter a toy that's clearly meant to simulate a human being. We would be the first to admit to a total lack of experience with dolls, and we don't mean to imply any condemnation of anyone who's ever enjoyed a good time with one. We just want to be honest about our own bias, arbitrary though it may be.

You might wonder why blow-up dolls strike us as distasteful while realistic dildos or artificial vaginas do not. Perhaps we're comfortable with dildos and sleeves because they are almost totemic symbols of human sexuality, and they've been around in one form or another since the beginning of human history. Perhaps it's simply that we're habituated to our products, and we know that they provide pleasure. We certainly recognize that someone walking into our store and facing a row of penis-styled dildos, complete with bulging veins and testicles, might consider our distinguishing between dildos and blow-up dolls to be so much self-serving hair-splitting, but we still feel the distinction is valid.

ABOUT APHRODISIACS   The notion that certain herbs, roots, foods or spices have the power to heighten sexual desire and improve sexual performance has a powerful appeal, and aphrodisiacs have been tried and true money-makers down through the ages. There's absolutely no scientific evidence for the notion that any particular substance enhances sexual energy, but there's bound to be a certain placebo effect for anyone who wants to believe in a passion pill. There's no harm done if you eat honey, drink ginseng potions or quaff oysters, all in the name of boosting your libido. Some so-called aphrodisiacs, however, are more dangerous. Spanish Fly, a preparation of crushed beetles, which has been touted as an aphrodisiac for centuries, is toxic, highly irritating to the urogenital tract, and potentially poisonous. (Products currently sold through adult mail-order companies under the name Spanish Fly contain harmless ingredients.) The worldwide belief that ground rhinoceros horn is an aphrodisiac has led to the near extinction of the rhino. And countless snake-oil salespeople have lightened innocents folks' wallets with their promises to "restore vigor" or "improve sexual performance" with one magical compound after another.

POSITIVE TRENDS IN TOY DESIGN   With several complaints off our chest, it's only fair to stop and acknowledge the positive changes that have taken place in novelty-toy design since the late eighties. For one thing, color has come to the world of battery vibrators. Once available only in hospital white, battery vibrators are now produced in a dazzling rainbow of colors. Interior decorators take note—you can match a vibrator to the decor of every room in your home. This may seem like a minor development, but simply offering a greater color selection bespeaks an acceptance of sex toys as consumer products. As former retail clerks, we can testify that nothing normalizes a purchase for a nervous customer better than weighing the decision as to which color to choose.

The materials sex toys are made out of have been evolving constantly since the mid-eighties. Until then, dildos were made of hollow vinyl or solid rubber and neither looked nor felt particularly lifelike. After the Family Jewels company developed their realistically detailed dildos made

out of a soft, resilient rubber, the realistic trend swept through the novelty industry, resulting in a wide range of dildos and artificial vaginas made out of a pleasingly pliable rubber. In the early nineties, jelly rubber came on the scene, and this clear, pink or orange bubbly rubber has been used to produce dildos, plugs and battery vibrators that resemble soft drinks or gum drops. Next in line was the type of jelly rubber we refer to as "jelly jewel," a sleek, elastic, nonporous material available in rich glowing colors. Jelly jewel rubber is used to cushion battery vibes and plugs and to create brilliantly colored nonvibrating toys. The bright, playful colors of jelly rubbers are a nice way to sidestep the issue of what skin tone dildos should be in. Materials under development include ever-more-stretchy rubbers and silicone blends.

The motors used in battery vibrators are also undergoing a serious upgrading as American manufacturers work to compete with the higher quality Japanese vibrators. Battery vibrator motors are being made ever-smaller and more powerful, which allows for more versatility in product design. Best of all, adult manufacturers such as California Exotic Novelties are responding to customer and supplier feedback and designing toys that people have always been asking for—for instance, a vibrator that plugs into a car cigarette lighter, a remote-controlled bullet vibe and a rechargeable battery vibrator. Not all of these toys live up to their billing in the early stages of development, but it's great that manufacturers are responding to genuine consumer desire, rather than tossing another slew of nubby French Ticklers our way.

The adult industry suffers from a good deal of racism, reflected in the dearth of diversity in X-rated videos and in the packaging of sex toys. Penis-shaped dildos and vibrators are primarily available in Caucasian skin tones, or what is referred to in product catalogs as "Eurasian" or "Flesh" color. In recent years, realistic dildos have been produced in a greater range of skin tones, but by and large in the adult world, the experience of white men is primary, the stereotype of hugely hung black men looms as a counterpoint, and Latins or Asians simply don't exist. This makes it all the more pleasing that slight strides are being made in the nineties. California Exotic Novelties has come out with a line of products featuring the popular African-American actor and director Sean Michaels. Doc Johnson has launched its *Fantasias Latinas* line of Spanish-language products. While these are baby steps, we're hopeful that simple market economics will inspire the adult industry to continue using a broader range of images in their packaging.

Finally, we're happy to say that imagination and a sense of humor are more and more evident in sex-toy design and packaging. You can buy toys designed for couples to enjoy together—whether the Acrobat Triple Stimulator, which allows a man to experiment with double penetration on his female partner, or the Headmaster, which allows two men to share the same vibrating sleeve. You can buy battery vibrators shaped like bananas, vibrators that glow in the dark, vibrators disguised as lipsticks and vibrators shaped like scorpions with long, flexible tails. The sheer entertainment value of these toys can break the ice for people intimidated by the idea of buying a sex toy.

Entrepreneurs

We admit to a bias in favor of other small businesses, and some of our favorite suppliers are themselves the owners of cottage industries. Some of these people got into their line of work purely by chance, some found that what started as a hobby turned into an occupation, and some are our former customers who became convinced they could design a better mousetrap and went into business for themselves.

Many of the most beautiful dildos in existence are produced by small manufacturers. Our wooden and glass dildos are sculpted by craftspeople who enjoy this erotic outlet for the imagination. Our silicone dildo manufacturers include a homeopathic healer, a former construction worker, a ceramics molder and a computer programmer. In the early seventies, Gosnell Duncan of Scorpio Products became interested in the idea of creating a more pleasing dildo than was gener-

ally available after attending several workshops on sexuality and disability in his capacity as president of his local chapter of the National Spinal Cord Injury Foundation. He worked with a chemist friend at General Electric (apparently, G.E. does bring some good things to life) for several years before developing his final formula. Gosnell hadn't intended to sell his dildos outside the disabled community, but word spread to the sex boutiques, and an industry was born.

Other silicone manufacturers decided to tackle silicone molding because they enjoyed Scorpio's products, appreciated silicone's superiority to other materials, and knew that Scorpio's limited supply of silicone dildos was not satisfying the growing demand. Silicone molding is a somewhat exacting and labor-intensive profession. We've heard countless individuals over the years claim, "I could do that," but only a handful have had the tenacity to follow through. These businesses may be small, but they've made a huge contribution to the pleasure experienced in bedrooms around the world.

Leather work is another field that's full of entrepreneurs. Many of the most beautifully crafted whips and restraints available are handmade by individuals who were inspired to go into business because they couldn't find the products they craved in any stores. Stormy Leather, now a nationwide wholesaler of dildo harnesses, restraints, toys and leather clothing for men and women, was founded in the owner's bedroom with one sewing machine and a commitment to creating comfortable, functional dildo harnesses for women to wear.

Our suppliers also include a woman who imports ostrich feathers and hand dyes them, a couple in Berkeley who makes wooden massage tools, and an electrical engineer who's produced an electric vibrator adapter known as the Humdinger, which adds a throb to the vibrator's usual continuous hum. These entrepreneurs will never be able to command the resources, the marketing power or the gross sales of Doc Johnson or Hitachi, but we'd like to salute them for doing their bit to make the world a more sexually fulfilling place.

CHAPTER 18

Safer Sex

Safer sex is the term used to describe sexual activities that minimize the risk of spreading sexually transmitted diseases. This chapter may seem redundant since many of the activities you've read about so far qualify as safer sex. Masturbating, playing with sex toys, massage, sharing fantasies and erotica are all safe and creative ways to enjoy sex. One of our motivations in writing this book was to illustrate the dozens of ways one can enjoy sex without engaging in high-risk activities. In chapters where we describe somewhat risky activities, we've incorporated easy ways to practice them safely.

Nonetheless, we would be remiss in omitting basic information about sexually transmitted diseases, since the more information you have, the better able you are to make decisions regarding your own sexual health. What's more, we jump at the opportunity to get excited about safer sex accessories. Too often they are treated purely as a necessary evil: weapons and armor in the war on disease, rather than as sex toys, deserving the same enthusiasm we lavish on vibrators and dildos.

The definition of safer sex can be expanded to include another area that directly impacts our sexual health—contraception. Although we consider birth control an important responsibility in a sexually active person's life, we have chosen not to enumerate the many forms of contraception in this chapter. There are entire books devoted to this subject alone; they treat the issue with the attention, thoroughness and respect it deserves. Keep in mind as you read, however, that condoms are an established and reliable method of contraception when used correctly. Their admirable versatility must be one of the reasons condoms are a four-hundred-and-fifty-million-dollar industry in the United States alone!

Just the Facts Ma'am

Sexually Transmitted Diseases or STDs

Estimates reveal that one in six people in the U.S. has an STD. There are over fifty known diseases that can be transmitted through sexual activity; chlamydia, gonorrhea, genital warts, herpes, hepatitus B, syphilis and AIDS are among the most common. Itching, nausea, painful urination, vaginal discharge, fatigue, skin changes, rashes and sores on or near the genitals can be signs or symptoms of an STD, and you should visit your doctor or a health center immediately if you suspect you may have contracted one.

If you're sexually active, but don't always practice safer sex, it's a good idea to get tested for STDs on a regular basis. Chlamydia, for example, is the most common STD in the U.S. largely because up to twenty percent of men and eighty percent of women show no symptoms when they contract the disease. Although chlamydia is easily treated with antibiotics, if a woman's infection remains untreated, it can lead to Pelvic Inflammatory Disease, possibly resulting in infertility or ectopic pregnancies.

If you're diagnosed with an STD, your doctor will give you specific guidelines for treatment. Bacterial infections, such as gonorrhea, chlamydia and syphilis, can be treated with antibiotics. Viral infections aren't necessarily curable. Genital warts are removed via lasers or freezing, since the virus that causes them can't be treated. If you haven't been vaccinated for hepatitis B and become infected, your initial infection can be treated with gamma globulin, but the disease may remain in your system. Both herpes and AIDS are incurable at this time, though anti-virals can suppress the severity of herpes outbreaks, and ongoing breakthroughs in the treatment of AIDS are increasing the chances of a person's long-term survival.

AIDS

WHAT IS IT? AIDS stands for Acquired Immunodeficiency Syndrome. The "acquired" means the HIV virus must be transmitted to you somehow; "immunodeficiency" refers to the virus attacking your immune system. The HIV virus destroys your immune system's ability to combat disease. The person who dies from AIDS actually succumbs to an opportunistic infection (such as pneumocystis or Kaposi's sarcoma) that a healthy individual's immune system would fight off.

TRANSMISSION The virus, known as HIV (Human Immunodeficiency Virus) is transmitted when infected bodily fluids—most commonly blood or semen—come into contact with open cuts or mucous membranes. Unprotected (no condom) penis/vagina and unprotected penis/anus sex are the most common methods of transmission. Shar-

ing blood, such as when intravenous drug-users share needles, is another common method of transmission. The virus cannot be transmitted by mosquitoes (or other insects), a handshake, toilet seats, clothes, phones, food handlers or sneezing. While it's present in trace quantities in sweat, saliva, urine or tears, there's no evidence that it can be transmitted by these fluids.

GETTING TESTED You can take a blood test at any hospital and at many free clinics that will tell you whether or not you have been exposed to the HIV virus. FDA-approved home tests have just come on the market and are being advertised on TV and in major magazines, and retail between twenty and forty dollars. Home tests come with instructions and tools for you to take a blood sample and return it to a central lab. You can call a few days later to hear the results. Home tests are anonymous and convenient, and the results are delivered to you by phone counselors. You may prefer, however, to take an HIV test at a clinic where counselors will be on hand to advise you should the results come back positive.

If you've had unprotected sex, you should wait at least six months before taking the HIV test. It can take up to six months for you to develop HIV antibodies (the proof that you've been infected), so testing any sooner may produce a false negative result. False positive test results are also not uncommon, so if you test positive once, your doctor or clinician will administer a second, more sophisticated blood test to confirm your HIV status. While there's no cure for AIDS at this time, an HIV-positive diagnosis is not an automatic death sentence. An ever-widening range of treatments, most recently a group of drugs known as "protease inhibitors," can keep the virus in check, and some HIV-positive individuals are well into their second decade of living with the infection.

A Word about Latex Accessories

Introducing latex barriers—condoms, gloves, dams, cots—into your sex play is the easiest and most effective way to minimize the risk of transmitting bodily fluids or of otherwise coming into contact with the viruses and bacteria that cause sexually transmitted diseases. These supplies are inexpensive, reliable and easy to find. Between two to four percent of the population, however, is allergic to latex. We'll discuss the alternatives—polyurethane or lambskin condoms, nitrile gloves and Saran Wrap—later in this chapter.

We know that whatever barrier you choose, with a little practice, you'll be snapping on the gloves and lubing up those condoms as if you'd been doing it all your life. You can find latex condoms, cots and gloves in pharmacies, medical or dental supply houses and sex boutiques. You're more likely to find dental dams at dental supply houses or sex boutiques than at the local drugstore.

Latex should only be used with water-based lubricants. Oils and oil-based lubes will destroy rubber and render latex barriers utterly useless. Make sure you use water-based lubricants, and don't be confused by lubes labeled "water-soluble"—these often contain oils. When in doubt, read the ingredients.

Condoms

You're probably thinking, "Oh no, not another lecture on using condoms." Actually, we're more interested in singing the condom's praises than in wagging our fingers at anyone. After all, condoms are the most widely available, inexpensive, and well-known sex toy in existence, and these days they come in almost as many sizes, colors and flavors as ice cream.

Who wouldn't be proud to use a toy with such a colorful history? Apparently you could have found one over fifteen thousand years ago, as a French cave painting of a man wearing a sheath suggests. Egyptian men wore condoms as a sign of rank three thousand years ago, while tribeswomen in South America fashioned themselves a female condom made out of a cut-off seed pod. Our favorite legend credits the Greek's mythical King Minos with the invention of the condom. Apparently the king had a tendency to ejaculate scorpions and snakes into his partners, so his right-hand man, Daedalus, invented a female receptacle into which the King could shoot his deadly semen. From scorpions to venereal disease to HIV, the condom has a noble history of protecting our sexual health.

If you're planning to sweet talk your sweetie into using a condom, why not try another name? At one time or another, condoms have been known as diving suits, phallic thimbles, life-savers, dibbers, preservatives, gloves, letters, hats and johnny bags. Remember to use your "frog-skins" during vaginal or anal intercourse, oral sex and on any shared sex toys.

Latex Condoms

There's a reason drugstore shelves overflow with latex condoms in every size, thickness and color—they're a convenient, affordable, highly effective barrier against disease transmission, as well as a popular contraceptive. Most latex condoms break because they're used incorrectly. The typical failure rate is about twelve percent, but researchers contend that if used correctly and consistently this would drop to about two percent. One British study revealed that out of three hundred men asked to demonstrate how to put on a condom, twenty percent failed because they tried to unroll it from the inside out.

So even though you might have the instructions memorized, if you're blaming faulty condoms, you may just need more practice. Both men and women can enjoy this homework exercise: On your next visit to the drugstore pick out an assortment of condoms, go home and play with them! If you don't have a willing penis handy, try putting them on a vibrator, vegetable, toothpaste dispenser, bedpost, anything that grabs you. The idea is to practice putting them on and to test their durability, so don't be afraid to get rough with your condoms. Take different sizes, colors, flavors, lubed or unlubed on a test drive to find the condom that's right for you—you might find that one particular brand feels better, tastes better or is just easier to use. If you're allergic to nonoxynol-9, a detergent often added to lubricants, make sure your condom lube doesn't contain this ingredient.

I always carry several condoms in my car, my wallet and my Day Runner Organizer (and to think people think I'm anal because I like being organized)!

I always put a condom on my dildo when I use it on someone else and almost always when I use it on myself. I like the texture.

How to Put on a Condom

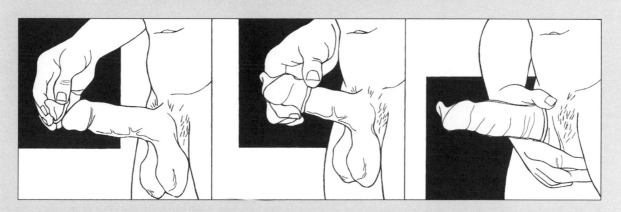

- Use condoms that have been stored in a cool, dry place. Check the expiration date printed on the package. If the condom looks brittle, sticky or discolored, throw it out.
- Open the package gently. You don't want to puncture the condom in your hurry to liberate it!
- Put a drop or two of extra water-based lube inside the tip of the condom. This aids in the unrolling and increases sensation for the penis.
- Before you start unrolling the condom, squeeze the air out of the receptacle tip, since air bubbles can cause condoms to break. Condoms without a reservoir tip require about one half inch free at the tip to catch the come.
- As you're holding the tip of the condom over the penis or dildo, check to make sure the latex will be emerging from the inside of the ring as you roll down.
- Unroll the condom down to the base of the penis. Pull back the foreskin of an uncircumcised penis before covering the glans. Apply generous amounts of water-based lubricant to the outside of the condom and to your partner's genitals before penetration. Condoms are easiest to apply when the penis is hard, but can be applied to a soft penis—just continue to roll the condom down the shaft as the penis hardens.
- Remember to hold on to the base of the condom when withdrawing so the condom doesn't slip off the penis. Withdraw before losing your erection.
- Throw used condoms away. They are not reusable. Use a new condom for each act of penetration.

I once used a cut-open condom to lick my girlfriend's newly pierced nipple. That was great because it was so sensitive and erotic for her.

If you're afraid the condom might slip off, pull it down so it fits over your testicles. A little too much lubricant inside the condom could be causing the slippage. You can try a Mentor condom, which has a post-it strength adhesive at its base (it peels right off, trust us). If you're worried about a condom breaking, try wearing two thin condoms at once for extra protection. If a condom breaks while you are having intercourse, don't panic. Stop what you're doing and apply some contraceptive foam—the spermicide in the foam may also kill any

viruses present. Don't douche or otherwise attempt to "wash out" your vagina or anus, as this will only push pre-come or semen further inside.

Polyurethane Condoms

Lots of people are atwitter about the condoms of the nineties. The Avanti male condom and the Reality female condom are made out of polyurethane, a plastic material twice as strong as latex. Check out all the features of this wonder material: It's thinner than latex, which means greater sensitivity for users. It's compatible with oil-based lubricants, so people who can't distinguish between water-based, water-soluble and oil-based lubes don't have to worry about their

The Cream of the Crop

♦ *Beyond Seven.* Thin, nearly transparent and slightly slimmer than standard size.

♦ *Crown Skinless Skin.* Thin and strong.

♦ *Gold Coins.* These unlubricated American condoms are great for oral sex and come in a cute foil wrapper (the only one you can open without using any hands).

♦ *Kimonos.* Thin and strong.

♦ *Kimono Sensation.* Little nubs along the inside of the condom are designed to increase sensation for the wearer.

♦ *Maxx.* Marketed as slightly bigger than regular condoms, they are wider at the head, which makes them good for uncircumcised penises or men with thick penises.

♦ *Mentors.* Worried it might slip off? This condom features a post-it style adhesive at the base of the condom. Apply a little lube if you're having trouble peeling off the condom.

♦ *Pleasure Plus.* At the time of our writing, this popular condom is unavailable, but keep your eyes open for its reappearance. It features a baggy pouch at the tip (more comfortable for uncircumcised men) that massages the penis with each stroke.

♦ *Sheik Elite.* Strong.

♦ *Sheik Mint.* Flavored and unlubricated.

condoms breaking down anymore. It's odorless and doesn't contain the proteins that cause some individuals to be allergic to latex. It transmits heat better and is more resistant to damage from heat and light. If you think that all sounds too good to be true, you're right. While polyurethane represents the first major advance in condom technology in seventy years, and has tremendous potential, the condoms themselves are still far from perfect.

It appears that in an effort to provide an alternative condom for latex-sensitive users, the FDA put the cart before the horse and approved Avanti's release before testing was completed. Unfortunately several studies have reported Avanti's breakage rate to be more than four times that of latex condoms. Although polyurethane is techni-

cally stronger than latex, the plastic is much less elastic, which results in a higher breakage rate. If you're allergic to latex, but don't want to fret about your condom breaking, try layering a latex condom over the Avanti. The FDA is still in the process of testing the Avanti, and only recommends the polyurethane condom to individuals with latex allergies. The Avanti, however, is expected to pass testing in the near future and to be approved for labelling as a device that protects against pregnancy or sexually transmitted diseases.

Other complaints that have surfaced about Avanti involve its larger than standard size. Since polyurethane won't stretch as much as latex, the Avanti is made a bit wider than latex condoms—this can result in a slippage problem. Avanti condoms are also considerably more expensive than latex condoms.

As for the female condom, the Reality is almost as hard to warm up to as its male counterpart. The Reality is a six-inch-long tube (as long as a condom, but wider), with one sealed end and a flexible, plastic ring at each end. The woman inserts one ring into her vagina, much like a diaphragm, while the ring around the opening remains anchored outside, resting flat against the labia.

There are several advantages to the female condom: It's great for those with latex allergies; women can take responsibility for its use; the condom can be inserted ahead of time; a man may find the loose fit of the female condom gives him increased sensation; and the coverage provided by the outer portion may help prevent transmission of STDs such as herpes or genital warts. The female condom is also suitable for anal use; just make sure the outer ring doesn't slip inside the anus (it's helpful to leave about one inch of the condom hanging outside the anus). The insertive partner should be careful to use shallow thrusts—since the Reality condom is not as long as the rectum, longer thrusts may stress the condom.

The reported disadvantages of the Reality condom at this point concern how difficult it is to use correctly (you're familiar with the phrase "reality sucks"?). Here are some helpful hints: Position the inner ring carefully or the condom may twist; use enough lube or the condom will

CONDOM SHOPPING CHECKLIST

✔ *Material.* Latex condoms are the most effective barriers against the transmission of disease, but some people are allergic to latex. If you have latex allergies, consider trying a polyurethane condom. Never use lambskin condoms for safer sex.

✔ *Size.* Large condoms are just over two inches wide while the "snug" variety are just under two inches. The minimum length for condoms is six and a half inches, but longer ones can exceed eight inches. The polyurethane condom is wider and shorter than standard latex.

✔ *Thickness.* Thinner condoms may feel great but aren't necessarily as strong as their thicker brethren. They do pass the basic air-inflation tests, but have a tendency to break more often than other condoms. If you're new to condom use, start out with the thicker variety.

✔ *Lubrication.* Many people don't like the taste of lubricated condoms and there are plenty of unlubricated ones available. If you're allergic to nonoxynol-9, avoid condom lubes with this ingredient. Use lubed condoms for intercourse, especially if you don't have any additional lube on hand.

✔ *Texture.* Some condoms (Kimono Sensation) come with little nubs on the inside designed to stimulate the wearer's penis and some with ribbing on the outside, ostensibly to stimulate the receptive partner's vagina or anus. You may or may not be able to distinguish these subtle sensations.

✔ *Flavor.* Condoms come in a variety of flavors, from mint to chocolate to tutti-frutti. If you're planning an evening of oral sex, we guarantee these'll spice up the occasion.

✔ *Color.* Most condoms are available in a clear or semi-clear color, but you can find condoms in every color of the rainbow as well as glow-in-the-dark.

✔ *Special Features.* Do you want it to stick to the base of the penis? Cover the testicles? Massage the tip of the penis? Read the condom's package to determine whether it has any special feature.

✔ *FDA approval.* If you're not sure whether the condom has been approved by the FDA for use in prevention of disease or pregnancy, check the label.

stick to the penis; make sure not to insert the penis or dildo between the condom and the vaginal wall; hold the outer ring in place to keep it from slipping into the vagina; and remove it very carefully to prevent ejaculate from leaking out. In addition, the outer ring may irritate the external genitalia while the internal "one size fits most" ring may not fit you. Finally, don't use the Reality condom in combination with a latex condom—they will stick together.

I felt like we were having sex with a grocery bag and the crinkly noise was a bit of a turn-off.

We're not trying to rain on your parade if you're a polyurethane fan; we just want to tell you what we know about these products, since it can be hard to get at the facts amidst all the hype. If you're allergic to latex, polyurethane is definitely your best bet.

Lambskin condoms

Made from the intestines of sheep, lambskin condoms should never be used for safe-sex purposes, as viruses may permeate small imperfections in the membrane's surface. Use latex condoms only, or wear a latex condom over a lambskin one if you're allergic to latex.

Basic Safer Sex Guidelines

♦ Viruses and bacteria cannot pass through latex.
♦ Use condoms every time you have either vaginal or anal intercourse. You may want to use unlubricated (or try flavored) ones for oral sex as well.
♦ Put condoms on sex toys used by more than one person for any type of penetration or on toys that go from anus to vagina.
♦ Use dental dams or a cut-open condom or glove as a barrier during oral/vaginal or oral/anal sex.
♦ Use only water-based lubricants with latex (including condoms, gloves, dams, cots and diaphragms). Never use oil or petroleum-based products with latex.
♦ Never reuse latex.
♦ Keep latex stored in a cool, dry place.

Dental Dams

These six-inch squares of latex are used by dentists during oral surgery and have been co-opted for safer oral sex purposes. Dental dams offer an adequate—if somewhat thick—barrier between your tongue and your lover's labia and/or anus. Fortunately, there are a few thinner dams being manufactured (Glyde Lollyes and Lixx) in a variety of flavors. An equally effective and easier-to-obtain alternative is a condom. Snip off the tip and then cut along one side of the condom. Open it up and voilà—you've got a very thin dam. You can do the same thing with a latex glove by snipping off the fingers and cutting open the side with the thumb. Plastic wrap is another option—although it hasn't received the testing that latex has, at least one study has determined that Saran Wrap is impermeable to virus-sized particles.

How to Use Dental Dams

♦ Rinse off the dam before use. It's covered in a fine powder that can irritate the genitals.
♦ The lickee or the licker holds the dam in place over the genitals while the licker performs. A little lube on the side next to the genitals will increase sensation. Try sucking in little air bubbles with your mouth and snapping the bubble back against the skin for a unique sensation.
♦ Don't inadvertently reverse the dam—only one side of the dam should come into contact with the genitals. Use a pen to mark a nonreversible letter (like *K* or *B,* don't use *A* or *X*) on the dam. This will help you find the right side if the dam is dropped.
♦ Throw away dams when finished. They are not reusable.

If you want your hands free, you can fashion yourself some plastic wrap underwear by first unrolling the sheet around your hips, then dipping it down between the thighs so it covers the labia and anus, and back up around the hips. Plastic wrap is so clingy it sticks together nicely. The alternative to plastic wrap undies is a dam harness. The harness has two leg straps with snaps to secure the dam in place over the vulva.

Dams are available in colors and flavors and can be purchased from dental supply houses and some sex boutiques and catalogs.

Gloves

Gloves feel like a second skin when worn, and once you've lubed them up, they can be a slippery smooth delight sliding over skin or in and out of orifices. Use gloves for any situation in which your finger or hand will be contacting mucous membranes, from fingering your partner's clit to giving a hand job, to fisting (use plenty of lube for the latter). Make sure your nails are trimmed, your hands free of any rings or items that might pierce the glove, and that your glove is long enough to cover the part of your hand or arm that will come in contact with mucous membranes. Do not reuse gloves.

Latex gloves are another medical tool co-opted as an exotic safe-sex toy. Rinse the powder off the gloves before using them, as it can irritate. Standard latex examination gloves can be found at most drugstores.

Nitrile gloves offer those with latex allergies a synthetic alternative to rubber. They are stronger, thinner, can be used with oil-based lubes, come in a powder-free version and are available in different sizes. These can be harder to find than latex gloves, check with sex boutiques or condom retailers.

I like gloves for penetrating my female partner. It is so nice to take them off and instantly have a clean hand to touch again.

I think gloves make the fingers/hand slicker and keep lube wetter longer.

Finger Cots

Cots are like miniature latex condoms for your fingers. If you plan on stimulating or penetrating someone with one finger only, this would do the trick. It's also a perfect size for smaller toys—butt plugs, mini-vibrators or small dildos, although you'll need to tie something around the base of the cot to make sure it doesn't roll off.

Gloves are great because your hands don't get pruney and your fingernails aren't as sharp. I've used these on women. I don't see the point of finger cots. Gloves are just as easy and give you more options.

Erotic Safer Sex

I work for a dentist. Why on earth would I want to use a dental dam for anything other than a root canal? I want to lick her...not latex.

The majority of people today are not what you'd call enthusiastic about safer sex. Many are resigned to the practice, but approach it with about as much enthusiasm as they would a trip to the dentist. Some folks resent being told what they "should" be doing in the bedroom; some feel a certain sense of immunity; some just write off safer sex as a big nuisance.

You alone are responsible for your sexual health. We can tell you how to try to make sex safer as well as easy, fun, interesting, exciting and erotic, but only you can make the words a reality. One good place to start is with your own attitude about safer sex. It's easy to complain about the taste or feel of condoms, but with a little creative research and imagination, you might change your opinions.

You're probably reading this book searching for a few good ideas or a fresh approach—why not embrace safe sex like you would any other toy or technique—with a playful spirit and a willingness to experiment?

I'm lucky that I've always liked latex—I used gloves long before most people ever heard of them.

Black, shiny rubbers on my white skin fetishize my dick as if it were a much larger dildo.

To illustrate our point, and to give you a place to start, we've listed some common complaints about latex, along with our suggestions for turning a potential problem into a playful activity.

Find me a condom that tastes like café mocha and then we'll talk! Thanks to the growing number of flavored latex supplies, your next oral sex adventure can be as tasty as a good café mocha. Mint condoms are perfect for an after-dinner blow job, while the bubble gum dams might bring out the naughty schoolgirl in you. This is great news for folks who find the actual taste and smell of latex less palatable. If you don't like the taste of lubricated condoms, buy them unlubricated and apply your own favorite lube. Think about how many tastes you've acquired in your life—perhaps coffee, beer, your lover's juices—latex too can be an acquired taste. After you've played with safer sex accessories for a while, you may develop a Pavlovian response!

Even the smell of some types of condoms turns me on.

With the right condom/flavored lube it's kinda neat to give a blow job with a condom, though latex does still taste yucky alone.

I could never understand what people meant by "eroticizing" latex until I bought a latex dress. I got so turned on by the snug, supportive feel of rubber on my body that now just about any kind of latex turns me on.

Condoms reduce sensitivity. Certainly nothing will feel exactly the same as naked skin, but you can learn to enjoy the new and different sensations offered by a condom. You may discover that condoms reduce friction and make your erection last longer. If you're having trouble maintaining an erection with a condom, try masturbating with different kinds to find the ones that feel the best—eventually your body will become conditioned to respond to this different kind of stimulus. And remember, not all condoms are identical—they vary in size, shape, texture, color and taste—so there's bound to be at least one out there with your name on it! Japanese condoms tend to be thinner than American brands, so you may want to start with these to maximize sensation. You might enjoy condoms that fit more snugly because they keep your penis harder longer. Or maybe you find that contoured condoms—those that balloon a bit at the top and then become narrow below the head—increase sensation. The Kimono Sensation condom with nubs on the inside may provide just the extra stimulation you need.

When you're with a partner and you're worried about not getting enough stimulation with a condom, you can always have him or her manually stimulate you until you're close to coming, then apply the condom for the duration of your sex play. Or you can see if your partner is interested in trying the Reality female condom, which can be used vaginally or anally.

Women should experiment too. The more comfortable and competent you are with applying condoms, the better it will feel to your partner.

Condoms become "unlubed" quickly and rub painfully during intercourse. This is nothing a spare bottle of lube and a spray bottle with water in it won't fix. Having extra lubricant on hand is essential. And many people don't realize that water will reactivate the lube as it starts to dry up. A spray bottle or a bowl of water by the bed will do the trick.

It's so awkward to stop what we're doing and whip out the latex. Try not to think of it as stopping, but as expanding what you're doing. Don't you already pause once in a while to dim the lights or find the vibrator? You don't have to think of it as a chore, but as part of the fun. Try fantasizing when you're alone about using latex with your partner, imagining different ways you'd like to try the condom, dam or glove. That way, when the

time comes, you'll have a few tricks up your sleeve. Have your safer sex supplies at the ready so you don't spend time searching around. We heard tell of one woman who liked to keep a glove stashed under the top of her stocking so a hand traveling up her thigh would encounter it before going any further. Play with your toys together—your partner can put a condom on himself or herself, acting the exhibitionist, or you can put it on for him or her as part of your foreplay, teasing as you go. You could practice different ways of applying the condom. When using your mouth, for example:

♦ You'll probably want to use an unlubricated condom.

♦ Open the condom and unroll it slightly.

♦ Form your lips into an O and place the condom between your upper and lower lips, in front of your teeth. Make sure the condom is facing the right direction so it unrolls correctly.

♦ Hold on to the penis or dildo with one hand, then place your mouth on the penis or dildo, tightening your lips and pushing down on the rim.

♦ Push from your neck to unroll the condom down the shaft.

As with many of the toys or activities we suggest in this book, part of the difficulty of incorporating safer sex accessories into your sex life stems from embarrassment or awkwardness when trying something new. A sense of humor is crucial, and can help you ease into a new activity (as long as you're not laughing at someone else's unwitting expense). Colored condoms or the glow-in-the-dark variety might underscore the playfulness and fun of the activity.

Some of my lovers have been reluctant to use condoms. At the risk of sounding preachy, if a sexual partner refuses to use a condom—or any other kind of safer sex accouterments—at your request, ultimately it shows a lack of regard for sexual health. Being sexually assertive is something that doesn't come naturally to many of us, so it's important to be prepared for situations like this. There are several good books that teach sexual assertiveness and specify how to ask for safe sex. Most of these stress the value of coming to terms with your wants and needs beforehand and school you on how to avoid common pitfalls like over-aggressiveness or defensiveness.

Benefits of Safer Sex

♦ It's a show of respect for both your own and your partner's sexual health.
♦ It gives you peace of mind.
♦ Condoms can help erections last longer (thereby prolonging intercourse or masturbation).
♦ Condoms can be effective contraceptives if used properly.
♦ It curbs the spread of sexually transmitted diseases.
♦ It keeps your sex toys clean.
♦ Latex barriers are ideal for those who might find sexual fluids unappealing.
♦ Latex barriers offer a unique tactile sensation, especially when used with lubricant.
♦ It frees you from having to rely exclusively on your partners knowing or telling the truth about their sexual histories.
♦ It facilitates communication about sex.
♦ It allows you to be creative in your sex play.
♦ It can introduce an element of humor into the bedroom.
♦ It has resulted in words like *anal sex* and *intercourse* becoming commonplace in the media.

Here are some of our customers' approaches:

My one rule is: no condom, no sex.

When I start getting close to someone I initiate a safe-sex talk. I state my sex history and that I have herpes.

One very simple tactic is to reassess your approach, making the proposition as appealing as possible. For example, instead of the cold, direct approach:

Now it's time for you to put on the condom.

We can't have sex without condoms.

Try a nasty, yet equally direct approach:

I know exactly which condom will feel great on you.

There's a condom with your name on it itching to get out of my pocket.

Safe sex with you is something I've fantasized about.

It might help for you to make a list of what your specific personal rules are when it comes to safer sex, so you'll be ready when the time comes. For example, you might list something like, "I don't want to go down on someone without a barrier," or "I will only perform fellatio with a condom." If your partner is unwilling, be empathetic and suggest you compromise with some alternatives that are acceptable to both of you. She may not want to use a dam, so you'll both masturbate instead. He may refuse to use a condom, but you feel okay about giving him a hand job. It might be awkward at first, but confidence and comfort will come with practice.

Try to raise the subject of safer sex in conversations outside the bedroom. This way you can feel each other out before your judgment gets blurred during a lip-locked passionate embrace. If you're finding yourself tongue-tied when it comes to asserting your intention to use dental dams, pull one out and show it to your partner. Talk about how you feel; maybe you're nervous, shy, embarrassed or intimidated—if you feel silly, say so. Find out how your partner feels as well. Maybe gloves remind her of a bad root canal, but the promise of a slow, smooth and slippery genital massage will undoubtedly give her something much better to think about. Often just being honest about the situation can ease the tension. It provides an opportunity to air your concerns or fears, clear up any misconceptions, and reassure the person that you're doing this out of concern for both of you! Not to mention it gives you something new and different to look forward to.

I think of latex gloves as the key to my chastity belt. No gloves, no prize.

Risk Management

Since the onset of AIDS, "risk reduction guidelines" were established to help people understand which activities presented a greater risk of transmitting bodily fluids.

Activities in the *unsafe* category generally involve semen or blood coming into direct contact with mucous membranes in the rectum, vagina or mouth. Activities in the *possibly unsafe* category are less likely to transmit the virus. Activities in the *possibly safe* category either involve contact with low-risk fluids, such as saliva and urine, or will not transmit the virus unless your latex barrier breaks. The *safe* category reflects activities that involve no exchange of bodily fluids and are completely safe. For example, using a condom during intercourse reduces the chance of transmission, but that the condom may break means that intercourse is not entirely safe. Studies have discovered traces of the virus in other bodily fluids such as saliva, urine and tears, but not in high enough quantities to be considered infectious. Vaginal secretions may be infectious under certain conditions, which is why contact with vaginal secretions is considered possibly safe. For example, if the secretions come into contact with open sores or cuts, there's a risk of viral transmission. Or, if you're experiencing a vaginal infection, there is a higher concentration of the virus in your secretions.

For more detailed information, we suggest you contact the AIDS hotline (800-342-2437), or peruse one of the many excellent books available on the subject.

Beyond Guidelines

One of the fundamental limitations of many safer sex raps is their focus on how to avoid contracting a disease, rather than how to avoid transmitting a disease. "Learn how to stay squeaky clean," the underlying message goes, "so you don't have to join the ranks of the untouchables." It's understandable that the focus of STD education would be on restricting the spread of disease, but where does this leave those of us who already have sexually transmitted diseases, yet have no desire to embrace celibacy?

Safe Activities

massage
hugging
mutual masturbation (touching your own
   genitals)
dry kissing
tribadism, dry humping, frottage
fantasy
voyeurism, exhibitionism
phone/computer sex
sex toys (provided condoms are used if toys
   are shared)
bathing together

Possibly Safe Activities

French kissing
anal intercourse with condom
vaginal intercourse with condom
fisting with glove
cunnilingus with latex barrier
fellatio with condom
rimming/analingus with latex barrier
finger-fucking vaginally or anally with latex
   glove or cot
watersports (urine on unbroken skin)

Possibly Unsafe Activities

cunnilingus without a barrier
finger-fucking without a barrier
fellatio without a condom
sharing sex toys without cleaning or
   changing condoms in between uses
fisting without a glove
rimming/analingus without a latex barrier

Unsafe Activities

anal intercourse without condom
vaginal intercourse without condom
blood contact
unprotected cunnilingus during menstruation

It's quite common for the average sexually active adult to take this us/them perspective to heart, and to divide the world of potential partners into those people they judge to be at risk for disease and those they judge not to be at risk. We were quite depressed at the number of our questionnaire respondents who, when asked about their experience with safer sex accessories, answered something to the effect of, "I know my partners, so we don't have to bother with the precautions that other people have to follow." Countless health professionals have explained that it's not who you have sex with, but what sexual activities you engage in that separates risky behavior from safe behavior. Is anybody listening?

People are listening, all right, but they're listening selectively. After all, media reports frequently aggravate the misconception that a wide gulf exists between a tragic caste of disease-ridden adults and "the rest of us clean folks." Take the infamous 1982 *Time* magazine cover story on herpes, entitled "The Scarlet Letter." Similarly, HIV has been labeled in a variety of ways over time—from a gay virus, to an intravenous drug-user's virus, to a low-income woman of color's virus. People seem to believe that the virus itself is selective about the sexuality and socio-economic status of the body it invades, rather than recognizing that infection rates rise more rapidly in different populations at different times during the course of an epidemic. What's going on here? Massive denial, that's what. Sexually transmitted diseases of all kinds are rampant in the American population, and the notion that anyone belongs to a "safe" stratum of society is ridiculous.

For instance, an article in the July 6, 1989 *New England Journal of Medicine* reported that more than sixteen percent of Americans between the ages of fifteen and seventy-four—an estimated thirty million people—were infected with herpes simplex II. Two-thirds or more of these were estimated to be unaware that they were infected with the virus or that they had the potential to transmit it asymptomatically, i.e., without actually experiencing an outbreak. Chlamydia is the most common STD in America, spreading particularly fast among people under twenty-five. AIDS, still widely viewed as a gay white man's disease, is rampantly on the rise among African Americans, Latinos and young people.

Acknowledging the prevalence of STDs in all classes and communities and setting up effective prevention methods is going to require a major overhauling of our social attitudes and proscriptions around sex. Our sex-negative culture is one of the prime culprits in the spread of disease. Sex is shameful, and having an STD identifies you as a sexually active individual, which is shameful. Telling a partner identifies you not only as sexually active (shameful), but as someone who's sick. Being sick is also shameful in our society, where the punishing viewpoint, "If you're sick, it's your own fault" still holds sway. All this shame results in secretiveness, and secretiveness results in further transmission.

The AIDS epidemic provides a distressing example of the inherent limits of public health campaigns to impose behaviorial changes in the context of a sex-negative society. Despite the ubiquity of AIDS-prevention campaigns within the gay community and a decreasing rate of new infections throughout the late eighties, more and more gay men are reporting "falling off the safe sex wagon" in the nineties. In an alarming trend, the rate of new infections is creeping back up again, especially among young men, and recent optimism about the efficacy of new AIDS treatment drugs may well result in backsliding to unsafe sex practices.

Societal unwillingness to be explicit about sexual activities often results in public health warnings being painted with such a broad brush that people wind up throwing in the towel and taking no precautions whatsoever. Individuals with genital herpes may be advised to use latex barriers every time they have sex, due to the outside chance of asymptomatic transmission. The "use condoms every time" injunction is the cornerstone of AIDS-prevention efforts, accompanied by laudable campaigns to eroticize latex. But blanket regulations can backfire. Just as teenagers who are urged to choose abstinence over sex are more likely to wind up pregnant than those who are provided with a more comprehensive range of options, adults who are urged to use latex barriers for every sexual encounter are likely to cheat. It's the American Way to seesaw wildly between extremes of abstinence and abandon: One more box of cookies tonight and I'll give up all fat and sugar tomorrow.

Individuals who weigh the specific risks of each encounter, and modify the safer sex approach they choose to take accordingly, stand a much better chance of sustaining a safer sex lifestyle for the long haul. For instance, you might decide that since you always know when a herpes outbreak is coming on, the risk of asymptomatic transmission is low enough that you'll forgo using a dental dam for oral sex. You might decide that you're willing to perform fellatio without a condom as long as you haven't flossed in the past few hours. And we hope that you'll insist on using a condom for vaginal intercourse with someone you've just met. We intentionally use the terms *risk management* and *risk reduction*, rather than *risk elimination* to encourage you to take an active, dynamic approach to protecting your sexual health.

STDs and Your Self-Image

Due to our culture's sex-negativity, contracting an STD can really do a number on both your general and your sexual self-esteem. Common mental tapes include: "It's all my fault, I'm being punished for being sexual; if only I hadn't (fill in the blank) this would never have happened; I'm ruined, violated, no longer whole; no one will want me now that I'm a vector of disease." Compare the dramatic negativity of these thoughts with how you'd feel if you'd simply caught the flu from a coworker, and you'll have a sense of how extraordinarily vulnerable we all are around our sexuality.

It's common for people to experience a decrease in sexual desire immediately after contracting a disease. Some people stop masturbating, let alone engaging in partner sex.

One of the hardest things for me about my chronic herpes outbreaks was that I went from feeling very positive about my labia to viewing them as a painful, sore, disgusting part of my body. It seemed to me that all my genitals did was let me down, and the less I had to think about or touch them, the better.

What's sad about this is that you are effectively denying yourself access to one of your greatest sources of healing. While it's natural to feel a decrease in sexual energy when you're otherwise physically debilitated, you should try not to let this extend into a total shutdown of sexual activity. Honoring your right to be sexually active can be physically healing: Sex reduces stress, provides a cardiovascular workout, strengthens your pelvic

muscles, and otherwise creates an all-over glow. Exercise is frequently recommended for people suffering from any kind of disease, so what better therapy for an STD than sexual exercise? Honoring your right to be sexually active can also be emotionally healing. Negative sexual feelings easily segue into an overall negative self-image. If you can keep the perspective that you have an unalienable right to sexual pleasure, your health and self-esteem will benefit directly.

While it may seem flagrantly Pollyanna-ish to speak of the positive ramifications of contracting an STD, it's true that certain silver linings can emerge if you let them. Many people find that STDs have taught them to be more open and communicative with sexual partners, as they can no longer simply initiate sex with new partners without some sort of preliminary discussion. While honesty entails risking rejection, it's also one sure-fire way to separate creative, compassionate women and men from narrow-minded, fearful girls and boys.

Chronic, incurable diseases, such as herpes or AIDS, also force you to take a healthier approach to your entire life, to do what you can to reduce stress and to build up your immune system.

Finally—we saved the best for last—an STD can pull you out of a behavioral rut like nobody's business. Suddenly, you're forced to appreciate the fact that sex can be oh-so-much-more than commingling body fluids and sticking one body part into another orifice. A whole new world of toys, fantasy play and full-body sensation can be yours if you'll let it.

I used to love fucking up the ass and getting fucked, because of the intimacy and sometimes roughness of the gesture. After I got anal herpes, from my days of unprotected sex, it became painful to get fucked and was a turn-off. Now I'm mostly a top (I wear a condom) or I delicately perform ass play on myself. Sometimes I squat on my partner's finger, gently jiggling against my prostate, so I can control the depth of the action. This is the hardest load I shoot. Being witnessed and having my partner's help in bringing me off makes me feel a rush of sexual appetite.

I first started making my partners use rubber gloves just so I wouldn't have to be distracted by worrying about cuts in their fingers and infecting them and all that. The unexpected bonus was that I love the way gloves turn a human hand into a slick, smooth little creature— sometimes I pretend I'm getting fucked by a seal.

If you're receptive to the possibility, a heightened consciousness around STDs can inspire a unique level of sexual self-awareness. Whether you have an STD, your partner has an STD, or you have no idea what the true status of your partner's health is, it's up to you to make the call as to how to behave. Coming to terms with and identifying your personal safer sex guidelines is a golden opportunity—a chance for you to appreciate the myriad possibilities of your entire body, to face your fears, to name your desires and to celebrate the triumph of sexual energy over ignorance and shame.

Sex for Fun

We thought about calling this book *Sex for Fun* for a while because it expressed so simply and concisely the message we wanted to impart to our readers. By now you're probably tired of hearing us tell you that sex should be playful, experimental, communicative and celebratory. But nowhere is this more worth repeating than in the conclusion to our chapter on safer sex. We've given you the information, the tools and (we hope) the motivation to go out and play safely, but only you can take those latex products out of your medicine cabinet and treat them like the real sex-enhancing, communication-building, confidence-inspiring, turn-on toys they were meant to be!

Censorship

Just as reliable as the natural urge to express our sexuality is the societal urge to censor these expressions. In this chapter, we'll take a look at recent American trends in sexual censorship and give you tips on what you can do to stand up for freedom of expression.

"Unnatural" Acts

Before we discuss the restrictions applied to sexual expression, it's worth noting that sexual activities between consenting adults are restricted in extremely punitive ways under the law of the land. Until 1961, all fifty states had criminal laws against various forms of consensual sex between unmarried adults. While many laws were repealed during the seventies, as of January 1997, twenty-five states—half the states in the union—still have laws on their books criminalizing unmarried cohabitation; "fornication," defined as sex between unmarried couples; and consensual "sodomy," defined as oral and/or anal intercourse.

What do these laws really mean? In eleven states around the country, married couples who engage in oral or anal sex in the privacy of their homes are committing a criminal act, usually a felony. In Rhode Island, an unmarried man and woman engaging in anal sex can receive anywhere from seven to twenty years in prison. In Michigan, two women were sent to prison in 1967 for enjoying oral sex in the privacy of their tent in a state park. In South Carolina, "the abominable crime of buggery" (not defined in the statute) is punishable by five years in prison. Lest you think that these antiquated statutes remain on the books only because they haven't been questioned in recent years, remember the infamous *Bowers v. Hardwick* ruling of 1986. In a five to four decision, the Supreme Court ruled that same-sex couples engaging in "sodomy" don't have a constitutional right to privacy and upheld Georgia state laws, in which consensual oral or anal sex between same-sex couples is a felony offense. No wonder we received the following letter:

> *After teaching human sexuality courses at the technical school and university levels for many years, I quit because I cannot discuss in open and honest ways all of the wonderful ways of pleasuring oneself and one another without incurring the wrath of the Georgia state legislature and the school system in which I work.*

Most frequently, "sodomy" laws are used to discriminate against gays and lesbians in housing, employment or child custody cases, but they can be used to discriminate against unmarried heterosexuals as well. Given the Supreme Court's proven reluctance to uphold the right to sexual privacy on a federal level, the best bet for repealing oppressive sodomy laws is on the state level. Check out our resource listings under "Freedom of Expression" to learn what you can do to help decriminalize the pursuit of sexual pleasure.

Obscenity and the Law

Sexual expression becomes a crime when the materials that are produced, whether writings or images, are legally classified as "obscene." Obscene materials are exempt from the First Amendment guarantees of free speech. The legal definition of obscenity, and the inevitably subjective interpretations of this definition, determine what sexual materials we have access to and what materials we can create.

The Supreme Court definition of obscenity, which has been in effect since their 1973 *Miller v. California* ruling, allows states to regulate sexual materials according to their own community standards, provided the regulations be restricted to works that "taken as a whole, appeal to the prurient interest in sex," that portray sexual conduct in "a patently offensive way," and that "taken as a whole, do not have serious literary, artistic, political or scientific value." Only materials that are found by judges or jurors to meet each of the "three prongs" of this definition of obscenity may be deemed obscene.

Needless to say, these criteria are breathtakingly vague. The dictionary defines "prurience" as "an inordinate interest in matters of sex," while the Supreme Court has helpfully added that prurient interests are those that are "sick and morbid," as opposed to "normal and healthy." Add the arbitrariness of defining "patently offensive" or determining whether a photograph has *serious* scientific value, versus merely scientific value, and you have the recipe for inevitable First Amendment violations.

The Golden Age

During the seventies, the flowering sexual revolution and women's movement created something of a Golden Age of sexual freedom of expression. President Johnson's Commission on Obscenity and Pornography reported in 1970 that pornography had no discernible negative effects, recommended the repeal of most obscenity laws and called for improved sex-education programs across the nation (Nixon vehemently rejected the Commission's findings). An abundance of magazines and books were published to satisfy people's desire for sexual information and depictions of sexual behavior. Early X-rated movies included work by directors and producers who were committed to pushing the envelope of sexual expression with serious dramas, and the success of sexually explicit mainstream films such as *Last Tango in Paris* and *Midnight Cowboy* suggested that Americans were finally "grown up" enough to embrace a popular culture that addressed sex in thoughtful and provocative ways.

The Reagan-Bush Years

Alas, the pendulum swung in the eighties with the dawn of the Reagan-Bush era and the rise of the so-called Religious Right. Reagan convened the U.S. Attorney General's Commission on Pornography, a.k.a. the Meese Commission, to try to find the causal link between pornography and social ills that President Johnson's Commission had been unable to ferret out over a decade earlier. The Meese Commission, an eleven-member panel of whom six were anti-pornography activists, obediently came to the conclusion that porn was a very bad, harmful thing indeed (not before publishing their voluminous 1986 report, fifteen percent of which consisted of excerpts from pornographic writings and plot summaries from X-rated videos).

The Commission's report concluded that pornography inspires sexual violence and abuse, a finding that was immediately disputed by several of the sociologists whose research the report misrepresented and by two of the Commission's female members. These women—psychiatrist Judith Becker, whose career was devoted to studying and treating victims and perpetrators of sex crimes, and Ellen Levine, editor of *Women's Day* magazine—formally dissented from the Commission's report. They pointed out that the Commission suffered from limited funds, took no time to do independent research, and held heavily biased hearings–the majority of their "witnesses" were self-described "victims of pornography." In a public statement, Becker and Levine noted, "To say that exposure to pornography in and of itself causes an individual to commit a sexual crime is simplistic, not supported by the social-science data, and overlooks many of the other variables that may be contributing causes."

Yet the Commission's detractors were ignored and the Justice Department, duly inspired with a mission to crack down on porn, created the National Obscenity Enforcement Unit. Under Reagan and Bush, this unit developed a sophisticated strategy to take on the heavyweights of the adult industry. They targeted a handful of video manufacturers and distributors and harassed them with obscenity indictments in multiple jurisdictions. Since obscenity is defined according to community standards, the Justice Department set up sting operations to ensure jury trials in conservative communities: For example, FBI agents would pose as consumers and place mail orders for videos to be delivered to Oklahoma City, Dallas or Salt Lake City.

These multiple jurisdiction law suits are a double whammy. First, most distributors can't afford the expense of mounting legal defense in several different states simultaneously, and the Justice Department counted on the fact that either the companies would agree to stop distributing videos, or they would drain all their financial resources on legal bills and go out of business.

Second, if obscenity charges did stick in more conservative jurisdictions, companies could then face possible federal racketeering charges for interstate trafficking in obscene materials. While state obscenity convictions are usually misdemeanor charges, racketeering is a federal felony charge, which can result in large fines, long prison sentences and the seizure of business assets. It would be difficult to guess how many millions of dollars and hours of staff time the Justice Department spent on the campaign to put adult distributors out of business.

One company that suffered a huge amount of federal harassment and lived to tell the tale is PHE, the parent company of one of the nation's largest adult mail-order catalogs, the Adam and Eve catalog. PHE, located in North Carolina, was established in 1970 by two graduate students in family planning who saw the need for a mail-order condom catalog. Over the years, the company added novelties, lingerie, magazines and videos, and grew large enough to attract the attention of the federal government. Between 1986 and 1993, the Justice Department waged a campaign to put Adam and Eve out of business, indicting the company on criminal obscenity charges in North Carolina, Utah, Kentucky and Alabama.

Fortunately, PHE had the resources and the commitment to fight back and win. Unlike many video distributors who have no particular investment in the products they produce, and whose defense frequently boils down to "I know this video is a tasteless piece of crap, but dammit I've got a First Amendment right to sell it," PHE's founder Phil Harvey stands behind his product line. He employs a panel of sex therapists and psychotherapists who screen every product under consideration for the Adam and Eve catalog to guarantee the absence of "prurient appeal" and the presence of "scientific value." PHE successfully defended itself against every obscenity indictment, and its 1993 civil suit against the Justice Department for harassment and selective prosecution led to the government being enjoined from further harassing indictments.

Growing public awareness of these bullying tactics (exposed in the 1991 ACLU publication *Above the Law: The Justice Department's War against the First Amendment*) and the advent of a new administration led the Justice Department to shift its focus. The multiple jurisdiction law suits and federal raids on adult businesses that were commonplace in the early nineties have come to an end. The new nineties' strategy revolves around "protecting" helpless women and innocent children from the "degrading" effects of sexually explicit materials.

Legal Tactics

Just in case the average American (several million of whom are on Adam and Eve's mailing list) might not appreciate the tax dollars that are being poured into the type of obsessive prosecutions

PHE endured, the Justice Department justifies its activities with the time-honored rationale: "We need to protect our children." One Justice Department unit that oversees the fight against porn is named the Child Exploitation and Obscenity Section. A recent head of this unit left his job for the greener pastures of Donald Wildmon's American Family Association.

The specter of a vast commercial empire of child pornography helps to keep the wheels of the federal anti-porn bureaucracy turning even though the existence of this empire is as yet unproven. Lawrence A. Stanley convincingly argues in "The Child Porn Myth," his 1989 article in the *Cardozo Arts & Entertainment Law Journal*, that there's no commercial production or sale of child pornography in this country—kiddie porn exists only as a cottage industry of images produced and shared among a small group of pedophiles. Yet claims by the Religious Right and the government, linking the sexual exploitation of children to the mainstream adult industry, or indeed to any sexually explicit imagery, make up in emotional power what they lack in accuracy.

Most recently, a series of ostensible Child Protection Acts have provided the cover for a new form of adult-industry harassment. The Child Protection Restoration Act of 1990 imposes record-keeping requirements on both the producers and distributors of sexually explicit images. Producers are required to maintain records proving that every model or performer who is photographed or filmed engaging in explicit sexual conduct was over eighteen at the time the photos or filming took place. These records need to include a photocopy of a picture ID. A disclosure label, attesting to the date of production and the address where the records are kept, must be attached to every video and included on every book or magazine. Distributors or retailers aren't required to keep copies of these records, but they are liable for felony charges if they knowingly distribute materials depicting actual intercourse, masturbation (including "genital fondling through clothing"), "bestiality" or "sadistic or masochistic abuse" that don't have the required disclosure labels.

On the face of it, this seems like a reasonable means of ensuring that minors are not employed in pornography. Yet the Child Protection Restoration Act, designed expressly to intimidate adult producers, publishers and retailers, will have an impact on the entire spectrum of sexually explicit materials. Only persistent negotiations by the American Booksellers Association and the Free Speech Coalition (the adult industry's First Amendment rights organization) insured that the law wouldn't be implemented retroactively. Given the impossibility of tracking down and documenting all models and performers from prior years, retroactive implementation would have criminalized and effectively banned a huge volume of materials ranging from X-rated videos to sexual self-help books to medical textbooks to photographic art books in one fell swoop.

The threat of prosecution under the Child Protection Restoration Act will have a chilling effect, not only on what gets produced, but on what retailers are willing to risk carrying. Given the practical constraints that limit booksellers or video store owners from personally reviewing all the materials they carry, and given the ongoing confusion about what materials are covered under the new law, even independent, open-minded retailers may well decide that it's safest simply to avoid stocking sexually explicit imagery.

In a climate in which a mega-chain such as Wal-Mart refuses to carry CDs with covers or lyrics it deems objectionable, while Blockbuster shuts out all NC-17 or X-rated tapes, preemptive censorship is steadily narrowing the range of images and writings that get commercial distribution. Most regrettably, the first casualties of laws ostensibly designed to protect children are often children's sex-education materials. Even before the Child Protection Restoration Act, nude photos of children have increasingly been deemed obscene in a range of court cases, and sex-ed books such as the European classic *Show Me* have been withdrawn from U.S. distribution.

Adult video, magazine and toy producers went to considerable expense to set up record-keeping systems and develop disclosure labels under the terms of the Child Protection Restoration Act and have been using these as required since July 1995. A year later, Congress was on the harassment trail again, with a law (tacked onto an unrelated spending bill in October 1996) expanding the definition of child pornography. This law makes it a felony to produce, distribute, sell or possess pictures or drawings that "appear to" involve or "convey the impression" of a minor engaging in sexual activity.

In other words, child pornography is no longer limited to images of *actual* sexual activity performed by people under the age of eighteen, it is now defined as any image that *implies* or *simulates* sexual activity. So an X-rated video starring a twenty-one-year-old actress in pigtails getting a spanking for being a "naughty girl" could conceivably be branded kiddie porn. Obviously, this nonsensical law has implications not merely for the adult industry, but for mainstream publishers, Hollywood filmmakers, art museums and ad campaigns. Free speech and First Amendment groups are challenging this bill.

No Senator or Congressperson wants to vote "for" child pornography, so anti-pornographers try to build a moral highground for their efforts to suppress the free exchange of sexually explicit materials by claiming that they are simply trying to combat the scourge of kiddie porn. There is, however, no documented commercial child-porn industry in this country.

The real target of these Child Protection Acts is the adult industry—yet pornographers are the first to agree that child pornography is criminally abusive. We'd be thrilled if the government were to turn its attention to protecting children from the appalling poverty and abuse that so many suffer, but it's difficult to see how pouring millions of tax dollars into preventing a married couple in Utah from receiving a mail-order porn video or raising a hue and cry over a Calvin Klein ad campaign truly combats the physical, emotional and sexual abuse of the nation's children.

Another popular tool of the censors is the so-called "third party liability bill," which puts forth the utterly ludicrous proposition that manufacturers and retailers should be held liable for crimes committed by anyone who purchases their wares. In 1992, the Senate Judiciary Committee approved the Pornography Victims' Compensation Act, a bill which would have entitled the victim of a sex crime to sue producers, distributors and retailers of books, magazines and videos purported to have inspired the crime. Although this Act never reached a vote in the full Senate, similar bills claiming a causal link between enjoying sexually explicit materials and performing criminal acts have been considered by a number of state and local legislatures (inspired by those two Energizer bunnies of censorship, Andrea Dworkin and Catharine MacKinnon).

The positive legacy of the aborted Pornography Victims' Compensation Act was the forging of alliances between publishers, distributors, retailers, media people and First Amendment groups. Powerhouse anti-censorship organizations such as Feminists for Free Expression sprang up in response to this threat to freedom of speech, and numerous mainstream journalists and editors took a stand in defense of the constitutionality of sexually explicit materials.

The Canadian Supreme Court's *Butler* decision of 1992 provides a textbook example of what can go wrong when governments step in to "protect" their citizenry from "obscene" materials. Inspired by ordinances Catharine MacKinnon and Andrea Dworkin had drafted stateside, linking pornography to sexual discrimination against women, *Butler v. the Queen* mandates that Canadian Customs seize all materials that officials deem to be "degrading" or "dehumanizing" to women.

Canadian Customs officials have taken the ruling as carte blanche to seize feminist, gay and lesbian writings crossing the border and to target gay and lesbian bookstores for ongoing harassment. The lesbian erotic magazine *Bad Attitude* was one of the first publications to be seized, and has been followed by countless other volumes from *Hot, Hotter, Hottest* (detained before it proved to be a chili pepper cookbook) to safer sex handbooks to, you guessed it, two of Andrea Dworkin's own books.

The recent passage of the 1996 Telecommunications Act, in which Congress sweepingly declared all "indecent" materials on the Internet to be illegal, is yet another poorly reasoned attack on First Amendment rights. We refer you to the High-Tech Sex chapter for more details on this recent attempt to censor the latest technology.

Self-Censorship

Censorship efforts don't merely limit access to sexually explicit materials, they limit what materials get produced. The mainstream producers of porn are resistant to abandoning a formulaic approach to plot and content for fear of creating works that could be deemed "obscene" in another state. In a Catch-22 scenario, the censorship of sexually explicit materials limits the extent to which these materials can evolve into a more artistic genre that fewer people might consider worthy of censorship. While the hate-mongers of the Religious Right are hardly likely to consider this a tragedy, or to identify distinctions between cutting-edge, provocative porn and assembly-line dreck, sex consumers everywhere suffer the consequences.

Books

How do obscenity prosecutions affect what gets produced? Publishers of mainstream sex manuals err on the side of caution and avoid explicit photos in their books—if you've ever seen a sexual-positions book in which all the images are carefully framed to keep genitals out of sight, you're familiar with how surreal the result can be.

When Canadian government officials spread the word that materials that feature "excessive ejaculation...interpreted as the simultaneous ejacu-

lation of two or more people on the body of another person" and "boot-licking in a sexual context" are likely targets for customs seizures, it's pretty easy to figure out why *Penthouse* magazine instructs story writers to avoid "excessive come on the face" along with bondage and discipline.

Given the U.S. Congress' obsession with "Protecting The Children," it's not surprising that stories related to adolescence or reflections on budding sexual feelings would never make it into mainstream porn—no matter how many of us had our adult eroticism forged during the teen years.

Adam and Eve, as we mentioned earlier, employs a staff of psychologists whose job it is to put a seal of approval on catalog products, guaranteeing that they won't appeal to the "prurient" interests of any "normal" adults. When *The Good Vibrations Guide to Sex* was first considered for possible inclusion in the Adam and Eve catalog, reviewers rejected it for fear that our discussion and illustrations of vaginal fisting and bondage put the book you're reading into the danger zone. Fortunately, with a little advocacy on the part of staff sex therapists, they reconsidered, and our book is carried in the Adam and Eve catalog. We don't blame the folks at Adam and Eve for being cautious, given the intense scrutiny they've been subjected to, but the fact that a self-help manual that some readers find almost *too* wholesome is deemed dangerously transgressive within the adult industry, gives you some sense of the schizophrenic effects of censorship.

Videos

The Justice Department's single-minded persecution of major adult video distributors in the late eighties produced a firestorm of preemptive self-censoring throughout the industry. If a plot device or sexual activity led to a video's conviction on obscenity charges somewhere in the country, the device or activity would be added to the informal, yet rigid, set of boundaries beyond which porn producers would not venture.

Forbidden activities include the predictable: bestiality, urination and defecation. They also include female ejaculation (ejaculate is mistaken for urine) and vaginal or anal fisting—the placement of any more than three fingers in the vagina is considered an appallingly unnatural act.

Censorship in Strange Places

At Good Vibrations, we've encountered plenty of censorship, and we've become accustomed to editing our ads to be palatable to readers of mainstream magazines—this often involves racking our brains for alternatives to common red-flag words such as *sexual, sensual* and *erotic*. We're always shocked at how censorship knows no political bounds and how we can be censored where we least expect it. For instance, throughout the eighties, *Ms.* magazine refused to run a classified ad for our catalogs, despite the fact that a 1986 feature article about sex toys for women was filled with praise for Good Vibrations. First they asked that we remove all references to "vibrators" from our ad text, but after we rewrote our ad, we were told that actually the name "Good Vibrations" itself was just too racy to run in their periodical. In another bizarre bit of censorship, *Playboy* magazine rejected a classified ad for The Sexuality Library catalog, our catalog of erotic and educational books and videos, singling out books on menstruation, safer sex, gay sex and masturbation to be "most objectionable." Apparently, in Hef's Magic Kingdom, Playmates don't menstruate, play with latex, play with each other or jerk off.

such as *Opening of Misty Beethoven* and *Private Afternoons of Pamela Mann*, were also vigorously edited to remove any potentially controversial chunks of plot or dialogue. As an analogy, try to imagine taking classic films of American cinema, such as *Chinatown* or *The Godfather*, and excising all the scenes in which sex and violence are linked. The resulting videos were a shadow of their former selves, rendered practically incomprehensible due to lack of continuity. While the threat of federal persecution has eased in recent years, and directors such as Paul Thomas, John Leslie and others are involved in more imaginative X-rated movie-making, the fate of porn's Golden Oldies is a sad reminder that X-rated video will never have a chance to grow up as long as censorship restricts it to the perpetual adolescence of lowest-common-denominator conformity.

Toys

While sex toys don't fall under any constitutional protection and have been ignored by federal legislators, several states have their own laws prohibiting the sale of "obscene devices." And, to avoid the vagaries of community standards, these statutes explicitly define an obscene device as "a device including a dildo or artificial vagina, designed or marketed as useful primarily for the stimulation of human genitals." Yup, in the states of Texas, Georgia, Louisiana, Mississippi and Kansas, sex toys are currently commercial contraband, although Kansas and Texas do allow the sale of sex toys for therapeutic and medical reasons. It's not quite clear where citizens of Kansas or Texas are supposed to go to buy their medically approved dildos, nor whether they'd need a doctor's note.

Due to these laws, adult bookstores in states such as Texas find themselves in the ludicrous position of labeling all their vibrators, artificial vaginas and blow-up dolls as "novelties only." In other words, someone selling a battery vibrator is

Any hint of nonconsensual activities is avoided; to this end bondage and genital-sex scenes are rarely, if ever, combined in the same film. Profanity is scrupulously avoided, to the point where ejaculations such as "Oh God, I'm coming!" are edited out. Drugs and violence have all been white-washed out of modern porn, while images of brand-name products are edited out as well (brand-name sex toys are a welcome exception to the rule!). And interracial sex scenes are almost impossible to find, thanks to the community standards of certain Southern states where depictions of interracial sex have been enough to get such videos deemed obscene.

In the early years of X-rated film, some directors framed explicit sex scenes within a context of dramatic, passionate plots. Rape and murder were tackled head on in videos such as *Anna Obsessed* and *Midnight Heat*, videos with all the moody complexity of Hollywood film noir. Needless to say, these classic films were among the first to go under the editor's knife in the early nineties when distributors were fleeing the threat of prison or bankruptcy. Other far more light-hearted classics, supposed to pretend that whoever purchases the vibrator is buying it purely as a gag gift and will never put the "novelty" anywhere near the genitals.

Other states have their own prohibitions restricting the exchange of accurate information related to sex toys. Under California state law, if you sell sexual products and you explain how best to use and enjoy them, you run the risk of being brought up on charges of "pandering." According to a California statute that dates back to 1919, soliciting a sex act on another's behalf in exchange for monetary compensation is a felony offense—the statute doesn't specify that the "other" must be a human being, so sex toys are covered under this law. Here again, distributors resort to labelling all sex toys "for novelty use only."

Zoning

Most of the statutes criminalizing the purchase of "obscene devices" date back to the seventies, when the increasing number of adult bookstores and massage parlors opening in major cities inspired opponents to devise whatever legislation they could dream up to limit the success of these businesses. Later, zoning laws became the method of choice for controlling adult retailers. Many cities and towns have zoning ordinances that restrict the location of adult-oriented businesses—specifying that they must be a certain number of feet from schools, churches, residential neighborhoods, etc.

At Good Vibrations, we ran afoul of similar zoning restrictions when we opened our second store in Berkeley in 1994. We had applied for a permit as a "book and gift store," as this is how our San Francisco store is zoned. A local resident complained that our store more closely resembled the description of adult-oriented businesses per the city zoning ordinance, namely "businesses which predominantly engage in the sale of products or materials which appeal to a prurient interest or sexual appetite of the purchaser or user." There's that word *prurient* again! When we went before the zoning administrators, we were informed that any business with more than twenty-five percent of its inventory in sexual products was considered an adult business, but that given our educational mission, they'd allow us to carry up to fifty percent of sexually related inventory before being deemed an adult business.

We found ourselves in the ridiculous situation of measuring the square footage of our fixtures and splitting hairs over which of our products constituted "adult" versus "educational" materials. Our suggestion that the language of the ordinance was clearly subjective and open to interpretation, and that even a lingerie store could be seen as a business that "appeals to sexual appetites," was not warmly received. We learned that a condom shop that had opened near Berkeley's college campus was similarly forced to limit condoms to less than twenty-five percent of their inventory and promptly went out of business.

In Good Vibrations' case, we were able to rally community support, which tipped the scales in our favor. Customers, friends and colleagues deluged the Berkeley city council with faxes, phone calls, e-mail and letters of support. The local media had a field day, and five days later, city officials bowed to community pressure and reinstated our permit.

Other adult-oriented businesses in other communities are not always so fortunate. Many people instinctively approve of zoning laws; after all, they're regarded as keeping adult businesses away from school children, rather than as violating First Amendment rights. Many people who sprang to Good Vibrations defense did so because they considered us to be "different" from "sleazy" adult bookstores with video viewing booths. In the eyes of many citizens, however, these fine distinctions would be purely academic, and any outfit distributing sexually explicit materials should be forced to hit the road. It's important to bear in mind that zoning laws are frequently the thin end of the wedge in attempts to legislate adult businesses right out of town. Whether zoning laws are being invoked to clean up Manhattan's Times Square, to remove X-rated videos from a mall's video store, or to keep a Good Vibrations from opening in your home town, we urge you to look beyond the anti-porn hysteria to make reasoned judgments of your own.

What You Can Do

You can participate in the fight against censorship both on a national and local level. Check out the freedom of expression organizations in our resource listings. These national organizations can keep you updated on upcoming federal legislation, and it's crucial that you let your Congressperson know how you feel on all censorship-related bills. Don't assume that challenges to First Amendment rights fall along party lines; whether the administration is Democratic or Republican, the individual right to privacy remains a tenuously held privilege.

Working for change on the local level can take a bit more courage, since this may entail contacting friends and neighbors to let them know you support access to sexual materials. Since definitions of obscenity and zoning ordinances are influenced by community standards, it's particularly important that you speak out on the local level.

You can also combat censorship by flexing your consumer dollar. If you enjoy a certain X-rated director's work, ask your local video store to order more of his or her videos, and tell all your friends to consider renting them as well. If you crave porn videos with greater diversity in performers and body types, you need to be willing to pay more for independent features than you will for mainstream porn. If one bookstore in your town carries sex books but another doesn't, patronize the sex-positive establishment and let them know you appreciate the range of their selection. Seek out the retailers who present the products and information you crave.

In your defense of sexually explicit materials, you're bound to grapple with your own preconceptions and subjective interpretations. Just as one man's porn is another man's erotica, one woman's utterly irredeemable filth is another woman's entertaining night on the town. You're certainly entitled to your own responses and opinions, and in fact we urge you to tease out and identify what does and doesn't give you pleasure in the videos, books, magazines and toys you encounter. We hope, however, you'll maintain the point of view that it's better for there to be a wide-ranging variety of sexual materials than it is to shut down or ban any one genre. The mainstream adult industry suffers from a certain "outlaw" complex—folks who are producing commercial porn are definitely lowest in the pecking order of First Amendment defense. The hypocrisy of having their work publicly scorned and politically persecuted, yet privately consumed in mass quantities, has resulted in an understandable amount of cynicism. As a result, adult-industry people have an incentive to circle their wagons and reject change rather than to expand the possibilities of their genre. Change will only come slowly and in direct response to consumer demand.

We recognize that it's much easier to say nothing than to stand up and identify yourself as someone who doesn't think that anal sex is a "crime against nature," who is happy that the town bookstore carries sex manuals, or who enjoys renting porn from the neighborhood video store. Yet as long as individuals remain silent about the books we read, the videos we watch and the toys we enjoy, our rights to privacy and the pursuit of pleasure will continue to be threatened.

Endnote

We hope you've enjoyed reading this book, that it made you laugh and turned you on. Most of all, we hope it inspired you to expand your own sexual boundaries. By this, we don't mean we'll feel like failures if you don't want to tackle at least four new sexual positions or try at least six new sex toys as soon as you finish the last page. We would be happy if you simply felt encouraged to communicate more about sex.

The most revolutionary aspect of our work is not the nature of the products we sell or the way we sell them—it's the fact that we talk about sex. Enthusiastic, forthright, frank talk about sex is in desperately short supply in our society, and our customers tell us they're grateful for the opportunity we provide to speak freely about a subject that is shrouded in mystification. If you've felt similarly gratified by what you've read, we'd like to ask a favor of you in return.

You can help advance sexual expression on a grassroots level if you're willing to take some personal risks. It takes courage to identify your sexual feelings, fantasies and fears without apologies, rationalizations or excuses. One of the biggest contributors to sexual shame and ignorance is people's reluctance to stand up and name what brings them pleasure. It's easier to fall silent than to ask a lover to touch you in specific ways. It's easier to dismiss activities as immature, dangerous or politically incorrect than to examine the source of your preconceptions. It's easier to make assumptions about somebody else's sexual preferences than to acknowledge what fuels your own fantasies. It's easier to critique that "tedious" X-rated movie or that "trite" porn magazine than it is to identify the moment during viewing when your pulse speeded up or to point to the photo that made your juices start flowing. It's easier to pretend that your siblings don't have sex than it is to compare notes on how you've been influenced by the cultural messages you all received while growing up. Yet if you take the risk of speaking up about sex, a whole new world of perceptions and possibilities will open before you.

Why not try talking to a lover, a friend, a coworker or a relative about sex in a way you never have before? Tell your lover the plot of your most powerful fantasy. Ask your best friend to take your kids to the movies so that you can stay home and masturbate. Interview your mother and your father as to how they learned about sex. Present a vibrator at your sister's bridal shower. Swap condom recommendations with a coworker. You may be surprised at how exhilarating it is to acknowledge yourself as a sexual person, and at how eagerly those around you respond to any encouragement to express sexual feelings and opinions.

We understand that many people feel that sex is a private matter, and that public discourse threatens to devalue it. The truth is, our society's tacit agreement to keep silent about where and how we get pleasure has created a situation in which the individual right to privacy is under siege and the right to free expression is subject to constant legislative threats.

The enjoyment of sex is a basic human right that we'd like to see guaranteed to all. When we were first working on this book, we used to joke that the final chapter should be entitled "We'd Like to Teach the World to Come," but perhaps a more accurate title would be "We'd Like to Teach the World to Communicate." Better communication leads to increased sexual pleasure, which, in turn, promotes health, self-esteem, intimacy, creativity and joy. The world would unquestionably be a better place if sexual pleasure were more abundant. While we can't necessarily realize our dream of putting a vibrator into the hands of every U.N. representative or penetrating the nation's corridors of power with dildos and lubes, we can offer you encouragement, praise and our heartfelt wishes for a lifetime full of all the sexual pleasure you desire.

Appendix: Survey

We invite you to fill out as much of the attached questionnaire as you wish. We're not looking for statistics—we simply want to get a sense of what sexual activities you're enjoying, so that we can best represent your experience in future editions of this book. We want to know what kind of sex you like and why you like it! If you're willing to share your responses (anonymously, of course), send your completed questionnaire to:

GV Guide Survey
938 Howard Street #101
San Francisco, CA 94103

1) Sexual Arousal and Response
Please describe your experience of any or all of the following:
Women: orgasm, multiple orgasm, ejaculation, G-spot stimulation
Men: orgasm, multiple orgasm, orgasm without ejaculation, prostate stimulation

2) Masturbation
a. What's your earliest memory of masturbating (consciously engaging in sexual self-stimulation)?
b. Describe your favorite method of masturbating.
c. Did you/do you have fears or anxieties about masturbation? What are they?
d. Do your masturbation habits change when you're single or coupled? How?

3) Sex Play
a. What are your favorite sexual activities that don't involve penetration? Describe your favorite one or two (massage, tribadism/dry humping, cunnilingus, fellatio, sixty-nine, rimming, mutual masturbation, etc.).
b. Please describe any other sex games you enjoy (talking dirty, phone sex, computer sex, exhibitionism, voyeurism, sex with more than one partner, S/M, etc.).

4) Penetration
a. Please describe your experience with vaginal and/or anal penetration. Which of the following do you particularly enjoy: a penis, fingers, fist, dildos, plugs, vibrators, anal beads, etc.?
b. What additional stimulation do you enjoy during penetration: clitoral, anal, prostate, nipple, etc.?
c. What are your favorite positions for penetration?
d. Do you use lubricant: why or why not? If you do, what kind?

5) Sex Toys
Describe your most enjoyable and most disappointing experiences with a sex toy (battery-operated vibrators, plug-in massagers, dildos, buttplugs, double dildos, cock rings, ben wa balls, French Ticklers, etc.) alone and with a partner.

6) Fantasies
a. Please describe your favorite fantasy.
b. What's your favorite time to fantasize?
c. If you use books, magazines or videos to enhance your fantasies, please describe how.

7) Communication
Are there specific ways in which you like to initiate a sexual encounter or ways in which you like a partner to initiate? If so, what are they?

8) Safer Sex
Please describe your experience with safer sex accessories, if any (condoms, dental dams, gloves, Saran Wrap, etc.). If you do not practice safer sex, please tell us your reasons.

We may choose to quote from portions of these questionnaires. All quotes will be anonymous. If you do not wish to be quoted, even anonymously, please tell us.

Resources

We have verified the following information with regard to addresses and phone numbers, but we cannot guarantee the delivery of goods or services as stated in each listing. Bear in mind that many of the mail-order companies listed here will request a signed statement that you are over twenty-one years old before they will send you a catalog.

Shopping Guide

Sex Toys

Adam and Eve
Mail-order catalog of toys, videos, lingerie: Free
PO Box 800
Carrboro, NC 27510
919/644-1212
800/274-0333
http://www.aeonline.com

Blowfish
Mail-order catalog of toys, books and videos: Free
2261 Market Street, #284
San Francisco, CA 94114
415/285-6064
800/325-2569
http://www.blowfish.com

B. R. Creations
Mail-order catalog of custom-made corsets with newsletter: $7.00
PO Box 4201
Mountain View, CA 94040
415/961-5354
br corsets@aol.com
http://www.best.com/~manx/brcreations.html

Come Again Erotic Emporium
Retail store
Video catalog of toys and lingerie: $24.95
Book and fetish publications catalog: $4.00
353 East 53rd Street
New York, NY 10022
212/308-9394

Eve's Garden
Retail store (woman-oriented) and mail-order catalog of toys, books and videos: Free with call
119 West 57th Street #420
New York, NY 10019-2383
212/757-8651
800/848-3837
evesgarden@focusint.com
http://www.evesgarden.com

Gauntlet
Retail stores offering piercing information and supplies
   8722 Santa Monica Boulevard, 2nd Floor
   West Hollywood, CA 90069
   310/657-6677

   2377 Market Street
   San Francisco, CA 94114
   415/431-3133

   144 5th Avenue, 2nd Floor
   New York, NY 10011
   212/229-0180

   23 Rue Keller
   Paris, France 75011
   011-331-4700-7360

Gauntlet
Mail-order catalog of body jewelry: $5.00, with sample of *PFIQ* magazine: $15.00
2215-R Market Street #801
San Francisco, CA 94114
415/252-1404
800/RINGS-2-U
mailorder@gauntlet.com
http://www.gauntlet.com

Good Vibrations
Retail stores of toys, books and videos
1210 Valencia Street
San Francisco, CA 94110
415/974-8980

2504 San Pablo Avenue
Berkeley, CA 94702
510/841-8987

Good Vibrations
Mail-order catalog of toys and videos: Free
938 Howard Street, Suite 101-GB
San Francisco, CA 94103
415/974-8990
800/289-8423
goodvibe@well.com
http://www.goodvibes.com

Grand Opening!
Retail store and mail-order catalog of toys, books
and videos: Free
318 Harvard Street, Suite 32
Arcade Building, Coolidge Corner
Brookline, MA 02146
617/731-2626
grando@tiac.net
http://www.grandopening.com

In Harmony
Mail-order catalog of sensual products: Free
5600 West Lovers Lane, Suite 116-380
Dallas, TX 75209
800/691-3324

Intimate Treasures
Mail-order catalog of toys and videos, plus
subscription to "catalog of catalogs": $5.00
PO Box 77902
San Francisco, CA 94107
415/863-5002
http://www.intimatetreasures.com

It's My Pleasure
Feminist gift shop of toys, books and videos
4258 Southeast Hawthorne Boulevard
Portland, OR 97215
503/236-0505

Lovecraft
Retail stores and on-line catalog of toys, books,
videos and lingerie
63 Yorkville Avenue
Toronto, Ontario
Canada M5R 1B7
416/923-7331
http://www.regsex.com/lovecraft

2200 Dundas Street East
Mississauga, Ontario
Canada L4X 2V3
905/276-7331

Loveseason
Retail stores and mail-order catalog of toys, books,
videos and lingerie: $4.00
4001 198th Street SW #7
Lynnwood, WA 98036
206/775-4502
800/500-8843

12001 NE 12th Street
Bellevue, WA 98005

Mercury Mail Order/MMO
Retail store and mail-order catalog of toys for
men: $5.00
4084 18th Street, Dept GV
San Francisco, CA 94114
415/621-1188
888/879-6669
http://www.gaysf.com

Passion Flower
Retail store of toys, books, videos and lingerie
Mail-order catalogs of lingerie/leather: $3.00 each
4 Yosemite Avenue
Oakland, CA 94611
510/601-7750
passion@passionflwr.com

Pleasure Chest
Retail store of toys and clothing. Ninety-six-page
mail-order catalog of toys and videos: $17.95
7733 Santa Monica Boulevard
West Hollywood, CA 90046
213/650-1022 (retail)
800/753-4536 (mail order)
http://www.thepleasurechest.com

Romantasy
Retail store of toys, books, videos and lingerie
Mail-order catalog of toys and lingerie: $5.00;
corset catalog: $12.00
199 Moulton Street
San Francisco, CA 94123
415/673-3137
800/922-2281
info@romantasy.com
http://www.romantasy.com

Sybian (for women) and Venus II (for men)
Info on high-tech stimulation machines: $3.00
PO Box 354
Monticello, IL 61856
217/762-2141
800/253-6135
abco@net66.com
http://www.sybian.com

Toys in Babeland
Retail store and mail-order catalog of toys, books
and videos: Free
707 East Pike Street
Seattle, WA 98122
206/328-2914
800/658-9119
letters@babeland.com
http://www.babeland.com

Voyages Catalog Group
Mail-order catalog of toys, videos and other adult
catalogs: $10.00
PO Box 78550
San Francisco, CA 94107
415/863-4822
http://www.voyages.com

Xandria Collection
Lawrence Research Group
Mail-order catalog of toys, books and videos: $4.00
leather catalog: $5.00; lingerie catalog: $2.00
165 Valley Drive
Brisbane, CA 94005
415/468-3812
800/242-2823

Leather and S/M Products

Adam and Gillian's Sensual Whips and Toys
Mail-order catalog: $5.00
The Utopian Network
PO Box 1146-GV
New York, NY 10156
516/842-1711
siradam@ix.netcom.com
http://www.catalog.com/utopian

Cupid's Treasures
Retail store and mail-order catalog of fetish
clothing and toys: Free
3519 North Halstead
Chicago, IL
312/348-3884

Dream Dresser
Retail stores of fetish clothing, shoes and toys
8444-50 Santa Monica Boulevard
West Hollywood, CA 90069
213/848-3480

1042 Wisconsin Avenue, NW
Washington, DC 20007
202/625-0373

Dream Dresser
Mail-order catalog of fetish clothing, shoes: $10.00
PO Box 16158
Beverly Hills, CA 90209
800/963-7326
http://www.dreamdresser.com

Fantasy World Products
Mail-order brochure of fabric restraints, whips and
blindfolds: SASE
PO Box 609
Webster, NY 14580

Heartwood Whips of Passion
Mail-order catalog of hand-crafted cats and
floggers: $6.00
412 North Coast Highway #210
Laguna Beach, CA 92651
714/376-9558

Lashes by Sarah
Mail-order catalog of hand-crafted cats and
floggers: $5.00
2336 Market Street #39
San Francisco, CA 94114
415/206-9447
lashes@sirius.com

Mr. S Leather Company & Fetters USA
Retail store and two-hundred-page mail-order
catalog of fetish clothing and toys: $20.00
310 7th Street
San Francisco, CA 94103
415/863-7764

Second Skin
Retail store of fetish clothing and toys
521 Rue Saint Philip
New Orleans, LA 70116
504/561-8167
ssleather@aol.com

SORODZ
Mail-order catalog of hand-crafted whips,
rods and paddles: $5.00
PO Box 10692
Oakland, CA 94610
510/839-2588
sorodz@aol.com

Stormy Leather Inc.
Retail store of fetish clothing, shoes and toys
1158 Howard Street
San Francisco, CA 94103
415/626-1672
info@stormyleather.com
http://www.stormyleather.com

Safer Sex Supplies

Condomania
Retail stores and mail-order catalog of safer sex
supplies: Free
 7306 Melrose Avenue
 Los Angeles, CA 90046
 213/933-7865
 800/926-6366
 http://www.condomania.com

 3066 Grand Avenue
 Coconut Grove, FL 33133
 305/445-7729

758 Washington Boulevard
South Miami Beach, FL 33139
305/531-8597

351 Bleecker Street
New York, NY 10014
212/691-9442

Rubber Tree
Mail-order catalog of safer sex supplies and
literature: $1.00 with SASE
4426 Burke Avenue North
Seattle, WA 98103
206/663-4750

Books and Audios

Alamo Square
Publishes and distributes books on S/M, leather
and fetish topics
Mail-order brochure: Free with SASE
PO Box 14543
San Francisco, CA 94114
415/252-0643

Isadora Alman
Audio tapes ($15) and booklets ($5) about connecting
with others, communication skills and sexual enjoyment
3145 Geary Boulevard #153
San Francisco, CA 94118
415/386-5090
isadora@sfbayguardian.com
http://www.askisadora.com

Alyson Publications
Publishes gay and lesbian sexual self-help and
erotic books
Catalog: Free
40 Plympton Street
Boston, MA 02118
213/871-1225
800/525-9766

Blue Moon Books
Publishes erotic fiction and nonfiction sex books
Catalog: Free
61 Fourth Avenue
New York, NY 10003
212/505-6880.
800/535-0007
bluoff@aol.com
http://www.bluemoonbooks.com

Carroll & Graf
Publishes erotic art, sexual self-help and Victorian
smut books
Catalog: Free
260 5th Avenue
New York, NY 10001
212/889-8772

Circlet Press
Publishes erotic science fiction books with S/M
and alternative sexuality themes
Mail-order brochure: Free with SASE
1770 Massachusetts Avenue #278
Cambridge, MA 02140
617/864-0492
circlet-info@circlet.com
http://www.circlet.com/circlet/home.html

Cleis Press
Publishes erotic fiction and nonfiction sex books
of interest to lesbians, gays, bisexuals and
transgendered readers
Mail-order catalog: Free
PO Box 14684
San Francisco, CA 94114
(415) 864-3385
800/780-2279
sfcleis@aol.com

Daedalus Publishing Company
Publishes and distributes books on S/M, leather
and fetish topics
Mail-order brochure: Free
584 Castro Street, Suite 518
San Francisco, CA 94114
415/626-1867
daedalus@bannon.com
http://www.bannon.com/daedalus

Down There Press
Publishes sexual self-help and erotic books
Mail-order catalog: Free with SASE
938 Howard Street, Suite 101-GB
San Francisco, CA 94103
415/974-8985
http:/www.goodvibes.com/dtp/dtp.html

Gay Sunshine Press/Leyland Publications
Publishes gay male sexual self-help and erotic books
Mail-order catalog: Free with SASE
PO Box 410690
San Francisco, CA 94141

Greenery Press
Publishes nonfiction guides for the sexually
adventurous
Mail-order catalog: Free with SASE
3739 Balboa Avenue #195
San Francisco, CA 94121
verdant@crl.com
http://www.bigrock.com/~greenery

Passion Press
Produces erotic fiction and nonfiction audio tapes
Mail-order brochure: Free
PO Box 277
Newark, NJ 94560
800/724-3283

The Sexuality Library
Mail-order catalog of sex books and videos: Free
938 Howard Street, Suite 101-GB
San Francisco, CA 94103
415/974-8990
800/289-8423
goodvibe@well.com
http://www.goodvibes.com

Videos

Betty Dodson, Ph.D.
Selfloving books and videos
PO Box 1933
Murray Hill Station
New York, NY 10156

Fatale Video
Erotic lesbian videos, lesbian-made
415/454-3291

Femme Productions, Inc.
Erotic videos from a woman's perspective
Mail-order catalog: Free
PO Box 268
Prince Street Station
New York, NY 10012
800/456-5683
http://www.royalle.com

Focus International, Inc.
Mail-order catalog of sexual self-help videos: Free
1160 East Jericho Turnpike
Huntington, NY 11743
516/549-5320
800/843-0305
sex-help@focusint.com
http://www.sex-help.com

Multi-Focus, Inc.
Distributes educational films, videos and slides in human sexuality
Mail-order catalog: Free
1525 Franklin Street
San Francisco, CA 94109
415/673-5100
800/821-0514

Tiger Rose Distributing
Erotic lesbian videos, lesbian-made
Mail-order brochure: Free
PO Box 609
Cotati, CA 94931
707/578-3336

Magazines and Zines

Adult Video News
Monthly trade magazine of the adult film industry: news, reviews and gossip
AVN Publications
6700 Valjean Avenue
Van Nuys, CA 91406
818/786-4286

Anything That Moves
Quarterly magazine "for the uncompromising bisexual"
2261 Market Street #496
San Francisco, CA 94114
415/703-7977x2

Bad Attitude
Quarterly lesbian magazine with S/M emphasis
PO Box 390110
Cambridge, MA 02139

Black Sheets
Three issues/year of sex, humor and popular culture. Kinky, queer, intelligent and irreverent
PO Box 31155
San Francisco, CA 94131
415/431-0171
BlackB@ios.com
http://www.queernet.org/BlackBooks/

CELEBRATE the Self
Solo sex techniques for men
PO Box 8888
Mobile, AL 36689
334/380-0606
800/304-0077

Diseased Pariah News (DPN)
Quarterly magazine of HIV humor and irony
c/o Men's Support Center
PO Box 30564
Oakland, CA 94604
510/533-3412
dpn@netcom.com

Eidos Magazine
Quarterly newspaper of sexual freedom for all orientations and lifestyles
PO Box 96
Boston, MA 02137-0096
617/262-0096
eidos4sex@pipeline.com
http://world.std.com/~kip/eidos.html

Fat Girl
A 'zine for fat dykes and women who want them
2215-R Market Street #197
San Francisco, CA 94114
415/522-8733
selene@sirius.com
http://www.fatgirl.com/fatgirl

Inciting Desire
A semi-annual 'zine for all sex styles
PO Box 7428
Santa Cruz, CA 95061

Lezzie Smut
Quarterly lesbian magazine
Hey Grrrlz! Productions
PO Box 364-1027 Davie Street
Vancouver, British Columbia
Canada V6E 4L2
604/324-7688
lezzie@cspo.queensu.ca
http://www.digital-rain.com/~lezzie

Libido
Quarterly literary sex magazine
PO Box 146721
Chicago, IL 60614
773/275-0842
800/495-1988
rune@mcs.com
http://www.indra.com/libido

Loving More
Quarterly magazine on responsible
nonmonogamy
PEP Publishing
PO Box 4258
Boulder, CO 80306
305/543-7540

Paramour
Quarterly magazine of essays, erotic art and
fiction
PO Box 949
Cambridge, MA 02140
617/499-0069
paramour@xensei.com
http://www2.xensei.com/paramour

Pucker Up
Biannual queer 'zine
PO Box 4108
Grand Central Station
New York, NY 10163
718/486-6966
BlkDogNY@aol.com

Sandmutopia Guardian
Quarterly S/M magazine for all sex styles
c/o Utopian Network
PO Box 1146
New York, NY 10156
516/842-1711
siradam@ix.netcom.com
http://www.catalog.com/utopian

Spectator Magazine
California's weekly sex news, reviews and pictorials
PO Box 1984
Berkeley, CA 94701
510/849-1615
bold1000@aol.com

Tantra
Quarterly magazine on sex and spirituality
PO Box 10268
Albuquerque, NM 87184
505/898-8246

Taste of Latex
Three issues/year pansexual fetish magazine
DM International
PO Box 16188
Seattle, WA 98116

Yellow Silk
Annual literary journal of erotic art, fiction and
poetry
PO Box 6374
Albany, CA 94706
510/644-4188

Newsletters

Masquerade
Bimonthly erotic newsletter of reviews, interviews
and fiction
801 2nd Avenue
New York, NY 10017
MasqBks@aol.com

Men's Confidential
Monthly newsletter of health, sex and fitness news
for older men
33 East Minor Street
Emmaus, PA 18098
800/666-2106

Sex Over Forty
Quarterly newsletter on sex and aging
PO Box 1600
Chapel Hill, NC 27515

Trust, the Handballing Newsletter
Quarterly newsletter on anal fisting
PO Box 14697
San Francisco, CA 94114

Sex Information and Referrals

Hotlines

SEX INFORMATION AND REFERRALS

Louanne Cole's "Sex Matters" Advisor Line
900/773-9463 ($1.00/minute)

San Francisco Sex Information 415/989-7374

Seattle Sex Information 206/328-7711

HEALTH

AIDS/CDC national hotline 800/342-2437

AIDS national hotline in Spanish 800/344-7432

AIDS TTY Service for the Deaf 800/243-7889

American Social Health Association Healthline
(to order free publications) 800/972-8500

Herpes Resource Center (to order publications)
800/230-6039

National herpes hotline 919/361-8488

National STD hotline 800/227-8922

SEXUAL ASSAULT

Incest Survivors Anonymous 310/428-5599

National Child Abuse Hotline 800/422-4453

National Domestic Violence Hotline 800/799-7233

Survivors of Incest Anonymous 410/282-3400

For rape crisis hotlines in most cities, look under
"crisis hotline" in the telephone directory.

Safer Sex Organizations

Condom Resource Center
Nonprofit coordinating condom education and
National Condom Week: 2/14-2/21 annually
Men's Support Center
PO Box 30564
Oakland, CA 94604
510/533-3412

Eros, The Center for Safe Sex
Safer sex club for gay men
2051 Market Street
San Francisco, CA 94114
415/864-3767
cluberossf@aol.com
http://www.gaysf.com

Mother Goose Productions
Info on SF Bay Area bi, lesbian and gay safer sex
parties: Free with SASE
PO Box 3212
Berkeley, CA 94703

Professional Organizations

American Association of Sex Educators,
Counselors and Therapists (AASECT)
Listing of AASECT-certified therapists and
counselors: Free with SASE
PO Box 238
Mount Vernon, IA 52314
319/895-8407

Sexuality Information and Education Council of
the United States (SIECUS)
Information on available bibliographies and other
services: Free with SASE
130 West 42nd Street, Suite 350
New York, NY 10036
212/819-9770
siecus@siecus.org
http://www.siecus.org

Society for the Scientific Study of Sexuality (SSSS)
Membership information: Free with SASE
PO Box 208
Mount Vernon, IA 52314
319/895-8407

Freedom of Expression Organizations

American Civil Liberties Union
Nonprofit offering educational and legal services
to defend First Amendment rights
132 West 43rd Street
New York, NY 10036
212/944-9800

Cal-ACT (Californians Against Censorship
Together)
Grassroots anti-censorship group fighting for
freedom of expression
Membership (and monthly newsletter): $20.00
1800 Market Street #1000
San Francisco, CA 94102
calact@netcom.com
http://www.blowfish.com/~calact

Committee to Preserve our Sexual Liberties
Publishes monthly digest of items related to
sexual liberties
PO Box 422385
San Francisco, CA 94142

Electronic Frontier Foundation
Nonprofit protecting civil liberties on-line
1550 Bryant Street #725
San Francisco, CA 94103
415/436-9333
ask@eff.org
http://www.eff.org

Feminists for Free Expression
Nonprofit anti-censorship organization
PO Box 2525
Times Square Station
New York, NY 10108
212/702-6292
ffe@aol.com
htp://www.well.com/user/freedom

National Coalition Against Censorship
Nonprofit, publishes *Censorship News* four
times/year
275 7th Avenue
New York, NY 10001
212/807-6222
ncac@netcom.com
http://www.ncac.org

Spectrum Institute
Nonprofit legal organization fighting
discrimination against unmarried couples
PO Box 65756
Los Angeles, CA 90065
213/258-8955

Sex and Disability Resources

The Disability Rag
This publication regularly covers sexual issues
PO Box 145
Louisville, KY 40201
502/894-9492

It's Okay!
International quarterly on sex and disability
Sureen Publishing
PO Box 23102
124 Welland Avenue
St Catherines, Ontario
Canada L2R 7P6

Lawrence Research Group
Special Edition Catalog for Disabled People: $4.00
165 Valley Drive
Brisbane, CA 94005
415/468-3812
800/242-2823

Sexuality and Disability Training Center
A group of health professionals exploring the
relationship of physical disability to sexuality,
publishes the *Journal of Sexuality and Disability*
Boston University Medical Center
88 East Newton Street
Boston, MA 02118
617/638-7358

Transgender and Cross-Dressing Resources

American Educational Gender Information Service
Hotline, information, referrals and archives on
transgender issues
Publishes quarterly journal *Chrysalis*
PO Box 33724
Decatur, GA 30033
770/939-0244
aegis@mindspring.com
http://www.ren.org/rafil/aegis.html

Cross-Talk
Monthly magazine of news, information and
commentary for cross-dressers
PO Box 944
Woodland Hills, CA 91356
818/907-3053
kymmer@xconn.com

ETVC (Educational TV Channel)
Hotline, information and referrals on
cross-dressing and gender issues
Publishes bimonthly newsletter of national and
local resources
PO Box 426486
San Francisco, CA 94142
415/564-3246

FTM
Information and peer support for female-to-male
transsexuals and cross-dressers
Publishes quarterly newsletter ($15.00/year) and
resource guide ($5.00)
5337 College Avenue #142
Oakland, CA 94618
510/287-2646
FTM News@aol.com
http://www.ftm-intl.org

International Foundation for Gender Education
Publishes quarterly *Transgender* magazine
PO Box 229
Waltham, MA 02154
617/894-8340
ifge@world.std.com

Transsexual News Telegraph
Quarterly magazine of transsexual culture
41 Sutter Street #1124
San Francisco, CA 94104

S/M Organizations

Eulenspiegel Society
Publishes quarterly magazine *Prometheus*
PO Box 2783
Grand Central Station
New York, NY 10163
212/388-7022
tes@dorsai.org
http://www.tes.org

National Leather Association, International
Provides referrals to local chapters
584 Castro Street #444
San Francisco, CA 94114
614/470-2093
nlaintl@aol.com

Society of Janus
PO Box 426794
San Francisco, CA 94142

Threshold
2554 Lincoln Boulevard #1004
Marina Del Rey, CA 90291
818/782-1160

Other Organizations

Bisexual Resource Center
Information and referrals pamphlet:
$1.00 with SASE
Publishes *Bisexual Resource Guide*
PO Box 639
Cambridge, MA 02140
617/424-9595

IntiNet Resource Center/Sacred Space Institute
Resource list on responsible nonmonogamy:
Free with SASE
PO Box 4322
San Rafael, CA 94913
415/507-1739
pad@well.com

Lifestyles Organization
Promotes alternative lifestyles and sexuality;
sponsors annual Lifestyles Convention
PO Box 6978
Buena Park, CA 90622
714/821-9953
Lifestyles@Playcouples.com
http://www.playcouples.com

NASCA (North American Swing Club Association)
International organization of swing clubs,
publications and events
PO Box 7128
Buena Park, CA 90622
714/229-4870
nasca@deltanet.com
http://www.nasca.com

Workshops

Body Electric School
Workshops on erotic spirituality (including
Tantric, Taoist and Sufi traditions)
for men and women
6527-A Telegraph
Oakland, CA 94609
510/653-1594

E-Sensuals
On-line directory of Tantra teachers and
workshops, on-line catalog of Tantra products
PO Box 1818
Sebastopol, CA 95472
707/823-3063
800/982-6872
e-sensuals@tantra.com
http://www.tantra.com

EroSpirit Research Institute
Workshops and videos on erotic spirituality for
gay men
Mail-order catalog: Free
PO Box 3893
Oakland, CA 94609
510/428-9063
800/432-3767 (video orders)
kramer@erospirit.org
http://www.erospirit.org

Human Awareness Institute
Workshops on love, intimacy and sexuality
1730 South Amphlett Boulevard #225
San Mateo, CA 94402
415/571-5524
info@hai.org
http://www.hai.org

QSM
Classes on S/M for all sexual orientations
Mail-order catalog of books and magazines: Free
PO Box 880154
San Francisco, CA 94188
415/550-7776
info@qualitysm.com
http://www.qualitysm.com

Carol Queen
Workshops on eroticizing safe sex, sexually
explicit writing, "talking dirty" and exhibitionism
for the shy
2215-R Market Street #455
San Francisco, CA 94114
415/978-0891
CarolQueen@aol.com

Sacred Space Institute
Workshops on nonmonogamy, Tantra
and sexual healing
PO Box 4322
San Rafael, CA 94913
415/507-1739
pad@well.com

Bibliography

Nonfiction

Female Sexuality

Awakening Your Sexuality: A Guide for Recovering Women by Stephanie Covington (HarperCollins Publishers/HarperSanFrancisco, 1991). Sexual issues relevant to women recovering from alcohol or chemical dependency.

Becoming Orgasmic by Julia Heiman and Joseph LoPiccolo (Simon & Schuster/Fireside, 1986). A structured program of self-discovery for women who have never had orgasms.

The Black Women's Health Book edited by Evelyn White (Seal Press, 1994). A comprehensive health book with a good discussion of sexuality.

Courage to Heal by Ellen Bass and Laura Davis (Harper & Row, 1988). A guide to healing for women survivors of child sexual abuse.

Courage to Heal Workbook by Laura Davis (Harper & Row, 1990). An interactive workbook for male and female survivors of child sexual abuse.

Cunt Coloring Book by Tee Corinne (Naiad Press, 1989). A coloring book of forty-two drawings of women's genitals (previously *LabiaFlowers*).

Eve's Secrets: A New Theory of Female Sexuality by Josephine Lowndes Sevely (Random House, 1987, o/p). Discusses female ejaculation and describes the physiological symmetry between male and female sexual organs.

Femalia edited by Joani Blank (Down There Press, 1993). Thirty-two full-color photographs of women's genitals.

For Yourself: The Fulfillment of Female Sexuality by Lonnie Garfield Barbach (Penguin Group/Signet, 1975). A guide for women who have never had orgasms or who wish to enhance their sexual responsiveness.

Forbidden Flowers by Nancy Friday (Simon & Schuster/Pocket Books, 1975). The author's second collection of women's sexual fantasies.

The G-Spot and Other Recent Discoveries about Human Sexuality by Alice Kahn Ladas, Beverly Whipple and John D. Perry (Bantam Doubleday Dell/Dell, 1982). A discussion of the G-spot, including first-person accounts about G-spot stimulation and female ejaculation.

Lesbian Passion by JoAnn Loulan (Spinsters Ink, 1987). Discusses lesbian sexual etiquette, sex toys, safer sex and sex and recovery.

Lesbian Sex by JoAnn Loulan (Spinsters Ink, 1984). An excellent primer on female anatomy, sexual response, lesbian sexual activities and communication with partners.

Lesbian Sex Book by Wendy Caster (Alyson Publications, 1993). A comprehensive guide to lesbian sex in the nineties, arranged by topic.

Making Out: The Book of Lesbian Sex and Sexuality by Nina Rapi (Pandora, 1992). A modern manual illustrated with color photographs.

My Secret Garden by Nancy Friday (Simon & Schuster/Pocket Books, 1973). A groundbreaking collection of women's sexual fantasies.

New Our Bodies, Ourselves by the Boston Women's Health Collective (Simon & Schuster/Touchstone, 1992). A wide-ranging source book on all aspects of female sexuality and sexual health.

New View of a Woman's Body by the Federation of Feminist Women's Health Centers (Feminist Health Press, 1991). A self-help classic, including an expanded definition of the clitoris and color photographs of women's genitals.

Ourselves, Growing Older by Paula Brown Doress and Diana Laskin Siegal (Simon & Schuster/Touchstone,1987). A source book on female sexuality and sexual health specific to the concerns of women over thirty-five.

The Playbook for Women about Sex by Joani Blank (Down There Press, 1982). An interactive play/workbook designed to enhance sexual self-awareness.

Sapphistry: The Book of Lesbian Sexuality by Pat Califia (Naiad Press, 1988). Features an excellent discussion of communication skills, a diverse range of sexual techniques and a good section on disability.

Shared Intimacies: Women's Sexual Experiences by Lonnie Barbach and Linda Levine (Bantam Doubleday Dell/Bantam Books, 1980). Interviews with over one hundred twenty women about their sexual activities, attitudes and feelings.

Women on Top by Nancy Friday (Simon & Schuster/Pocket Books, 1991). A collection of women's sexual fantasies in which women play a dominant role. Also available as an audiocassette.

Male Sexuality

Circumcision: What It Does by Billy Ray Boyd (Tatterhill Press, 1990). Facts about circumcision.

Gay Sex: A Manual for Men Who Love Men by Jack Hart (Alyson Publications, 1991). A comprehensive guide to gay sex in the nineties, arranged by topic.

How to Make Love All Night: The Male Multiple Orgasm and Other Secrets of Prolonged Love by Barbara Keesling (HarperCollins Publishers/ Harper Perennial, 1994). Exercise regime teaching techniques to achieve and control the timing of orgasm without ejaculation.

Male Multiple Orgasm Audio by Jack Johnstone (self-produced, 1995). Techniques of ejaculation control.

Men in Love by Nancy Friday (Bantam Doubleday Dell/Dell/Laurel, 1980). A collection of primarily heterosexual male sexual fantasies.

Men Loving Men: A Gay Sex Guide and Consciousness Book by Mitch Walker (Gay Sunshine Press, 1994). Sex manual featuring erotic photography and a historical section on gay male sex in other cultures.

The Multi-Orgasmic Man by Mantak Chia and Douglas Abrams Arana (HarperCollins Publishers/Harper-San Francisco, 1996). An illustrated guide to achieving multiple orgasms based in Taoist teachings.

The New Joy of Gay Sex by Charles Silverstein and Felice Picano (HarperCollins Publishers, 1992). An updated reference book on gay male sexuality.

New Male Sexuality: The Truth about Men, Sex and Pleasure by Bernie Zilbergeld (Bantam Doubleday Dell/Bantam Books, 1992). Encouragement and advice on concerns including performance anxieties, erection difficulties and desire discrepancies (previously published as *Male Sexuality,* 1978).

The Playbook for Men about Sex by Joani Blank (Down There Press, 1981). An interactive play/workbook designed to enhance sexual self-awareness.

Sex: A Man's Guide by Stefan Bechtel, Laurence Roy Stains (Rodale Press, 1996). Engagingly written advice on one hundred thirty different sexual topics.

Sexual Solutions: A Guide for Men and the Women Who Love Them by Michael Castleman (Simon & Schuster/Touchstone, 1983). An informative, down-to-earth guide aimed at men in heterosexual relationships.

Masturbation

First Person Sexual edited by Joani Blank (Down There Press, 1996). A collection of masturbation stories by men and women of all orientations.

Masturbation, Tantra and Selflove by Margo Woods (Mho & Mho Works/Omphaloskepsis Press, 1981). A discussion of channeling sexual energy through masturbation.

Men Loving Themselves: Images of Male Self-Sexuality by Jack Morin (Down There Press, 1988, o/p). A photo-study of twelve diverse men expressing their feelings about masturbation.

More Joy of Solo Sex: An Advanced Guide by Dr. Harold Litten (Factor Press, 1996). Advanced techniques of male masturbation.

Sex For One: The Joy of Selfloving by Betty Dodson (Crown Publishers/Harmony Press, 1987). A reassuring, entertaining guide to the techniques and pleasures of masturbation, with erotic line drawings by the author (expanded from previously self-published works, *Liberating Masturbation* and *SelfLove and Orgasm*).

Solo Sex: Advanced Techniques by Dr. Harold Litten (Factor Press, 1992). A friendly, creative guide to the varieties of male masturbation.

Sex Manuals

101 Nights of Great Romance by Laura Corn (Park Avenue Press, 1996). A creative couple's book with different suggestions for exploring sensuality and building intimacy on each sealed page.

101 Nights of Great Sex by Laura Corn (Park Avenue Press, 1995). A creative couple's book with different suggestions for exploring sexual intimacy on each sealed page.

Anal Pleasure and Health by Jack Morin (Down There Press, 1986). The one-and-only guide to eliminating anal tension and enjoying anal stimulation.

Anne Hooper's Kama Sutra: Classic Lovemaking Techniques Reinterpreted for Today's Lovers by Anne Hooper (Dorling Kindserly, 1994). A modern adaptation of the classic Indian sex manual with color photographs of heterosexual lovers.

Anne Hooper's Ultimate Sexual Touch: The Lover's Guide to Sensual Massage by Anne Hooper (Dorling Kindserly, 1995). Genital and full-body touch techniques are illustrated with color photographs of heterosexual lovers.

The Clitoral Kiss: A Fun Guide to Oral Sex for Men and Women by Kenneth Ray Stubbs (Secret Garden, 1993). A collection of oral sex tips and techniques for men and women.

Enabling Romance: A Guide to Love, Sex and Relationships for the Disabled by Ken Kroll and Erica Levy Klein (Crown Publishers/Harmony Books, 1992). A one-of-a-kind guide covering sexual concerns and techniques for people with a variety of disabilities. Features interviews and a thorough resource list.

Erotic Massage: The Touch of Love by Kenneth Ray Stubbs (Secret Garden, 1989). General techniques for massaging the entire body, presented in clear language and with excellent illustrations.

Exhibitionism for the Shy by Carol Queen (Down There Press, 1995). Tips for dressing up, showing off, talking sexy and communicating your desires with a partner.

Fantasex: A Book of Erotic Games for the Adult Couple by Rolf Milonas (Putnam/Perigee Books, 1983). A collection of sexual scenarios and suggestions for role-playing.

For Play: 150 Sex Games for Couples by Walter Shelburne (Waterfall Press, 1993). A collection of provocative games and sexual techniques.

Good Vibrations: The Complete Guide to Vibrators by Joani Blank (Down There Press, 1989). The ultimate guide to selecting, enjoying, maintaining and introducing your partner to a vibrator.

Guide to Getting It On: A New and Mostly Wonderful Book About Sex by Goofy Foot Press (Goofy Foot Press, 1996). A humorous, playful discussion of a variety of sexual interests and activities.

Hot Monogamy: Essential Steps to More Passionate, Intimate Lovemaking by Dr. Patricia Love and Jo Robinson (Penguin/Plume, 1994). An exercise book for monogamous couples who want to improve sexual intimacy, communication and technique. Also available as an audiocassette.

Love without Limits: Resource Guide for the Responsible Non-Monogamist by Deborah Anapol (InterNet Resource Center, 1992). An encouraging guide to negotiating multi-partner relationships with respect and integrity.

Mindblowing Sex in the Real World: Hot Tips for Doing It in the Age of Anxiety by Sari Locker (HarperCollins Publishers/Harper Perennial, 1995). Sex-positive guide geared toward twentysomething heterosexuals.

More Than Just Sex by Daniel Beaver (Aslan Publishing, 1992). An excellent guide to sexual communication geared toward couples in long-term relationships.

The Oral Caress: The Loving Guide to Exciting a Woman by Robert W. Birch, Ph.D. (PEC Publications, 1996). An enthusiastic, illustrated guide to cunnilingus.

Sex Toy Tricks: More Than 125 Ways to Accessorize Good Sex by Jay Wiseman (Greenery Press, 1995). Sex toy tips.

Sexual Pleasure by Barbara Keesling (Hunter House, 1993). An excellent guide to using sensate focus exercises to solve common sexual dysfunctions, written by a former sex surrogate (previously *Sexual Healing*).

Talk Sexy to the One You Love by Barbara Keesling (HarperCollins Publishers, 1996). An exercise program that teaches you how to create and use an erotic vocabulary.

The Ten Commandments of Pleasure: Erotic Keys to a Healthy Sexual Life by Susan Block (St. Martin's Press, 1996). Advice from a popular radio and talk show personality on how to sexually satisfy yourself and a mate.

Tricks by Jay Wiseman (Greenery Press, 1993). Compendium of simple tips for "making good sex better."

Trust: The Hand Book by Bert Hermann (Alamo Square Press, 1991). The definitive guide to anal fisting.

The Ultimate Kiss by Jacqueline and Steve Franklin (Media Products, 1982). A guide to oral sex techniques illustrated with explicit photographs. Dated (no safer sex information), yet written with timeless enthusiasm.

The Ultimate Sex Guide by Anne Hooper (Dorling Kindersley, 1992). Contemporary heterosexual manual with color photographs. Sex-positive albeit somewhat sexist.

Eastern Sexual Techniques

The Art of Sexual Magic by Margo Anand (Jeremy P. Tarcher/Putnam, 1995). An accessible guide to Tantric lovemaking.

The Encyclopedia of Erotic Wisdom by Rufus Camphausen (Inner Traditions, 1991). Over one thousand cross-referenced entries related to esoteric and ancient sexual practices.

The Great Book of Tantra: Translations and Images from the Classic Indian Texts by Indra Sinha (Inner Traditions/Destiny Books, 1993). Reproductions of paintings and carvings depicting Tantric positions and deities accompanied by explanations of Tantra's symbolism.

The Illustrated Perfumed Garden adapted by Jan Hutchinson, Kirsty McKenzie and Ken Brass (HarperCollins Publishers, 1996). Modern adaptation of the classic sixteenth-century Arabian sex manual illustrated with color photographs of a heterosexual couple demonstrating sexual positions.

Sacred Sex: Ecstatic Techniques for Empowering Relationships by Jwala (Mandala, 1993). A Tantric sex guide.

Tao of Love and Sex: The Ancient Chinese Way to Ecstasy by Jolan Chang (Penguin Group/Arkana, 1991). A guide to the basic principles of Taoist sexual techniques, including how to control ejaculation and the distinction between ejaculation and orgasm in men.

The Yin-Yang Butterfly: Ancient Chinese Sexual Secrets for Western Lovers by Valentin Chu (Putnam/Jeremy P. Tarcher, 1993). An engaging historical overview of Taoist sexual traditions, including detailed techniques for modern lovers.

S/M and Power Play

The Bottoming Book by Catherina A. Liszt and Dossie Easton (Greenery Press, 1995). An illustrated guide to submission.

Coming to Power: Writings and Graphics on Lesbian S/M edited by SAMOIS (Alyson Publications, 1982). A groundbreaking collection of essays, erotica and fantasy related to lesbian S/M.

Consensual Sadomasochism: How To Talk About It and How To Do It Safely by Sybil Holiday and Bill Henkin (Daedalus, 1996). An expert guide to S/M.

Different Loving: An Exploration of the World of Sexual Dominance and Submission by Gloria Brame (Random House/Villard Books, 1993). In-depth interviews with over one hundred primarily heterosexual practitioners of S/M.

Kinky Crafts: 101 Do-It-Yourself S/M Toys edited by Lady Green (Greenery Press, 1995). A how-to book about creating your own S/M toys.

Learning the Ropes: A Basic Guide to Safe and Fun S/M Lovemaking by Race Bannon (Daedalus Publishing, 1992). A reassuring and informative how-to book for couples of all sexual orientations.

Leatherfolk: Radical Sex, People, Politics and Practice edited by Mark Thompson (Alyson Publications, 1991). A diverse and provocative collection of essays by some of the best writers in the gay and lesbian S/M community.

Leatherman's Handbook II, Updated Second Edition by Larry Townsend (Carlyle Communications, Ltd, 1989). A classic guide to S/M for gay men, including instructional information and erotic first-person accounts.

Lesbian S/M Safety Manual edited by Pat Califia (Lace Publications, 1988). A thorough guide to keeping S/M emotionally and physically safe, relevant to men and women of all sexual orientations.

The Loving Dominant by John Warren (Masquerade/Rhinoceros, 1994). A comprehensive guide to dominance and submission.

Miss Abernathy's Concise Slave Training Manual by Christina Abernathy (Greenery Press, 1996). A how-to of slave training.

The Original Leatherman's Handbook by Larry Townsend (LT Publications, 1977, reissued 1993). Of historical interest, describing the gay male leather community of the seventies.

The Second Coming edited by Pat Califia (Alyson Publications, 1996). A collection of essays, stories and fantasies (the follow-up to *Coming to Power*).

Sensuous Magic: A Guide for Adventurous Couples by Pat Califia (Masquerade Books, 1993). A nonthreatening, accessible guide to S/M for couples of all sexual orientations.

Sexual Magic: The S/M Photographs by Michael Rosen (Shaynew Press, 1986). Over fifty photographs of S/M play, accompanied by the subjects' personal reflections.

Sexual Portraits: Photographs of Radical Sexuality by Michael Rosen (Shaynew Press, 1990). Portraits of practitioners of body modification, bondage and S/M, accompanied by the subjects' personal reflections.

*The Sexually Dominant Woman: A Workbook for Nervous Beginner*s by Lady Green (Greenery Press,1992). A step-by-step guide to planning, negotiating and carrying out a female dominant S/M scene (geared toward heterosexuals).

SM 101: A Realistic Introduction by Jay Wiseman (Greenery Press, 1992). A thorough guide to S/M equipment and techniques, focusing on physical safety and geared toward heterosexuals.

Some Women edited by Laura Antoniou (Masquerade, 1995). A collection of writings from female practitioners of S/M.

The Topping Book by Catherine A. Liszt and Dossie Easton (Greenery Press, 1995). An illustrated guide to dominance.

Safer Sex

The Complete Guide to Safer Sex by staff of the Institute for the Advanced Study of Human Sexuality (Barricade Books, Inc, 1992). A valuable guide to learning healthy sexual behavior, with current information about the transmission and prevention of AIDS.

How to Persuade Your Lover to Use a Condom...And Why You Should by Patti Breitman, Kim Knutson and Paul Reed (Prima Publishing, 1994). An accessible, realistic guide to countering possible arguments against using a condom.

Lesbians Talk (Safer) Sex by Sue O'Sullivan and Pratibha Parmar (Scarlet Press, 1992). An even-handed presentation of the debates raging around safer sex guidelines for lesbians.

Safer Sexy: The Guide to Gay Sex Safely by Peter Tatchell (Cassell, 1994). Explicit color photographs illustrate this gay male sex guide.

Sex Facts

Advocate Advisor by Pat Califia (Alyson Publications, 1991). A collection of Pat's witty and wise advice columns addressing gay sexual etiquette.

Ask Me Anything by Marty Klein (Simon & Schuster/Fireside, 1992). A sex therapist presents reassuring, realistic answers to his clients' most frequently asked questions.

How They Do It by Robert Wallace (William Morrow, 1980). A highly entertaining guide to the mating habits of a variety of animal species.

The Kinsey Institute New Report on Sex by June Reinisch. (St. Martin's Press, 1990). An excellent reference guide to all aspects of human sexuality, loaded with interesting statistics and national survey results.

Let's Talk Sex by Isadora Alman (Crossing Press, 1993). Advice on meeting and mating by San Francisco's own "Ann Landers of Lust."

Sex Information, May I Help You? by Isadora Alman (Down There Press, 1984). A blend of sex education and fiction, chronicling the adventures of a group of volunteers who staff a sex information switchboard.

Sexual Slang: Words, Phrases and Idioms from AC/DC to Zig-Zag by Alan Richter. (HarperCollins Publishers, 1995). An edifying and entertaining reference book, compiled by a professional lexicographer.

Directories

The Black Book: The Guide for the Erotic Explorer edited by Bill Brent (Black Book/Amador Communications, 1996). A user-friendly, national directory of sex-related businesses and organizations, updated annually.

Safer Planet Sex: The Handbook by Tuppy Owens (self-published, 1994). An international guide to sex-related destinations and activities.

On-Line Guide Books

Erotic Connections: Love and Lust on the Information Superhighway by Billy Wildhack (Waite Group Press, 1994). Guide to sex on-line with an extensive listing of BBSs.

The Joy of Cybersex: An Underground Guide to Electronic Erotica by Phillip Robinson and Nancy Tamosaitis (Prentice Hall/Brady Publishing, 1993). Includes reviews of software, adult CD-ROMs and on-line bulletin boards.

Net.Sex: The Complete Guide to the Adult Side of the Internet by Candi Rose and Dirk Thomas (Sams Publishing, 1995). A guide to Usenet News groups, e-mail and downloading pictures.

The Penthouse Guide to Cybersex by Nancy Tamosaitis (Penthouse International, Ltd, 1995). A guide to on-line sex (an updated version of *The Joy of Cybersex*), packaged with a CD-ROM sampler.

Children/Teens/Parents

Changing Bodies, Changing Lives edited by Ruth Bell (Random House/Vintage Books, 1987). A comprehensive guide to puberty and adolescence written for fourteen to nineteen year olds and filled with quotes from teenagers.

How Sex Works by Elizabeth Fenwick and Richard Walker (Dorling Kindserly, 1994). A comprehensive, respectful guide for teens illustrated with color photographs.

It's Perfectly Normal: Changing Bodies, Growing Up, Sex and Sexual Health by Robie H. Harris (Candlewick Press, 1996). Sex-education book for seven to fourteen year olds, with cartoon illustrations.

A Kid's First Book about Sex by Joani Blank (Down There Press, 1983). A lively presentation of sex information for young children—one of the few books that discusses sexuality as distinct from reproduction. Illustrated.

The Period Book: Everything You Don't Want to Ask But Need to Know by Karen and Jennifer Gravelle (Walker Publishing Company, 1996). Information on the physical, emotional and social changes that accompany puberty, cowritten by a teenager.

The Playbook for Kids about Sex by Joani Blank (Down There Press, 1982). An interactive play/workbook that encourages sexual awareness in children (text is the same as in *A Kid's First Book about Sex*).

Talking with Your Child about Sex: Questions and Answers for Children from Birth to Puberty by Mary Calderone and James Ramey (Random House/Ballantine Books, 1982). Presents the questions children ask about sex along with practical answers for their parents.

Two Teenagers in Twenty: Writings by Gay and Lesbian Youth edited by Ann Heron (Alyson, 1994). A collection of essays (only some are about sex) by gay and lesbian teens.

What You Can Do to Avoid AIDS by Ervin "Magic" Johnson (Random House/Times Books, 1992). Inclusive and respectful in tone, this is the only explicit AIDS-prevention book geared specifically to teens.

What's Happening to My Body? Book for Boys; What's Happening to My Body? Book for Girls by Lynda Maderas (Newmarket Press, 1987). Written for pre-teens, these informative guides to the changes brought on by puberty are reassuring.

Older Adults

Love and Sex after Sixty by Robert Butler and Myrna Lewis (Ballantine, 1993). Good discussion of how aging affects sexual desire and lovemaking.

My Parents Never Had Sex: Myths and Facts about Sexual Aging by Doris Hammond (Prometheus Books, 1988). A discussion of how culture, religion and society have created certain stereotypes around sex and aging.

The Pause: Positive Approaches to Menopause by Lonnie Barbach (Penguin/Signet, 1994). Includes a good discussion of sexuality.

Sex Over 40 by Saul Rosenthal (Putnam/Jeremy P. Tarcher/Perigee Books, 1987). Information and practical advice on maintaining a satisfying sex life, focusing on the value of communication and experimentation.

Sexual Health in Later Life by Thomas Walz and Nancee Blum (DC Heath/Lexington Press, 1987). A sex-positive approach to maintaining sexual desire and staying sexually active despite the effects of aging or chronic illness.

The Time of Our Lives: Women Write on Sex after 40 edited by Dena Taylor and Amber Sumrall (Crossing Press, 1993). An anthology of prose and poetry from straight and lesbian contributors.

Transgendered

In Search of Eve: Transsexual Rites of Passage by Anne Bolin (Bergin & Garvey Publishers, 1988). An anthropological study of sixteen male-to-female transsexuals, accessible to laypeople as well as academics.

Information for the Female-to-Male Crossdresser and Transsexual by Lou Sullivan (Ingersoll Gender Center, 1990). A unique guide, including historical background, tips on "passing," information on hormone therapy and surgery.

Mirrors: Portraits of a Lesbian Transsexual by Geri Nettick with Beth Elliot (Masquerade/Rhinoceros, 1996). Biography of a male-to-female transsexual.

The Transsexual's Survival Guide: To Transition and Beyond by JoAnn Altman Stringer (Creative Design Services, 1990). Written by a transsexual woman, this thoughtful resource book deals with emotional, economic and legal issues.

The Transsexual's Survival Guide, Volume 2 by JoAnn Altman Stringer (Creative Design Services, 1992). Written by a transsexual woman.

Transvestites and Transsexuals: Toward a Theory of Cross-Gender Behavior by Richard F. Docter (Plenum Press, 1988). A respectful academic work based on ten years of sociological research.

The Uninvited Dilemma: A Question of Gender by Kim Elizabeth Stuart (Metamorphous Press, 1991). A well-researched, up-to-date work, featuring interviews with transsexuals.

Cultural Studies/Sexual Politics

Bi Any Other Name: Bisexual People Speak Out edited by Loraine Hutchins and Lani Kaahumanu (Alyson Publications, 1990). A collection of seventy bisexual coming-out stories.

Caught Looking: Feminism, Pornography and Censorship by the FACT Book Committee (Inland/LongRiver Books, 1988). A groundbreaking collection of essays by feminist writers challenging censorship, illustrated with sexually explicit art.

Dagger: On Butch Women edited by Lily Burana, Roxxie and Linnea Due (Cleis Press, 1994). Anthology of short stories and essays.

Defending Pornography: Free Speech, Sex and the Fight for Women's Rights by Nadine Strossen (Doubleday/Anchor, 1995). A feminist perspective on the dangers of censorship.

Disorders of Desire: Sex and Gender in Modern American Sexology by Janice Irvine (Temple University Press, 1990). Details the professional and political agendas that have shaped the evolution of the scientific study of sex.

An End to Shame: Shaping Our Next Sexual Revolution by Ira Reiss (Prometheus Books, 1990). A sociological indictment of the problems created by our sex-negative culture.

Erotic Impulse: Honoring the Sexual Self edited by David Steinberg (Putnam/Jeremy P. Tarcher/Perigee Books, 1992). A wide-ranging collection of writings on sexuality from noted novelists, poets, therapists and sexperts.

The Erotic Mind: Unlocking the Inner Sources of Sexual Passion and Fulfillment by Jack Morin (HarperCollins Publishers/Harper Perennial, 1995). Explains the four cornerstones of eroticism and teaches how to make sex more enjoyable. Also available in audiocassette.

Eyes of Desire: A Deaf Gay and Lesbian Reader edited by Raymond Luczak (Alyson Publications, 1993).

The Femme Mystique edited by Lesléa Newman (Alyson Publications, 1995). Short stories, essays and photographs of femmes.

Forbidden Passages: Writings Banned in Canada (Cleis Press, 1995). Fiction and nonfiction.

The Girl Wants To: Women's Representations of Sex and the Body edited by Lynn Crosbie (Coach House Press, 1994). Female artists and writers explore contemporary sexuality through fiction, poetry, song lyrics and comics.

Good Sex: Real Stories from Real People by Julia Hutton (Cleis Press, 1992). A fascinating collection of sexual oral histories from sixty diverse men and women.

Hard Core: Power, Pleasure and the Frenzy of the Invisible by Linda Williams (University of California Press, 1989). A provocative analysis of hard-core pornography written by a feminist film critic.

History Laid Bare: Love, Sex and Perversity from the Ancient Etruscans to Warren G. Harding by Richard Zacks (HarperCollins Publishers/Harper Perennial, 1995). A highly entertaining collection of sex trivia and history.

Intimate Matters: A History of Sexuality in America by John D'Emilio and Estelle B. Freedman (Harper Perennial, 1988). Three hundred years of American sexual mores.

Men Confront Pornography edited by Michael Kimmel (New American Library/Dutton, 1990). A collection of essays from men with wide-ranging attitudes toward pornography.

Mystery Dance: On the Evolution of Human Sexuality by Lynn Margulis and Dorion Sagan (Simon & Schuster/Touchstone, 1992). Biology, genetics and psychology are woven together in this explanation of the evolution of human sexuality.

Pleasure and Danger: Exploring Female Sexuality edited by Carole S. Vance (Routledge & Kegan Paul, 1990). A seminal text of the "feminist sex wars" containing papers presented at a controversial 1982 feminist conference.

Post Porn Modernist by Annie Sprinkle (Art Unlimited, 1993). Annie chronicles her career in massage parlors, adult films and performance art in a book that is part autobiography, part photo album.

The Prehistory of Sex: Four Million Years of Human Sexual Culture by Timothy Taylor (Bantam Doubleday Dell, 1996). Attempts to decipher the mystery of Stone Age sex.

Public Sex: The Culture of Radical Sex by Pat Califia (Cleis Press, 1994). Pat's collected essays on pornography, S/M, sexual repression, and other topics.

Red Light: Inside the Sex Industry by Sylvia Plachy and James Ridgeway (Powerhouse Books, 1996). Interviews with male and female American sex industry workers.

Sex and the Bible by Gerald Larue (Prometheus Books, 1983). An explanation of biblical texts relating to sex and the somewhat arbitrary ways these texts have been interpreted.

Sex in History by Reay Tannahill (Scarborough House, 1992). An engaging exploration of sexual attitudes and practices in the major world civilizations from prehistoric times up to the present day.

Sex Work: Writings by Women in the Sex Industry edited by Frédérique Delacoste and Priscilla Alexander (Cleis Press, 1987). A candid and provocative collection of writings by female sex workers.

Sex: Real People Talk about What They Really Do by Harry Maurer (Penguin, 1994). A compilation of a wide range of personal sex histories (previously titled *Sex: An Oral History*). Also available as an audiocassette (Passion Press).

Susie Bright's Sexual Reality: A Virtual Sex World Reader by Susie Bright (Cleis Press, 1992). A collection of insightful essays on everything from sex during pregnancy to being a panelist on *Donahue*.

Susie Bright's Sexual State of the Union by Susie Bright (Simon & Schuster, 1997). Essays on sex and pop culture.

Susie Bright's Sexwise by Susie Bright (Cleis Press, 1995). A collection of essays, interviews and reviews.

Susie Sexpert's Lesbian Sex World by Susie Bright (Cleis Press, 1990). A witty, irreverent collection of Susie's "Toys for Us" columns from *On Our Backs* magazine.

Sweet Talkers by Kathleen K. (Masquerade/Richard Kasak, 1994). A peek into the phone-sex industry.

Talk Dirty to Me: An Intimate Philosophy of Sex by Sallie Tisdale (Bantam Doubleday Dell/Anchor, 1994). An exploration of pornography.

Vice Versa: Bisexuality and the Eroticism of Everyday Life by Majorie Garber (Simon & Schuster/Touchstone, 1995). A provocative exploration of sexual identity.

Wild Women Don't Wear No Blues: Black Women Writers on Love, Men and Sex edited by Marita Golden (Anchor Books, 1994). A collection of essays.

Women of the Light: The New Sacred Prostitute edited by Kenneth Ray Stubbs (Secret Garden, 1994). Nine sex workers offer special insight into the spiritual and healing aspects of their work.

Books about Videos

Coming Attractions: The Making of an X-Rated Video by Robert J. Stoller and I.S. Levine (Yale University Press, 1993). A nonjudgmental account, featuring interviews with cast and crew.

Only the Best: Jim Holliday's Adult Video Almanac and Trivia Treasury by Jim Holliday (Cal Vista International, 1986). Comprehensive and thoughtful reviews from an insightful porn reviewer.

Porn: Myths for the Twentieth Century by Robert J. Stoller (Yale University Press, 1991). Candid interviews with twelve actors and directors in the porn business.

Video Sex: Create Erotic and Romantic Home Videos with Your Camcorder by Kevin Campbell (Amherst Media, 1994). A guide to do-it-yourself erotic home movies.

X-Rated Videotape Guides, Volumes 1, 2, 3, 4 and 5 edited by Robert Rimmer and Patrick Riley (Prometheus Books, 1986, 1991, 1993, 1994, 1995). Reviews, plot summaries and lists of X-rated movies from the late-seventies to the present.

Fiction

Woman-Authored

Alida: An Erotic Novel by Edna MacBrayne (Parkhurst Press, 1981). The erotic adventures of an older woman.

Black Satin by Joan Elizabeth Lloyd (Carroll & Graf, 1995). Novel.

Deep Down: The New Sensual Writing by Women edited by Laura Chester (Faber and Faber, 1988). Short story anthology.

Erotic Interludes: Women Write Erotica edited by Lonnie Barbach (Harper Perennial, 1986). Short story anthology.

Fever edited by Michele Slung (Harper Perennial, 1994). Short story anthology.

Ladies Own Erotica by The Kensington Ladies Erotica Society (Simon & Schuster/Pocket Books, 1984). Short story anthology.

Look Homeward Erotica by The Kensington Ladies Erotica Society (Ten Speed Press, 1986). Short story anthology.

Pleasures: Women Write Erotica edited by Lonnie Barbach (Harper Perennial, 1984). Short story anthology.

The Pleasures of Jessica Lynn by Joan Elizabeth Lloyd (Carroll & Graf, 1996). Novel.

Slow Hand: Women Write Erotica edited by Michele Slung (HarperCollins Publishers, 1992).

Touching Fire: Erotic Writings by Women edited by Louise Thorton, Jan Sturtevant and Amber Sumrall (Carroll & Graf, 1989). Short story anthology.

Lesbian

Afterglow: More Stories of Lesbian Desire edited by Karen Barber (Alyson Publications, 1993). Short story anthology.

Behind Closed Doors by Robbi Sommers (Naiad Press, 1993). Short story collection.

Breathless by Kitti Tsui (Firebrand, 1996). Short story collection.

Bushfire: Stories of Lesbian Desire edited by Karen Barber (Alyson Publications, 1991). Short story anthology.

Getting There by Robbi Sommers (Naiad, 1995). Short story collection.

Getting Wet: Tales of Lesbian Seduction edited by Carol Allain (Women's Press, 1992). Short story anthology.

Heatwave: Women in Love and Lust edited by Lucy Jane Bledsoe (Alyson Publications, 1995). Short story anthology.

Hog Heaven: Erotic Lesbian Stories by Caressa French (Crossing Press, 1994). Short story collection.

Kiss and Tell by Robbi Sommers (Naiad Press, 1993). Short story collection.

More Serious Pleasures: Lesbian Erotic Stories and Poetry edited by the Sheba Collective (Cleis Press, 1991). Short story and poetry anthology.

A Movement of Eros: 25 Years of Lesbian Erotica edited by Heather Findlay (Masquerade/Richard Kasak, 1996). Short story anthology.

Once Upon a Time: Erotic Tales for Women edited by Michael Ford (Masquerade/Richard Kasak, 1996). Short story anthology.

Riding Desire: An Anthology of Erotic Writing edited by Tee Corinne (Banned Books, 1991). Short story anthology.

The Rosebud Sutra by Valentin Cilescu (Masquerade/Rosebud, 1994). Novel.

Players by Robbi Sommers (Naiad Press, 1990). Novel.

Provincetown Summer by Lindsay Welsh (Masquerade/Rosebud, 1992). Short story collection.

Serious Pleasure: Lesbian Erotic Stories and Poetry edited by the Sheba Collective (Cleis Press, 1991). Short story and poetry anthology.

Tangled Sheets: Stories and Poems of Lesbian Lust edited by Rosamund Elwin and Karen X. Tulchinsky (Women's Press, 1995). Short story anthology.

Virgin Territory edited by Shar Rednour (Masquerade/Richard Kasak, 1995). Short story anthology.

Virgin Territory 2 edited by Shar Rednour (Masquerade/Richard Kasak, 1997). Short story anthology.

Gay Men

2069 Trilogy: *2060, 2069 + 1, 2069 + 2* by Larry Townsend (Masquerade/Badboy, 1995). Science fiction novels.

The Badboy Erotic Library, Volumes 1 and 2, edited by Michael Lowenthal (Masquerade/Badboy, 1995, 1994 respectively). Short story anthologies.

The Best of the Badboys edited by Michael Lowenthal (Masquerade/Richard Kasak, 1995). Short story anthology.

Executive Privileges by Sutter Powell (Masquerade/Badboy, 1996). Short story collection.

Happily Ever After: Erotic Tales for Men edited by Michael Ford (Masquerade/Richard Kasak, 1996). Short story anthology.

Hot Living: Erotic Stories About Safer Sex edited by John Preston (Alyson Publications, 1985). Short story anthology.

Mad Man by Samuel Delaney (Masquerade/Richard Kasak, 1994). Novel.

Mr. Benson by John Preston (Masquerade/Badboy, 1992). Novel with S/M theme.

The Scarlet Pansy by Anonymous (Masquerade/Badboy, 1994). Novel.

Tales of the Dark Lord by John Preston (Masquerade/Badboy, 1992). Short story collection.

Wired Hard: Erotica for a Gay Universe edited by Cecilia Tan (Circlet Press, 1994). Short story anthology.

Smut

Autobiography of a Flea by Anonymous (Carroll & Graf, 1983). Novel.

The Best of the Erotic Reader (Carroll & Graf, 1996). Short story anthology.

The Captive Flesh by Cleo Cordell (Black Lace, 1993). Novel.

Carrie's Story by Molly Weatherfield (Masquerade, 1995). Novel.

Emmanuelle by Emmanuelle Arsan (Grove Press, 1971). Novel.

Erotic Reader: Collections of Previously Banned Fiction, Volumes 1-5 (Carroll & Graf, 1988-1993).

Fanny Hill by Anonymous (Carroll & Graf, 1990). Novel.

Healing Passion by Portia Da Costa (Black Lace, 1995). Novel.

The Pearl (Random House/Ballantine, 1996). Short story anthology.

Romance of Lust by Anne-Marie Villefranche (Carroll & Graf, 1995). Short story anthology.

Scandale d'Amour by Anne-Marie Villefranche (Carroll & Graf, 1995). Two novels.

Souvenir d'Amour by Anne-Marie Villefranche (Carroll & Graf, 1995). Short story collection.

Multicultural

Erotique Noire: Black Erotica edited by Miriam DeCosta Willis, Reginald Martin, Rose Ann Bell (Doubleday/Anchor, 1992). Short story anthology.

The Mammoth Book of Erotica edited by Maxim Jakubowski (Carroll & Graf, 1994). Short story anthology.

The Mammoth Book of International Erotica edited by Maxim Jakubowski (Carroll & Graf, 1996). Short story anthology.

On a Bed of Rice: An Asian American Erotic Feast edited by Geraldine Kudaka (Bantam Doubleday Dell, 1995).

Pleasure in the Word: Erotic Writing by Latin American Women edited by Margarite Fernandez (White Pine, 1993). Short story anthology.

Speaking in Whispers: African American Lesbian Erotica by Kathleen E. Morris (Third Side Press, 1996). Short story collection.

Under the Pomegranate Tree: The Best New Latino Erotica edited by Ray Gonzalez (Simon & Schuster/ Washington Square Press, 1996). Short story anthology.

European

The Ages of Lulu by Almudena Grandes (Grove Press, 1994). Novel.

Behind Closed Doors by Alina Reyes (Grove Press, 1996). Novel.

The Butcher by Alina Reyes (Grove Press, 1995). Novel.

Philosophy in the Boudoir by The Marquis de Sade (Creation Books/Velvet, 1795). Novel.

The Pleasure Chateau by Jeremy Reed (Creation Books/Velvet, 1994). Novel.

The She Devils by Pierre Louys (Creation Books/Velvet, 1995). Novel.

The Whip Angels by Anonymous (Creation Books/Velvet, 1995). Novel.

Series

Best American Erotica 1993 edited by Susie Bright (Macmillan, 1993). Short story anthology.

Best American Erotica 1994 edited by Susie Bright (Simon & Schuster/Touchstone, 1994). Short story anthology.

Best American Erotica 1995 edited by Susie Bright (Simon & Schuster/Touchstone, 1995). Short story anthology.

Best American Erotica 1996 edited by Susie Bright (Simon & Schuster/Touchstone, 1996). Short story anthology.

Best Gay Erotica 1996 edited by Michael Ford, selected by Scott Heim (Cleis Press, 1996). Short story anthology.

Best Gay Erotica 1997 edited by Richard Labonté, selected by Douglas Sadownick (Cleis Press, 1997). Short story anthology.

Best Lesbian Erotica 1996 edited by Tristan Taormino, selected by Heather Lewis (Cleis Press, 1996). Short story anthology.

Best Lesbian Erotica 1997 edited by Tristan Taormino, selected by Jewelle Gomez (Cleis Press, 1997). Short story anthology.

Flesh and the Word: An Anthology of Gay Erotic Writing edited by John Preston (New American Library/Plume, 1992). Short story anthology.

Flesh and the Word 2: An Anthology of Gay Erotic Writing edited by John Preston (New American Library/Plume, 1993). Short story anthology.

Flesh and the Word 3: An Anthology of Gay Erotic Writing edited by John Preston and Michael Lowenthal (Penguin/Plume, 1995). Short story anthology.

Herotica: A Collection of Women's Erotic Fiction edited by Susie Bright (Down There Press, 1988). Short story anthology.

Herotica 2: A Collection of Women's Erotic Fiction edited by Susie Bright and Joani Blank (New American Library/Plume, 1992). Short story anthology.

Herotica 3 edited by Susie Bright (Penguin/Plume, 1994). Short story anthology.

Herotica 4 edited by Marcy Sheiner (Penguin/Plume, 1995). Short story anthology.

Herotica 5 edited by Marcy Sheiner (Penguin/Plume, 1996). Short story anthology.

Herotica 6 edited by Marcy Sheiner (Penguin/Plume, 1997). Short story anthology.

Science Fiction & Futuristic

Alien Sex edited by Ellen Datlow (Penguin, 1990). Short story anthology.

Feline Fetishes: Erotic Tales of Science Fiction edited by Corwin (Circlet Press, 1993).

Forged Bonds: Erotic Tales of High Fantasy edited by Cecilia Tan (Circlet Press, 1993).

Mate by Lauren Burka (Circlet Press, 1992). Short story anthology with S/M theme.

Off Limits: Tales of Alien Sex edited by Ellen Datlow (St. Martin's Press, 1996). Short story anthology.

Selling Venus: Futuristic Tales of the Age-Old Tradition of Exchanging Sex for Money edited by Cecilia Tan (Circlet Press, 1995). Short story anthology.

Telepaths Don't Need Safe Words by Cecilia Tan (Circlet Press, 1992). Short story anthology with S/M theme.

Gothic

Blood Kiss: Vampire Erotica edited by Cecilia Tan. (Circlet Press, 1994) Short story anthology.

Daughters of Darkness: Lesbian Vampire Stories edited by Pam Keesey (Cleis Press, 1993). Short story anthology.

Erotica Vampirica edited by Cecilia Tan (Circlet Press, 1996). Short story anthology.

Sons of Darkness: Tales of Men, Blood and Immortality edited by Michael Rowe and Thomas Roche (Cleis Press, 1996). Short story anthology.

Women Who Run with the Werewolves: Tales of Blood, Lust and Metamorphosis edited by Pam Keesey (Cleis Press, 1996). Short story anthology.

S/M, Power Play

By Her Subdued by Laura Antoniou (Masquerade/Rhinoceros, 1995). Novel.

The Catalyst by Sara Adamson (Masquerade, 1992). Novel.

Doing It for Daddy edited by Pat Califia (Alyson Publications, 1995). Short story anthology.

Exit to Eden by Anne Rice (Random House/Ballantine, 1985). Novel.

The Heir and *The King* by John Preston (Masquerade, 1992). Two novellas.

Leatherwomen edited by Laura Antoniou (Masquerade, 1993). Short story anthology.

Leatherwomen 2 edited by Laura Antoniou (Masquerade, 1995). Short story anthology.

Macho Sluts by Pat Califia (Alyson Publications, 1988). Short story collection.

The Marketplace Trilogy: *The Marketplace, The Slave, The Trainer* by Sara Adamson (Masquerade/Rhinoceros, 1993, 1994, 1995 respectively). Erotic novels.

Meeting the Master: Stories of Mastery, Slavery and the Darker Side of Desire by Elissa Wald (Crown Publishers, 1995). Short story collection.

Melting Point by Pat Califia (Alyson Publications, 1993). Short story collection.

The Sleeping Beauty Trilogy: *Claiming of Sleeping Beauty, Beauty's Punishment, Beauty's Release* by Anne Rice writing as A. N. Roquelaure (New American Library/Plume, 1983, 1984, 1985 respectively). Novels.

S/M Futures edited by Cecilia Tan (Circlet Press, 1995). Short story anthology.

S/M Pasts edited by Cecilia Tan (Circlet Press, 1994). Short story anthology.

S/M Visions: The Best of Circlet Press edited by Cecilia Tan (Circlet Press, 1995). Short story anthology.

Story of O by Pauline Reage (Ballantine, 1973). Novel with S/M theme.

Literary and Historical

The Book of Eros: Arts and Letters from Yellow Silk edited by Lily Pond and Richard Russo (Random House/Crown Publishers, 1995). Short story anthology.

Coming Up: The World's Best Erotic Writing edited by Michael Perkins (Masquerade/Richard Kasak, 1996). Short story anthology.

Erotic Literature: Twenty-Four Centuries of Sensual Writing edited by Jane Mills (HarperCollins Publishers, 1993). Short story anthology.

Erotica: Women's Writing from Sappho to Margaret Atwood edited by Margaret Reynolds (Fawcett, 1990). Short story anthology.

The Literary Lover: Great Contemporary Stories of Passion and Romance edited by Larry Dark (Viking, 1993). Short story anthology.

The New Olympia Reader edited by Maurice Girodias (Blue Moon, 1993). Short story anthology, originally published in 1970.

The Penguin Book of Erotic Stories by Women edited by Richard Jones and Susan Williams (Penguin, 1995). Short story anthology.

Yellow Silk: Erotic Arts and Letters edited by Lily Pond and Richard Russo (Random House, 1990). Short stories and art from the magazine, *Yellow Silk*.

Uncategorizable

Erotic Edge: Erotica for Couples edited by Lonnie Barbach (Penguin/Dutton, 1994). Short story anthology.

Fermata by Nicholson Baker (Random House, 1994). Novel.

The Field Guide to Outdoor Erotica edited by Rob Moore (Solstice Press, 1988). Short story anthology about sex outdoors.

Noirotica: An Anthology of Erotic Crime Stories edited by Thomas Roche (Masquerade/Rhinoceros, 1996). Short story anthology.

On the Wings of Eros: Nightly Readings for Passion and Romance edited by Alicia Alvarez (Conari Press, 1995). Short story anthology.

The Sex Box: Man, Sex, Woman (Chronicle Books, 1996). Short story anthology.

Switch Hitters: Lesbians Write Gay Male Erotica and Gay Men Write Lesbian Erotica edited by Carol Queen and Lawrence Schimel (Cleis Press, 1995). Short story anthology.

Unmade Bed: Sensual Writing on Married Love edited by Laura Chester (HarperCollins Publishers, 1992). Short story anthology.

Vox by Nicholson Baker (Random House, 1992). Novel about phone sex.

American Masters

Henry Miller
Tropic of Cancer by Henry Miller (Grove, 1961). Novel.

Tropic of Capricorn by Henry Miller (Grove, 1961). Novel.

Anaïs Nin
Delta of Venus by Anaïs Nin (Simon & Schuster/ Pocket Books, 1979). Short story collection.

Little Birds by Anaïs Nin (Simon & Schuster/Pocket Books, 1986). Short story collection.

Marco Vassi
The Vassi Collection, Volumes 1-10 by Marco Vassi (Second Chance Press, 1993). A series of ten erotic novels.

Erotic Comedies by Marco Vassi (Masquerade, 1994). Short story collection.

Audio Erotica

The Butcher by Alina Reyes (Passion Press, 1995).

Cyborgasm: Erotica in 3-D Sound (Time Warner, 1993). Virtual 3-D audio on CD or cassette.

Cyborgasm 2: The Edge of the Bed (Time Warner, 1995). Virtual 3-D audio on CD or cassette.

Erotic Edge edited by Lonnie Barbach (Passion Press, 1995).

The Erotic Reader: Selected Excerpts from Banned Books (Passion Press, 1995).

Exit to Eden by Anne Rice (Random House, 1992).

Fermata by Nicholson Baker (Random House, 1995).

Herotica edited by Susie Bright (Passion Press, 1995).

Herotica 2 edited by Susie Bright and Joani Blank (Passion Press, 1996).

The Pearl: An Erotic Classic (Clivia Publishing, 1993).

The Pearl: Lady Pokingham (Clivia Publishing, 1993).

The Pearl: My Grandmother's Tale (Clivia Publishing, 1995).

The Sleeping Beauty Trilogy: *Claiming of Sleeping Beauty, Beauty's Punishment, Beauty's Release* by Anne Rice (Simon & Schuster, 1995).

Triple Passion: Fanny Hill, Fanny Hill's Daughter, Lady Chatterly's Lover (Passion Press, 1995).

Art

Fine Art Collections

The Art of Arousal by Dr. Ruth Westheimer (Abbeville Press, 1993).

Birds and Bees edited by Dugald Stermer (Harper-Collins Publishers, 1995).

Erotic Art by Drs. Phyllis and Eberhard Kronhausen (Carroll & Graf, 1993).

Erotic Art by Living Artists, Volumes 1 & 2 (Artnetwork, 1988 and 1992).

Erotic Art: From the 17th to the 20th Century edited by Peter Weiermair (Taschen, 1995).

Erotica, An Illustrated Anthology of Sexual Art and Literature, Volumes 1, 2 & 3 edited by Charlotte Hill and William Wallace (Carroll & Graf, 1992, 1993, 1996).

Erotica Universalis edited by Giles Neret (Taschen, 1995).

Folk Erotica: Celebrating Centuries of Erotic Americana edited by Milton Simpson (HarperCollins Publishers, 1994).

I Modi: An Erotic Album of the Italian Renaissance edited by Lynne Lawner (Northwestern University Press, 1989).

Let Them Eat Cheesecake: The Art of Olivia by Olivia de Beradinis (Ozone, 1993).

May I Feel Said He poem by ee cummings and paintings by Marc Chagall (Stewart, Tabori and Chang, 1995).

Patterns of Desire by Joyce Kozloff (Hudson Hills, 1990).

Plaisirs D' Amour: An Erotic Guide to the Senses by Elizabeth Nash (HarperCollins Publishers, 1995).

Silent Orgasm (Taschen, 1995).

Voluptario by Carlos Fuentes and Brian Nissen (St. Martin's Press, 1996).

Pillow Books

The Erotic Sentiment in the Paintings of China and Japan edited by Nik Douglas and Penny Slinger (Inner Traditions, 1990).

The Erotic Sentiment in the Paintings of India and Nepal edited by Nik Douglas and Penny Slinger (Inner Traditions, 1989).

Gay Pillow Book (HarperCollins Publishers, 1995).

The Illustrated Kama Sutra translated by Sir Richard Burton (Inner Traditions, 1991).

Japanese Art of Love (HarperCollins Publishers, 1994).

Kama Sutra Pillow Book (HarperCollins Publishers, 1994).

Lesbian Pillow Book (HarperCollins Publishers, 1995).

The Perfumed Garden translated by Sir Richard Burton (Inner Traditions, 1989).

Photography

Among Women by Tom Bianchi (St. Martin's Press, 1996).

Bizarre (Taschen, 1995).

The Body: Photographs of the Human Form edited by William Ewing (Chronicle Books, 1994).

Body Alchemy: Transsexual Portraits by Loren Cameron (Cleis Press, 1996).

Body and Soul: Black Erotica edited by Rundu Staggers (Crown Publishers, 1996).

Bunny's Honeys: Bunny Yeager, Queen of Pin-Up Photography (Taschen, 1994).

Dirty Windows by Merry Alpern (DAP, 1995).

Doris Kloster (Taschen, 1996).

Drawing the Line by Kiss and Tell (Press Gang, 1991).

Early Erotic Photography edited by Serge Nazarieff (Taschen, 1993).

Ebony Erotica (California Exotic Novelties, 1996).

Elmer Batters: From the Tips of the Toes to the Top of the Hoes (Taschen, 1996).

Eric Kroll's Beauty Parade (Taschen, 1996).

Eros (Stewart, Tabori and Chang, 1996).

Erotic By Nature edited by David Steinberg (Red Alder and Down There Press, 1988).

Femalia edited by Joani Blank (Down There Press, 1993).

Fetish Girls by Eric Kroll (Taschen, 1994).

Her Tongue on My Theory: Essays and Fantasies by Kiss and Tell (Kiss and Tell, 1994).

Jan Saudek: Life, Love, Death and Other Such Trifles by Jan Saudek (Art Unlimited, 1991).

Jeux de Dames Cruelle: 1850-1960 edited by Serge Nazarieff (Taschen, 1992).

Lesbian Sacred Sexuality edited by Diane Mariechild and Marcelina Martin (Wingbow Press, 1995).

LoveBites by Della Grace (GMP, 1991).

Lust: The Body Politic (Advocate, 1991).

Male Nudes by Women edited by Peter Weiermair (DAP, 1995).

Men/Women by Herb Ritts (Twin Palms, 1989).

Nothing But the Girl: The Blatant Lesbian Image edited by Susie Bright and Jill Posener (Cassell, 1996).

Nudes edited by B. Martin Pederson (Watson, 1996).

One Thousand Nudes edited by Michael Koetzle (Taschen, 1995).

Robert Mapplethorpe edited by Richard Marshall (Little, Brown and Company, 1988).

Secret: Fetish Photo Anthology edited by Jürgen Boedt (Glitter, 1996).

Sexual Art: Photographs That Test the Limits by Michael Rosen (Shaynew Press, 1994).

Wheels and Curves: Erotic Photographs of the Twenties edited by W. Honscheidt (Taschen, 1995).

Women En Large: Images of Fat Nudes edited by Laurie Edison and Debbie Notkin (Focus Books, 1994).

Videography

Thanks to Susie Bright for introducing us to many of the following videos.

Erotic Classics of the Seventies and Eighties

3 A.M. directed by Robert McCallum (Cal Vista, 1976). A great erotic tragedy with superior acting.

Autobiography of a Flea directed by Sharon McNight and the Mitchell Brothers (1976). A wonderfully naughty Victorian romp.

Behind the Green Door directed by the Mitchell Brothers (1972). Marilyn Chambers is spirited away from humdrum reality to live out her fantasies.

BiCoastal (Catalina, 1984). One of the few videos with a genuine bisexual perspective and sensitivity.

Cafe Flesh directed by Rinse Dream (VCA, 1982). Cafe Flesh presents a post-apocalyptic world divided between sex positives who are forced to perform for sex negatives.

Devil in Miss Jones directed by Gerard Damiano (VCA, 1972). Thought-provoking and arousing, with excellent performances.

Every Woman Has a Fantasy directed by Edwin Brown (VCA, 1984). John Leslie portrays a husband who dresses in drag to eavesdrop on his wife and her friends as they recount their sexual fantasies.

Felines directed by Daniel Daert (VCX, 1975). A French classic in which a bored wife seduces her husband away from his mistress with the help of a female houseguest.

Great Sexpectations (VCA, 1984). The career of a porn director is the center of this comedy.

Insatiable directed by Godfrey Daniels (Caballero, 1980). Marilyn Chambers as a woman with a voracious sexual appetite.

Nightdreams directed by Rinse Dream (Caballero, 1981). A surreal presentation of one woman's erotic delusions.

Other Side of Julie directed by Anthony Riverton (Cal Vista, 1978). When Julie discovers her husband, played by John Leslie, is earning their living as a gigolo, she decides to assert her own sexuality.

Outlaw Ladies directed by Henri Pachard (VCA, 1981). Five women aggressively pursue (and achieve) sexual satisfaction over the course of a day.

Platinum Paradise directed by Cecil Howard (Command, 1980). A day in the life of an escort, featuring Vanessa del Rio.

Playgirl directed by Roberta Findlay (Video-X-Pix, 1982). Veronica Hart as a female Don Juan.

Roommates directed by Chuck Vincent (Video-X-Pix, 1982). Samantha Fox, Kelly Nichols and Veronica Hart are the roommates whose sexual experiences run the gamut in this well-produced, thoughtful drama.

Talk Dirty to Me (Caballero, 1980) and *Nothing to Hide* (Cal Vista, 1981) directed by Anthony Spinelli. John Leslie and Richard Pacheco star in two buddy films loaded with sex and realistic relationships.

Tigresses (Video-X-Pix, 1979). Vanessa Del Rio and her girlfriends indulge their voracious sexual appetites in a film with a fantastic orgy finale.

V-The Hot One directed by Robert McCallum (Cal Vista, 1978). Wife/prostitute Annette Haven and husband/pimp John Leslie pull no punches in their tension-filled sex scenes.

Compilations

Compilation tapes are anthologies of memorable sex scenes from different movies. The videos listed here were all compiled by porn historian Jim Holliday.

Legends of Porn (Cal Vista, 1987). Scenes featuring X-rated celebrities such as Marilyn Chambers and John Holmes.

Love Scenes for Loving Couples (Cal Vista, 1988). Scenes of sex between heterosexual couples.

Only the Best Volume 1 (Cal Vista, 1986); *Only the Best Volume 2* (Cal Vista, 1989); *Only the Best Volume 3* (Cal Vista, 1990). Superior sex scenes from mainstream porn of the seventies and eighties (*Volume 3* includes clips from classic stag films).

Only the Best from Europe (Cal Vista, 1989). Superior sex scenes from European porn.

Only the Very Best on Film (VCA, 1993). Scenes from recent movies shot on film rather than video.

True Legends of Adult Cinema: Cult Superstars (VCA, 1993). More legendary performances from X-rated celebrities.

True Legends of Adult Cinema: The Erotic Eighties (VCA, 1993). Features the decade's greatest stars including Nina Hartley, Ginger Lynn and Barbara Dare.

True Legends of Adult Cinema: Unsung Superstars (VCA, 1993). Memorable performances from lesser-known actors and actresses.

Notable Directors of the Nineties

ANDREW BLAKE

Director Andrew Blake has won many fans with his glossy, stylized videos, all of which are notable for high production values, attractive performers, and minimal plots.

Desire (VCA, 1994). Beautiful people frolic among priceless art pieces in a West L.A. art gallery.

Femmes Erotiques (Studio A Entertainment, 1993). A visual treat featuring stylish fetish wear and futuristic sex toys.

Hidden Obsessions (BlueFrame Films, 1993). An erotic writer begins to explore her own fantasies.

House of Dreams (Caballero, 1990). Zara White is a woman compelled to act out her masturbation fantasies.

Night Trips 1 (Caballero, 1989). Tori Wells is a woman having trouble sleeping due to her exhausting erotic dreams.

Night Trips 2 (Caballero, 1990). A sex-obsessed woman allows her doctor access to her erotic dreams.

Secrets (Caballero, 1990). Ashlyn Gere is a Beverly Hills madam.

Sensual Exposure (Studio A Entertainment, 1993). A mistress-in-training is taken to the Manor House to learn her lessons.

PAUL THOMAS

Director Paul Thomas delivers satisfying plots, elicits strong performances and dedicates plenty of screen time to authentic female orgasms in some of the most compelling videos in the industry today.

Borderline (Vivid, 1995). Explores infidelity and betrayal in the tale of two-timing lovers in a small Mexican border town.

Justine: Nothing to Hide 2 (Cal Vista, 1994). An insatiable young woman, portrayed by the explosive Roxanne Blaze, unwittingly seduces her boyfriend's father. Winner of eight *Adult Video News* awards.

Lunachick (Vivid, 1996). Lust for revenge consumes therapist Tyffany Million when she discovers a female client has fallen for her boyfriend.

The Masseuse (Vivid, 1990). The unpredictable story of a masseuse whose virgin client persuades her to initiate him sexually, starring Hypatia Lee and Randy Spears.

The Swap 2 (Vivid, 1994). Two couples experiment with swinging in this witty, well-acted comedy about monogamy and its discontents.

Things Change: My First Time (Cal Vista, 1993) and *Things Change: Letting Go* (Cal Vista, 1993). Deidre Holland is the deliciously dominant lesbian whose girlfriend, portrayed by Nikki Dial, decides to experiment with men in this sensitive exploration of sexual discovery.

JOHN LESLIE

Director John Leslie's films aren't for the hearts-and-flowers crowd, but they deliver strong plots, tight editing and athletic, nasty sex between the hottest performers in the business.

Anything That Moves (VCA, 1992). The tale of two strippers who are best friends.

Bad Habits (VCA, 1994). Deidre Holland stands out in a film filled with scorching performances portraying a writer who can't kick the habit of anonymous sex.

Chameleons (Not the Sequel) (VCA, 1992). Deidre Holland and Ashlyn Gere star as a pair of form-shifting aliens in what many critics consider to be John Leslie's best film ever.

Dog Walker (Evil Angel Video, 1994). A lush, stylized drama about a disillusioned thief trying to sever his ties to the underworld.

Sexophrenia (VCA, 1993). This funny, dark and dirty film is set in a future dystopia where the only people who still have sex are society's rejects.

TYFFANY MILLION

Tyffany Million, whose high-octane sexual performances light up every video she's in, currently runs the only woman-owned and -operated production company in mainstream adult film—Immaculate Video Conceptions.

Dirty Little Mind directed by Jean-Pierre Ferrand (Immaculate Video Conceptions, 1995). Tyffany reveals her creative fantasies, which include a simmering anal rimming scene with Sean Michaels.

Generally Horny Hospital (Immaculate Video Conceptions, 1995). This genuinely funny soap opera spoof features Tyffany as Dr. Juicelyn Udders, Surgeon General.

I Touch Myself (Immaculate Video Conceptions, 1994). Six porn actresses explicitly detail their fantasies and reveal their favorite ways to maturbate.

Jailhouse Cock directed by Jean-Pierre Ferrand and Tyffany Million (Immaculate Video Conceptions, 1994). A raunchy, irreverent comedy about sexually rapacious female prison guards who terrorize their male inmates.

Mind Games (Immaculate Video Conceptions, 1995). Tyffany's a frustrated writer drawn into the sexual fantasies she overhears from the office next door.

ERNEST GREENE

Ernest Greene directs the Twist line of fetish and S/M films distributed by Ona Zee Productions. Explicit genital contact is rarely shown in films that also depict bondage and discipline, as producers fear legal repercussions, but these stylish videos of erotic power play generate plenty of heat.

Contract for Service (1994). Vanilla and leather sex are skillfully integrated by an all-female cast.

Lydia's Web (1994). This lesbian dungeon romp features sincere performances and exquisite fetish gear.

Prison World (1994). A mean prison warden tortures her female flock with a firm but loving hand.

Trained by Payne (1995). An inexperienced female bottom is given personal attention courtesy of the exacting Mistress Payne.

Notable Videos of the Nineties

Blue Movie directed by Michael Zen (Wicked, 1995). This film within a film spoofs the porn industry and features Jenna Jameson as a tabloid reporter determined to get the scoop on a cross-dressing porn director.

Deep Inside Nina Hartley (VCA, 1993). Our favorite feminist porn star introduces her favorite performances and talks candidly about her adventures in the industry.

Dinner Party directed by Cameron Grant (Ultimate Pictures, 1994). Guests at an elegant dinner party feast on their sexual fantasies in this beautifully produced film.

Latex directed by Michael Ninn (VCA, 1995). Superior camerawork, sexy fetish-wear and dynamic performances earned this futuristic saga numerous *Adult Video News* awards.

Man Who Loved Women (VCA, 1994). The first African-American director in porn, Sean Michaels takes to the streets in this faux-documentary filled with athletic sex.

Revenge of the Bi-Dolls directed by Josh Eliot (Catalina, 1994). An *Adult Video News* award-winning camp extravaganza with Chi Chi LaRue as a psycho nurse and porn legends Gloria Leonard and Sharon Kane as dueling divas.

Secret Life of Nina Hartley (VCA, 1994). Nina directs and stars in a comedy about a lonely secretary with a steamy fantasy life.

Sex (VCA, 1994) and *Sex 2* (VCA, 1995) directed by Michael Ninn. These skillfully shot tales of gorgeous celebrities trapped in a decadent world of stardom put Michael Ninn on the map.

Shock directed by Michael Ninn (VCA, 1996). More fetish fashions and uninhibited sex in the sequel to *Latex* with Jeanna Fine as a futuristic Marilyn Monroe.

Amateur

Amateur videos feature relatively inexperienced performers and include a more diverse range of body types than is found in mainstream porn. They offer a slice of sexual realism, but they're not for viewers who crave slick, well-produced fantasies.

Masturbation Memoirs, Volumes 1 and 2 (House O'Chicks, 1995). Women speak frankly about their sexual histories and demonstrate their favorite masturbation techniques in these sensitive documentaries.

San Francisco Lesbians, Volumes 1-6 (Pleasure Productions, 1992-1994). This series delivers a diverse group of butches, femmes, grunge babes and hippie chicks engaging in a range of activities.

Lesbian

Every mainstream video includes at least one "girl-girl" scene of sex between women, and many adult video companies produce "all girl" tapes. However, if you want to see genuine, hot lesbian sex, look for tapes produced by lesbian companies.

Bittersweet (House O' Chicks, 1993). An S/M vignette between a dominatrix and her live-in submissive, featuring play piercings and dildo-fucking.

Burlezk Live, Volume 1 (Fatale, 1987) and *Volume 2* (Fatale, 1990). Live footage of a lesbian strip club with performances by professional erotic dancers.

Clips (Fatale, 1988). Three short vignettes depict anal masturbation, safe-sex bondage and female ejaculation.

Erotic in Nature (Tigress, 1986). Two women enjoy a tender, sensual afternoon in the countryside.

Hayfever (Tigress, 1989). Country music, comedy, outdoor sex and a star turn by Nina Hartley.

Hungry Hearts (Fatale, 1989). Two lovers spend a romantic weekend in a hot tub, by the fire, and strapping on a dildo harness.

Private Pleasures/Shadows (Fatale, 1985). Two videos feature the same pair of lovers playing in a dungeon and enjoying vaginal fisting. Low on production values; high on sexual tension.

Safe Is Desire (Fatale, 1993). Lesbians at a hip San Francisco orgy demonstrate just how hot safer sex techniques can be.

Suburban Dykes (Fatale, 1990). Nina Hartley and Pepper are a bored suburban couple who hire Sharon Mitchell to spice up their sex life.

Gay

Gay male porn is frequently more diverse in style and content than straight porn. Our recommendations of some classics and a couple of recent stand-out videos are the barest tip of the iceberg.

All About Steve directed by Chi Chi LaRue (HIS Video, 1995). An all-male remake of *All About Eve,* this stylish parody about a porn star clawing his way to the top features some of the hottest stars of the nineties.

El Paso Wrecking Co. directed by Joe Gage (HIS Video, 1977). Gay truckers enjoy sex on the road.

Erotic Explorer directed by Josh Schafer (Schafer Films, 1994). This tender independent video shows how two male lovers use fantasy to turn each other on.

A Few Good Men directed by Steve Scott (Bijou Video, 1983). Homoeroticism in the barracks.

Inches directed by Steve Scott (Bijou Video, 1979). Al Parker, one of the greatest gay porn stars ever, stars as a young photographer about to break up with his lover.

Jumper directed by Chi Chi LaRue (HIS Video, 1992). A gay angel earns a brief return trip to Earth to sexually enlighten a series of men in this *Adult Video News* award-winning video.

Le Beau Mec directed by Wallace Potts (Le Salon, 1980). A fictional autobiography of a French hustler that is simultaneously raunchy and tender.

Powertool directed by John Travis (Catalina, 1986). Jeff Stryker is sent to prison, where tensions rise between prisoners and guards.

Sailor in the Wild directed by William Higgins (Laguna Pacific, 1980). The ultimate erotic road movie about a sailor on leave.

Skin Deep directed by Tom DeSimone (Laguna Pacific, 1983). An "Owl and the Pussycat" love story in which a porn novel writer who restricts his sex life to prostitutes meets his sexual and emotional match.

Feminist

Some women filmmakers, notably Candida Royalle of Femme Productions, take a feminist approach to creating heterosexual porn. Their films tend to be slower paced and less in-your-face than mainstream adult videos (i.e., no external come shots and fewer genital close-ups).

Cabin Fever directed by Deborah Shames (Deborah Films, 1993). A softcore rendition of a story from Lonnie Barbach's erotica anthology *Pleasures,* in which a woman is wooed by a handyman.

Christine's Secret directed by Candida Royalle (Femme, 1985). A city girl finds romance at a country inn.

Femme (Femme, 1984) and *Urban Heat* (Femme, 1985) directed by Candida Royalle. The first two Femme features have no plot, little dialogue, and move from one erotic scenario to another.

The Hottest Bid directed by Deborah Shames (Deborah Films, 1995). A fundraising auction in which women bid for hunky bachelors provides the backdrop for two couples' sexual awakenings.

My Surrender directed by Candida Royalle (Femme, 1996). The tale of a filmmaker, the incomparable Jeanna Fine, who helps improve other couple's sex lives, but has no romance of her own...until the right man breaks through to her.

Revelations directed by Candida Royalle (Femme, 1993). A young wife living in a sexually repressive society finds a stash of porn.

Rites of Passion directed by Annie Sprinkle and Veronica Vera (Femme, 1987). Annie's segment is a humorous exploration of Tantric sex, and Veronica's segment is a look at the secret fantasies of "Mr. Morality."

Sensual Escape directed by Gloria Leonard and Candida Royalle (Femme, 1988). Gloria's segment is a scene between two lovers planning sex for the first time, and Candida's presents one woman's recurring erotic dream.

A Taste of Ambrosia directed by Veronica Hart and Candida Royalle (Femme, 1987). In Veronica's segment, a couple demonstrates how to keep sparks flying in a long-term relationship, and Candida's segment depicts a couple facing interference from the woman's pet cats.

Three Daughters directed by Candida Royalle (Femme, 1986). The sexual escapades of three daughters as well as Mom and Dad.

The Voyeur directed by Deborah Shames (Deborah Films, 1995). In this softcore romp, a yuppie couple visit a Wine Country resort to recharge their sexual relationship.

Educational

How-to tapes featuring porn stars are explicitly designed to arouse viewers. Independently produced sex-education films, while not as titillating as mainstream X-rated videos, are frequently erotic as well as enlightening.

Ancient Secrets of Sexual Ecstasy for Modern Lovers (Higher Love Video, 1996). The world's most respected Tantra teachers offer a historical survey, and heterosexual couples demonstrate sexual techniques.

Becoming Orgasmic (Sinclair Institute, 1993). A preorgasmic woman is guided through techniques of self-discovery.

Carol Queen's Great Vibrations directed by Joani Blank (1995). Carol, author of *Exhibitionism for the Shy* and a Good Vibrations staffer, offers explicit vibrator demonstrations and tips for women and men alike.

Celebrating Orgasm (Betty Dodson, 1996). Betty offers private coaching in masturbation techniques to five different women ages twenty-six to sixty-three.

Complete Guide to Safe Sex directed by Laird Sutton (Multi-Focus, 1988). Describes how to have and negotiate safer sex and depicts real people using safer sex accessories.

Erotic Massage (Secret Garden, 1989). A guide to full-body and genital massage from Kenneth Ray Stubbs.

Expressions of Love from Paladin Productions (Multi-Focus, 1981). A married couple takes time to experiment sexually.

The Fine Art of Anal Intercourse (VCR, 1985). Porn stars Erica Boyer and Marc Wallace discuss and demonstrate anal intercourse.

Fire on the Mountain: An Intimate Guide to Male Genital Massage directed by Joseph Kramer (EroSpirit, 1993). If you make it through the New Age rap you'll be rewarded with the ultimate hand-job lesson demonstrated by two men.

Going Down to Bimini directed by Laird Sutton (Multi-Focus, 1978). A heterosexual couple enjoys a sensuous Caribbean interlude that culminates in mutual orgasm.

Good Vibrations, Part 2 directed by Patti Rhodes Lincoln (Video Team, 1992). A mainstream adult video about incorporating vibrators into partner sex. Notable for the use of electric vibrators and for depicting a man reaching an orgasm with a wand vibrator (*Good Vibrations, Part 1* contains inaccurate information).

How to Female Ejaculate (Fatale, 1992). A group of five women discuss their experiences of female ejaculation and then demonstrate in a very fluid circle-jerk.

How to Perform Fellatio (VCR, 1985). Porn actress Karen Summer demonstrates her tried-and-true oral sex techniques on two male subjects, and a wonderful time is had by all.

Incredible G-Spot (Merlin/Park Avenue Publishers, 1995). Laura Corn provides heterosexual couples with enthusiastic, practical instruction in locating and stimulating the G-spot.

Jim and Vern directed by Laird Sutton (Multi-Focus, 1976). A gay male couple integrates Tantric breathing and meditation with explicit sex.

Learning the Ropes (Ona Zee Productions, 1992). A series of S/M instructional tapes from Ona Zee and Frank Weegers, addressing both emotional issues and technique.

Nice Girls Don't Do It directed by Kathy Daymond (1990). A short art film on the subject of female ejaculation, packing a lot of information and some great visuals into thirteen minutes.

Nina Hartley's Guide to Anal Sex (Adam & Eve, 1996); *Nina Hartley's Guide to Better Cunnilingus* (Adam & Eve, 1994); *Nina Hartley's Guide to Better Fellatio* (Adam & Eve, 1994). Porn star Nina Hartley delivers accurate anatomical information and demonstrates techniques with male and female pals with her trademark humor, enthusiasm and professionalism.

A Ripple in Time directed by Laird Sutton (Multi-Focus, 1974). Sally, fifty-three, and Ed, sixty, enjoy leisurely lovemaking, which includes vibrator use during intercourse.

Selfloving (Betty Dodson, 1991). A filmed version of Betty's Bodysex workshop, in which a group of ten women discuss sexual self-image and feelings before Betty leads them in a guided masturbation ritual.

Sex: A Lifelong Pleasure (Focus International, 1993). A high-quality, Dutch-produced series narrated by a male and female sex therapist while on-screen couples demonstrate the techniques discussed.

Sex After 50 narrated by Lonnie Barbach (Focus International, 1991). An excellent survey, enhanced by honest, funny interviews with men and women from fifty to ninety. No explicit sex.

Sexual Secrets: A Sex Surrogate's Guide to Lovemaking (Access Instructional Media, 1993). A guide to partner sex and an inside look at what sex surrogates do with their clients.

Sexuality Reborn narrated by Ben Vereen (Kessler Institute for Rehabilitation, 1993). Five couples dealing with spinal cord injuries discuss and demonstrate their sexual techniques (available only through the Kessler Institute).

Sluts and Goddesses directed by Maria Beatty and Annie Sprinkle (1992). Annie's diverse female cast explores erotic energy from a New Age perspective, and the video culminates in Annie's five-minute orgasm.

Videos for Lovers: Behind the Bedroom Door (Educational Video, 1993-1996). With over a dozen volumes to date, this series features real-life couples discussing their sex lives and demonstrating their favorite activities.

CD-ROM Discography

Anne Hooper's Ultimate Sex Guide (Dorling Kindserly, 1996). This excellent sex-education disc features high-quality multimedia, in depth reference sections, instructions on technique and an interactive program that helps you develop your own sexual profile.

The Dinner Party (Ultimate Interactive, 1994). No interactivity, but nice soundtrack and visual presentation of the scenes from Cameron Grant's video *Dinner Party*.

Diva X: Ariana (Pixis, 1996). A unique interface (TFUI) allows the viewer to manipulate hand, tongue, sex toy or penis controls while a "Diva" responds in real time. You can also create, edit, save and download your activities on this technologically advanced game. Ariana is the first in the Diva series—each disc features a different woman.

The Dream Machine (New Machine Publishing, 1994). Simple interactive format—you view a series of film clips and then respond to questions that determine what your next clip will be. In this way, you tailor your fantasy to suit your individual sexual preferences.

The Dream Machine 2 (New Machine Publishing, 1996). More sophisticated graphics and special effects than its predecessor, along with a more challenging game.

Fetish (Edge Interactive, 1996). Over seven hundred stunning photographs focusing on eight women by the king of fetish photography, Eric Kroll. Features latex, bondage and S/M.

House of Dreams (New Machine Publishing, 1993). Not interactive, but you can pick and choose the order in which you see the film clips from Andrew Blake's most critically acclaimed film.

Latex: The Game (VCA Interactive, 1995). Explore a retro-future city and encounter erotic devices, a sexy cyber siren and secret rooms in one of the most challenging, graphically superb, interactive games.

Men in Motion (Rom Antics, 1995). Five hunky guys strip, share fantasies and some good sex instruction in this cute, moderately interactive game.

Space Sirens (Pixis, 1994). You're a sex slave trapped in an alien pod with a space siren and can't leave until you sexually satisfy her. Use hand and dildo controls to figure out ways to please your siren—but you lose if you come before she does.

Space Sirens 2: Megababes from Aija (Pixis, 1995). Similar premise to the original, with more arcadelike games and a much harsher sentence if you fail to satisfy the sirens.

Vampire's Kiss (Digital Playground, 1994). Minimal interactivity, but enjoy the gothic twist. Explore three rooms of a virtual castle and discover the erotic antics of the inhabitants.

Virtual Sex Shoot (Digital Playground, 1995). An admirable, early attempt to let the viewer direct—select and record the scenes you prefer (you can even choose from different camera angles), then playback your tailor-made video.

Index

MacKinnon, Catharine, 254
magazines, 202, 204-205, 254, 256, 258
Magic Connection, 102
Magic of Sex, 4
Mahler, Richard, 189
mail-order catalogs, 1, 7, 71, 73, 96, 97, 114, 146, 157, 163, 192, 208, 221, 223, 225, 230
mainstream publishers, 184
Making Love Better, 3
Male Sexuality, 3
Mammoth Book of Erotica, 185
Mapplethorpe, Robert, 187
marijuana, 69
massage, 31, 43, 77-81, 246; butt, 78; genital, 77, 78, 245; and lubricants, 69, 70; perineal, 121; prostate, 21; and self-image, 12
massage oil, 69, 70, 76, 79, 83; allergic reaction to, 78, 83
Masters and Johnson, 3, 24
masturbation, 6, 31, 45, 135, 175, 259; in the Bible, 51; books on, 3, 54-55; and experimentation, 49; and fantasy, 168, 172; and guilt, 54; and multiple orgasms, 27-28; negative attitudes towards, 36, 51-55, 64; with partner, 38, 43, 55; and pornography, 64, 194-195; as safer sex, 236, 245, 246; and self-esteem, 10-11; with sex toys, 49
Masturbation Hall of Fame, 64-65
Masturbation Home Page, 202
Masturbation Memoirs, 192
Masturbation Society, 65
Maxx, 240
McCallum, Robert, 189
media, 39, 210, 245; repressive attitudes, 12, 50, 51, 53; and self-image, 11
Meese Commission, 251-252
menopause, 33, 68, 70, 85, 121, 128, 144
Men's Confidential, 33, 177
Men's Cream, 62, 69
menstrual cycle, 68, 85, 93, 139, 144, 226

menstruation, 246
Mentor, 239, 240
Metzger, Radley, 189
Miami University, 65
Michaels, Sean, 190, 235
Michigan, 250
Michigan Womyn's Music Festival, 151
Midnight Cowboy, 251
Midnight Heat, 256
Miller, Henry, 185
Miller v. California, 251
Mindblowing Sex in the Real World, 4
Minos, 238
Mississippi, 256
Mitchell Brothers, 189
mitt, 82
modern primitive, 226
Morin, Jack, 3, 44, 179, 180, 214-215
Ms., 256
MTV, 211
multiple orgasm, 27-29
My Secret Life, 195

NASA, 70
National Masturbation Month, 56, 64-65
National Obscenity Enforcement Unit, 252
National Spinal Cord Injury Foundation, 235
Naughty Linx, 202
netiquette, 201, 206
Net Nanny, 206
New England Journal of Medicine, 247
New Joy of Sex, 95
newsgroup, 65, 202
New View of a Woman's Body, 3, 12, 15
Nin, Anaïs, 184, 185
Nina Hartley's Guide to Better Cunnilingus, 87
Nina Hartley's Guide to Better Fellatio, 88
nipple clamps, 113, 211, 214, 225-226; vibrating, 111. *See also* clamps

nipples, 78, 137, 225-226
nonoxynol-9, 73, 238, 241
North Carolina, 252

obscenity laws, 206, 251, 253-257
Octopus vibe, 107
odor, 85
Ogden, Gina, 29
older adults, 7, 9, 32-33, 85, 127
Onanism: Treatise of the Diseases Produced by Masturbation, 51-52
on-line services, 198, 199, 201, 203, 207
Only the Best, 194
Opening of Misty Beethoven, 256
Oprah, 39, 72
oral sex, 39, 84, 169, 245, 250. *See also* rimming
orgasm, 2, 4, 15-18, 21-22, 24-26, 135; and anal intercourse, 133-134; and clitoral stimulation, 8, 40, 123; discovery of, 6, 8, 202; and fisting, 122; and individuality, 5, 11, 15; and life changes, 30-32; and massage, 77; and masturbation, 58, 60-64; multiple, 27-28; oral sex, 86, 87, 89; and penetration, 119; simultaneous, 123; spontaneous, 29; and vibrators 97-98, 116; in X-rated videos, 191
Opening of Misty Beethoven, 256
Oster coil, 8
Our Bodies, Ourselves, 3, 55
Outcasts, 214

Pachard, Henri, 189
packing, 148, 160
paddles, 82, 211, 222
Page, Betty, 187
pagers, 176
pain, 214
Panasonic, 100, 229
Panasonic Massager, 139
paraurethral glands, 16
parents, 206; new, 30-32, 176, 204
Parents Place, 204
Passion Press, 186
PC muscle, 22, 27-28, 29, 31, 136

Selected Titles from Cleis Press

BEST LESBIAN EROTICA 1997

Selected by Jewelle Gomez
Tristan Taormino, Series Editor
$14.95 ISBN: 1-57344-065-5

Chrystos, Cherríe Moraga, Dawn Milton, Laura Antoniou, Donna Allegra, Heather Lewis, Carol Queen, Beth Brant, Jenifer Levin, Cheryl Clarke, Red Jordan Arobateau, Cecilia Tan, Kitty Tsui, Kathleen E. Morris, Karen Green, Jeannine DeLombard, Lauren Voloshen, Mickey Laskin, Vicki Lewis, Dolphin Julia Trahan, Bree Coven, Katya Andreevna, María Helena Dolan, Sandra Lee Golvin, Robin Bernstein
EROTIC STORIES

BEST GAY EROTICA 1997

Selected by Douglas Sadownick
Richard Labonté, Series Editor
$14.95 ISBN: 1-57344-067-1

Jack Fritscher, Pansy Bradshaw, D. Travers Scott, Scott O'Hara, Simon Sheppard, Lawrence Schimel, Gary Bowen, Ken Butler, Justin Chin, Kevin Killian, Cornelius Conboy, Emanuel Xavier, Robert Goldstein, J. Eigo, Michael Patrick Spillers, Al Lujan, Doug Mirk, Jameson Currier, Roberto Friedman, R.L. Kitzman, Ferd Eggan, Kelly McQuain, Tommi Avicolli Mecca
EROTIC STORIES

BEST GAY EROTICA 1996

edited by Michael Ford, selected
and introduced by Scott Heim
$12.95 ISBN: 1-57344-052-3

Scott O'Hara, Michael Rowe, Jameson Currier, Simon Sheppard, Carol Queen, Mark David M. Fennell, Stephen Greco, Thomas Roche, Mitch Cullin, M. Christian, Matthew Rettenmund, Owen Keehnen, Alex Jeffers, Rick Jackson, D. Travers Scott, Miodrag Kojadinovic', Michael Lassell
EROTIC STORIES

REAL LIVE NUDE GIRL
Chronicles Of Sex-Positive Culture
Carol Queen
$14.95 ISBN: 1-57344-073-6

Carol Queen's long-awaited collected writings on sex, pornography, prostitution and bisexuality. "The thinking person's sex queen, Carol Queen is a real live brilliant girl. For people who can't imagine what all the fuss is about sex, this is the book to read." —Annie Sprinkle, Pleasure Activist/Artist

SEX CHANGES
The Politics of Transgenderism
Pat Califia
$16.95 ISBN: 1-57344-072-8

Pat Califia's meticulously researched analysis of the contemporary history of transsexuality. Based on in-depth interviews with gender transgressors who "opened their lives, minds, hearts, and bedrooms to the gaze of strangers," this book combines a well-thought-out chronology with Pat Califia's hallmark candor and insight.

PUBLIC SEX
The Culture of Radical Sex
Pat Califia
$12.95 ISBN: 0-939416-89-1

Here are the best of Pat's writings—on porn, S/M, sex with youth, unmonogamy, and, of course, public sex! "*Public Sex* is the real thing without the tedious bullshit and self-serving obscurity that characterizes so much writing about sex." —Dorothy Allison, author, *Bastard Out of Carolina*

SEX WORK
Writings by Women in the Sex Industry
edited by Frédérique Delacoste and Priscilla Alexander
$16.95 ISBN: 0-939416-11-5

The original collection of writings by street prostitutes, exotic dancers, nude models, escorts, porn stars and massage parlor workers—honest, astute, and sexually explicit, this is the book that coined the phrase "sex work."

BODY ALCHEMY
Transsexual Portraits
Loren Cameron
$24.95 ISBN: 1-57344-062-0

An intimate, remarkable self-portrait of a female-to-male transsexual by an emerging transsexual photographer. "Andy Warhol, Robert Mapplethorpe, Dianne Arbus among many others have all trained their lenses on the transgendered figure. Never have the transgendered seriously photographed their own. Not until Loren Cameron, that is." —Kate Bornstein, author, *Gender Outlaw*

I AM MY OWN WOMAN
The Outlaw Life of Charlotte Von Mahlsdorf, Berlin's Most Distinguished Transvestite
Charlotte von Mahlsdorf
Translated by Jean Hollander
$12.95 ISBN: 1-57344-010-8

"Move over Quentin Crisp: A naked civil servant is nothing compared with the German boy in a dress…" —*Out* magazine. "As a child, Lothar Berfelde loved to wear an apron and polish porcelain. Given his druthers, he would have chosen to live quietly in the 19th century, perhaps as a housekeeper in a well-appointed home near Berlin. Instead, his life took a bumpier course…." —*Time*

DAGGER
On Butch Women
Edited by Lily Burana, Roxxie, Linnea Due
$14.95 ISBN: 0-939416-82-4

Pat Califia, Carol Queen, Susie Bright, JoAnn Loulan, Donna Minkowitz, Achy Obejas, Diane DiMassa, Joan Hilty, Trina Robbins. Photographs by Phyllis Christopher, Della Grace, Morgan Gwenwald, and Jill Posener. "Looking for a simple one-dimensional view of butch lives and loves? Keep looking. Dagger is a down and dirty discussion on butch diversity. Wanna listen in?"—Leslie Feinberg, author, *The Transgender Warriors*